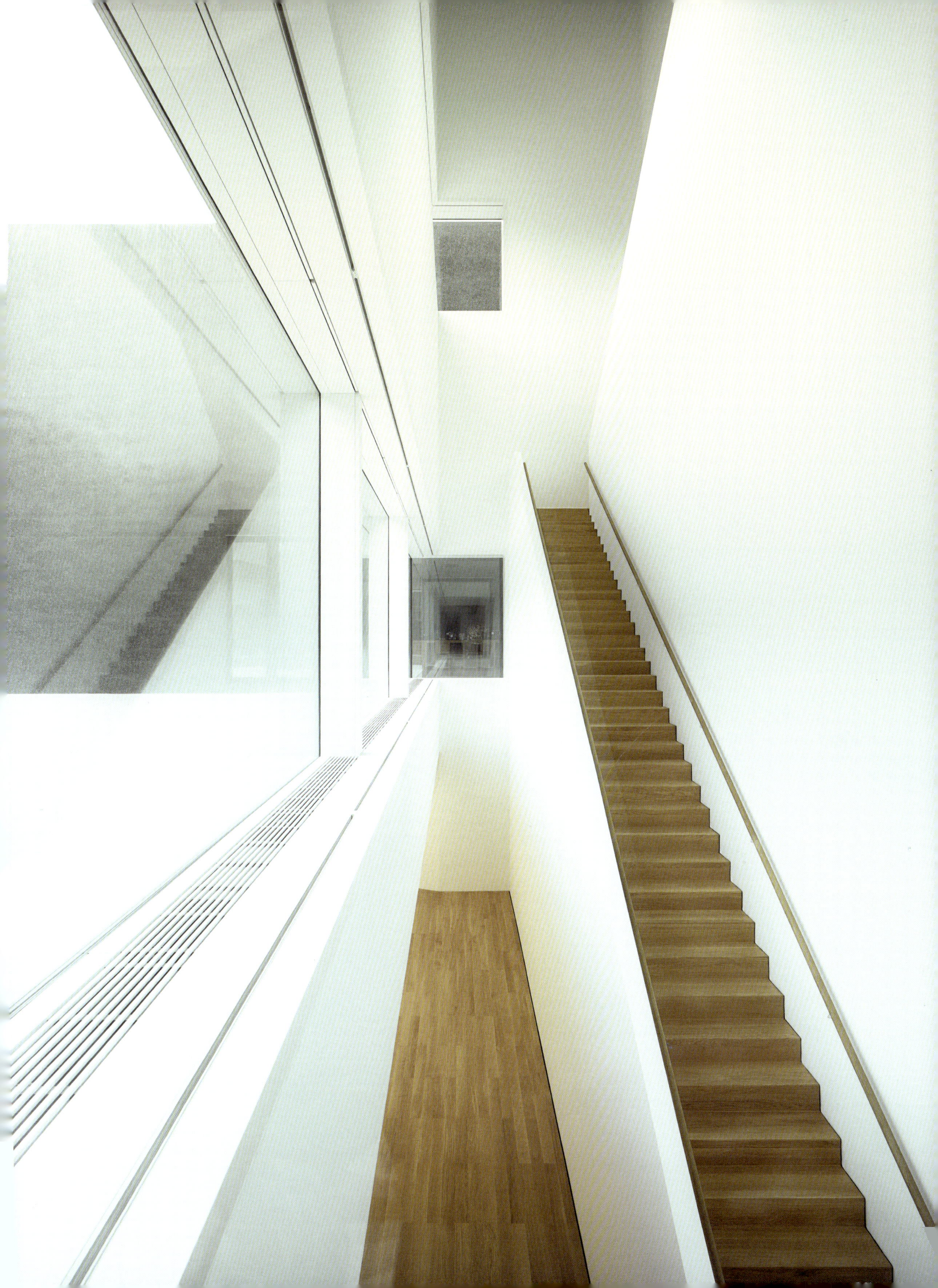

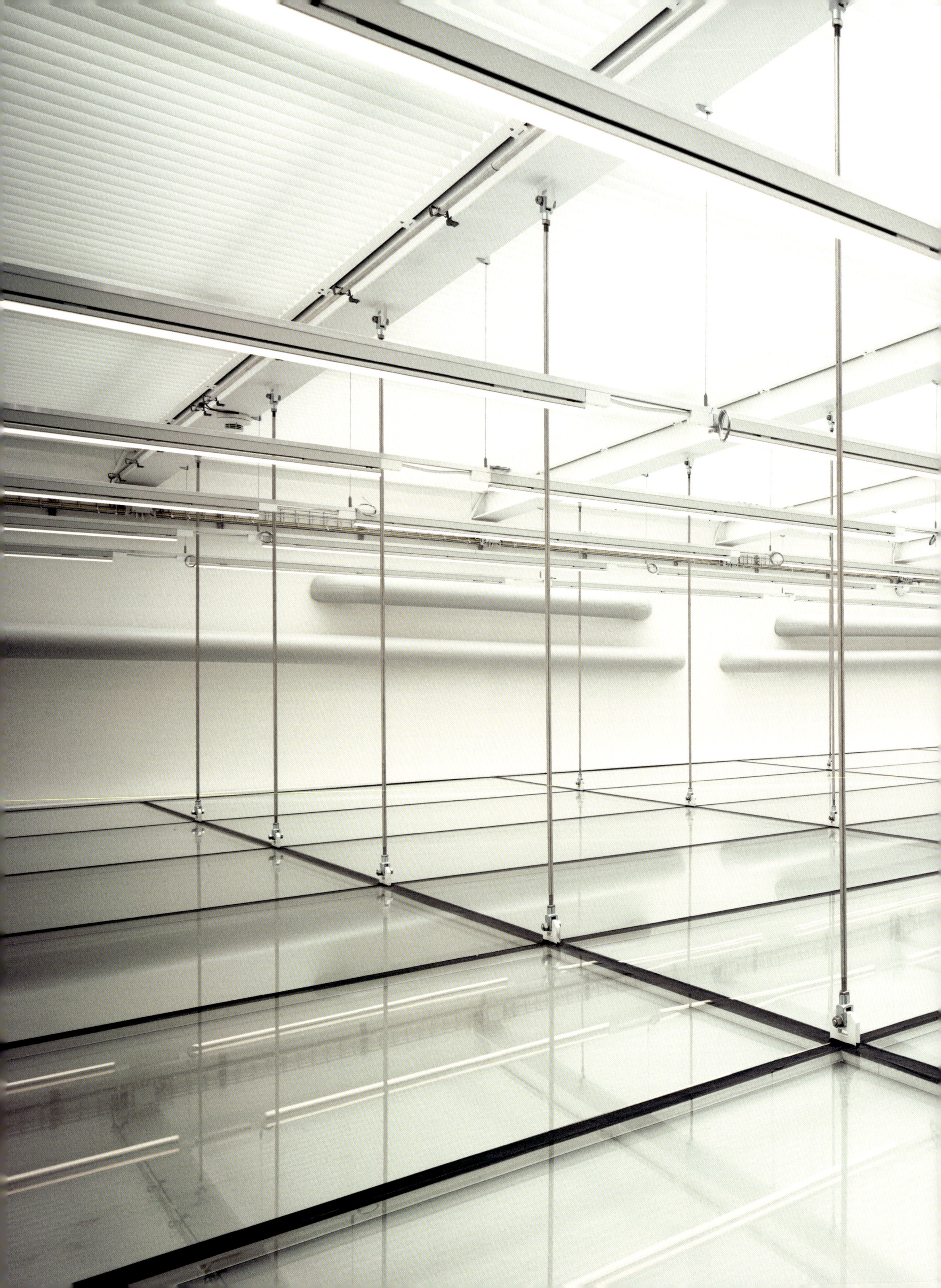

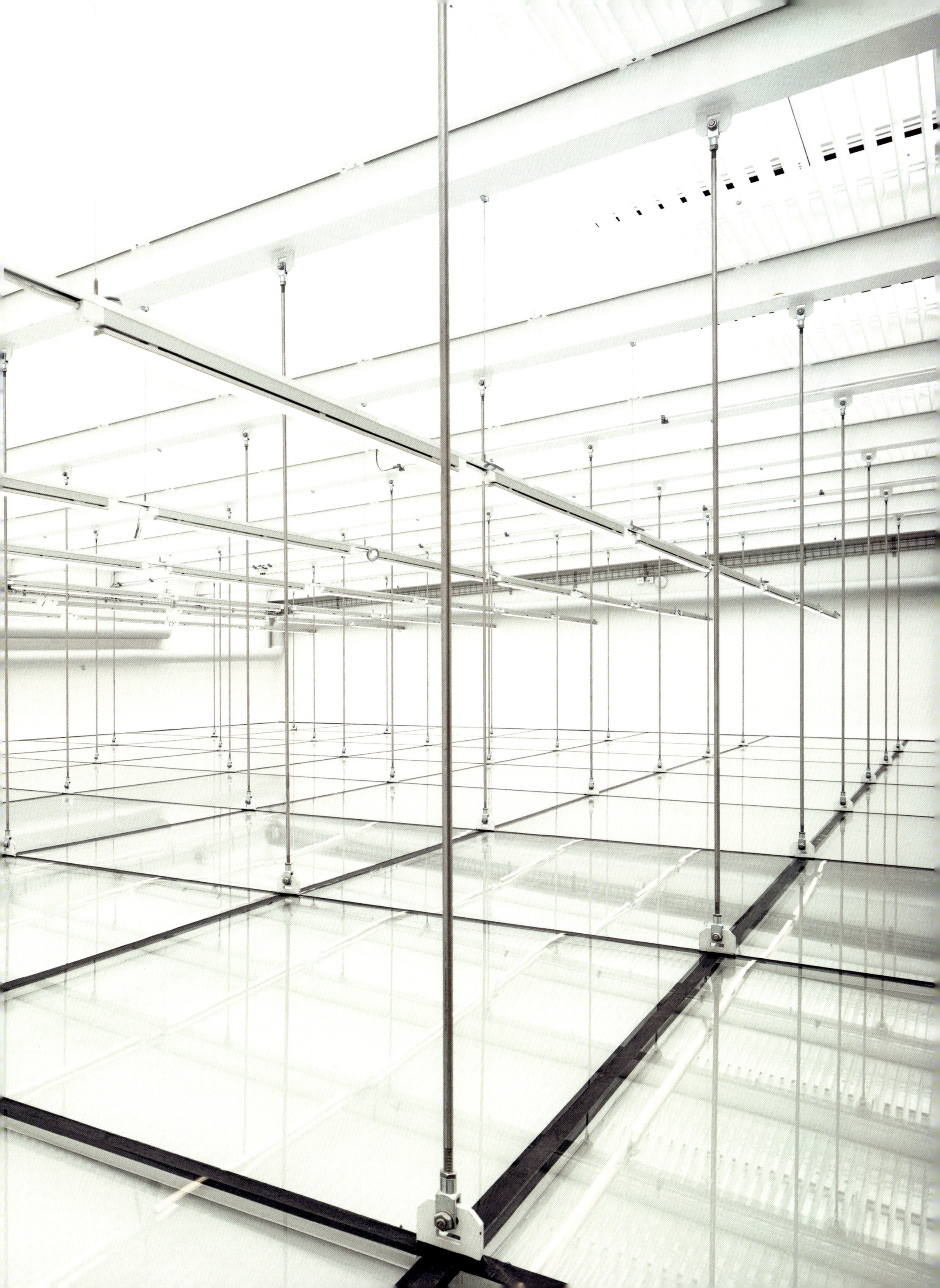

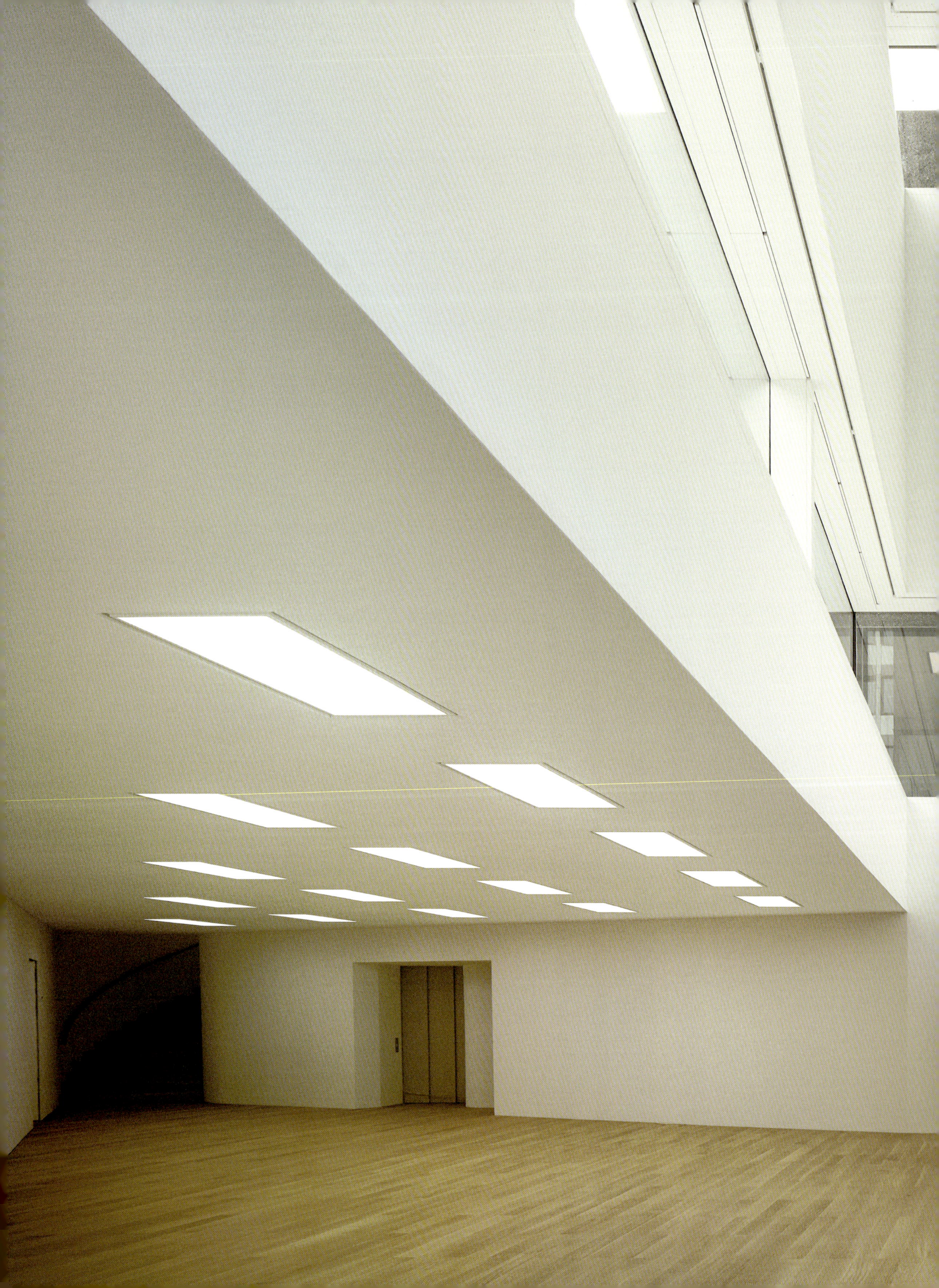

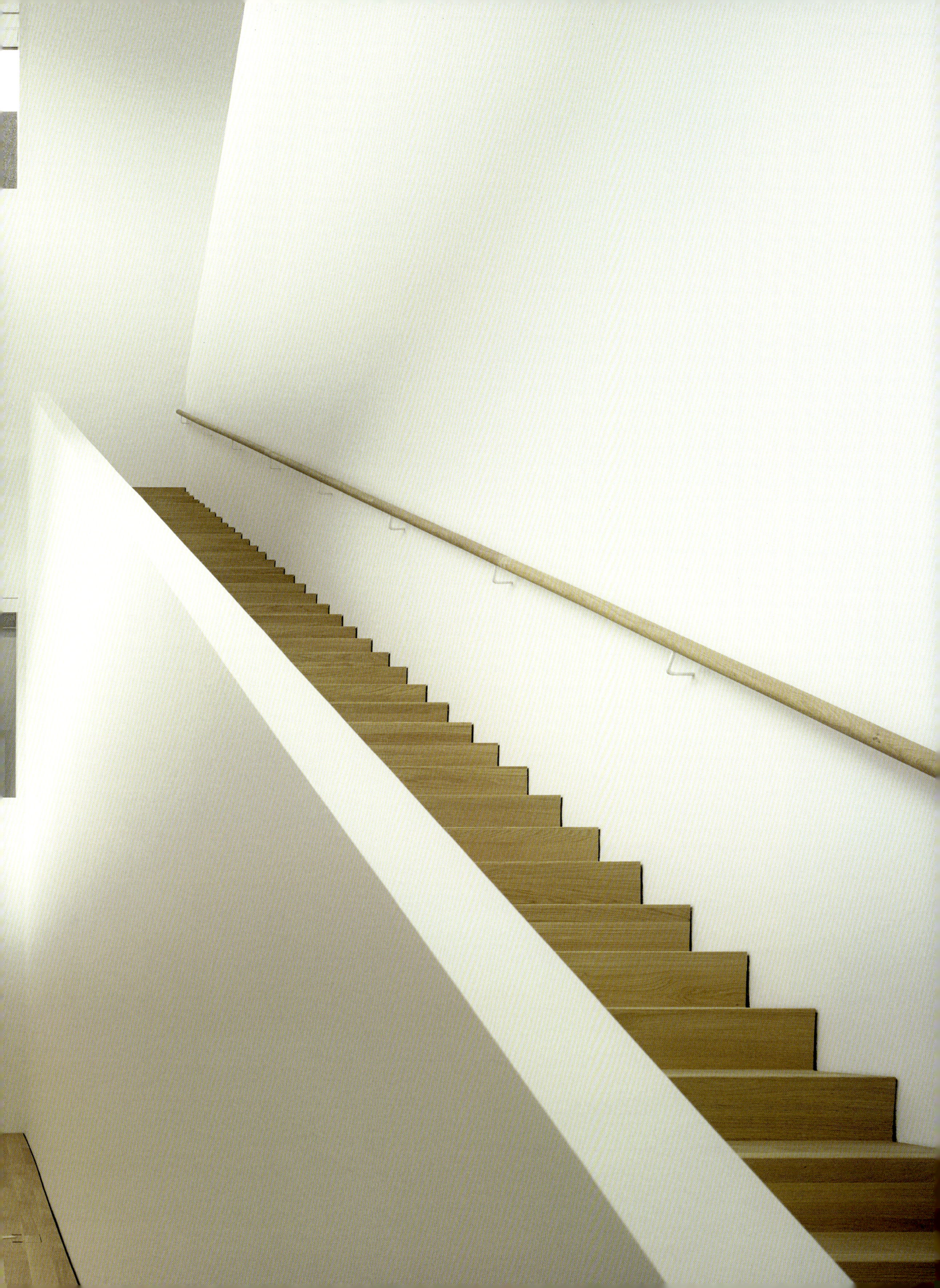

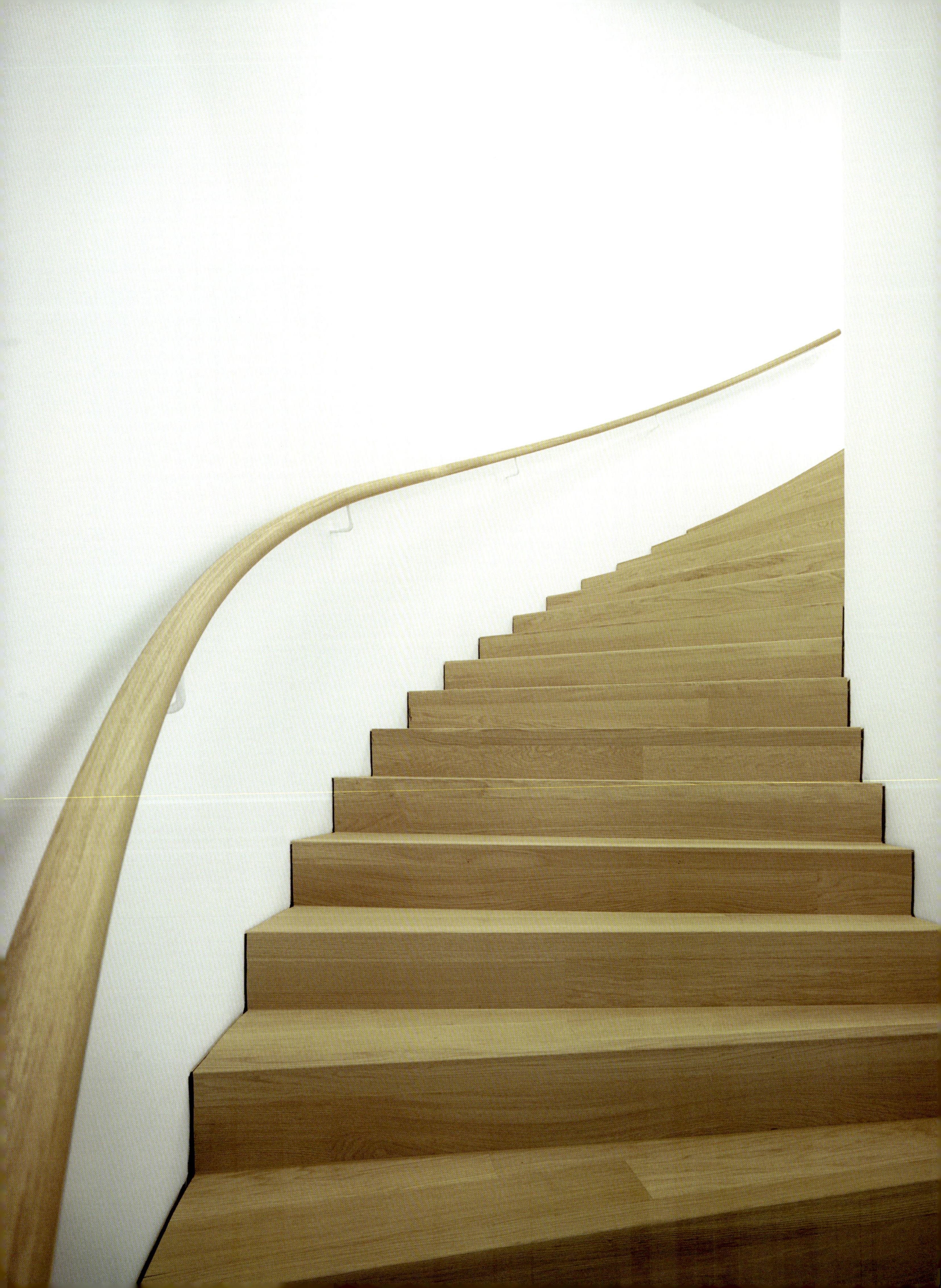

It’s always just a matter of seeing ...
You can paint anything.
Seeing if what you are doing
is good or not, is more difficult.
But it’s the only thing that matters ...

Seeing
is after all the decisive act,
which ultimately puts producer
and viewer on equal footing.

Gerhard Richter, 1990

Hilti Art Foundation

The Collection

Vol. 2

Art from 1950 to the Present Day

HIRMER

Preface
Michael Hilti

In 2005, for the first time, we ventured to present some 60 works from our family collections, newly named the Hilti Art Foundation, to a larger public at the Kunstmuseum Liechtenstein. The collections have been growing steadily ever since, and in 2015 we mounted a second exhibition of selected works, this time in the galleries of our own museum. These developments were inspired by the wish to make the collections permanently accessible to the public in the form of changing exhibitions. When I speak of family collections presented under the name of the Hilti Art Foundation, I am referring to the Martin Hilti Family Trust, into which the collection of my sister, Ursula Zindel-Hilti, was integrated when she passed away in 2016, as well as the collection belonging to myself and my wife, Caroline. We have now taken the next step of publishing a comprehensive catalogue to allow in-depth study of our collections and provide greater insight into their development through the inclusion of acquisition dates.

It is perhaps of interest to trace the emergence of our collections. My parents always had works of art at home, not with the intention of building a collection but simply because they loved living with art. These were largely works by masters of earlier periods. It was only late in life that our father acquired two paintings by Emil Nolde, *Dunkles Meer* (vol. 1, cat. 12), *Blumengarten* (vol. 1, cat. 11), as well as Paul Gauguin's *Entre les lys* (vol. 1, cat. 2). Upon his death in 1997, our family decided to keep the collected work intact, rather than dividing it up, with the objective of using it as the wellspring of a family collection devoted to classical modernism. My wife's private collection stems from her delight in art and from encounters with our English friend and art dealer Richard Nathanson, whom we met through my work in London in 1974.

Private collectors have the privilege of being able to pursue goals that are different from those of public institutions. We need not be guided primarily by art historical considerations; we are free to decide. Our collections are an expression of this freedom; they testify to our preferences, to what we consider important and outstanding. A closer look at our work will reveal that we have always aimed to collect art that is informed with a certain sense of harmony and balance, art that not only stimulates perception and inspires new thoughts, but that is, above all, a joy to look at – in short, art that is a pleasure to live with. For us, collecting has never meant speculation; it has always been a matter of affinity and quality – art as part of everyday life, self-evident, loved and integrated. In this spirit, I hope that you, too, will share the emotion and passion that we feel for these works when you study our catalogue.

I would like to take this opportunity to thank our curator, Uwe Wieczorek, for his invaluable support over the past 16 years in building up and expanding the collections, the advisory board of the Hilti Art Foundation, Angela Schneider and Claudia Steinfels, as well as the galleries and auction houses for repeatedly drawing our attention to interesting works.

On the Joy of Collecting

Uwe Wieczorek

Curator

Volume 2 of the Hilti Art Foundation's collection is the chronological sequel to Volume 1 of 2019, which is devoted to the art of Classical Modernism (1880–1950), specifically paintings, collages, gouaches and sculptures. In contrast, the 120 selected works in Volume 2 additionally include reliefs, kinetic objects, light sculptures, photography and objects made of materials alien to traditional sculpture. Spanning the period from 1950 to the present day, Volume 2 signals a hopeful perspective for the future development of the collection. The time span coincides with the lives of the Liechtenstein collectors Michael and Caroline Hilti, for whom the art they collect represents a vibrant contemporaneity. In fact, the present volume contains works from *their* collection alone, testifying, even more so than the works of the Martin Hilti Family Trust in Volume 1, to a highly personal interest in art, motivated more often than not by spontaneous impulses and nurtured not only by the works themselves but also by those who have created them. The Hilti family cultivate and cherish contact with the artists whose works they collect, leading to the acquaintance and, in some cases, close friendship with such artists as Max Bill, Gotthard Graubner, Gottfried Honegger, Imi Knoebel, Hanns Kunitzberger, Heinz Mack, Sean Scully, Keith Sonnier, Klaus Staudt and Thomas Struth. Social encounters foster the felicitous experience of discovering in these works a correspondence to their own wish, as expressed in Michael Hilti's foreword, to find harmony and balance, sensual appreciation and spiritual inspiration. The desire to share their experience with others prompted the family's decision to build a museum that would house the Hilti Art Foundation. Inaugurated in May 2015, it partners with the existing Liechtenstein Art Museum in Vaduz and has since organised several temporary exhibitions of selected works from the collection.

A brief glance at the present publication suffices to reveal the wide-ranging, open diversity, both in content and aesthetics, of the art contained herein. This is no doubt indebted to the sheer boundlessness of the art produced since 1950 but also to the mindful care with which the two collectors pursue a broad spectrum of interests. To structure the content of the second volume, it made sense to start with the beginnings of the collection, followed by several focal points, specifically, *Zurich Concrete Artists, Between Europe and America, Europe circa 1960, The Düsseldorf Academy* and *Works after 1990*. The structure does not reflect strictly programmatic collecting, nor does it indicate a guideline for future acquisitions. Rather, it represents one of many possible ways of organising the collection at the present time, showing an order that is to be understood as permeable and flexible.

Interest in artists belonging to the circle of so-called *Zurich Concrete Artists* (cat. 1–21) derives not only from Liechtenstein's cultural proximity to Switzerland but also from the spirit of enterprise that propels the Hilti family's affinity with Concrete Art and Constructivism. That affinity was fostered by their friendship with Max Bill and especially Gottfried Honegger, which heightened their appreciation of Concrete Art, specifically the potential of geometry and its rules to generate compositions that are striking for their harmony of colour and shape. The first acquisitions date from the 1980s, modest holdings that have grown steadily over the past decades with the works of Bill and Honegger complemented by those of Camille Graeser, Richard Paul Lohse and Verena Loewensberg, so that the collection now holds an important group of works providing considerable insight into Concrete Art.

The rules of geometry have often been a source of artistic inspiration, as demonstrated by such artists as Josef Albers and Zurich-born Fritz Glarner (cat. 22–24). Like so many other artists of the European avant-garde, they left their native continent and went to the United States to escape the threat of political violence and war. There, they both found themselves attracted to a concrete visual syntax, Albers through his encounter with Central American art and architecture, Glarner through his study of Piet Mondrian (vol. 1, cat. 34), whom he had already met in Paris and who did not immigrate to New York until 1940. Glarner returned to Europe in 1971, while Albers spent the remainder of his life in the United States, creating art and also becoming an influential teacher.

The American sculptor Alexander Calder (cat. 25–27) is similarly indebted to Mondrian, who had a decisive impact on his late work. When Calder went to Paris in 1926, he met several artists, among them Joan Miró, Fernand Léger and, as mentioned, Piet Mondrian. The latter's variable arrangements of colour on the wall of his studio inspired Calder's abstract *Mobiles*, the first of which he created in Paris in 1931, thereafter continuing to produce them in France and later in the United States as well.

Keith Sonnier (cat. 28–31) also travelled to Paris from his native Louisiana. However, in 1967, he too was drawn to New York, by which time the compass needle of art had long since swung around to the North American metropolis. Stimulated by the buoyantly experimental art scene that he encountered there, Sonnier began working with neon light, glass and other materials to explore the terrain between Abstract Expressionism and Minimalism. In the 1970s, New York also became the artistic seedbed and workplace of the European painters Sean Scully (cat. 32–36) and Helmut Federle (cat. 37, 38).

Despite the widely divergent sources of inspiration and means of expression featured in the work of these artists, their nonfigurative painting shares a profoundly emotional and indeed romantic undercurrent, which is associated, in Federle's case, with Asian spirituality.

Neither European nor American artists were daunted by the Atlantic divide, both sides drawing inspiration from the other at an early stage. In 1940s New York, the fruitful pluralism of European immigrants and American artists created a vibrant climate of modernism, marked equally by mutual appreciation and competition, which proved, in the decades that followed, to be of great benefit to the development of art on both sides of the ocean.

Abstract Expressionism, known in Europe as Tachism or Art Informel, became the dominant "world idiom", as it were, of 1940s and '50s art in the Western world. It is exemplified at the Hilti Art Foundation by the work of Wols (vol. 1, cat. 77). However, around 1960, numerous artists on both sides of the Atlantic took a step back, eschewing gestural configuration and striving for a rational formal idiom, as demonstrated in the work of the European artists Victor Vasarely, Günter Fruhtrunk and François Morellet (cat. 39–45). Independently of one another, they drew on the tradition of Constructivism and Suprematism, specifically the art of Piet Mondrian and Kazimir Malevich, to create works informed with a radical turn through optical irritation or underpinned with playful irony.

An entirely different artistic concept motivated Lucio Fontana (cat. 46–48), born 1899 in Argentina of Italian descent. His *spazialismo* marks an artistic and intellectual caesura in Europe after the Second World War. The violent and radical act of slashing a white canvas drew immediate attention to the physical facts of material, surface, structure, space, time and light, or, as Fontana put it in his 1946 *Manifiesto Blanco*, to the "primary values of existence". His act paved the way to complete liberation from traditional concepts of a painting or a work of art. In response, around 1960, a generation of artists some thirty years younger came to widely diverse conclusions; among this generation were Yves Klein, Piero Manzoni, Dadamaino, Hans Bischoffshausen and the ZERO artists Otto Piene, Heinz Mack and Günter Uecker (cat. 49–51 and 54–61). A focus on material, surface, structure, space, time and light as well as form, movement and rhythm also characterises the work of Jean Tinguely, Gianni Colombo, Jan Schoonhoven, Klaus Staudt, Gerhard von Graevenitz and the neon installations of Maurizio Nannucci, the latter in combination with words and lettering (cat. 52, 53 and 62–72). These works of art offer a great wealth of visual and material qualities. In contrast, Peter Roehr's serial montages (cat. 73) confront the human eye with identical products of industrial mass production and mass imagery.

A look at the biographies of the artists represented in the collection of the Hilti Art Foundation reveals that the Art Academy in Düsseldorf played an important role for many of them, who trained and in some cases taught there as well. Under the direction of Friedrich Wilhelm Schadow (1788–1862), the Academy acquired an international reputation in the nineteenth century, attracting students from the United States, Russia and Scandinavia. Wilhelm Lehmbruck and August Macke (vol. 1, cat. 9 and 23) were among the German students who attended the Academy prior to the First World War, and Paul Klee (vol. 1, cat. 44–47) taught there from 1931 to 1933 after spending eleven years as a professor at the Bauhaus in Weimar and Dessau. The artistic doctrine of the Nazis and the ravages of war necessitated substantial reorientation after 1946, on the basis of which an art scene emerged in the decades that followed, its impact once again extending far beyond the borders of Germany into an international network that still prevails today. Piene, Mack and Uecker studied at the Academy in the 1950s, as did Gotthard Graubner (cat. 75–79) and Konrad Klapheck (cat. 83–85), who each took a fundamentally different conceptual approach. Graubner understood his nonfigurative works as painterly, condensed organisms of colour while Klapheck attached explicit colours to his precisely represented pictorial objects. Graubner also taught at the Academy, as did the sculptor Norbert Kricke (cat. 74) before him.

The critique of painting elicited widespread discourse towards the end of the 1950s in Europe and the United States and acquired traction at the Düsseldorf Academy not least because of Joseph Beuys, who was active there as a student from 1946 to 1953 and as a professor from 1961 to 1972. He declared that "it is already a mistake to even entertain the thought of buying a stretcher and canvas". Both as a student and professor at the Academy during the 1960s and 1970s, Gerhard Richter (cat. 80–82) kept his distance from Beuys, maintaining a basically appreciative attitude towards painting, despite a certain scepticism, and making no distinction between figuration and nonfiguration. Imi Knoebel (cat. 86–92), in turn, deliberately sought out Beuys as a mentor, benefiting from the freedom of his expanded concept of art, which included the politically informed idea of "social sculpture". Knoebel also took inspiration from the work of Mondrian and Malevich, specifically the universal language of geometry, which would become the artistic foundation of an experimental oeuvre that oscillates between picture, object and installation, and resonates with the nonfiguration of geometric abstraction and Art Informel. In 1968, Knoebel installed his now legendary *Raum 19* in the classroom that housed Joseph Beuys' master class in sculpture. His arrangement of fibreboard cubes and panels in concert with empty stretchers toyed with traditional notions of sculpture and painting.

Thomas Struth, whose work has recently been added to the collection of the Hilti Art Foundation (cat. 93–102), was also a student at the Düsseldorf Art Academy. Initially studying painting with Gerhard Richter, he later chose to devote himself to the field of photography under the tutelage of Bernd Becher, who had joined the Academy in 1976. The Düsseldorf School of Photography, founded by Becher with his wife, Hilla, has since produced many photographers of international standing. The acquisition of Struth's work, rooted in the medium of photography, has substantially broadened not only the aesthetic reach of the Hilti Art Foundation's collection but also its content, focused, as it is, on subject matter directly related to the contemporary phenomena of today's world.

The form and content of works collected in previous decades and indeed since Classical Modernism continue to resonate in the art dating from approximately 1990: the constructive approach of Willi Kopf (cat. 103, 104) and Hanna Roeckle (cat. 105); the works created by Giovanni Di Stefano (cat. 106, 107), whose performative character links them with chance, thus emphasising difference; the figuration of Karol Broniatowski (cat. 108, 109) and Julian Opie (cat. 110, 111), who capture the human figure in all its timelessness and topicality, its anonymity and singularity; the painterly approach of Callum Innes (cat. 112, 113) and Hanns Kunitzberger (cat. 114–116), marked by the finest of chromatic nuances; and the landscapes of Frank Thiel (cat. 117) and Stéphane Kropf (cat. 120), whose confrontational and alienating pictures sharpen our perception of both traditional genre and subject matter as such. Finally, attention turns to the East, to Japan and the art of Leiko Ikemura (cat. 118) and Mariko Mori (cat. 119), two women who bridged East and West early on in their careers, expressing their transcultural self-image in a wide variety of subjects and mediums.

Leaving aside orientation towards subject matter in Volume 2 to consider the overall aesthetics of the works contained herein, one can identify two dominant trajectories: concrete/constructivist and substantive/painterly. Accordingly, such artists as Bill, Loewensberg, Honegger, Calder, Sonnier, Knoebel, Graubner, Scully, Kunitzberger and Innes represent both quantitative and qualitative highlights in the collection. It is in their work above all that Michael and Caroline Hilti find the harmony and balance they so deeply appreciate and admire, their thoughts and sense perception additionally fostered by the creative diversity of such artists as Albers, Fontana, Schoonhoven, Fruhtrunk, Morellet, Klein, Manzoni, Uecker, Staudt and von Graevenitz. The fundamentally nonobjective world represented by these artists now stands in fruitful contrast to Thomas Struth's photographs of the visible world.

The connection between looking and thinking, seeing and appreciating is one of the great joys of self-realisation; the works of art collected by Michael and Caroline Hilti provide ample opportunity to cultivate that connection. It is also a privilege to be able to present these works to the public in the form of this catalogue as a source of information for personal use and companionship while visiting the museum of the Hilti Art Foundation. Together, Volumes 1 and 2 provide a representative insight into the current holdings of the collection.

My most cordial gratitude goes to the following people for their commitment, professionalism, reliability and support: Caroline, Michèle and Michael Hilti as well as all the members of the Hilti family and the Martin Hilti Family Trust. I am equally grateful to: Arnulf Appel, Marco Auderset, Monika Bergmann, Siegfried Brugger and Günter Hofer with the staff at MuseumsPartner, Claudia Büchel, Miles Champion, Kurt Dornig, Isabel Fehr, Shandor Hayde, Valentin Jeck, Günter König, Heinz Preute, Martin Rogy-Hinse, Julia Ryff, Catherine Schelbert, Angela Schneider, Claudia Steinfels, Cornelia Wieczorek, Thomas Zuhr and Rainer Arnold with the staff at Hirmer Verlag, and the many others who were indispensable despite not being named here.

The Authors

Dr. Angela Schneider
studied art history, classical archaeology and history at the University of Munich. From 1973 to 2008 she worked at the National Gallery in Berlin, first as a curator and from 1999 additionally as deputy director. There she planned and mounted numerous exhibitions of twentieth-century international art, including one-person shows of such artists as Pablo Picasso, Alberto Giacometti, Francis Bacon, Walter De Maria and Jannis Kounellis.
AS

Dr. Uwe Wieczorek
studied art history, classical archaeology and history of bookmaking at the University of Mainz. He worked for the Berlin State Museums, and from 1992 to 2003 he was director of The Collections of the Prince of Liechtenstein. Since 2003 he has been the curator of the Hilti Art Foundation in Schaan, Liechtenstein. He has planned and mounted exhibitions on art from the Renaissance to the twentieth century, as well as solo presentations of such artists as Franz Erhard Walther, Sean Scully, Gottfried Honegger and Gotthard Graubner.
UW

Dr. Julia Ryff
Studied art history, Byzantine art and French literature at the Ludwig-Maximilians-Universität, Munich and the Courtauld Institute of Art, London. While writing her doctoral thesis, she worked for the DFG (German Research Foundation) on the Grosse Deutsche Kunstausstellung (Great German Art Exhibition) at the Zentralinstitut für Kunstgeschichte, Munich. From 2014 to 2018 she worked at Christie's, Zurich in the departments of Impressionism, Classical Modernism and Post-War & Contemporary Art. Since 2019 she has been a specialist on Impressionism and Classical Modernism at Bonhams, London.
JR

Zurich Concrete Artists

Camille Graeser
Doppelte Komplementär-Relation
1965

001

Camille Graeser
1892 Carouge – 1980 Wald / Zurich

Oil on canvas
Signed verso: graeser
80 × 80 cm

Inv. no.: P87M / Acquired 2001

The Swiss artist Camille Graeser studied furniture-making and interior architecture with Bernhard Pankok in Stuttgart. Under the influence of Willi Baumeister and Oskar Schlemmer, he cultivated a rigorous and planar purism. After returning to Switzerland in 1933, he found a growing affinity with Concrete Art, the theory of which had already been elaborated in 1930 by Theo van Doesburg. He was a proponent of Zurich Concrete Art along with Richard Paul Lohse, Max Bill, Verena Loewensberg and others.

In 1944, in the bulletin *abstrakt + konkret*, Graeser attempted to define the concepts that would dominate his painting after 1945. "Concrete is the rigorously logical creation and composition of works of art, which have laws of their own. Concrete works with the scale and value of colour, form and line ..." For him, "concrete" also meant "purity, law and order".

Drawing also played an important role in Graeser's oeuvre, as demonstrated by a substantial legacy of works on paper. Drawings of ideas and visual concepts devised according to arith-metic principles of composition would become the source material of his paintings.

From the end of the 1950s, in works titled *Relation*, Graeser concentrated on the quantitative and physical relationship of plane and colour. *Doppelte Komplementär-Relation* (Twofold Complementary Relation) of 1965 visualises the order of complementary colours. The purple and yellow horizontals in the lower half of the painting convey dynamically rising movement while the red and green squares above impart calm and stasis. The painted areas are equally proportioned; the choice of colours aims at polarity. Here, Graeser is exploring the equality of volumes of colour and, formally, the equality of unequal entities. The composition of this *Relation* in square format is characteristic of Graeser's output in the 1960s. The combination of planes and stripes, and, in this case, the total design of the pictorial plane, makes these works reminiscent of flags.

JR

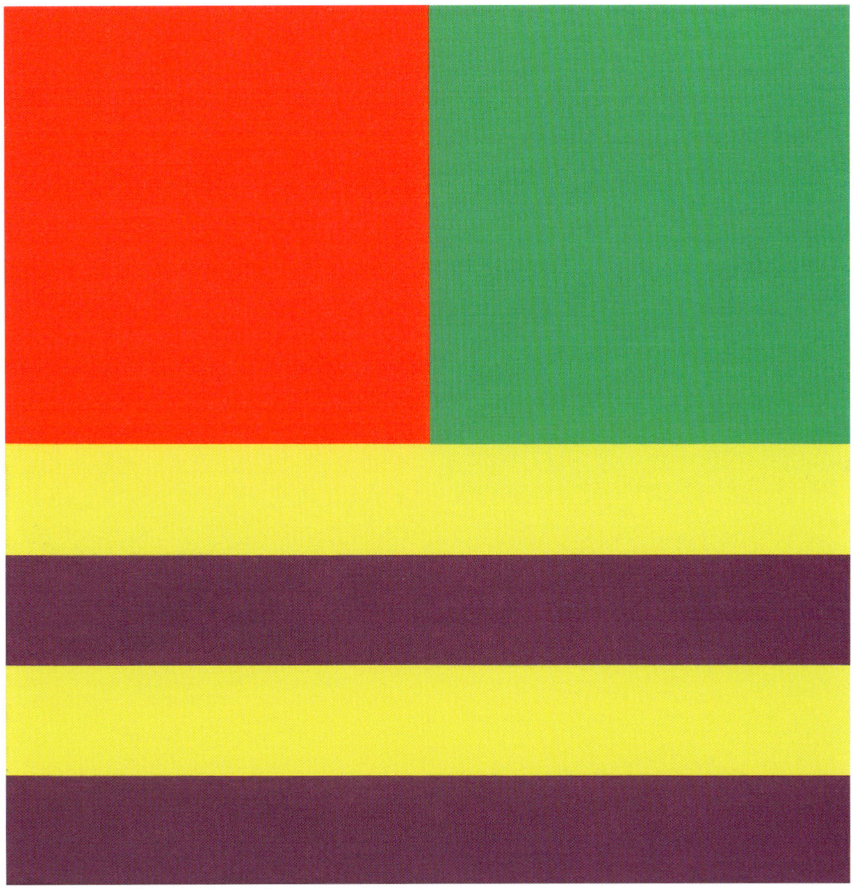

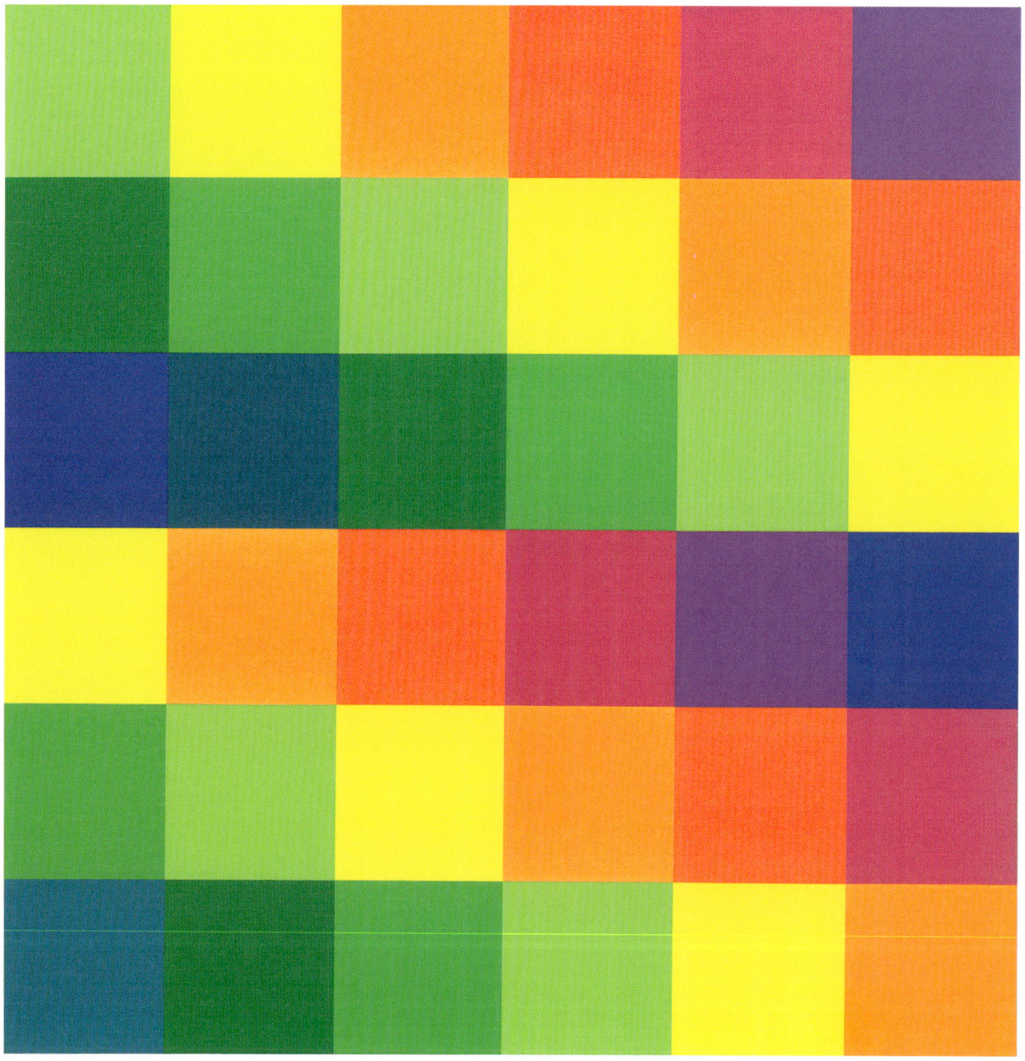

Richard Paul Lohse
1902 Zurich – 1988 Zurich

Oil on canvas
Signed, inscribed, titled and dated verso:
Richard P. Lohse Zurich Schweiz /
[title] / 1955/65 / III
120 × 120 cm

Inv. no. P260M / Acquired 2014

Richard Paul Lohse
6 systematische Farbreihen von blau zu blau
1955/1965

After training in commercial art at the Zurich School of Arts and Crafts in the 1920s, Richard Paul Lohse gravitated step-by-step towards Concrete Art, taking inspiration from studies in Cubism as well as Russian and Dutch Constructivism. In 1937 he and Leo Leuppi founded Allianz, an association of contemporary Swiss artists that would lead to the Zurich Concrete Artists group with Camille Graeser, Max Bill, Verena Loewensberg, himself and others. In the early 1940s, Lohse began to develop so-called serial and modular constructions based on squares and rectangles. Instead of relying exclusively on pictorial means, he worked out a method of strictly rational composition, featuring “the standardisation of pictorial means (the square), the parallelism of visual elements and margins, equal volumes of colour, steadily growing orders of colour, grouping, the principle of rotation, the identity of quantity and quality, [and] democratic pictorial structure.” Lohse applied this complex of visual properties directly to human society. “Owing to their flexible and dialectical character, serial and modular methods of composition are parallels of the expression and activities in a new social reality.” However, “integrating these new systems and methods of composition into society ... will not be possible until [people] acquire the capability of recognising in them an analogy to their own behaviour and self-understanding. The prerequisite is a nonhierarchical, transparent social structure.” Clearly, Lohse’s art is thus also impelled by a social-utopian component.

6 systematische Farbreihen von blau zu blau (6 Systematic Rows of Colour from Blue to Blue) belongs to the category of serial orders and is based on a 1955 sketch. It consists of six rows of six coloured squares each following a systematic sequence from blue to blue via several shades of green as well as yellow, orange, red, magenta and purple. Lohse shifted the sequence of colours two squares to the right in comparison to the preceding row, which becomes evident when focusing on the yellow squares. The colours appear only once per row, both vertically and horizontally, while the repetition of the ten different colours increases: blue, at the beginning and end of the rows, as well as purple and bluish green, each appear twice, magenta and dark green three times, red and medium green four times, orange and light green five times, and yellow six times.

The arrangement of the painting is not hierarchical and does not make a distinction between figure and ground. Each square of colour corresponds to the square format of the whole. The squares circulate rhythmically within that whole but can also be envisioned as a sequence that continues into space beyond the painting. Lohse described his expandable compositions as “limited-unlimited systems”. Thanks to the saturation and luminosity of the colours, the painting radiates a “positive” presence, although neither psychological interpretation nor a personal signature had any relevance for Lohse.

JR

Richard Paul Lohse
6 systematische Reihen in rot und grün mit Verdichtung nach innen

1955/1971

Richard Paul Lohse
1902 Zurich – 1988 Zurich

Oil on canvas
Signed, inscribed, titled and dated verso:
Richard Paul Lohse Zurich /
[title] / 1955/1971
150 × 150 cm

Inv. no. P261M / Acquired 2014

This is also one of Richard Paul Lohse's serial orders. The work shows six by six rows with red and green as bipolar colour values in a sequence of graded hues to yellow. The square fields in the diagonals of the work are dynamically proportioned – 5:5, 3:3, 1:1, 1:1, 3:3, 5:5 – while all the other fields are rectangular in the proportion of 3:5, 1:5, 1:5 and 3:5 or 5:3, 5:1, 5:1, 5:3 as well as 1:3, 1:3, 3:1, 3:1. The colours are laid out so that they never come into contact with another identical colour.

As in the preceding painting (cat. 2), the composition is governed by a stringent and rational logic. Every single element in the painting has its firm and immutable place. As Lohse explains, a spiritual law "dictates the creative spontaneity of the sequence. The process of designing the whole acquires the character of patient and prolonged laboratory work."

JR

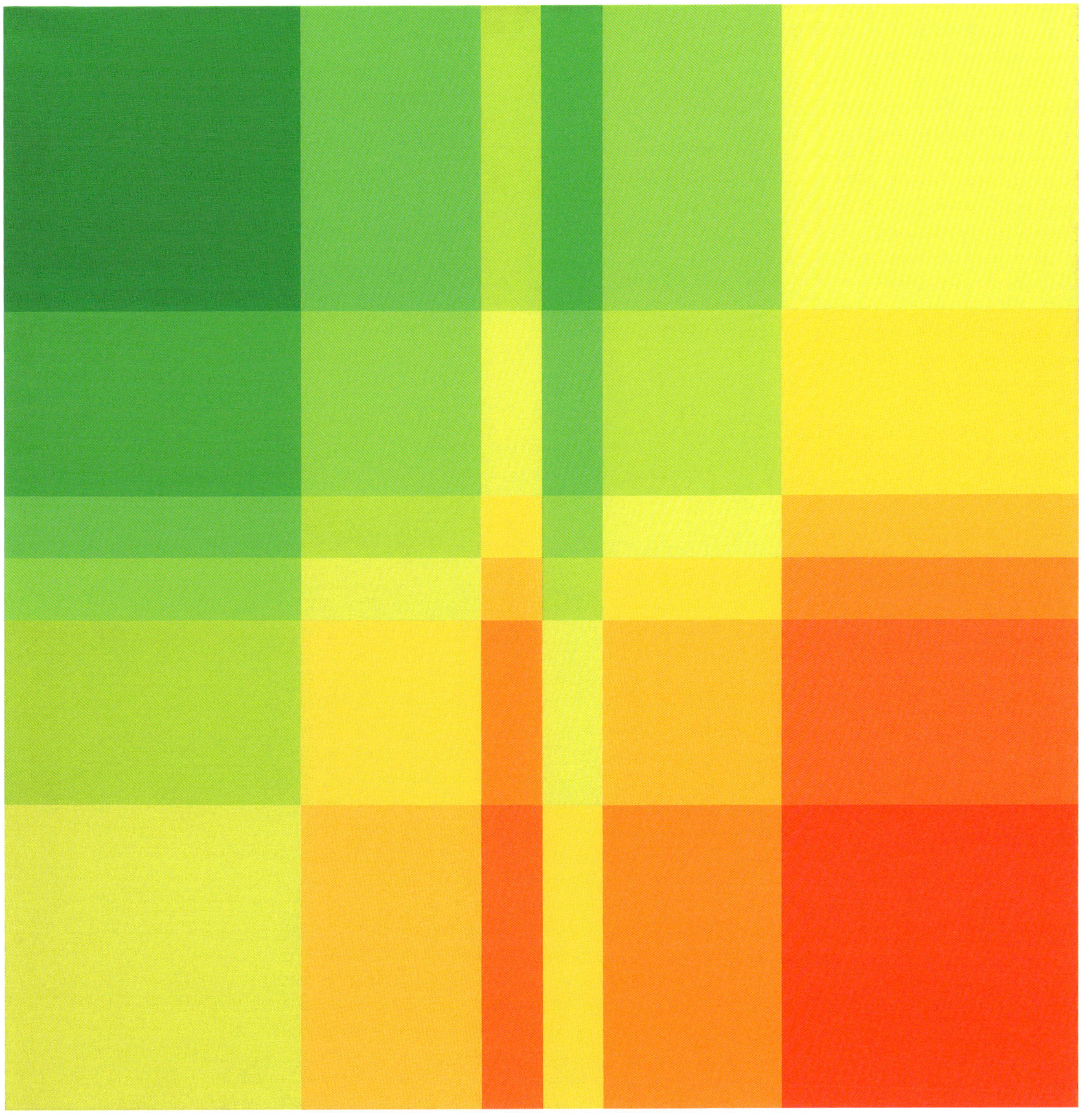

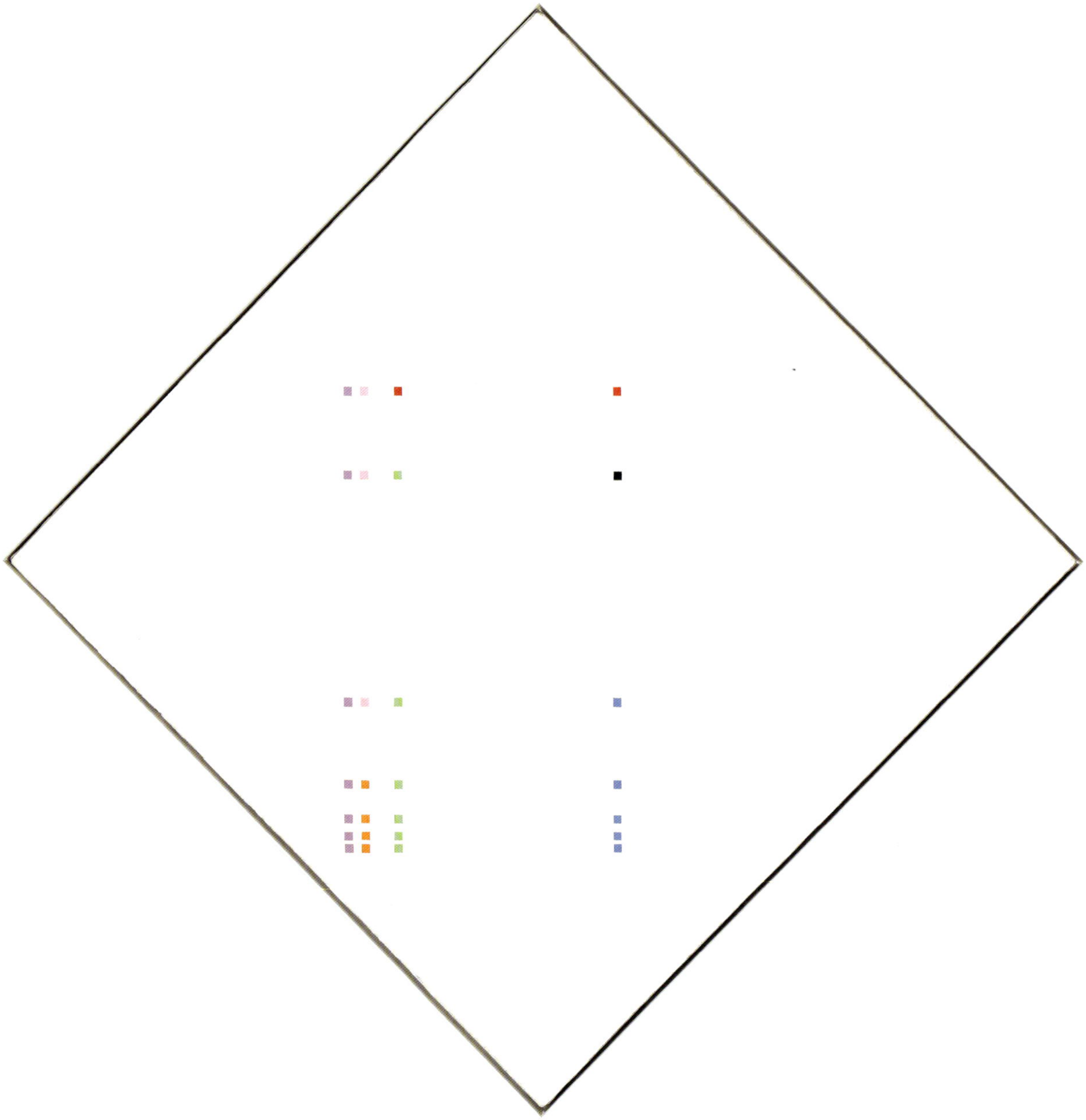

004

Max Bill
1908 Winterthur – 1994 Berlin

Oil on canvas
Signed, titled and dated on stretcher:
max bill Zurich / [title] / 1948
Signed and dated on canvas verso: bill 1948
79 × 79 cm (diagonal)

Inv. no. P74M / Acquired 2000

Max Bill
geordnete spannungen
1948

In 1927, Max Bill went to the Bauhaus in Dessau, where he studied with Josef Albers, László Moholy-Nagy, Oskar Schlemmer, Wassily Kandinsky, Paul Klee and others. They were important pioneers and representatives of modern art, each with different convictions and formal visions, ranging from constructivism and expressionism, abstraction and figuration to sensuality and spirituality. Within this wide-ranging framework, Bill forged a remarkably independent and cogent oeuvre, making him one of the most significant and certainly most influential students of the Bauhaus. On the basis of the ideas put forth in 1930 by Theo van Doesburg in the journal *Art Concret*, Bill – painter, sculptor, architect, graphic artist, designer and art theoretician – elaborated a definition, in 1936, of Concrete Art that would apply to aesthetic design across the board: works of Concrete Art show no external reference to natural phenomena; they are entirely divorced from reality; they are governed exclusively by their own laws; and they are not the result of abstraction.

Bill had already crossed the border to "concrete" nonfiguration in 1931, restricting his visual vocabulary to line, geometrical shape and the flat application of paint, with the occasional gradation of colours, modulated by varying their intensity. From 1932 to 1936 he was a member of the Parisian artist group Abstraction-Création, founded by Vantongerloo and Herbin, and including such artists as Arp, Delaunay, Van Doesburg, Kandinsky, Mondrian and Vordemberge-Gildewart. They all ascribed to the goal of creating an international forum for nonfigurative art through exhibitions and publications.

In an essay of 1949, Bill expressed the following thought: "The primal element of a visual work is geometry, the relationship of layers on a plane or in space. And just as mathematics is one of the essential means of primary thinking and thus of perceiving our surroundings, it is also one of the fundamental elements of a science of relations, of the relationship of thing to thing, group to group, movement to movement."

These thoughts have been visualised in the work *geordnete spannungen* (ordered tensions), created at almost the same time. On a white ground, Bill painted twenty-eight coloured squares, each 6 mm^2, in four or seven progressive rows depending on whether they are read vertically or horizontally. The proportions are based on the number 3 as the smallest unit and on 6 as the (square) module. Despite the stringent order that governs the rows, the work does not appear rigidly mathematical but rather poetic and playful, an impression generated especially by the small group size of the squares, the intriguing rhythm in which they follow each other, the asymmetrical arrangement and, finally, the colours that could as much be the result of deliberate choice as pure chance. In addition, the diamond format, also seen occasionally in Mondrian's work as of 1918, creates an impression of increasing dynamics. Above all, however, the painting shows a visual vibrancy and clarity, which characterises Max Bill's oeuvre as a whole.

UW

Max Bill
neun akzente aus quadratischem feld
1949–1951

005

Max Bill
1908 Winterthur – 1994 Berlin

Oil on canvas
Signed, titled and dated on stretcher:
max bill / [title] / 1949–51
Signed and dated on canvas verso: bill 1949–51
62.5 × 62.5 cm (diagonal)

Inv. no. P31M / Acquired 1996

Bill painted the diamond-format work *neun akzente aus quadratischem feld* (nine accents from a square field) between 1949 and 1951 while serving as the director at the Hochschule für Gestaltung in Ulm. Nine green-black circular fields are seen on a white ground primed in green; they are laid out like bowling pins and slightly fuzzy in outline because Bill dabbed the paint onto the canvas. A barely visible linear square runs parallel, between them and the edge of the picture. In addition, they are linked by a subtle net of smaller squares that abut each other at right angles in the middle of the circles. This work clearly reveals Bill's predilection for symmetrical compositions of rows, rhythmical planes, the grouping of geometric forms and the play of colours. The reduced aesthetic of his work, which also applies to his sculptures and architecture, bespeaks his focus on a sparing use of materials. The titles of the works also illustrate his desire to establish a connection between science and art, and to systematise the creative process. In the work that he created, Bill aimed to demonstrate his conviction that Concrete Art is the "pure expression of harmonic scale and laws" and, as such, the basis of a "fitting spiritual order". According to the artist's second wife, Angela Thomas, a renewed interest in this subject matter had inspired the decision to mount this painting on the wall of his studio shortly before he died.

JR

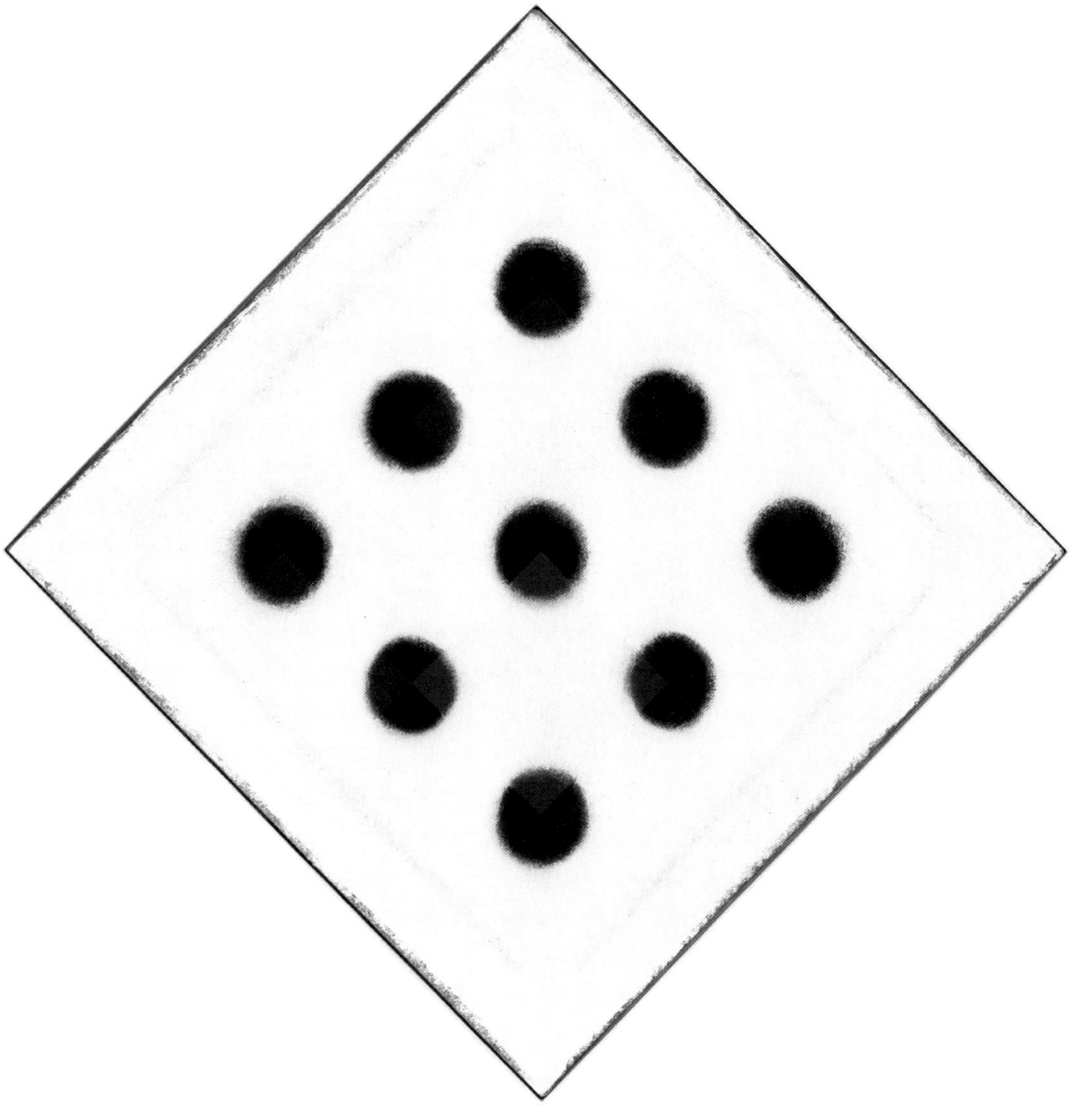

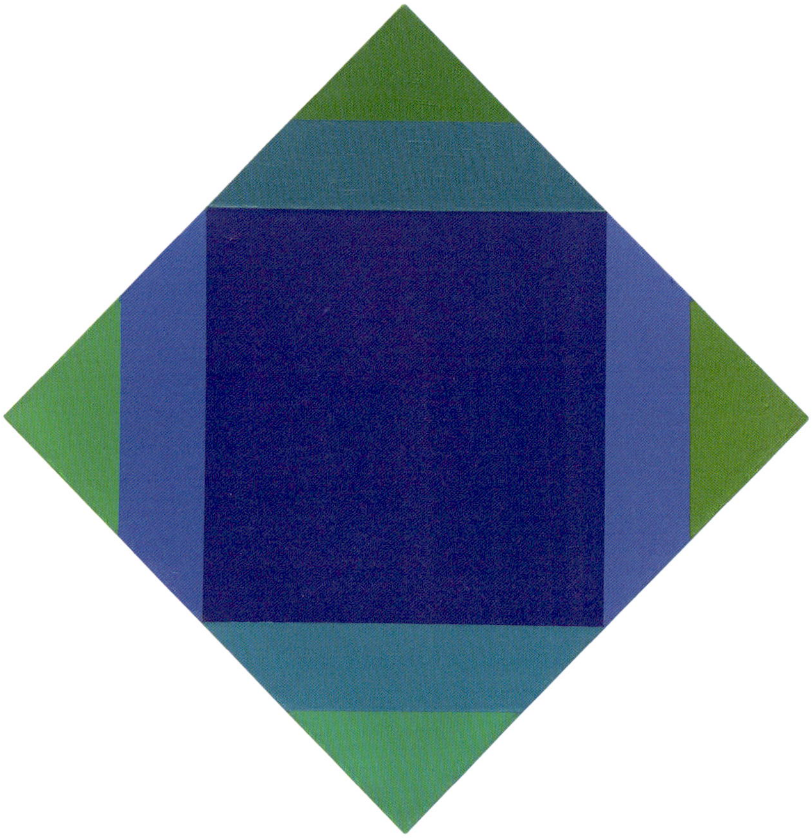

006

Max Bill
1908 Winterthur – 1994 Berlin

Oil on canvas
Signed, dated, titled and inscribed on stretcher:
max bill / 1972–74 / [title] / diagonal
Signed and dated on canvas verso: bill / 1972–74
33.5 × 33.5 cm (diagonal)

Inv. no. P35M / Acquired 1994

Max Bill

zerstrahlung von blau

1972–1974

Max Bill
unendliche schleife
1994–95

007

Max Bill
1908 Winterthur – 1994 Berlin

Granite
200 × 180 × 200 cm

Inv. no. S47M / Acquired 1998

The notion of an artistic configuration that would later be called *unendliche schleife* (endless loop) goes back, according to Max Bill, to the year 1935. The architect Marcel Breuer had asked him to devise a sculpture for a nonfunctional electric fireplace in a London exhibition venue. Bill envisioned an elementary, floating shape that would be set in motion by the draught from the chimney and would replace the flickering of the fire. An endless loop resulted from his experimentation, created by twisting the ends of a strip of paper by 180 degrees and then joining them together. The commissioned work never came about but the form Bill had found inspired a variety of iterations in different sizes and materials. For the 1936 triennial in Milan, Bill had craftsmen produce the first loop out of plaster, which hung suspended from the ceiling above a column. Not much later, he created a variation, 1.5 m in length, which he placed on the floor.

The properties of the endless loop fascinated Bill. Since it consists of only one plane, inside and outside, front and back are identical. Dietmar Guderian observed that from every point on the plane, every other point can be reached without stepping beyond the edge; moreover, infinite paths can be traced without changing direction. The edge of the loop forms one single line that runs parallel to itself. For Bill that meant the end of Euclidean geometry's theorem that parallel lines intersect in infinity. Here, the line, running parallel to itself, never intersects despite its infinite course. Only later did the artist discover that his endless loop had been prefigured by the Möbius strip, named after the Leipzig mathematician August Ferdinand Möbius (1790–1868). Bill had actually reinvented the phenomenon and, as he wrote himself, created "an art object out of a mathematical problem of topology".

Before implementing the version in stone, Bill had produced smaller models using paper, wire mesh or tin. After determining the exact shape and scale, he made a drawing as the basis for larger models in plaster or tin, after which he had the original produced in stone. The latter required highly specialised craftsmen who cut the shape out of a huge, solid monolith and then polished it. There are five variations of the *unendliche schleife*. The present one is the last and largest, made by the stonemasons Paolo Grassi, Silvio Santini and Mario Fruendi from Torano, near Carrara, out of red Assuan granite, a material that Bill particularly appreciated. Bill did not live to enjoy the final work, which was completed in 1995 under the guidance of his son Jakob Bill.

UW

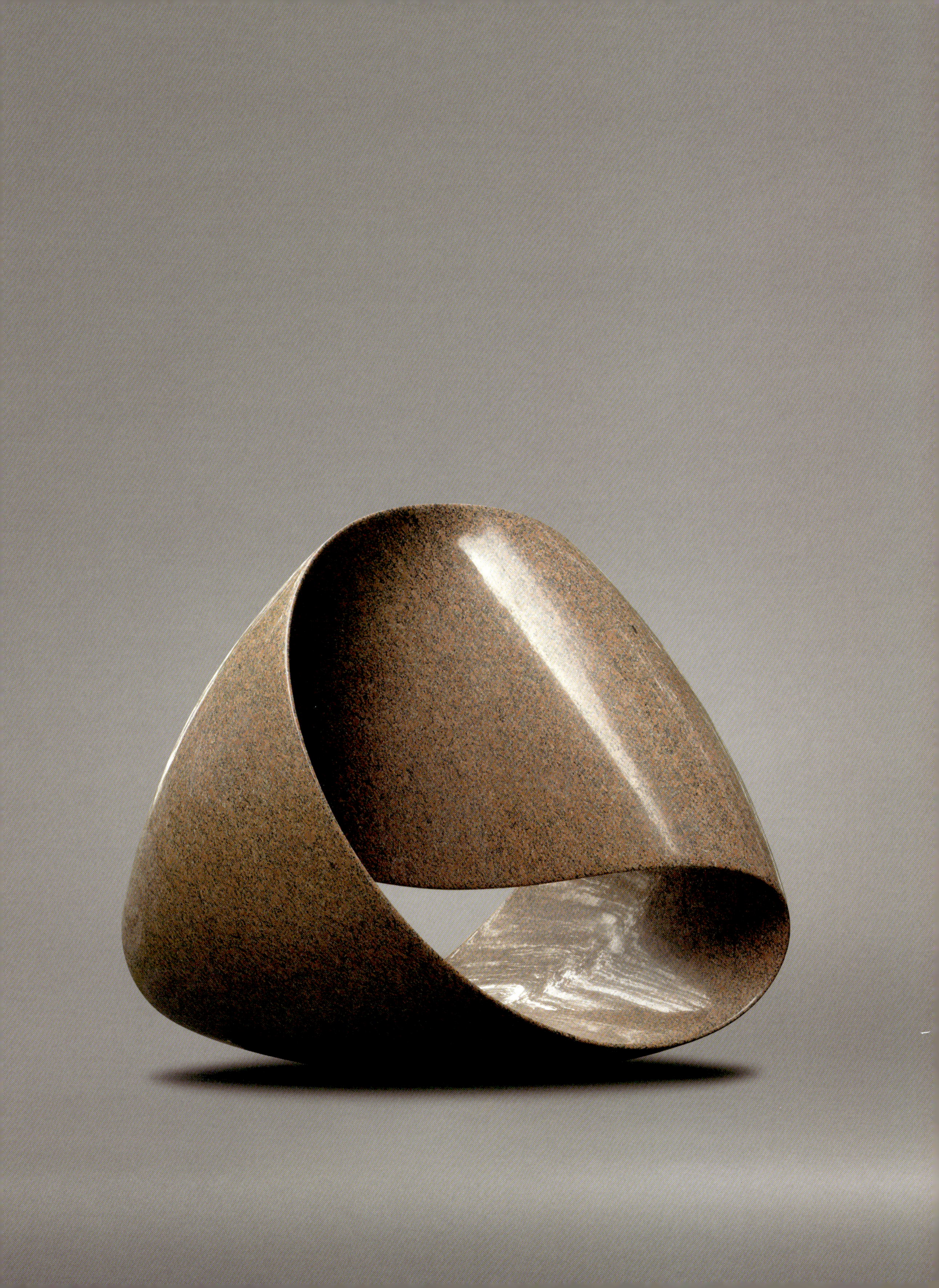

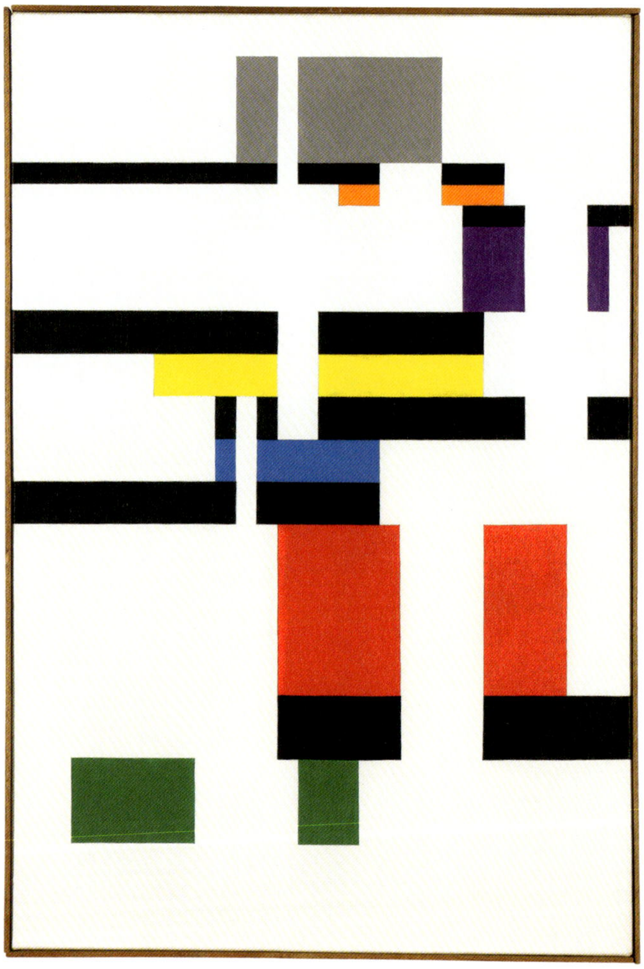

008

Verena Loewensberg
1912 Zurich – 1986 Zurich

Oil on canvas
Signed and dated on stretcher and on canvas verso: Loewensberg 44*
88 x 60 cm

Inv. no. P302M / Acquired 2016

Verena Loewensberg
Untitled
1948

*According to the catalogue raisonné, Verena Loewensberg subsequently mistook the date of the work.

Verena Loewensberg always felt an affinity with the "language of geometry", which led to her connection, while commuting between Zurich and Paris, with Max Bill and Georges Vantongerloo. Both artists were important sources of inspiration. Although she was later associated with the so-called Concrete artists in Zurich – not only Max Bill but also Camille Graeser, Richard Paul Lohse and others – she felt that the term "concrete", as defined by Theo van Doesburg in 1930, did not apply to her work; she preferred to describe it as "constructive". For her, the constructive language of geometry was always related to "mood" and therefore to feelings.

Loewensberg would begin with a preliminary study on graph paper, which she transferred to scale to the primed canvas. She then painted both shapes and background without the use of masking tape, wielding her paintbrush with great precision, applying colour after colour, layer after layer until she had achieved a seemingly homogeneous picture plane whose material quality was a consequence of both painting technique and the oil of the binder.

Loewensberg knew Van Doesburg personally and deeply appreciated his work despite her reservations regarding his definition of Concrete Art. In contrast to Mondrian's uncompromising restriction of his artistic vocabulary to horizontals, verticals and the primary colours of yellow, red and blue, Van Doesburg always worked with an expanded repertoire of shapes and colours, for instance, the triangle, which leads to diagonals, as well as the so-called secondary colours, orange, green and purple. In her untitled painting of 1948, with its clearly visible pencil lines and pinpricks caused by transferring the study to the canvas, Loewensberg combines rectangular stripes and fields in an orthogonal composition. Bands of grey, orange, purple, yellow, blue, red and green, each doubled on a white ground, are separated from top to bottom by bands or fields of black. In this way, black and white as well as all the colours and their complements are represented in the painting. The delicately balanced composition leaves ample room for the white ground and extends only partially to the edge of the picture plane, making the whole seem light and floating. Verena Loewensberg placed each of her shapes and colours with compelling, almost inexorable cogency, and yet they are delightfully casual in their interaction.

UW

Verena Loewensberg
Untitled
1947

Verena Loewensberg
1912 Zurich – 1986 Zurich

Oil on canvas
Signed on stretcher: Loewensberg
40 × 40 cm

Inv. no. P288M / Acquired 2016

This painting of 1947 demonstrates Verena Loewensberg's uninhibited, undogmatic treatment of form and colour. Large and small circles with segments varying in size and shape reference space far beyond the picture plane but also reach into it from outside, coalescing into a dynamic position. Yellow occupies the centre as a diagonal "figure", its shape a passive consequence of encroaching circular lines. But the energy of the colour activates the shape, which is embedded in a whirlwind of circles and segments in hues of unbroken purity: luminous green, red, blue and purple as well as white and black.

In the 1940s, Max Bill, whom Loewensberg perceived not as a teacher but as a "challenge", also experimented with variable circular shapes and segments. These elements had, in fact, already played an important role in Kandinsky's compositions. What's more, as a member of the artist group De Stijl, Georges Vantongerloo, whom Loewensberg knew well, aimed to counter the aesthetic stringency of his colleagues, above all Piet Mondrian's rigid grid of horizontals and verticals, by having lines of exquisitely tender airiness snake their way across the picture plane. Verena Loewensberg, younger than her colleagues, no doubt took inspiration from them, ultimately maturing into an artist whose compositions proved astonishingly diverse, distinctive and independent.
UW

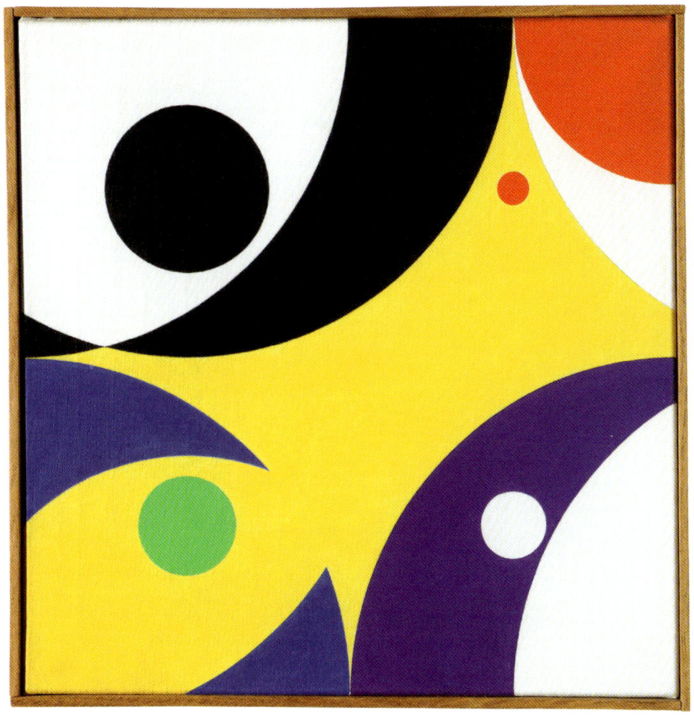

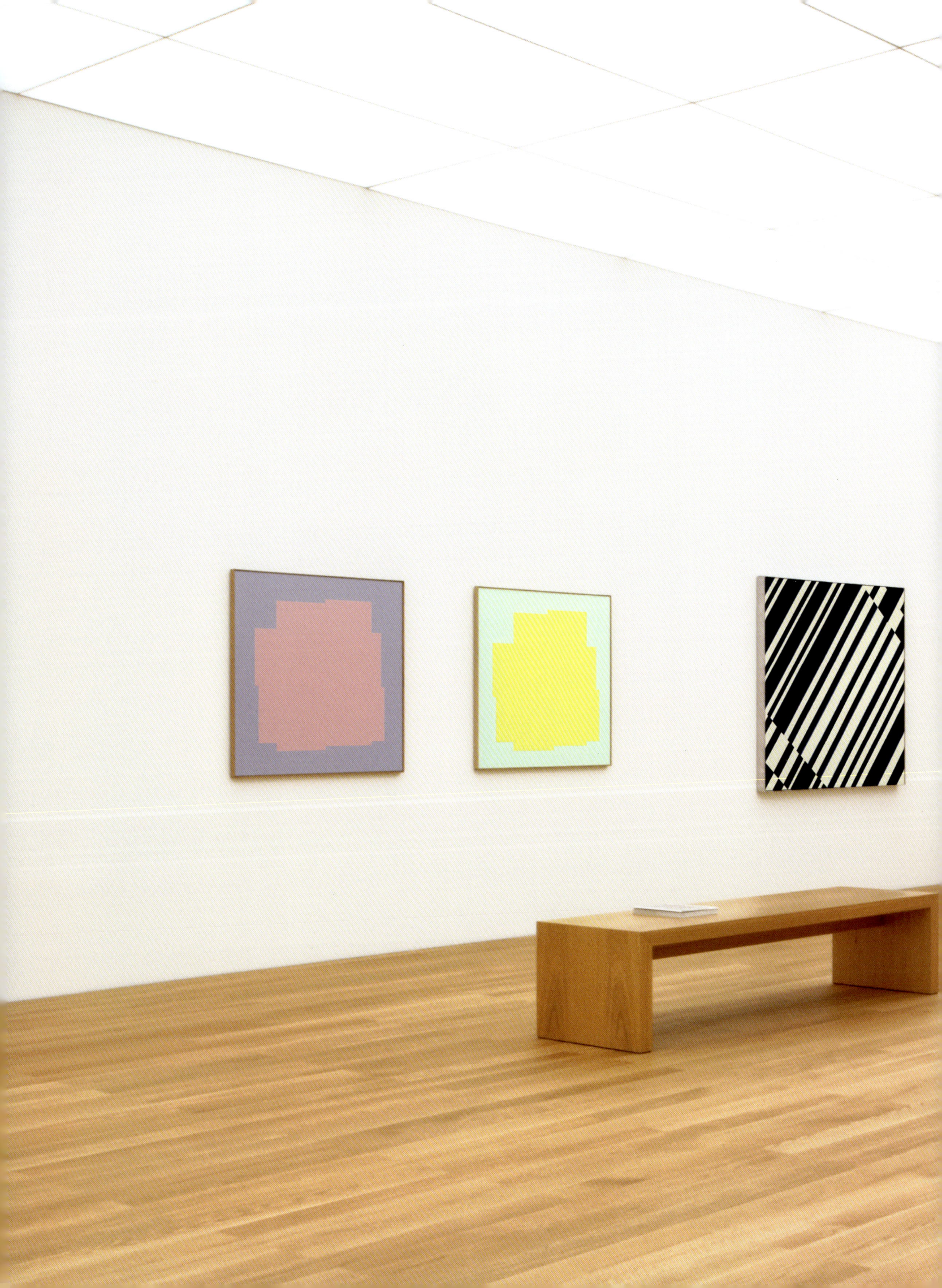

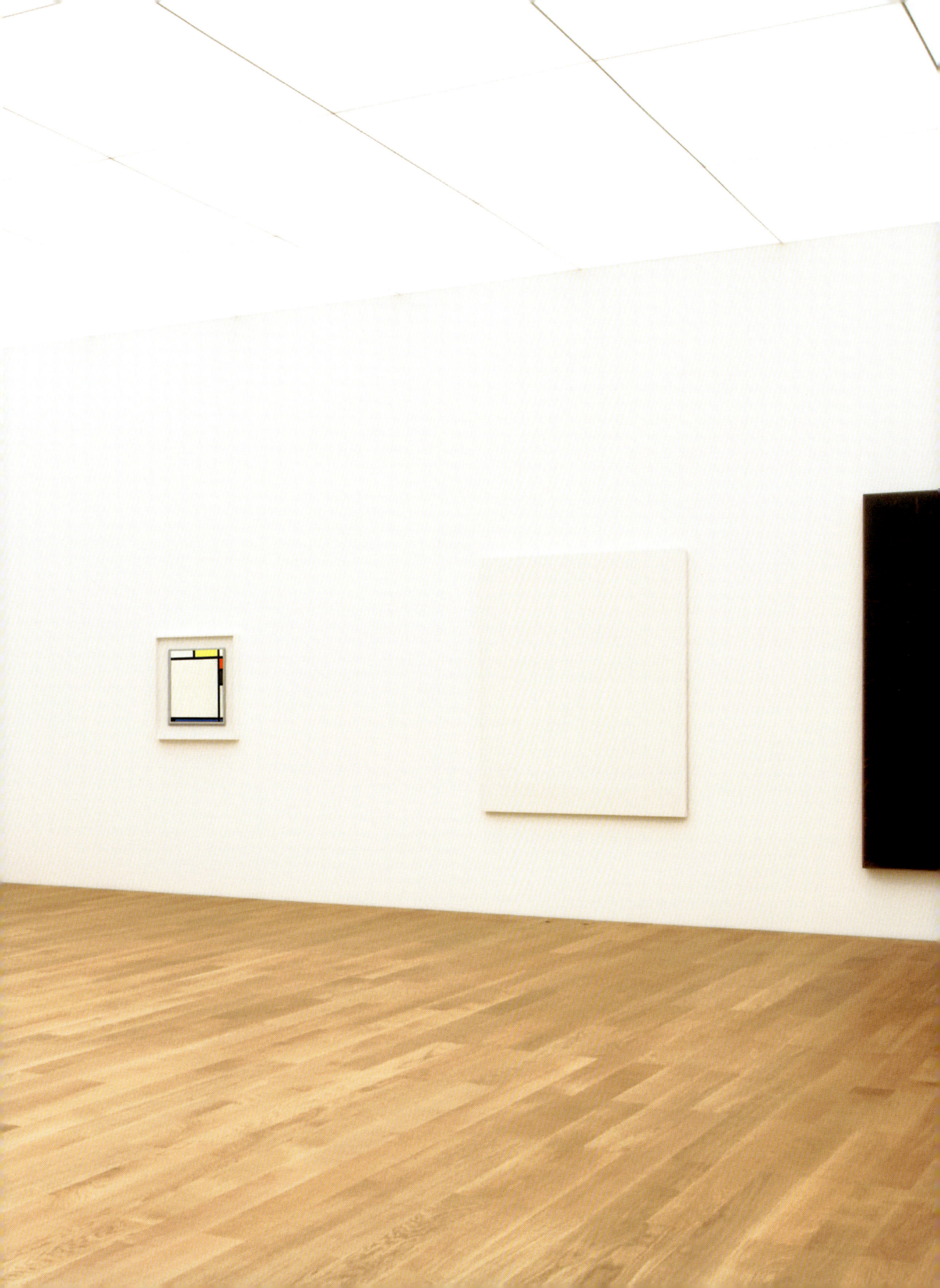

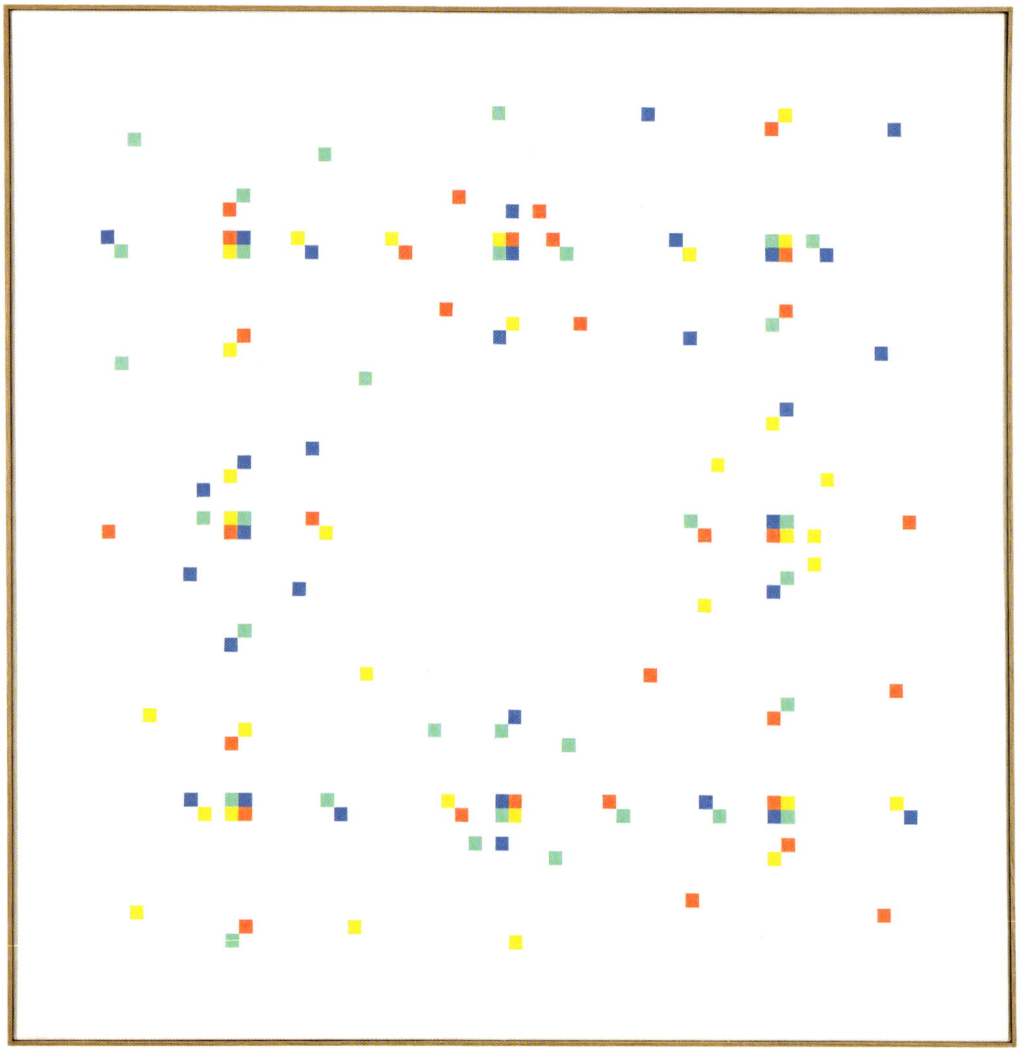

010

Verena Loewensberg
1912 Zurich – 1986 Zurich

Oil on canvas
Signed and dated on stretcher and on canvas verso: Loewensberg 77
110 × 110 cm

Inv. no. P305M / Acquired 2016

Verena Loewensberg
Untitled
1977

Verena Loewensberg
Untitled
1981

011

Verena Loewensberg
1912 Zurich – 1986 Zurich

Oil on canvas
Signed and dated on stretcher and on canvas verso: Loewensberg 81
100 × 100 cm

Inv. no. P246M / Acquired 2013

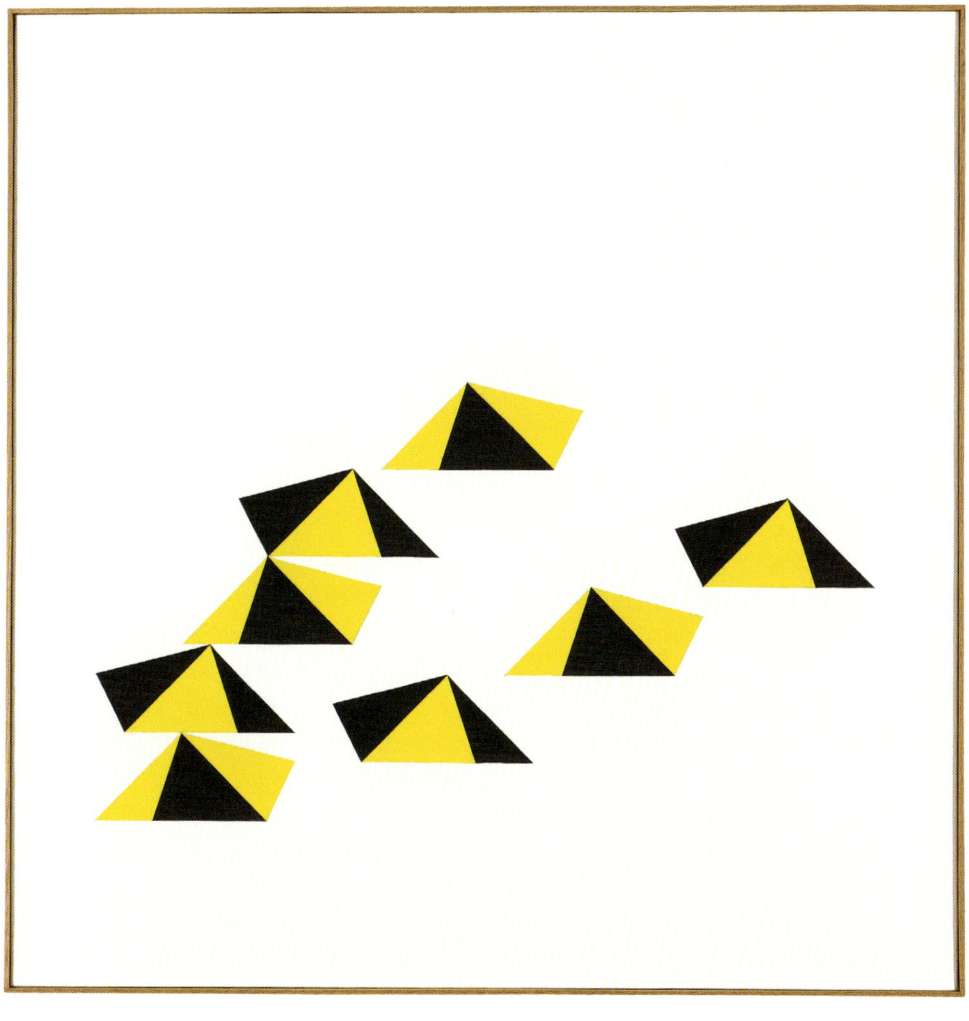

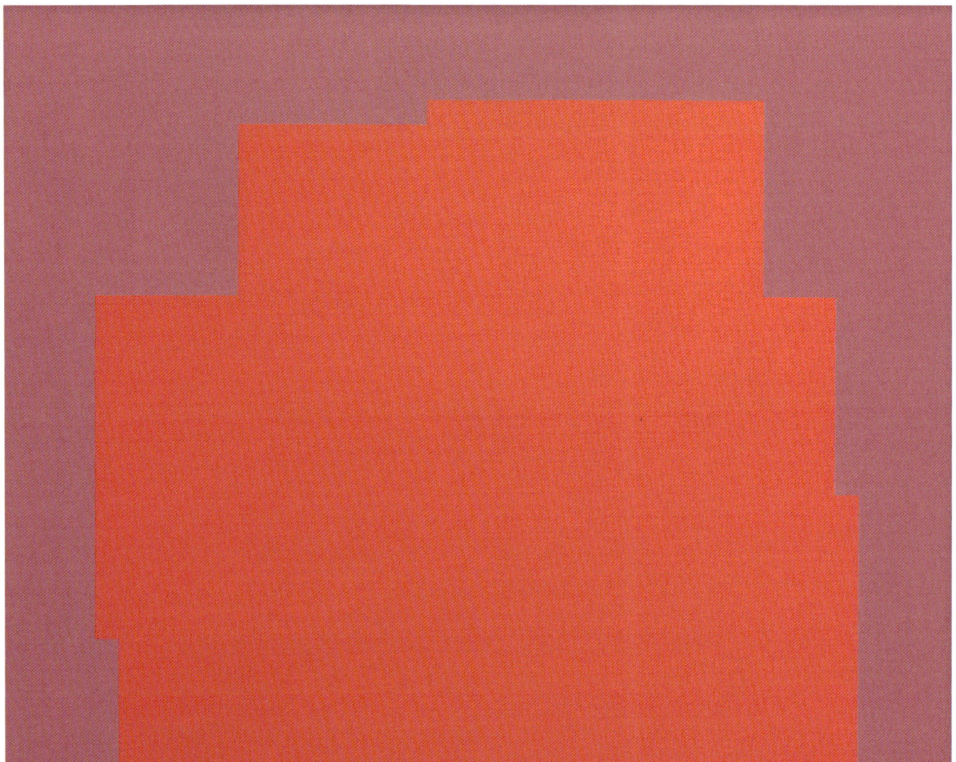

012

Verena Loewensberg
1912 Zurich – 1986 Zurich

Oil on canvas
Signed and dated on stretcher and on canvas verso: Loewensberg 84
100 × 100 cm

Inv. no. P247M / Acquired 2013

Verena Loewensberg
Untitled
1984

The series of twenty-nine works in two colours, painted between 1983 and 1986, that is, late in life, may well be considered Verena Loewensberg's ultimate artistic legacy. The series unites two ideas that she developed early in her career, the staggered rectangle and the dialogue between two colours. But these works also show a clarity, an almost floating tranquillity of form and subtlety of colour, that can only emerge after many years of artistic endeavour and experience.

All of these paintings, measuring 100 by 100 cm, present a monochrome shape on a monochromatic ground. The essentially orthogonal shape always has an irregular right-angled outline in a colour that is different from the background. On comparing these twenty-nine single works, one finds that none of the shapes are identical; they are each distinguished through immeasurably subtle variations in the number, position and depth of the angles that mark their outline. What's more, the dialogue between the colours, from starkly contrasting to gently refined combinations, is not governed by theory but exclusively by sensual response. These qualities define and heighten the singular appeal and value of this series.

Whether studied individually or as a whole, commitment to the works transcends their gripping visual impact, leading to concentration and, ultimately, meditation. A border crossing is conceivable – from the inner world of concrete forms and colours to a transcendental place of sublime weightlessness.

UW

Verena Loewensberg
Untitled
1984–85

013

Verena Loewensberg
1912 Zurich – 1986 Zurich

Oil on canvas
Signed and dated on stretcher and
on canvas verso: Loewensberg 84/85
100 × 100 cm

Inv. no. P248M / Acquired 2013

014

Verena Loewensberg
1912 Zurich – 1986 Zurich

Oil on canvas
100 × 100 cm

Inv. no. P249M / Acquired 2013

Verena Loewensberg
Untitled
1985

This is the last work painted by Verena Loewensberg. It is neither signed nor dated and, like all of her work, it has no title in order to give beholders the greatest possible freedom of perception and thought.
UW

Gottfried Honegger
Gestern
1957–58

Gottfried Honegger
1917 Zurich – 2016 Zurich

Oil on canvas
Signed and dated verso: HONEGGER 1957–1958
100 × 100 cm

Inv. no. P111M / Acquired 2000

In the early 1950s, the successful graphic artist Gottfried Honegger took up painting, first working in small format, cautiously and carefully probing what might be transferred from the visible world to the picture plane. He transformed his lyrically rendered objects of nature into signs and metaphors. It seems as if Honegger was looking not only on but also in things, as if trying to capture both outer form and inner structure at once, as if simultaneously embracing and disassembling the things of this world with his gaze and exploring them with an equally sensual and analytical eye.

Growing up as a child in Sent in the Lower Engadine where his mother came from, Honegger honed his perception, studying the wide-open landscape and single plants, striking cliff formations and the scales of pine cones. He learned that nature is as carefully ordered as it is chaotic. Everything perceived with open-minded curiosity would form the basis of an approach to form that prevailed throughout his later oeuvre.

The study of art complemented his insights drawn from nature. Honegger discovered not only the Cubists and Picasso, whose work he saw at Kunsthaus Zürich in 1932, but above all Juan Gris, who was, as Honegger writes, his model during the early years of his career. He "loved and admired his poetry, his warmth". *Gestern* (Yesterday), painted in Zurich and measuring one square metre, shows the influence of Gris, as exemplified in the floating serenity of simple, subtly composed shapes and colours in an abstract assemblage that draws on the tradition of nonfigurative painting. Honegger has laid the shapes out flat on the picture plane. Surrounded by a deep brown background, they seem to be embedded in the dark soil of the earth, like archaic treasures that must be sheltered and preserved. The composition emanates a quiet magic with its elements coloured like precious gems, its surfaces smooth or pastose and the light absorbed or gently glistening. On the one hand, we distinctly perceive items in relief and yet, on the other, we are deceived by the illusion of folds and cells set off against the background. Honegger explores the broad spectrum of painterly qualities between plane and space, between reality and fiction, between sense experience and mental conception, culled equally from nature and mind. *Gestern* is one of the last paintings the artist made before moving to the United States, before the "breakthrough of the monochrome" that would define his working years to come.
UW

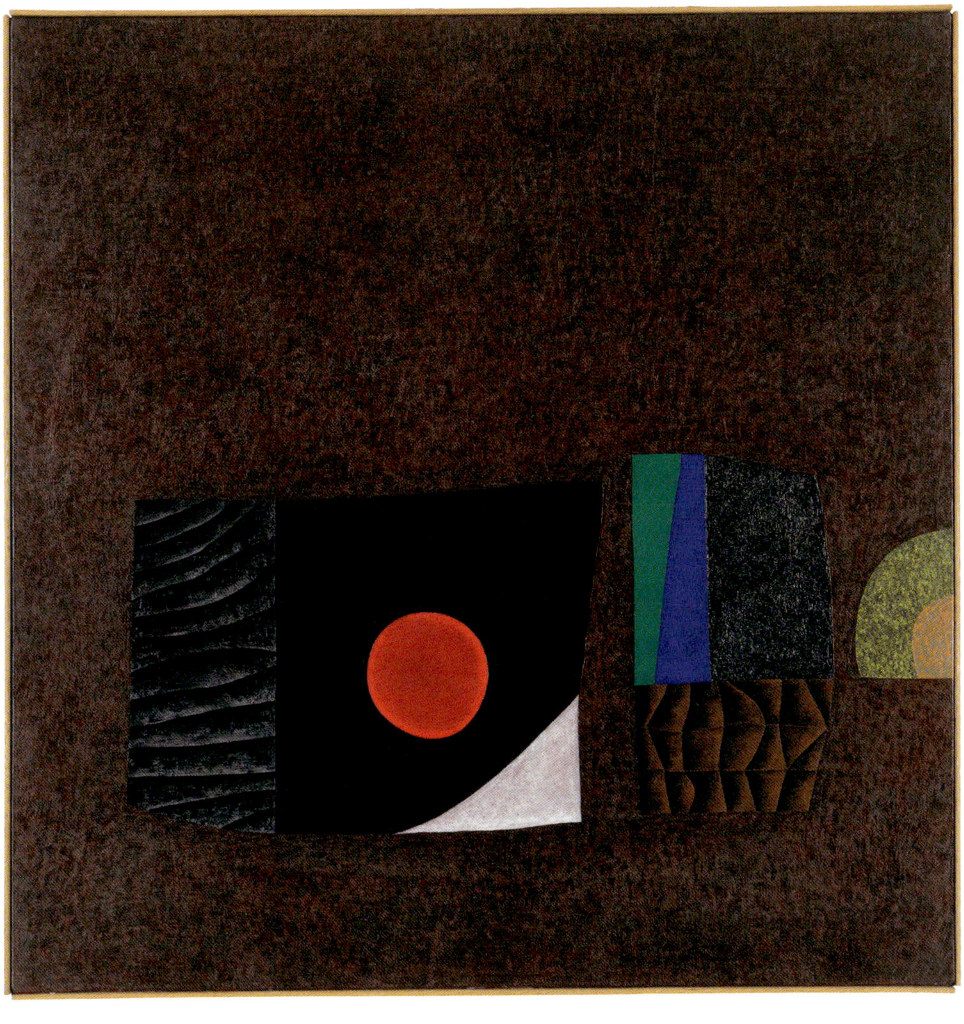

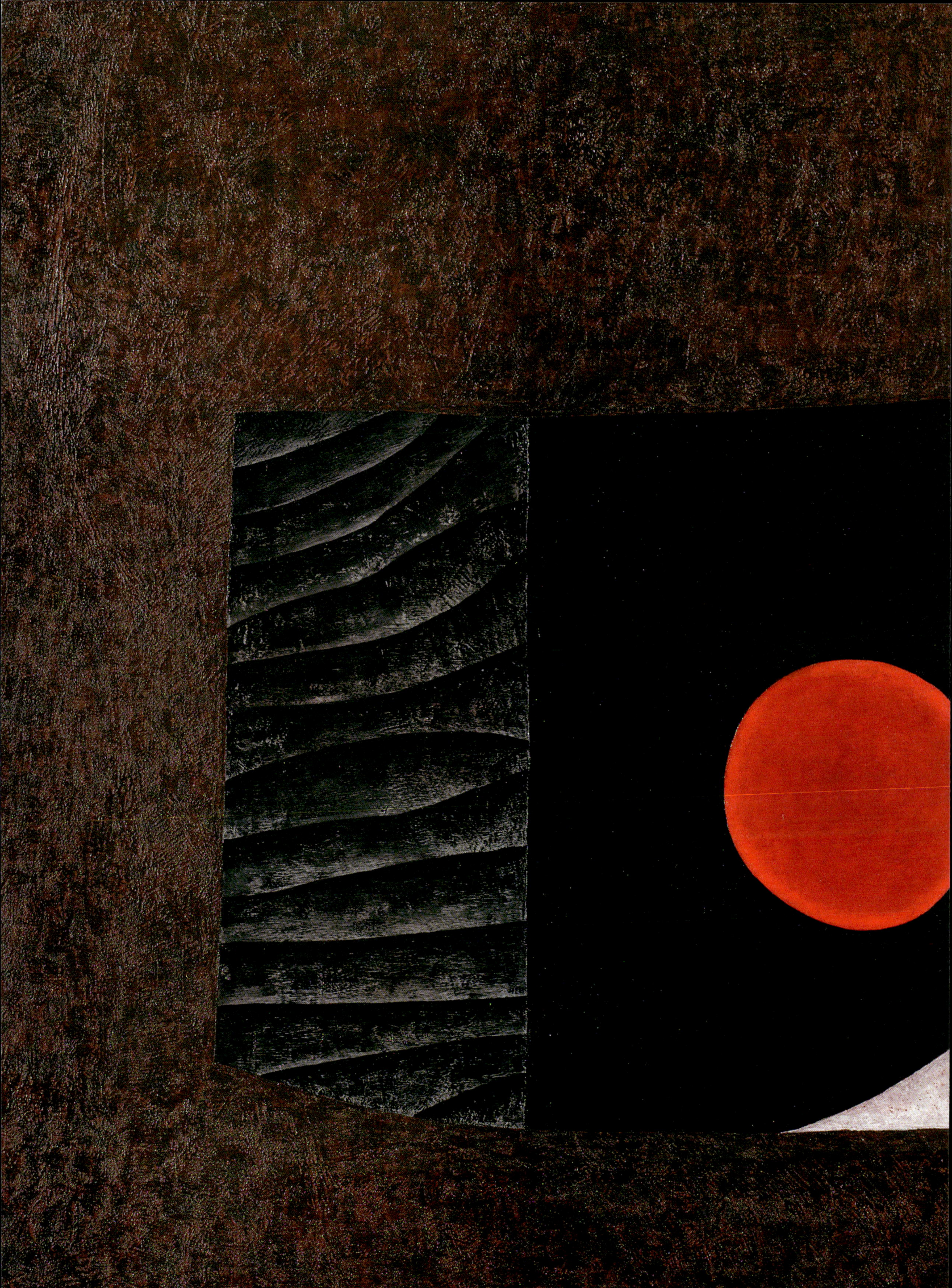

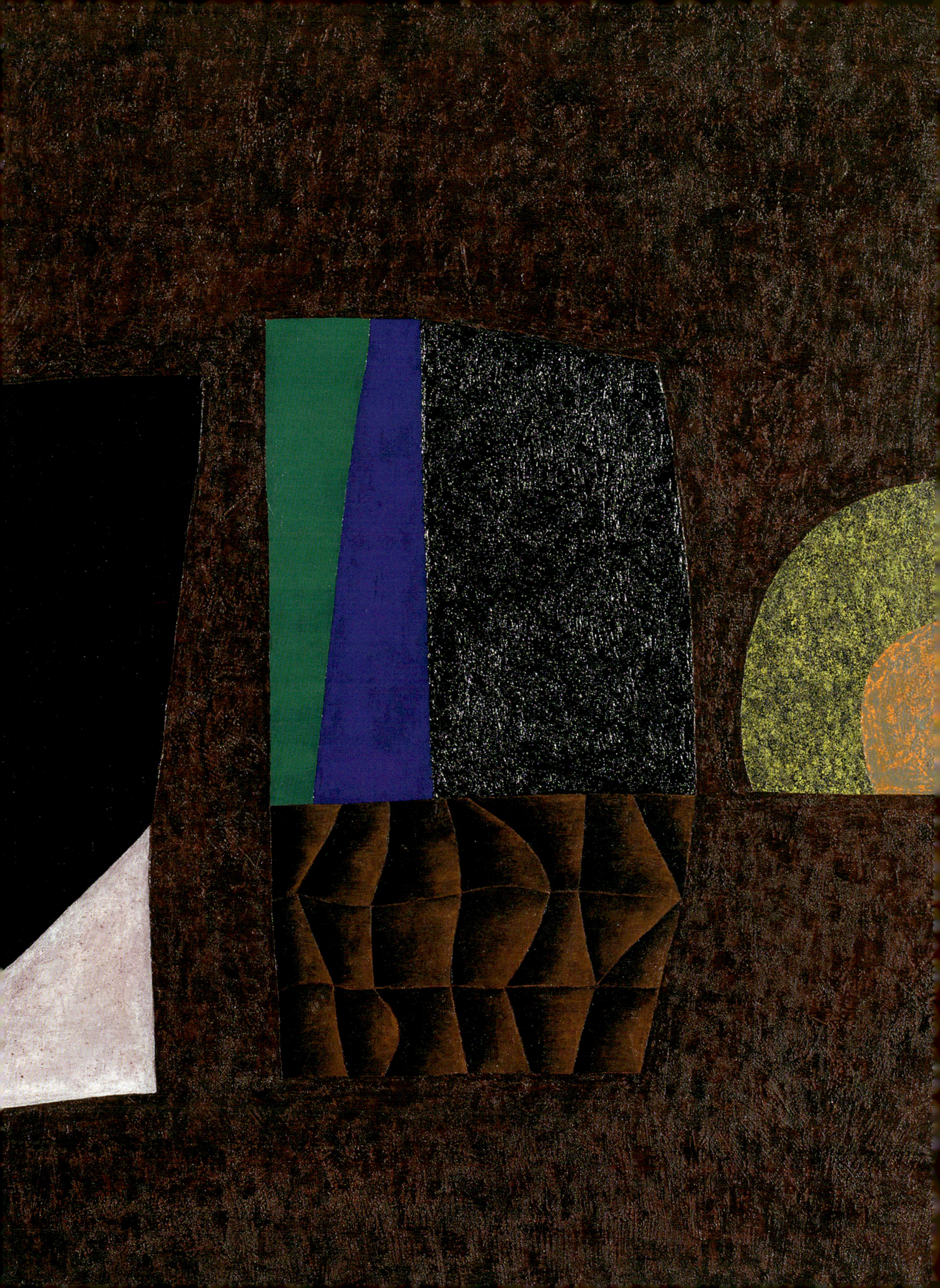

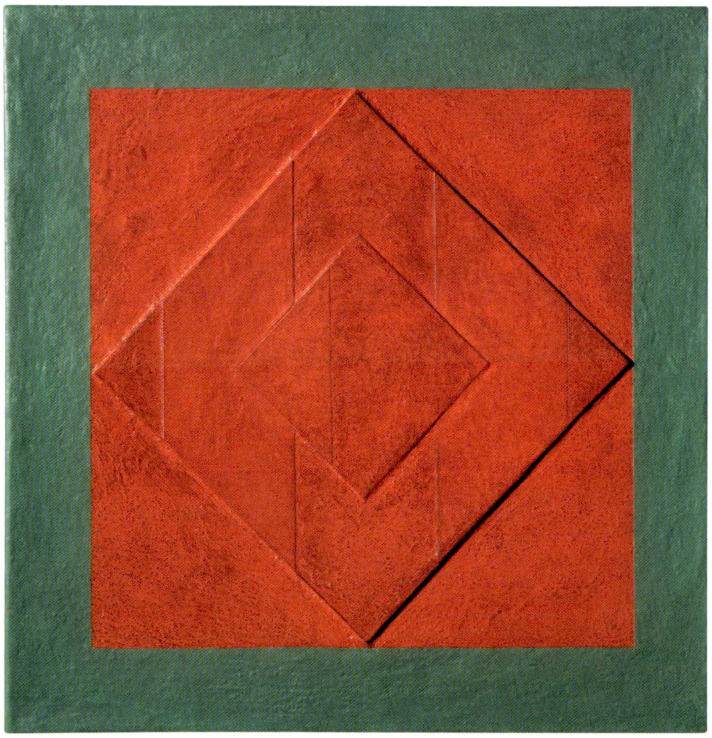

Gottfried Honegger
Untitled
1957

Gottfried Honegger
1917 Zurich – 2016 Zurich

Oil on cardboard on canvas
Signed and dated verso: HONEGGER 1957
42.5 × 42.5 cm

Inv. no. P112M / Acquired 2004

This small-format work of 1957, combining relief and collage, is the first in a series of *Tableaux Reliefs* that Gottfried Honegger continued to produce until the 1990s. They were essentially prefigured in the small-format, lyrical, abstract paintings made prior to 1957 (see cat. 15), in which patterns of folds and cells are still derived from the forms of nature and seem to be tangibly set off against the ground of the painting. Honegger transferred them to cardboard, thus taking a step from illusion to reality, from abstract to concrete nonfiguration on the basis of geometrical forms. Like that of his artist colleagues from Zurich, Max Bill, Richard Paul Lohse and Camille Graeser, his Concrete work is not entirely without precedent. Kazimir Malevich, Piet Mondrian and especially Theo van Doesburg spearheaded the notion. Van Doesburg had already coined the programmatic term "Concrete Art" in 1930, and in 1936 Max Bill specified that Concrete Art refers to "those works of art that have been made on the basis of their own intrinsic means and laws without any external reference to natural appearances, in other words, not through abstraction."

In this work, a wide green margin frames a centered square, to which Honegger applied two symmetrically up-ended, smaller red squares of cardboard. These are, in turn, articulated by vertical variations in level. The elements of this relief refer to nothing; they represent nothing but themselves – they are autonomous and concrete.

UW

Gottfried Honegger
Waria
1960

017

Gottfried Honegger
1917 Zurich – 2016 Zurich

Collage, oil on wood
Signed, inscribed, dated and titled verso:
HONEGGER / NEW YORK / 1960 /
TITEL: WARIA
152 × 152 cm

Inv. no. P178M / Acquired 2006

While living and working in New York for two years, from 1958 to 1960, Gottfried Honegger continued to experiment with the relief-collage, the first of which he had created in 1957 (see cat. 16). A successful exhibition at Martha Jackson Gallery (1960), in which he presented only red reliefs, gave him the impetus to abandon his profession as a commercial artist altogether and devote himself to fine art. Inspired by young artists in the United States, among them Clyfford Still, Franz Kline, Mark Rothko, Barnett Newman and his friend Sam Francis, Honegger started painting medium- and largeformat monochromes.

The square relief in the centre of the dark red picture *Waria* presents a free composition of geometrical elements, yielding a formal vocabulary on which Honegger would base his future work. It consists of squares, rectangles, triangles and trapezoids. For the artist, geometry provided the constructive foundation of life; it was the law that determines the form of all natural phenomena. In the years that followed, Honegger added circles and segments, cubes, spheres and cylinders to his formal vocabulary – in painting, sculpture, prints and drawings.

Waria is the first name of Honegger's wife, Warja Lavater, a graphic artist and illustrator born in Winterthur in 1913 († 2007 Zurich). Sam Francis acquired the picture in New York; it had previously been exhibited at Martha Jackson Gallery.

UW

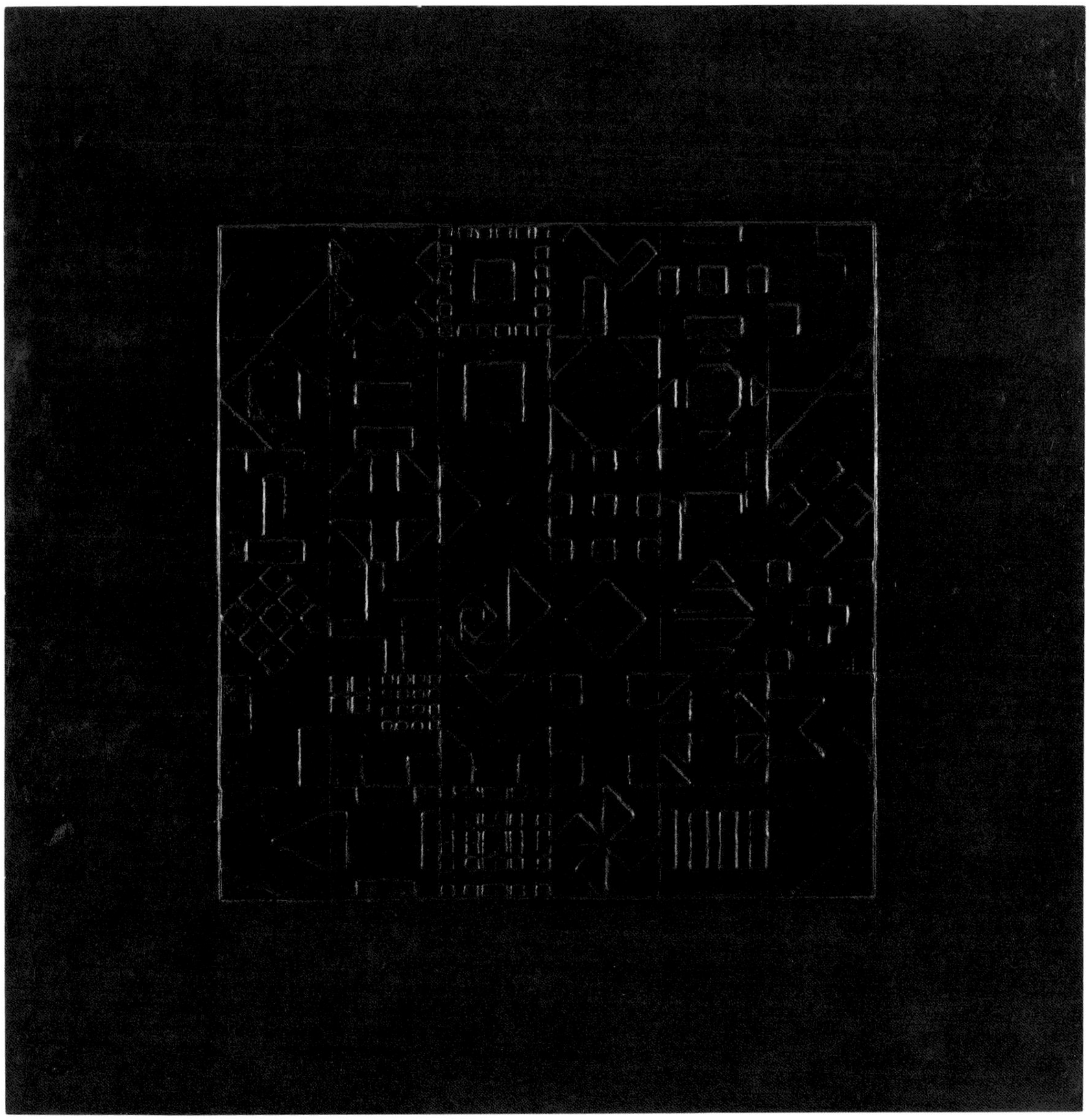

018

Gottfried Honegger
1917 Zurich – 2016 Zurich

Oil, acrylic, board on canvas
Signed, dated and inscribed on verso:
HONEGGER 1979 / Z.825.1
200 × 250 cm

Inv. no. P211M / Acquired 2009

Gottfried Honegger
Tableau-Relief Z.825.1
1979

As in other *Tableaux Reliefs*, the blurred relief of the adjoining edges creates irregularities in the grid of the cardboard module and lends the whole a haptic, sensual quality. Honegger happily welcomed the accidental modifications caused by the nature of his material and its manual treatment because he never quite managed to embrace the stringency of "geometrically defined art", which he felt was mandatory among Zurich's Concrete artists. However, what distinguishes his work from pure geometry based exclusively on scale and number is the use of monochrome, his tribute to each single colour as colour, whether it be a warm yellow that spreads throughout the entire painting or any other colour, presented exclusively for its own sake, as a sensual phenomenon.
UW

Gottfried Honegger
Tableau-Relief P 725
1973

019

Gottfried Honegger
1917 Zurich – 2016 Zurich

Oil, acrylic, board on canvas
Signed, dated and inscribed verso:
HONEGGER 1973 / P 725
250 × 200 cm

Inv. no. P117M / Acquired 2004

Gottfried Honegger integrated the aspect of chance into his paintings, as Hans Arp had already done, for instance, in 1916, when he created his *Rectangles selon les lois du hasard*, under the influence of an exhilarating Dadaist mood of creation. Inspired by Jacques Monod's scientific book *Chance and Necessity*, Honegger devised a system of random mathematics, "flexible and full of surprises". He began throwing dice to determine the arrangement of the cardboard squares glued to his pictures and assigned the size of the squares to a specific number, as in the present work. The random sequence of predetermined numbers resulted in a blank leftover patch. Honegger was particularly interested in these remainders, in what had not come out even, as it were, in these "random leftovers at a random place in the picture". He painted the white of the cardboard squares with a transparent wash while making the white of the leftover homogeneous and opaque.
UW

020

Gottfried Honegger
1917 Zurich – 2016 Zurich

Acrylic, board on canvas
Signed, dated and inscribed verso:
HONEGGER 1971 / Z 629
180 × 120 cm

Inv. no. P121M / Acquired 2004

Gottfried Honegger
Tableau-Relief Z 629
1971

Gottfried Honegger
Pliagen (1–16)
2002–2004

Gottfried Honegger
1917 Zurich – 2016 Zurich

Acrylic on aluminium
Signed under the plinth: Honegger
(dated and numbered)
Height: each c. 80 cm

Inv. no. S151M / Acquired 2004

Beginning in the 1960s Gottfried Honegger devoted himself to both painting and sculpture. Sphere and cube were the formal points of departure for his concrete, nonfigurative sculptures. Initially, he assigned an independent aesthetic value to his preferred materials of marble, granite, chrome and aluminium. By the 1990s, he could no longer ignore the extreme sense of unease that he felt about the invisible interior of the sculptures. He was particularly disturbed by the fact that the metal sculptures were hollow inside, and the material itself seemed much too "seductive" to him. Honegger began treating his sculptures not as body but as surface, so that nothing is hidden from view. In 1997 he created his first *Pliage*, 6.5 metres in height, out of iron, folded at right angles with circular segments cut out of it and in a setting of homogeneous blue.

Depending on the shape, the *Pliages* may have an inner and an outer side but both sides basically remain visible. Viewers should be able to decipher how the metal has been folded, bent or cut, and then mounted on the base. A moral attitude underlies this desire for "transparency"; artworks are expected to be analogous to an open, democratic society regardless of whether they have found a home in private or public space.

The sculpture chosen for reproduction here, *Pliage C 149*, is one of sixteen works, all identical in size and colour but each different in form. Honegger first designed them in cardboard, drafting the circular segments, resembling wind-filled sails, not with a compass but freehand, as in all of his *Pliages*. This explains the slight irregularities in contour. The viewer's vantage point determines whether *Pliage C 149*, its basic shape corresponding to a right-angled Z, is straight or round in outline, whether an impression of line or plane, light or shadow dominates. The segments, offset in height, lend the *Pliage* a delicately undulating S-shape. Honegger has created an artwork of elegant buoyancy with a sparing use of material means.
UW

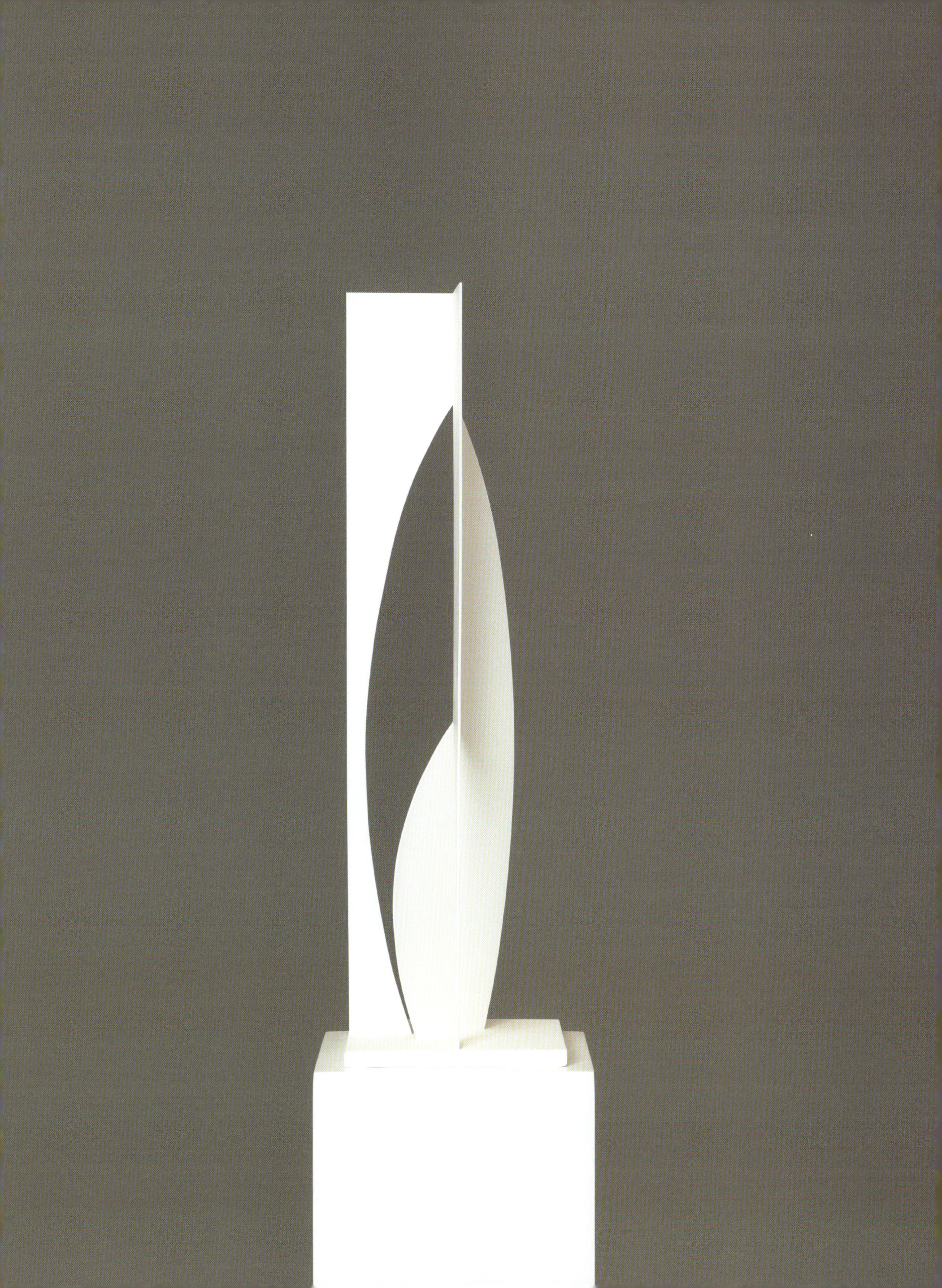

Between Europe and America

Josef Albers
Homage to the Square (Early Diary A)
1954

Josef Albers
1888 Bottrop – 1976 New Haven / Connecticut

Oil on Masonite
Initialled and dated upper right: A54
61 × 61 cm

Inv. no. P171M / Acquired 2006

The title of the painting could well suggest that Josef Albers was paying tribute to a geometric shape that has left an indelible mark on the history of art ever since Malevich painted a black square on a white ground (*Black Square*, 1915). Actually, during a long, successful career as a teacher at the Bauhaus in Weimar and Dessau and later at Black Mountain College and Yale University in the United States, Albers was always more interested in colour than in form. To show how "deceptive" colour can be, he created *Homage to the Square*, a series begun in 1950 and exemplary of his entire oeuvre. In it, he draws attention to the discrepancy between physical/objective reality and sensual/subjective appearance, the latter being inescapably influenced by context, specifically by the juxtaposition of different colours. Albers successfully aimed to hone our perception of colour and, by proxy, of the phenomena of the visible world in general.

The discovery of pre-Columbian art and architecture acquired in the course of numerous trips to Mexico in the 1940s not only heightened the artist's sense of colour. Having already taken the step from figuration to abstraction, Albers started designing compositions reduced to three or four superimposed squares. The pattern of the squares, although variable in size and scale, remained consistent from 1950 onwards. Deliberately restricting himself to this simple geometric shape in order to focus on colour, he squeezed his oil-based paint from the tube and applied it directly to the canvas with a palette knife. He invariably left a narrow margin unpainted along the inside edges of the aluminium frame, thereby clearly defining the picture as a plane. Albers described what happens on the picture plane as the "interaction of colour". This interaction is a given since we do not ordinarily see colours in isolation; they are always interacting, generating tension, vibrating and even creating an illusion of depth despite the flatness of the picture plane: for instance, dark colours are perceived as being closer to the front than light ones – a fact that already played a role in Mondrian's work (see cat. 34). Furthermore, even if the paint comes from the same tube, our perception of the colour changes depending on its neighbours.

Albers' paintings are concrete, matter-of-fact and of a contemplative serenity. They are not meant to represent personal expression of any kind but, rather, to demonstrate an extremely ambiguous phenomenon of visual perception. Regardless of how he combined his colours, Albers showed no preference for a particular chromatic harmony. Everything was possible, as in the real world. Through his investigation of colour, he came to the conclusion that "colour in my opinion behaves like man ... First in self-realisation and then in the realisation of relationships with others. ... We must combine both being an individual and being a member of society. ... You may conclude that I consider ethics and aesthetics as one."

UW

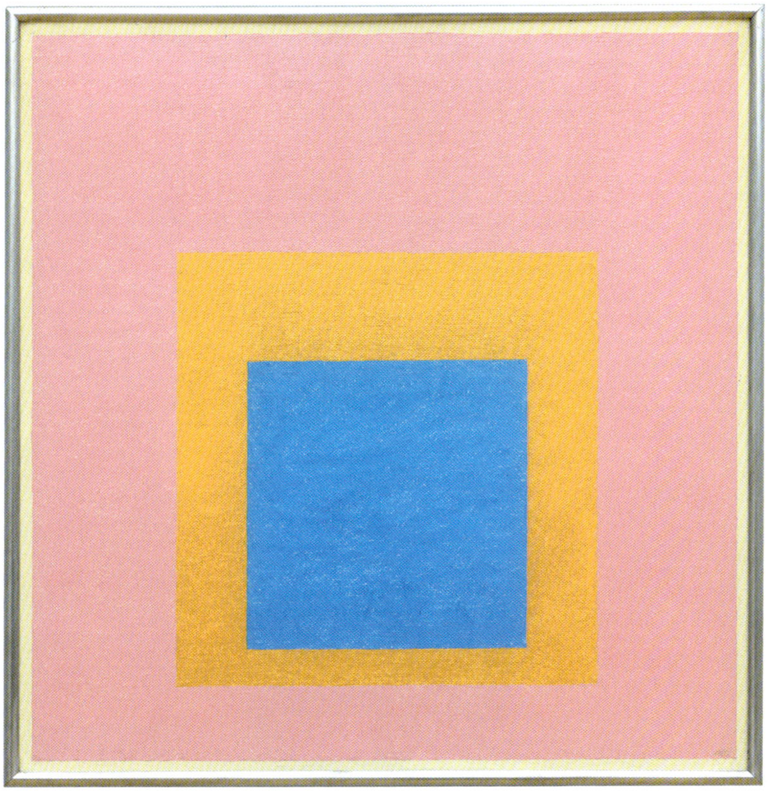

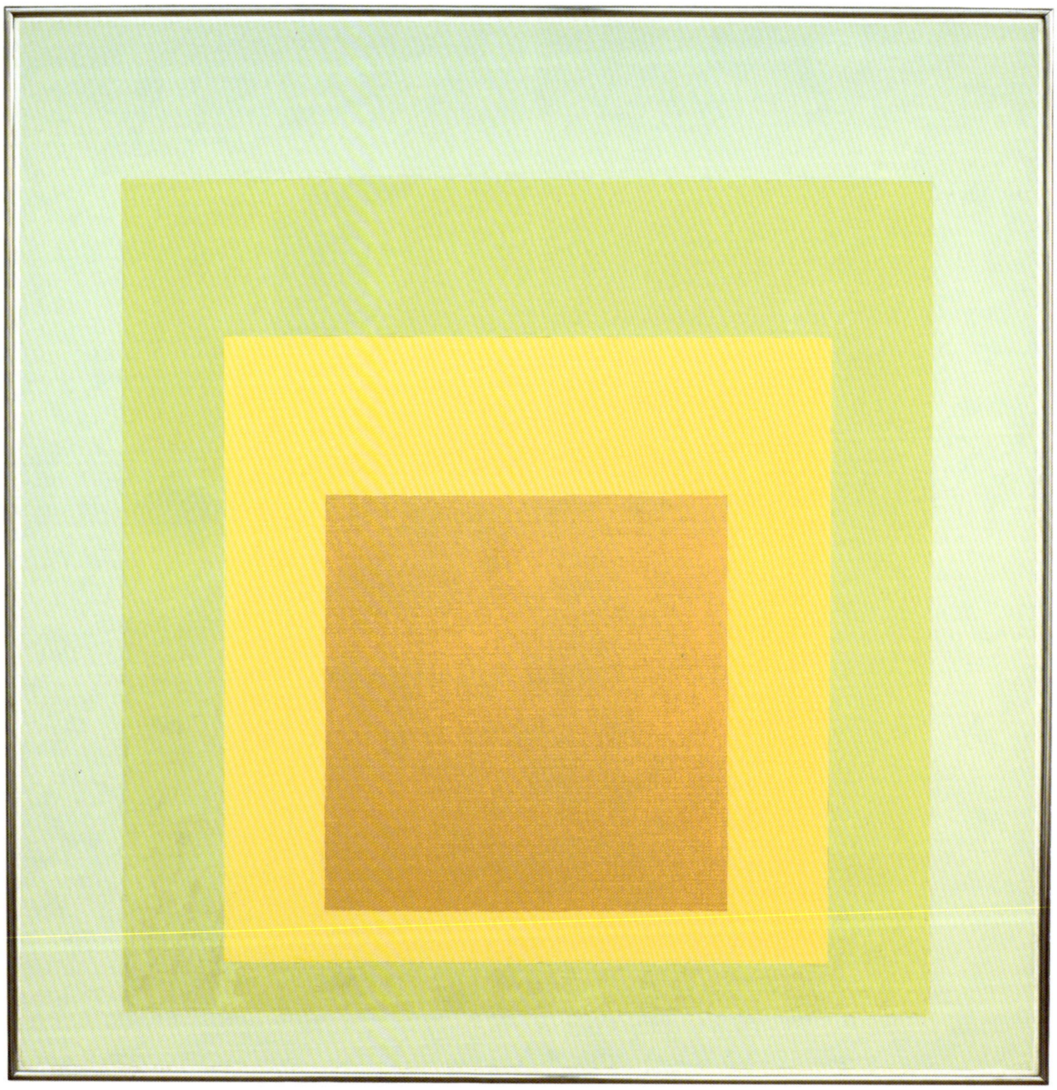

023

Josef Albers
1888 Bottrop – 1976 New Haven / Connecticut

Oil on Masonite
Initialled and dated upper right: A59
121.5 × 121.5 cm

Inv. no. P205M / Acquired 2009

Josef Albers
Homage to the Square
1959

Fritz Glarner
Relational Painting No. 58
1952

Fritz Glarner
1899 Zurich – 1972 Locarno

Oil on canvas
Signed and dated upper right:
F. GLARNER – 1952
51 × 41 cm

Inv. no. P271M / Acquired 2015

While living in New York with his American wife, Lucie, from 1936 to 1957, Fritz Glarner met fellow émigré Piet Mondrian (vol. 1, cat. 34). The two became close friends and enjoyed a vibrant exchange, intensified by being members of the American Abstract Artists group, which had been founded in 1936 to promote the American avant-garde. The years Glarner spent in New York seminally influenced his artistic development. It is there that he devised his theory of elementary geometrical forms, moving beyond Mondrian's stringent Neoplasticism, in particular, the restriction of composition to horizontals and verticals.

In 1941 Glarner coined the term Relational Paintings to designate the emphasis on interaction between plane, form and colour in his concrete paintings. Three characteristics define Relational Painting: a flat composition of differently proportioned rectangles completely devoid of illusionist perspective; the introduction of diagonals, as equivalents to horizontals and verticals, in order to generate a greater dynamic; and graded chromatic values that lend order to the relations between the elements of the composition. Beginning in the early 1940s, Glarner restricted his palette to red, yellow and blue complemented by the scale of hues from white to black.

The artist was still in New York when he painted *Relational Painting No. 58* in 1952. The composition is accentuated by blue, yellow and red fields, placed largely at the margins, thus leaving room in the middle for planes of white and grey. The properties of the paint alternate between pastose and smooth, glossy and mat, warm and cold. While the diagonals undermine the stringency of the horizontals and verticals, lending a dynamic to the composition, the whites and greys in the middle counteract the dynamics of the painting as a whole. The delicate balance between form, colour and structure yields a purely flat and harmonious composition.

For Fritz Glarner, painting, as the expression of mental states, embodies the ceaseless quest for a balance between the dichotomies of life. Glarner wanted to visualise not only the tension between opposite poles but also a potential synthesis, testifying to his conviction that the ultimate value of painting lies in its ability to reveal fundamental existential experience.

JR

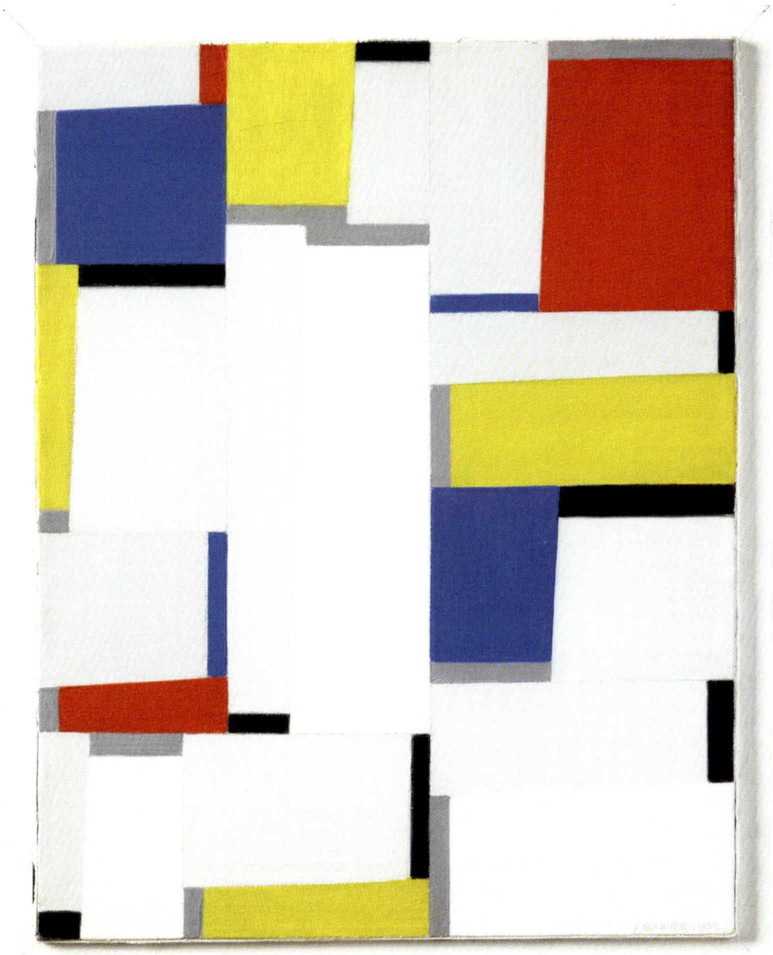

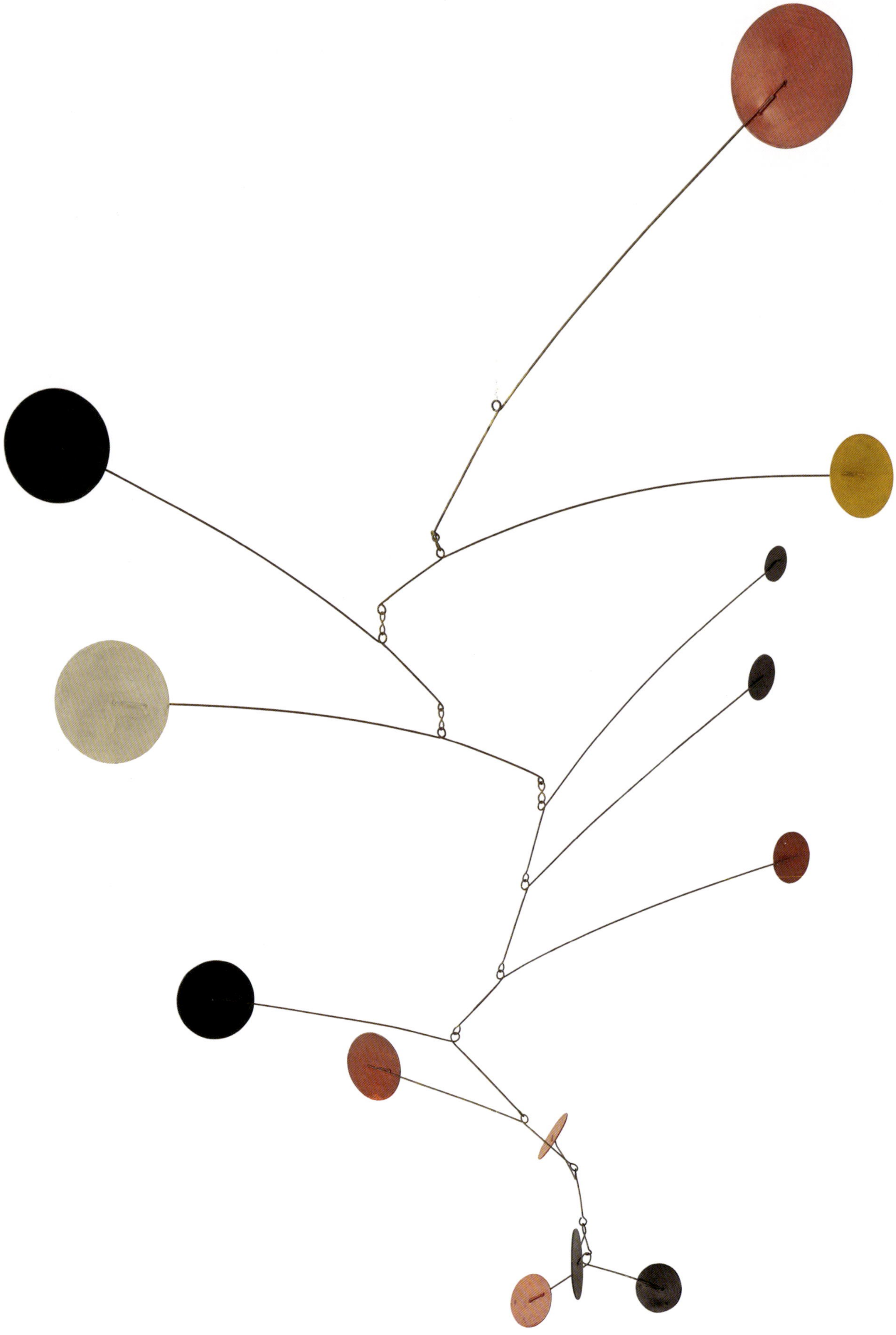

025

Alexander Calder
1898 Lawnton / Pennsylvania – 1976 New York

Sheet metal, wire, painted
86 × 71 cm

Inv. no. S316M / Acquired 2017

Alexander Calder
Untitled
1947

The great achievement of such artists as Vladimir Tatlin, Naum Gabo, László Moholy-Nagy and, not least, Alexander Calder consists of having set the hitherto static genre of sculpture in motion. Calder always took playful pleasure in experimenting with whimsical figures out of wood, textile and wire. He built an entire circus with reticulated acrobats twirling around in the air and defying gravity. He collected children's toys, a passion he shared with Joan Miró, one of his closest friends. They inspired each other, sharing a similarly creative inventiveness, much indebted to Paul Klee's enchantingly imaginative universe. But it was a visit to Piet Mondrian's Paris studio in 1930 that motivated Calder's decision to explore abstract art and the free play of nonfigurative forms. He was particularly impressed by coloured rectangles tacked on the wall. He would have liked to make them oscillate but Mondrian objected: the rectangles were to be combined into patterns on the picture plane. Nonetheless, Calder immediately applied the new artistic impulse to sculpture. He felt that from then on "the underlying sense of form" in his work was derived from "the system of the universe". He envisioned detached bodies floating in space, of different sizes and densities, diverse both in shape and movement. By 1931 he had already made his first *Mobiles*, the name he gave his fragile sculptures of metal, wood and wire as suggested by Marcel Duchamp. A stable base on the floor supported geometrical and biomorphic elements mounted on wires that moved in different directions when touched or affected by the airflow. Calder also suspended Mobiles from the ceiling, permitting them to move freely in space without the need of a support. He preferred black and white for his works, but complemented them with the primary colours that Mondrian used: red, yellow and blue.

"When I have used spheres and discs," Calder writes, "I have intended that they should represent more than what they just are. More or less as the earth is a sphere, but also has some miles of gas about it, volcanoes upon it, and the moon making circles around it, and as the sun is a sphere – but also as a source of intense heat, the effect of which is felt at great distances." While the orbits of the stars and planets can be calculated, Calder entrusts his "celestial bodies" to chance. Thus, the decisive property of his sculptures is not just motion alone but the effect of chance on movement, which defines their playful lightness and cheerful poetry, regardless of whether they are small or large in format, whether mounted in closed spaces or on public plazas.

UW

Alexander Calder
Untitled
1960

026

Alexander Calder
1898 Lawnton / Pennsylvania – 1976 New York

Sheet metal, wire, painted
15.9 × 28 cm

Inv. no. S54M / Acquired 1999

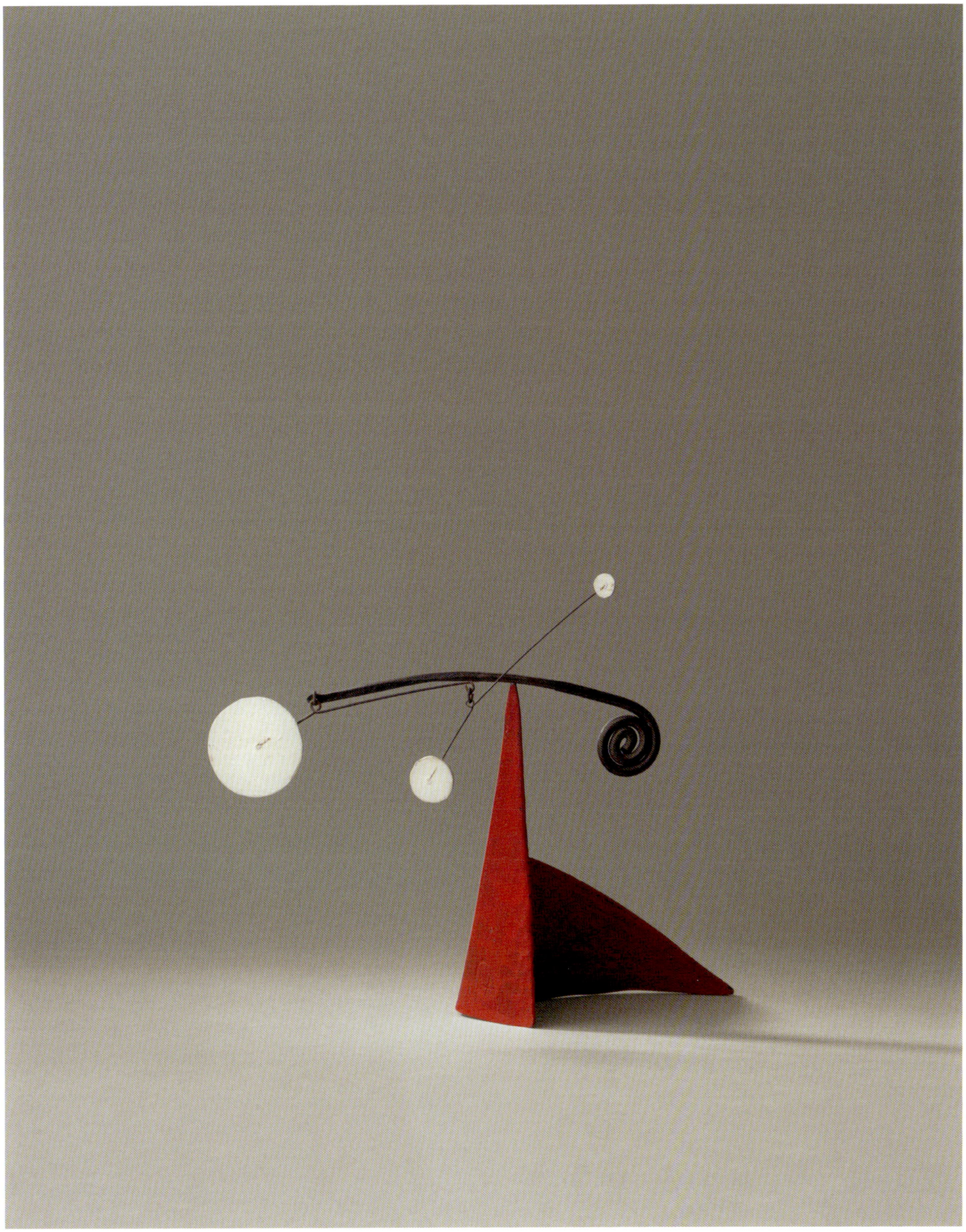

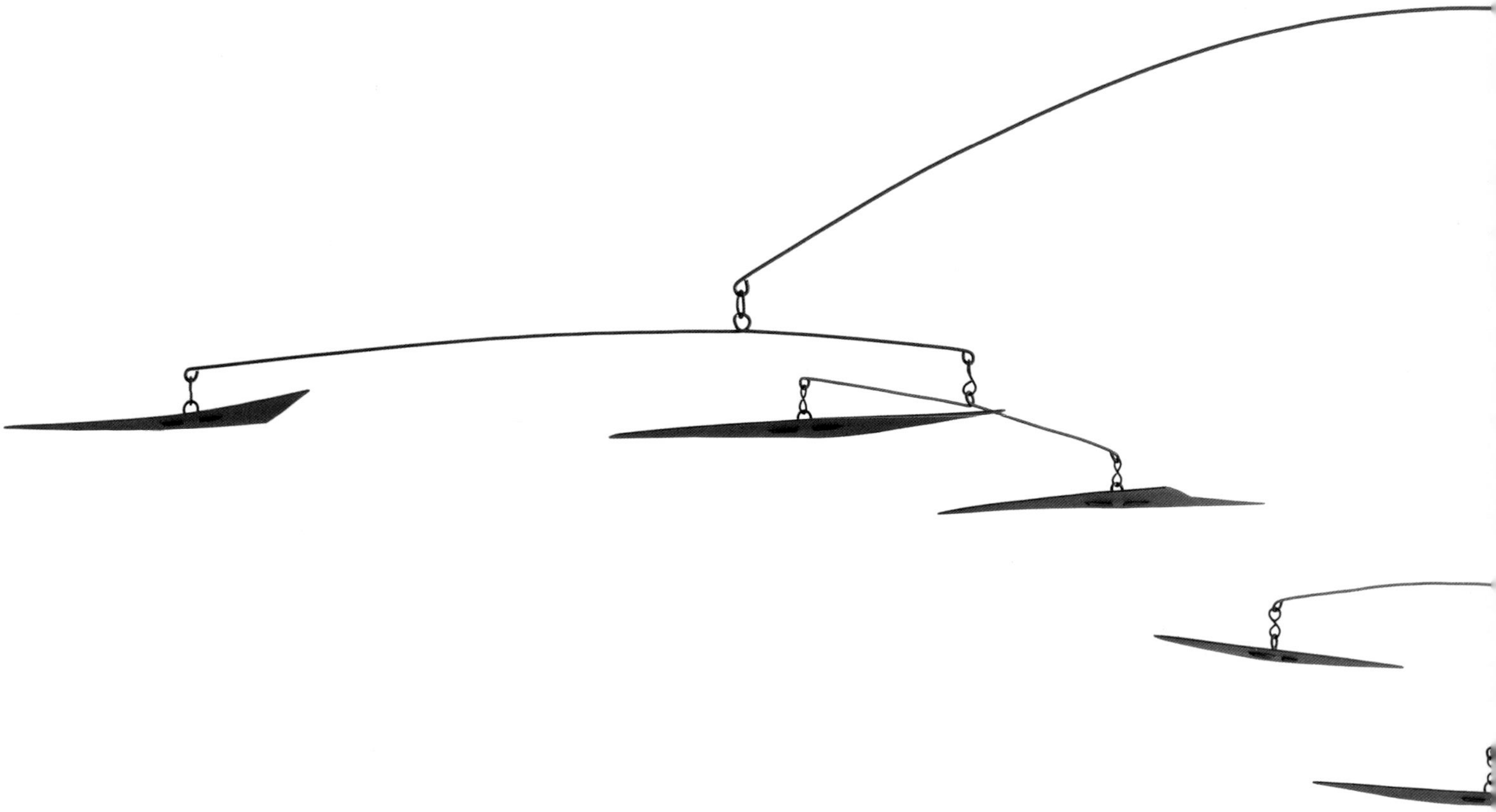

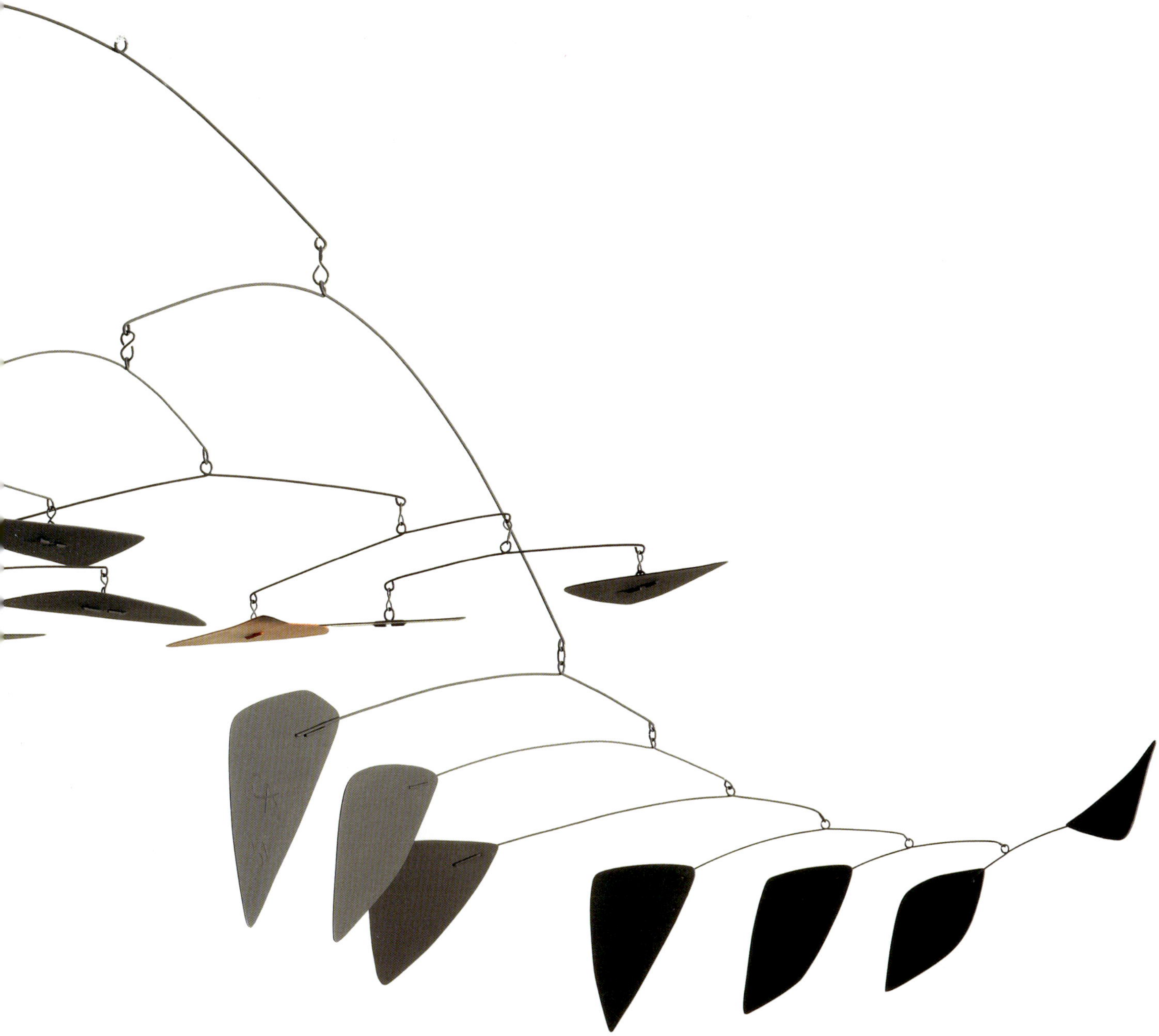

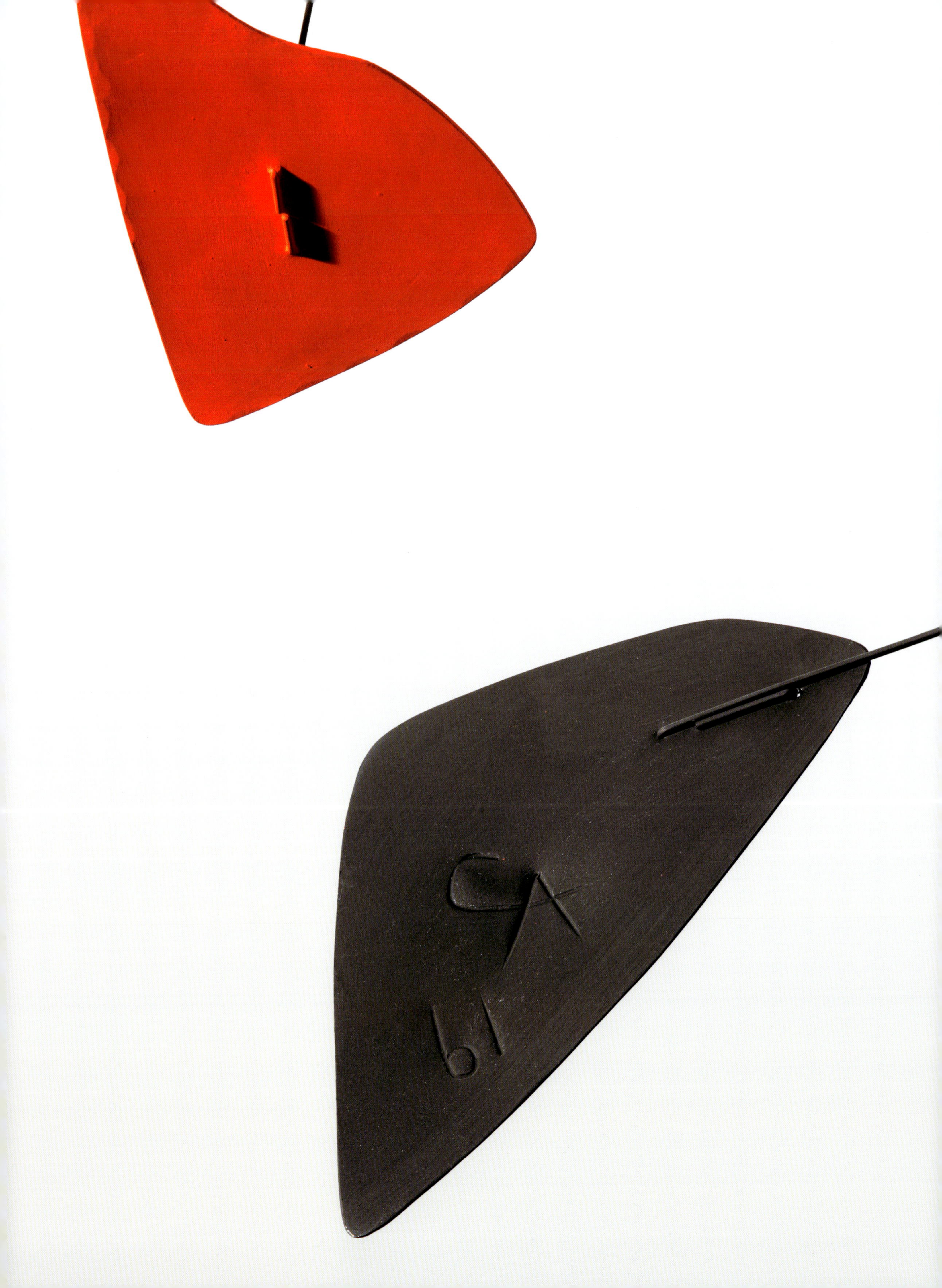

027

Alexander Calder
1898 Lawnton / Pennsylvania – 1976 New York

Sheet metal, wire, painted
Initialled and dated: CA (lig.) 61
68.6 × 223.5 cm

Inv. no. S156M / Acquired 2005

Alexander Calder
Lone Red Among Blacks
1961

Keith Sonnier
Lit Square – right side variation (2-M-N)
1969 (2015)

Keith Sonnier
1941 Mamou / Louisiana

Glass, neon, wiring, transformer
200 × 200 × 18 cm

Inv. no. S274M / Acquired 2015

Upon arriving in New York in 1967, Keith Sonnier encountered an interdisciplinary art scene, with young practitioners implementing their new ideas in such widely divergent fields as performance, dance, video and installation. They also began to make their art out of everyday materials. Sonnier was quick to become part of this avant-garde in SoHo. He too experimented with such widely diverse materials as radio transmitters, wire grids, plate glass, mirrors, latex, satin, light bulbs and neon. Sonnier continues to combine high-tech achievements with art forms drawn from many different and independent cultural contexts. His work has always been subject to constant change.

Sonnier produced three versions of *Lit Square*, each based on a 1969 drawing, with variations in the placement of the neon tubing. It was executed for the first time in 2015 according to the artist's instructions. The three versions of *Lit Square* have only been made once and are therefore unique; one of them is owned by the Australian National Gallery in Canberra.

Sonnier's in-depth involvement with neon goes back to the end of the 1960s when he began studying its technical, artistic and even philosophical potential. *Lit Square* consists of a square piece of plate glass measuring 200 by 200 cm. It is propped against the wall at a distance of 18 cm, creating a new, transparent and open space between the floor and the wall. The glass plate is divided into two symmetrical parts. The right half is delimited by a thin, orange neon tube that frames the shape of the glass while the black wiring in the left half curves gracefully down to the transformer placed in front of the glass plate. The rigid, luminous shape of the neon to the right is juxtaposed with the flexibility of the cable to the left. The right side references the art of Piet Mondrian, with which Sonnier was well acquainted, while one might interpret the left side as an ironic commentary on action painting in 1950s New York.

Lit Square radiates a soft, orange to salmon coloured light. The light of the neon tubing can be perceived as condensed and tangible colour. It reaches into the room, blends into it and becomes an immaterial, atmospheric phenomenon. "Light," Sonnier says, "can be presented not only as energy but also as matter." A distinctive poetry of palpable sensuality is inherent in the artificial character of this form of light. The experience of light that radiates and emanates is the point of departure for Sonnier's work. As he comments in an interview published in the magazine *Parachute* in 1977, "Those fluorescent light and glass pieces remind me a lot of driving in Louisiana. Coming back late at night and in the distance seeing a club somewhere through the fog. About the most religious experience I've ever had in Louisiana: coming back from a dance late at night and driving over this flat land and, all of a sudden, seeing these waves of lights going up and down in this thick fog. Just incredible!"
AS

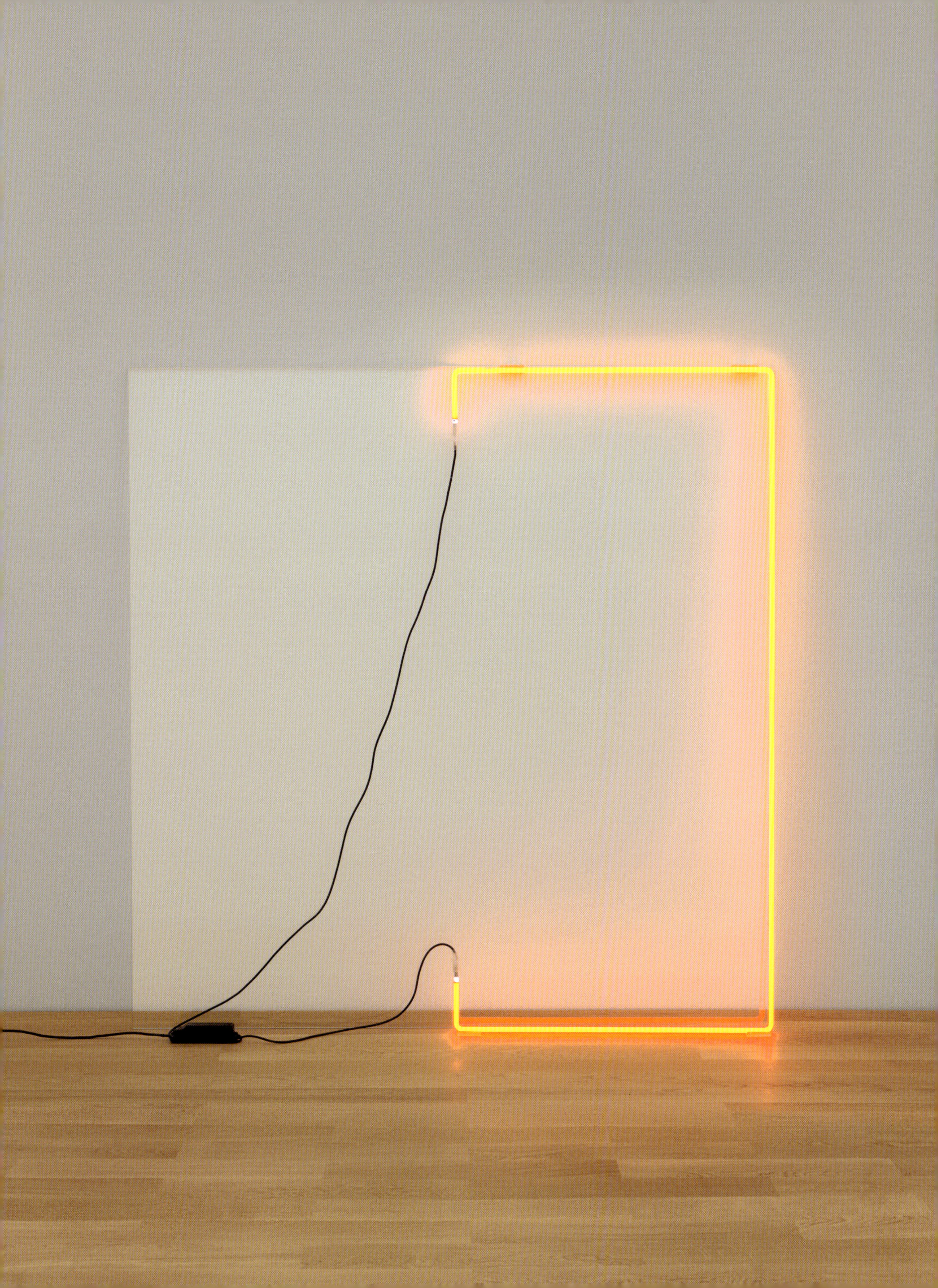

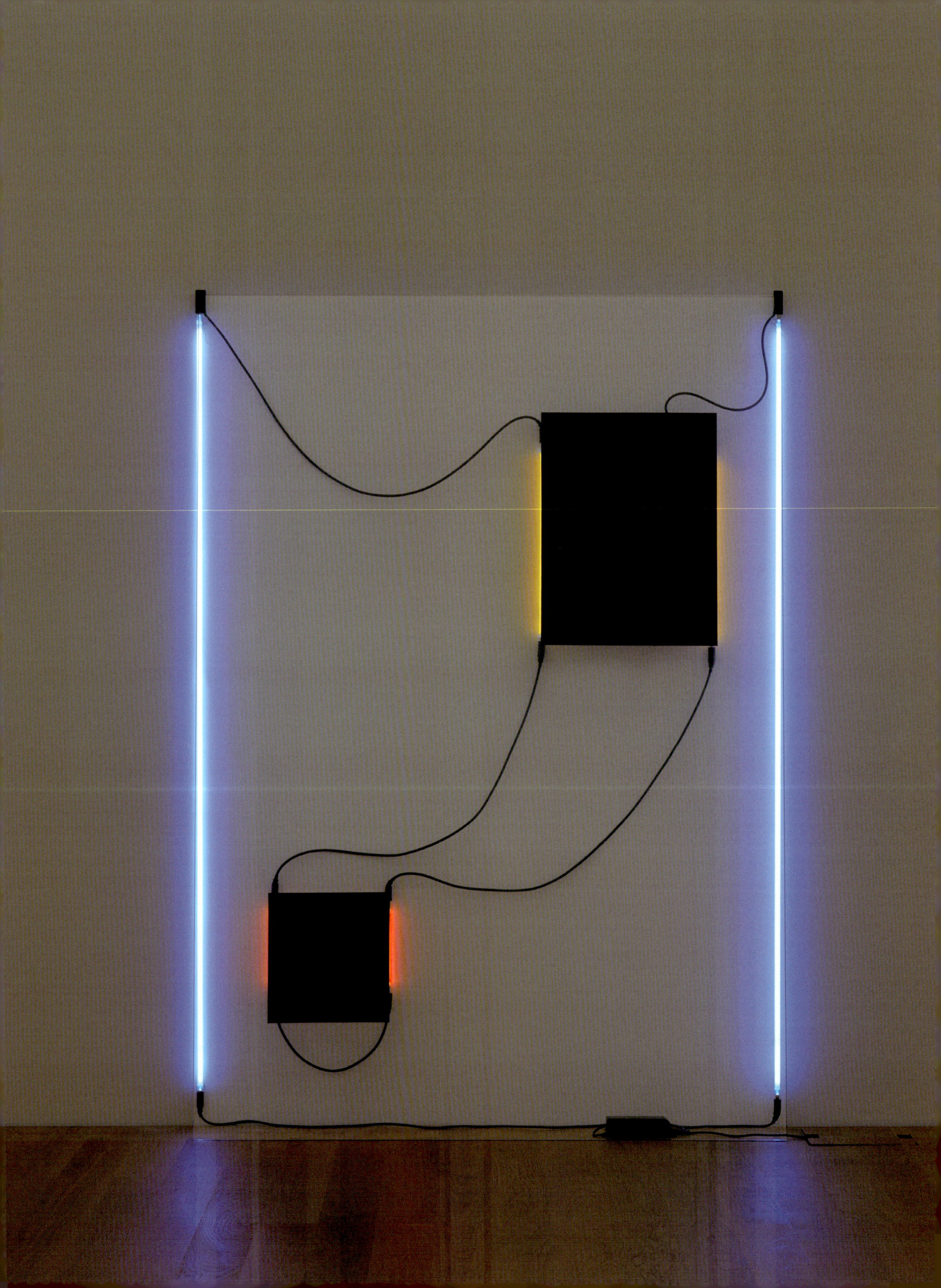

029

Keith Sonnier
Ba-O-Ba Krefeld IB
1977 (2015)

Keith Sonnier
1941 Mamou / Louisiana

Glass, enamel, neon, wiring, transformer
210.8 × 166.4 × 26.7 cm

Inv. no. S276M / Acquired 2015

All of the *Ba-O-Ba* sculptures are part of a series to which the artist has repeatedly returned over the years. The first one was created in New York in 1969. The series owes its name to the fact that Sonnier was familiar with Haitian slang from his childhood in Louisiana. *Ba-O-Ba* refers to being bathed in light, in colour or in the light of the moon. For Sonnier, it is crucial for viewers to be standing in the light when they face his work. Light is incorporated into these works not for its romanticising effect but above all to reveal the metaphysical potential inherent in the artificial and the industrial.

The materials in the *Ba-O-Ba* sculptures are panes of plain or mirrored glass in combination with luminous neon tubes and occasionally aluminium. Each iteration of the sculptures is based on a meticulously detailed plan, down to the way in which it is connected to the power and switched on. Only when the light quickens the material does it come to life, manifesting the intention of the artist and acquiring the presence that transforms it into a work of art. Taken in isolation, the parts of the whole – cables, transformers, glass and aluminium – are merely the quotidian trappings of modern life. The process of transforming an everyday object into a work of art cannot be gleaned from the work on display but it is nonetheless part of it.

Ba-O-Ba Krefeld 1B was conceived in 1977 on the occasion of the exhibition *Keith Sonnier: Argon- und Neon-Arbeiten* at Museum Haus Lange in Krefeld; it was implemented in 2015. Despite its statuary character (Storck, 1979), the colouring and transparency of the work give it the impression of being astonishingly light. The two verticals of mercury argon, emitting a diffuse and garish light blue, look as if they were incisions in the wall, as if they were hazardous rods that confine the inner structure and make it inaccessible. This structure consists of a pane of glass, supporting two rectangles, one large, one smaller, both painted in black enamel. They are connected by two undulating cables behind them, which almost makes them appear to be suspended in space. The yellow and red neon gas of the shorter rods, also affixed to the wall, radiates a diffuse mysterious light; the more transparent and not fully saturated red resembles a flame, which the poet Max Blagg, Sonnier's connoisseur and friend, compares to the gently burning natural gas vents in the western Mississippi Delta.

It is important to Sonnier that the *Ba-O-Ba* sculptures become part of the room in which they are on display. This is achieved by placing the large pane of glass at a slant, thereby connecting the floor and the wall with the sculpture. Both the panelled structure of the ceiling and the visitors are mirrored in the pane of glass: they stand in front of the work and are part of it at the same time.

The glass plate, measuring 210 by 166 cm and thus alluding to the venerable proportions of the golden section, may also be interpreted as a door, whose passage is blocked by the black rectangles. In a 2002 interview with Joachim Jäger, the curator of the exhibition at the Neue Nationalgalerie in Berlin, Sonnier said: "Well, maybe the romantic side of all the *Ba-O-Ba* works is that you enter directly into the realm of the sculpture. This concept is very much like the surrealistic idea of a world beyond. I keep thinking, for instance, of this image in the Jean Cocteau film *Orphée*, where you go through the mirror into the underworld. And this is very much how you enter into my work, into the realm of the sculpture: you go into the fourth dimension."

AS

Keith Sonnier
Expanded SEL VII
1978 (2006)

Keith Sonnier
1941 Mamou / Louisiana

Neon, wiring, transformer
230 × 170 × 10 cm

Inv. no. S233M / Acquired 2012

Sonnier's interest in "foreign" cultures goes back to his youth in Louisiana, which is a melting pot of Cajun French, American, Creole and African traditions. As a student at Rutgers University in New Jersey, Sonnier explored new forms of sculptural expression alongside his in-depth study of African art. His first travels took him to the Tokyo Biennial in 1970 and the New Delhi Triennial in 1971. In 1981 the Sarabhai Foundation invited him to spend several months in Ahmedabad in West India, where he worked with local craftsmen to build sculptures out of bamboo, a material common in both India and his native Louisiana. For him, India meant confrontation with a hitherto unknown culture: its divinities and its overwhelming intensity of colours, with pigments often stored in open vats. He described the experience in an interview of 2017: "I was, and am, very interested in learning about other cultures, other ways of being in the world; that's been an important element in my overall approach to art making."

Early Chinese calligraphy of the kind that embellished precious bronze vessels in ancient times is among the references that inform the *SEL* series, begun in 1978. However, Sonnier does not aim to assimilate and even less to imitate these early characters; it is their magical and ceremonial significance that has captured his imagination. Using the potential of modern technology, he seeks to invest his sculptures with comparable qualities. "I want them to have some mystery and awe, so that you don't quite know what they are."

Expanded SEL VII does indeed convey an atmosphere of magic and mystery, with diffuse colours shining into the distance and an open, formal structure of single signs in space. According to writer and performer Max Blagg, Sonnier is "a poet of curves and arches and colour". His neon tubes conjure seemingly floating, enigmatic configurations that evoke *shimenawa*, the thick ropes of straw at the entrance to Shintoist shrines. Such twisted, curved ropes on the buildings mark the border between sacred and secular areas.

Sonnier's colourful semiotic universe encourages a variety of interpretations. The large, light-red figure in the middle could be read as the head of a carp, a fish that still makes frequent appearances in Japan and China as a symbol of strength and perseverance and even as a pop figure. Legend has it that, after overcoming the rapids of the Yellow River and reaching the mythical Dragon Gate, the carp was rewarded by being transformed into a dragon, a mythical creature with a higher status. Particularly in China, dragons are considered celestial beings and primeval ancestors of humankind. Over the millennia, they have come to embody a variety of meanings and are now known primarily as harbingers of good luck.

The motifs in Sonnier's oeuvre are imbued with a Matissian elegance, perceptible in simple, singular forms and reinforcing the ambivalence that is crucial to these works. The motif of the portal from which to discover new spaces and cross metaphysical boundaries consistently plays a decisive role, not least in the more recent *Portal* series begun in 2015.

AS

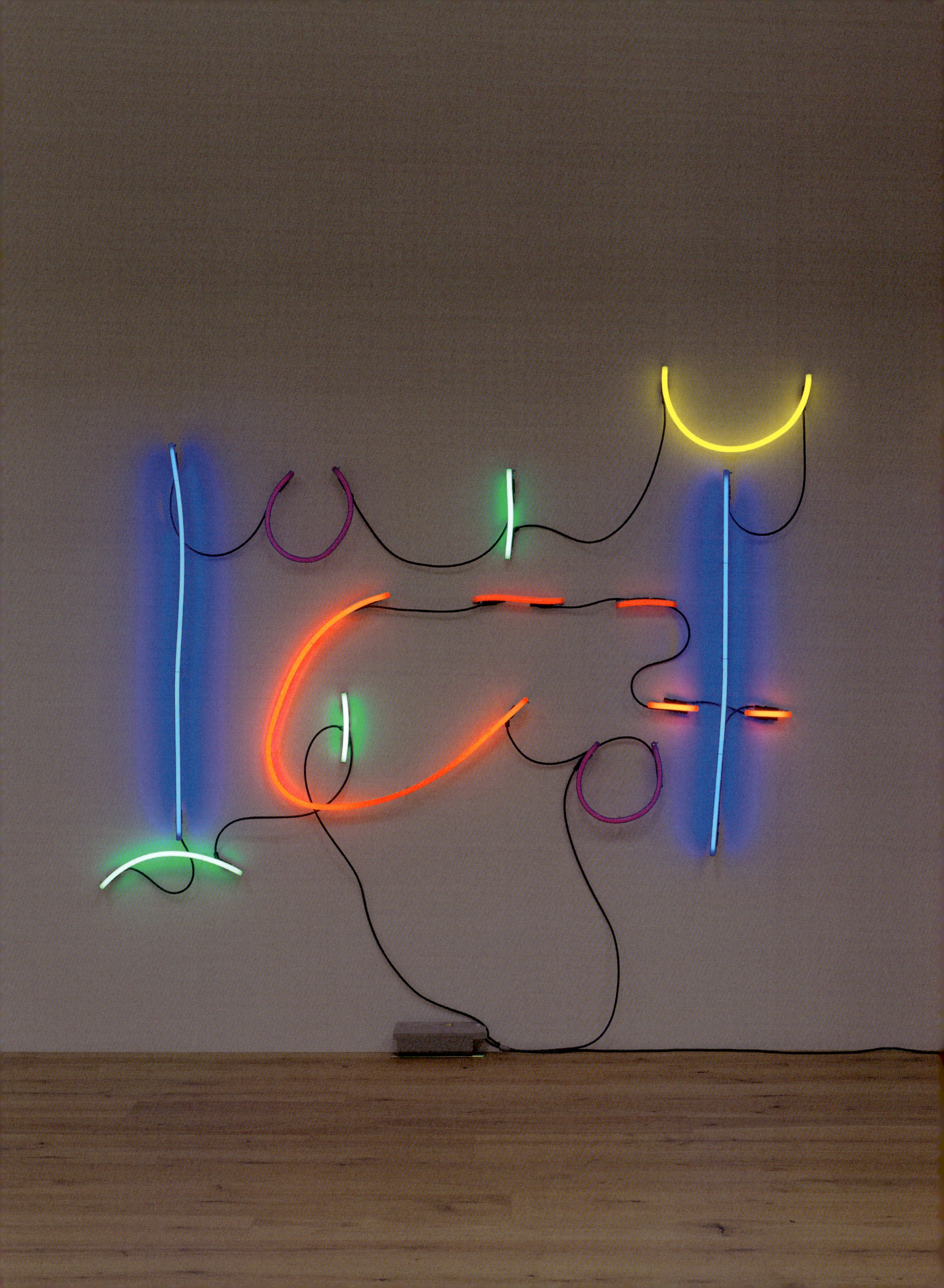

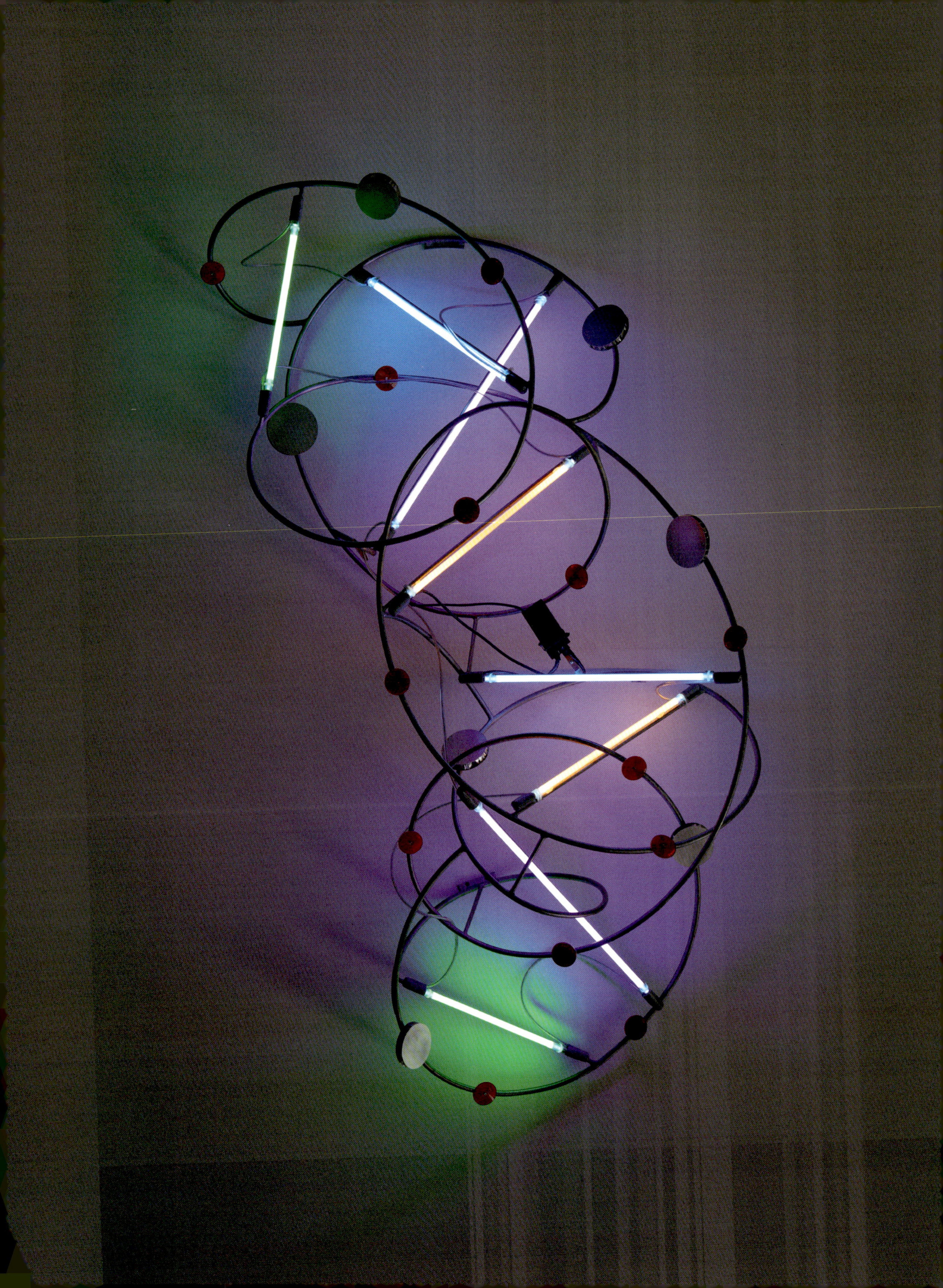

031

Keith Sonnier
1941 Mamou / Louisiana

Steel, neon, argon, wiring, transformer, reflector
112 × 208 × 56 cm

Inv. no. S282M / Acquired 2016

Keith Sonnier
Gran Twister
2012

Sonnier describes the titles of his works as "magic keys" to their understanding. Rather than being literary explanations of their subject matter, the titles are based on "certain ideas and associations". *Gran Twister* may refer to anything from a tornado to a tongue twister and is also the title of an American horror film, thus allowing for a wide variety of interpretations drawn, for instance, from nature, technology, the body or the media.

Gran Twister is a complex, contorted configuration that winds its circular way through space from top to bottom and bottom to top. Eight neon tubes placed between artistically welded steel rods "materialise" the movement of air in the devastating whirlwind that is called a tornado. One is reminded of the frenzied gestural painting in 1950s New York, as in the work of Jackson Pollock, but also, as Richard Shiff has observed, of the filigree structure of Wassily Kandinsky's works, which have been a vibrant and crucial part of the Solomon R. Guggenheim Museum's permanent collection since the 1930s.

This work is instantly striking for its fragility and dynamic movement. Affixed to the wall at only a few points, it is as captivating as it is unsettling. The red reflectors and the black, reflecting aluminium plates are fixed points in the bewildering gyrations of the composition through space, which lend the sculpture a touch of floral poetry despite a certain overall gruffness. This is partly a consequence of the variations in volume within the winding steel and also of the flowing, spreading neon and argon light. The green, purple and blue are related to distinctive colour combinations typical of thunderstorms and other celestial events. The light is at its most intense in the tubes themselves. Despite their restless arrangement, which makes them seem to be tipping over, they draw the gaze upwards, like a Jacob's ladder connecting heaven and earth, a motif that also plays a role in the *Ebo River Series* of 2016. In the words of Klaus Kertess, Sonnier is "smitten by the interface of technology and nature, and the toxic beauty of these virtual, abstract works forms a meditation on exactly that."

Gran Twister can also be installed horizontally and freely suspended in space. The sculpture then might be seen as a radiantly illuminated crown, a mysterious flying object, a floating celestial dome or an astral event. "Some kind of organism, work with a soul, an astral projection," was Sonnier's reply, when Richard Shiff asked him about the significance of mind and matter in his art.

AS

Sean Scully
Ada
1980

Sean Scully
1945 Dublin

Oil on canvas
Titled, signed and dated verso:
ADA / Sean Scully 1980
243.8 × 123.2 cm

Inv. no. P185M / Acquired 2007

In 1975 Sean Scully left London and moved to New York. There he initially focused on the characteristic stringency of Minimalism, established in the United States since the mid-1960s – although he always created his work in response to a subjective emotional impulse. *Ada*, a portrait-format work of 1980, actually shows little more than two vertical panels of horizontal, alternating brown and black stripes, essentially flat and hermetic in appearance. As in similarly reduced paintings of that time, apart from early figurative works such as *Cactus* of 1964, Scully did not paint in acrylic but rather in oils, which are more painterly in essence, more profound and challenging to handle. Their use indicates a deliberate alignment with the tradition of painting in the Western world since the Renaissance.

The catalogue raisonné (Marla Price, 2018, vol. II, p. 35) attributes the title of the painting to a suggestion of the writer, composer and collector Charles Choset (1940–1986). According to the artist, it refers to Vladimir Nabokov's novel *Ada or Ardor, A Family Chronicle*.
UW

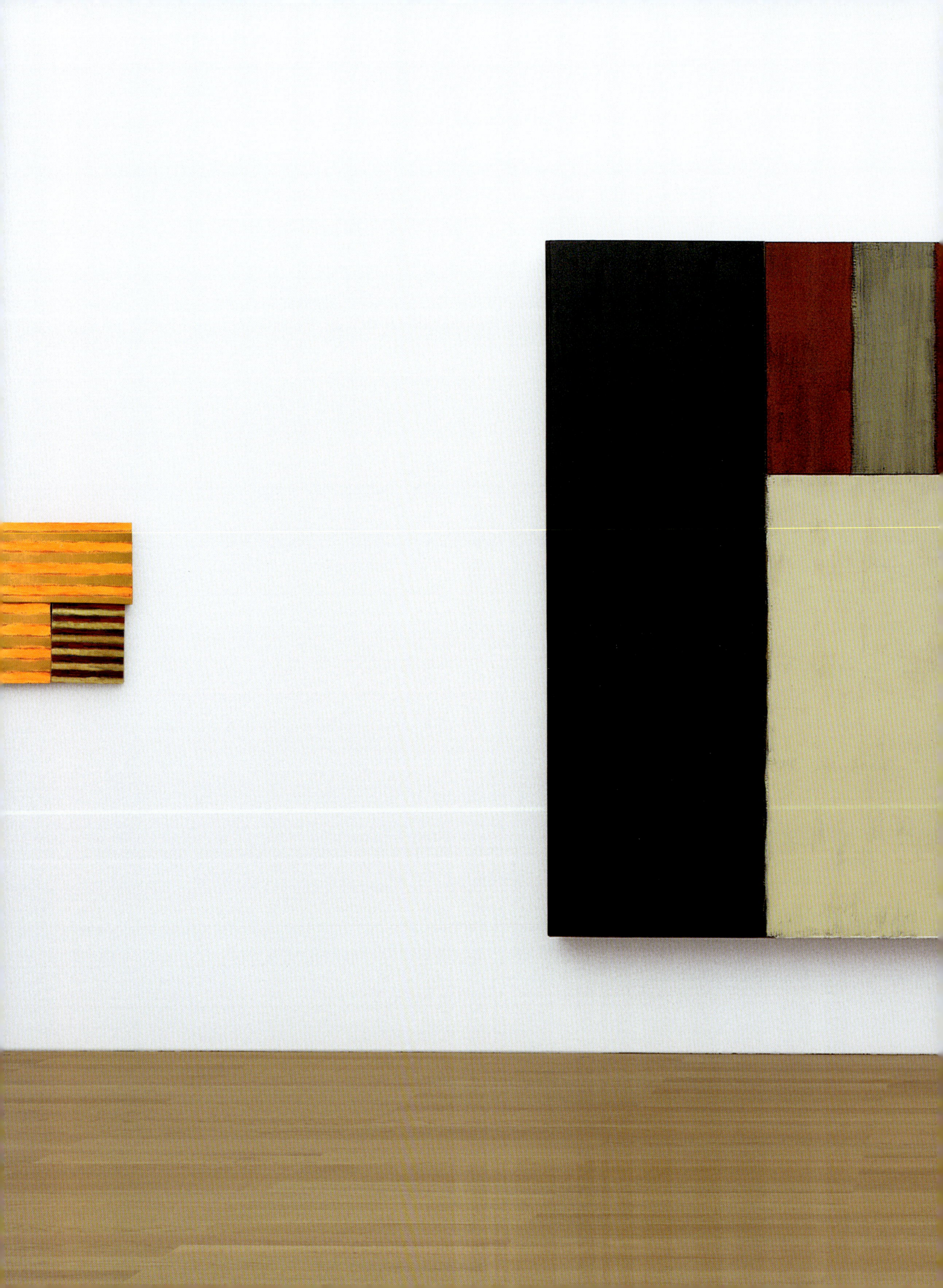

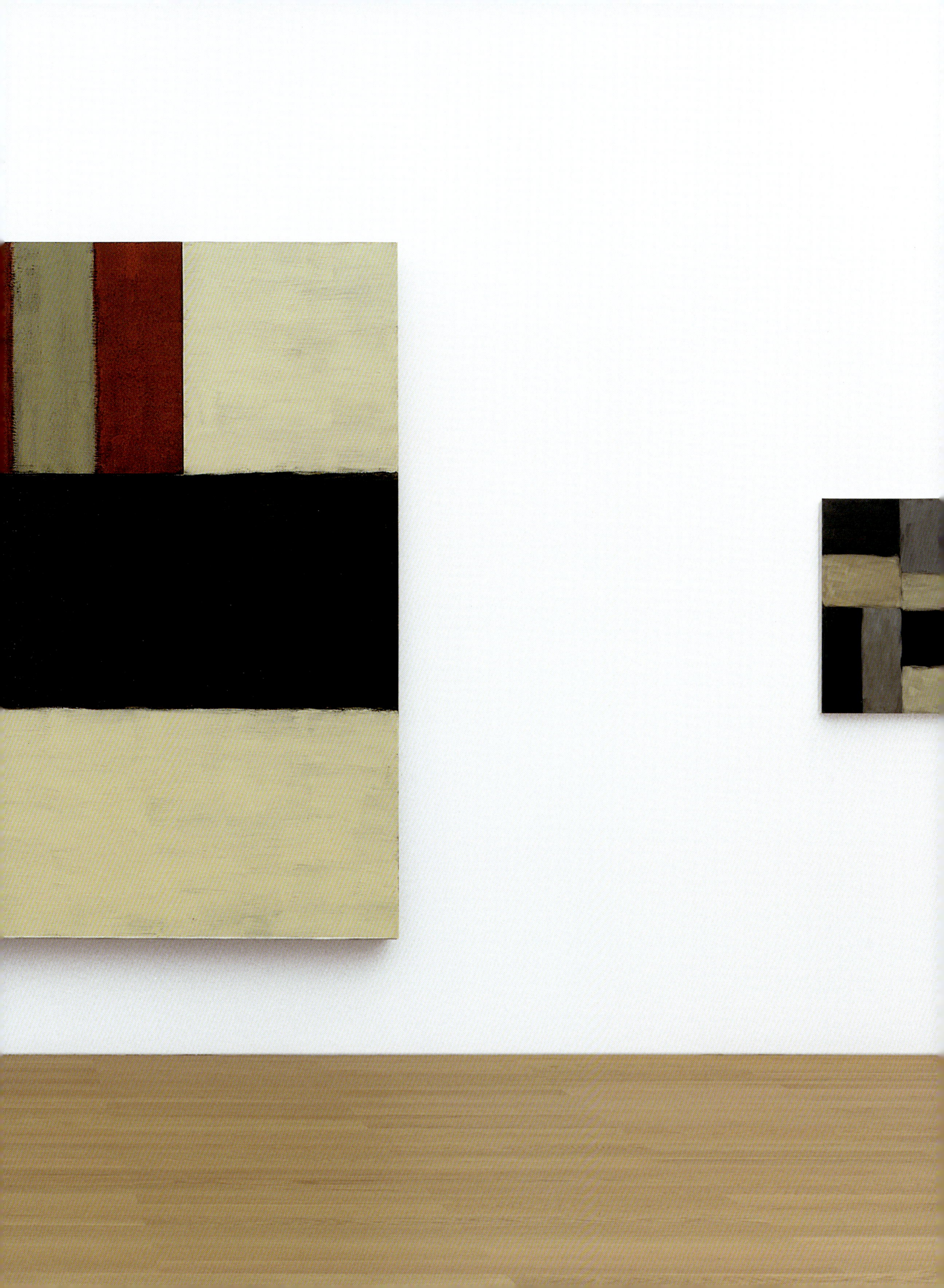

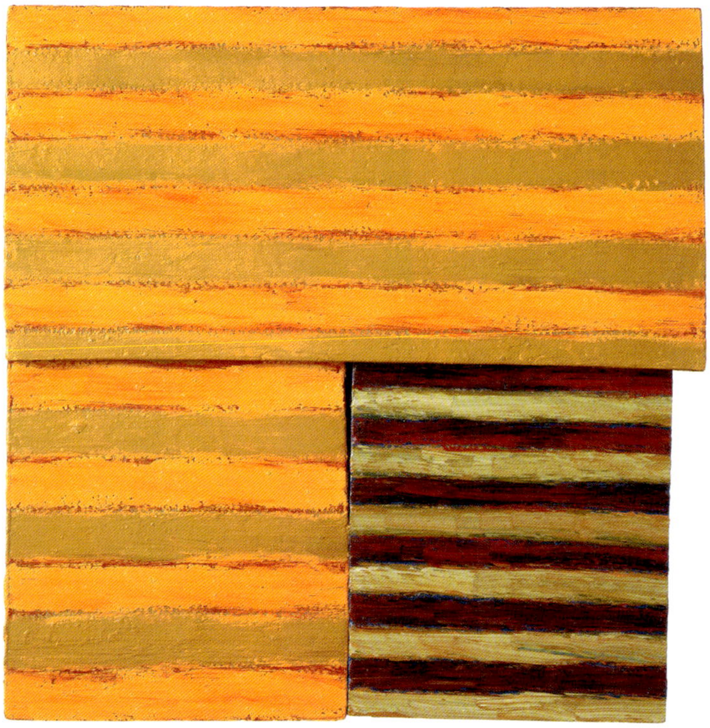

033

Sean Scully
1945 Dublin

Oil on wood
Signed and dated verso: Sean Scully 8.1982
53.3 × 53.3 × 7.6 cm

Inv. no. P252M / Acquired 2014

Sean Scully
Plum
1982

Given the nature of the minimalist paintings that Sean Scully created in New York in the late 1970s, he might well have been receptive to the potential of an increasingly conceptual artistic approach, especially in view of the then current preference for "elementary painting" and later, in the 1980s, the growing interest in "radical painting". These tendencies took an analytic, self-reflective approach to the actual tools of the trade, such as paintbrushes, support and paint. Phil Sims, Joseph Marioni, Olivier Mosset, Winston Roeth and other painters born, like Scully, in the 1940s followed this trajectory, studying Robert Ryman, Frank Stella and Brice Marden, as well as older artists like Barnett Newman, Agnes Martin and Ad Reinhardt. In contrast, Scully showed an unbroken confidence in the traditional means and forms of expression in painting. The rich body of work that he produced between 1981 and 1991 shows a voluptuous chromatic abandon and an additive, dynamic visual vocabulary that could be described as "baroque", although without the latter's distinctive penchant for symmetry. Thus, *Plum* is infused with a sense of harmony and balance despite the asymmetry of the overall composition with its imprecisely distinguished and tendentially skewed horizontals.

The incongruent and often unexpected juxtaposition of visual elements, characteristic of the work Scully produced in the 1980s, is combined with great sensuality as well as an expressive palette. Such qualities can already be observed in works by Henri Matisse. Comparison might also be made with the composition and structure of Frank Stella's paintings, such as *West Broadway* (1958, Basel Kunstmuseum) and the "shaped canvases" of the early 1960s. The vibrantly colourful and dynamic body of work that Scully produced in the 1980s cannot, however, eclipse the sombre and at times even melancholy emotionality of his palette, indicative of a romantic, profoundly sensitive artist.

UW

Sean Scully
Dreamland
1987

034

Sean Scully
1945 Dublin

Oil on linen
Titled, signed and dated verso:
Dreamland / Sean Scully / 1987
228 × 296.5 × 14 cm

Inv. no. P215M / Acquired 2009

In *Dreamland*, the additive composition of Sean Scully's small-format painting *Plum* (cat. 33) has burgeoned into a rectangular, positively architectural large format. Architectural structures already marked his work in the early 1970s: the bridges and roads, the industrial plants and facades of buildings that formed the backdrop of everyday life in northern England's Newcastle-upon-Tyne, where Scully was living at the time and which impressed themselves on his mind.

"Architectural" does not mean that the large-formats Scully made in the 1980s were walk-in pieces. Like all of his paintings, *Dreamland* is entirely wall oriented and created explicitly for visual appreciation. The architectural feeling that the work suggests comes both from the physical addition of its three single parts, combined to form a compact pictorial construction, and from the rigorous arrangement of vertical and horizontal fields. The impression of supports, loads and walls derives from a deliberate and systematic brushstroke that follows the longitudinal alignment of the fields and thus the basic structure of the whole.

However, colour is the crucial factor in the composition of this three-part work. It lends the painting presence and weight, and defines its architecture. Without colour, only the scantily sketched, underlying structure of lines would be left. Colour constitutes the picture as a picture, through its own self-contained aesthetic and compositional value. In contrast to the symmetry of the three-part construction, the colours have been applied asymmetrically, lending the composition a precarious though viable balance. By having the colours deviate from the symmetry of the visual structure, Scully underscores their aesthetic and compositional autonomy.

UW

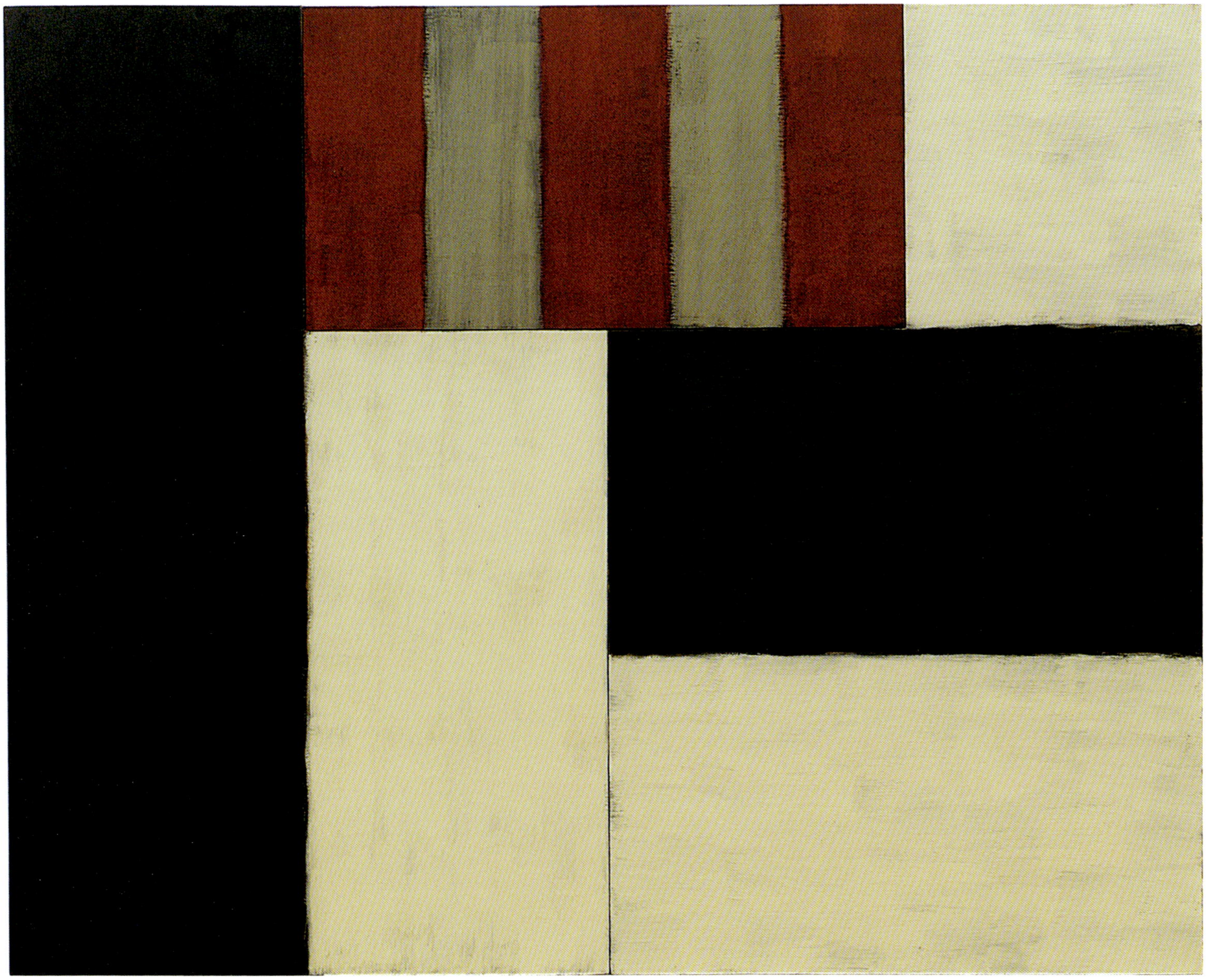

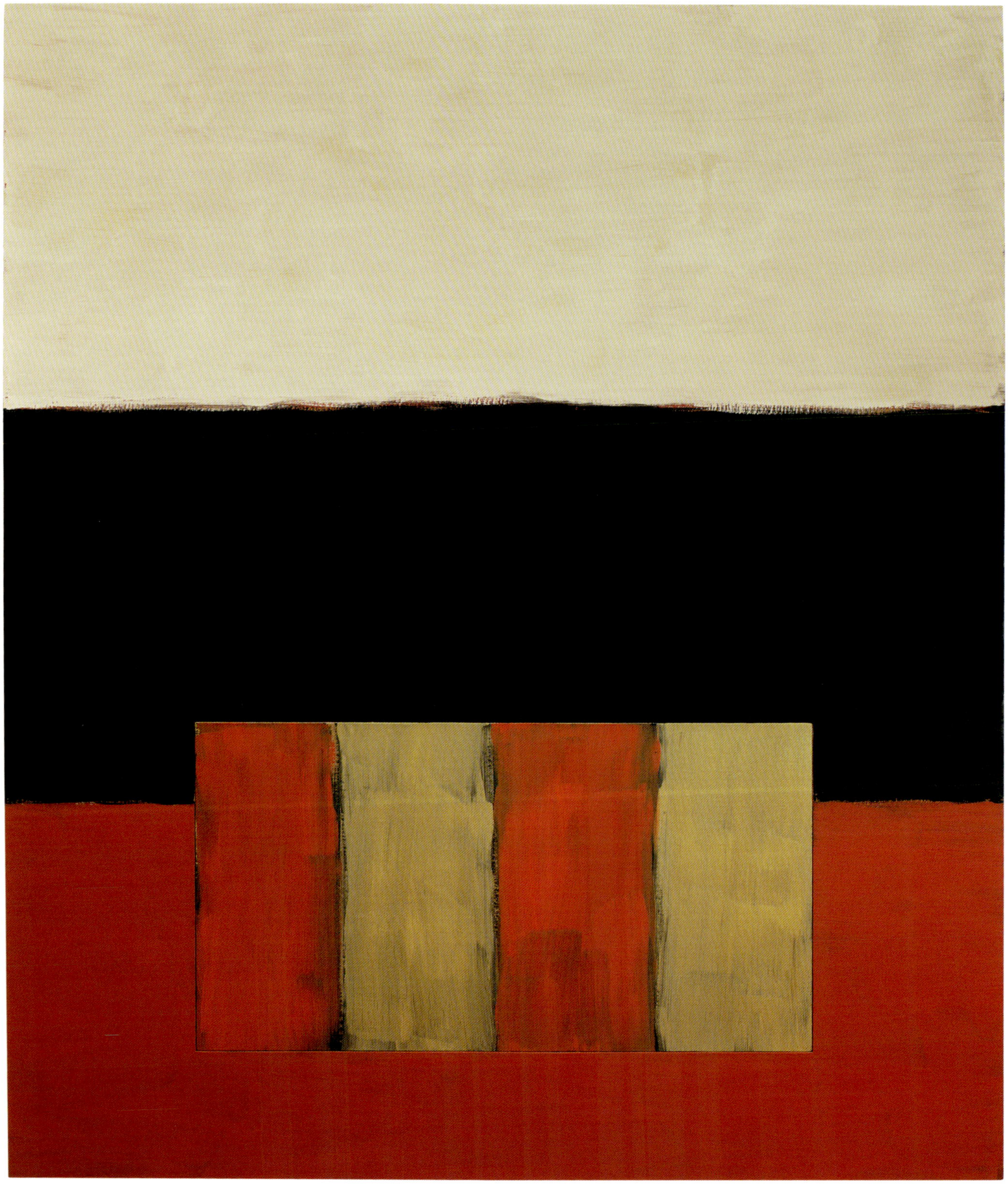

035

Sean Scully
1945 Dublin

Oil on linen
Titled, dated and signed verso:
SONG OF RED / 1999 / Sean Scully
244 × 213 cm

Inv. no. P97M / Acquired 2002

Sean Scully
Song of Red
1999

Sean Scully
Doric Grey
2012

036

Sean Scully
1945 Dublin

Oil on linen
Titled, signed and dated verso:
DORIC GREY / Sean Scully / 3.12
71.1 × 81.3 × 4.3 cm

Inv. no. P239M / Acquired 2012

As so often in Scully's oeuvre, the title of this small-format painting refers to the sensual impression made by a specific colour in a specific place; the impression may have been evoked by an ancient temple of Doric order in Greece or Italy.

UW

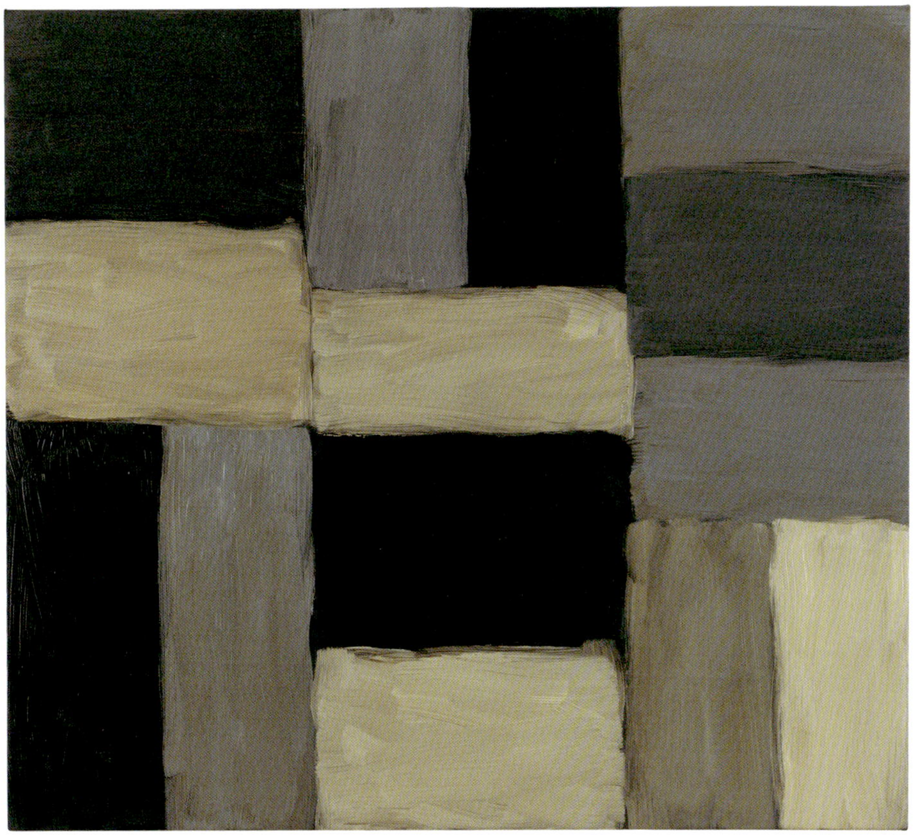

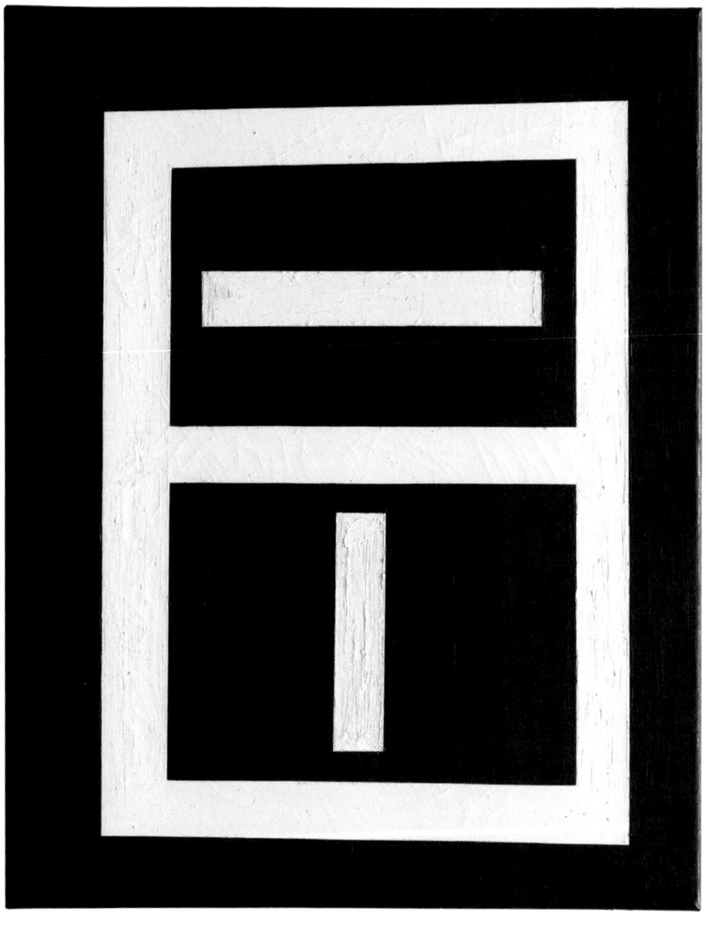

037

Helmut Federle
1944 Solothurn

Oil on canvas
Titled, signed and dated verso:
[title in capitals] / FEDERLE 84/86
50 × 40 cm

Inv. no. P184M / Acquired 2007

Helmut Federle
Zeichen der geteilten, eingeschlossenen Ganzheit
1984/1986

While still studying with Franz Fedier at the School of Commercial Art in Basel (1964–1969), Helmut Federle took trips to Afghanistan, India and Nepal. He studied the prehistoric civilisations of Asia and the characters of Asian writing, particularly Sanskrit. These studies exerted a profound influence on his painting and the geometric-abstract work he began producing in the mid-1970s. In New York, where he lived for four years (1979–1983), he focused primarily on postwar painting in the United States. In the course of the 1980s, Federle started collecting pre-Columbian and East Asian ceramics, variously presenting them in the context of his own work. He consciously defined his painting within the larger framework of a universal history of civilisation across times and eras.

The small-format painting *Zeichen der geteilten eingeschlossenen Ganzheit* (Sign of the Divided Enclosed Totality) is characteristic of Federle's work in the mid-1980s. The motif is clear-cut: a white, upended rectangular frame on a black ground divided in half horizontally, with a horizontal white band in the field on top and a vertical one in the field below. By the beginning of the decade, Federle had already reduced his palette to what he called suicide colours – black, white, grey and a broken yellow – but he wanted the psychological, existential components of his work to encounter "revisited, harmonising shapes", governed not by emotional logic but, rather, a logic that is immanent in the work itself. He extracted this from geometric abstraction's universal repertory of forms. However, geometric shapes are not governed by rigorous laws, nor do they reflect a fixed worldview, as was the case several times in the course of the twentieth century. Instead, they appear as fragile, self-questioning configurations. The present work is a case in point. The painterly brushwork stands in contrast to the angular outline of the white shape while the black ground, worked with a spatula, yields a relief-like structure that enters into conversation with the light. Moreover, a closer look reveals that the white figure also stands opposed to right angles and symmetry. Lengths, widths and angles subtly deviate so that none of the elements proves to be where anticipated by a fleeting glance.

Federle's divided, upended rectangle might be associated with the characters of Phoenician and East Asian alphabets but also with the Latin initials of the artist's own name. This would lend the work the significance of a sign, as indicated in the title. But the divided rectangle obviously encloses two diametrically opposed signs of orientation, a horizontal and vertical, which would, if they were united, form a new sign, for instance, a cross, ultimately combining antimonies to form a single whole. No matter how one chooses to interpret the work and its title, Federle has created a subtle "icon" of visual ambivalence that challenges us to take a close and careful look beyond the formal clarity of the composition.

JR

Helmut Federle
Two i, Undecided
1985

038

Helmut Federle
1944 Solothurn

Oil on cotton
Signed, dated and titled verso:
H. FEDERLE 85 TWO i, UNDECIDED
285 × 180 cm

Inv. no. P188M / Acquired 2007

Federle's large-format work *Two i, Undecided* of 1985 also shows white geometric shapes on a black ground. The composition consists of two pairs, a square and a rectangle, placed side by side vertically but in reverse order. The identical squares have the same width as the rectangles of uneven length but do not share the same axes despite relating vertically to their respective rectangle. Although placed vertically and parallel, the four elements prove to be asymmetrical and unstable because their axial shift varies, as do the distances between and around them. Moreover, if we suspend judgement, we can even conceive of a switch between figure and ground with the black becoming the shape, and the white shapes the ground. This work makes manifest Federle's ongoing study of the balance between geometrical shapes. In his own words: "My pictures are perhaps models that show there are no models."

The title *Two i* suggests that the two white shapes refer to the lowercase "i", consisting of a dot and a line or, in this case, a square and a rectangle, whose status in the painting is indecisive and precarious. *Two i* could also mean to "I"s, two identities in a state of permanent indecision.

JR

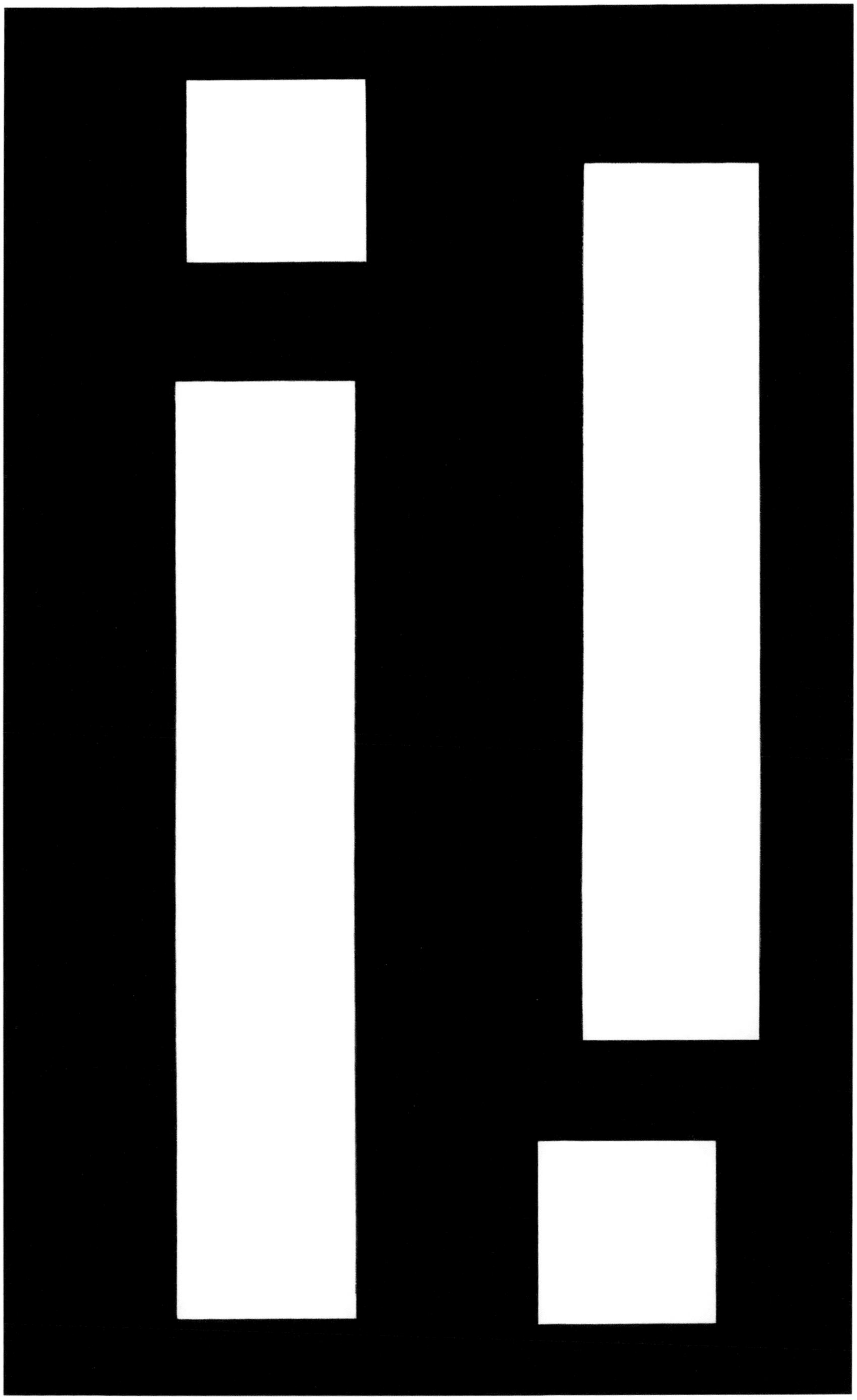

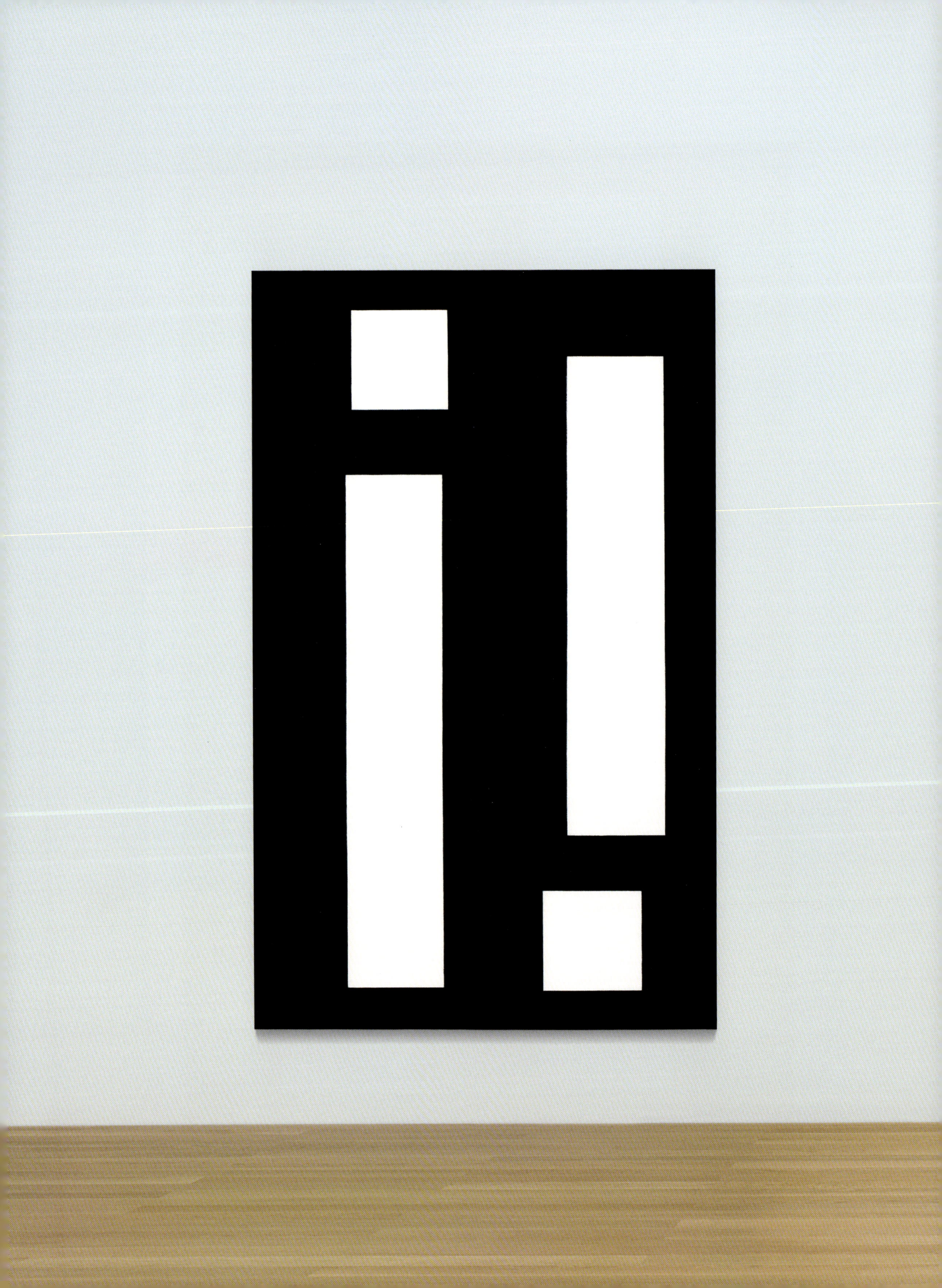

Europe circa 1960

Victor Vasarely
Procion
1959

Victor Vasarely
1906 Pécs – 1997 Paris

Oil on wood with relief
Inscribed, titled, dated and signed verso:
AK / "PROCION" + / 1959 / Vasarely
99.5 × 66 cm

Inv. no. P177M / Acquired 2007

Growing up in the context of Cubism, Constructivism and the Bauhaus, Victor Vasarely was to become a pioneer of Op Art, creating an oeuvre based on a "sculptural alphabet" of geometric shapes – squares, triangles, trapezoids, rods, circles, ellipses – in conjunction with six basic colours. The vast potential of combining these elements both visually and kinetically led to sculptural and dynamic compositions. Vasarely's lifelong interest in graphic patterns and spatial illusion was already manifest in the 1930s when he was working as a commercial artist in Paris; the first constructive geometric and abstract motifs appeared in his work in 1947. In 1951 he embarked on his "kinetic-abstract style", refining and honing it over the next few years. During his black-and-white period, from about 1951 to 1963, Vasarely focused on the opposition between black and white as the greatest possible colour contrast to further explore its effect on the relationship between figure and ground.

In *Procion* of 1959, nine black squares are laid out three by three on a white ground with corners extended at right angles and each with a white square in the middle. These black squares take up the lower two-thirds of the painting. The ground of the picture, that is, the white areas in between, also forms a grid which can in turn be perceived as a figure on a black ground. The upper third of the composition is dominated by a single, centred and conspicuously larger white square with corners extended at right angles and a black square in the centre. It is therefore the visual converse of the nine smaller squares below and is set off against the whole as a relief.

The opposition of black and white, of figure and ground, goes hand-in-hand with the contrast of positive and negative as well as the play between two and three dimensions. Our perception oscillates between two fundamentally different "readings". As Vasarely wrote in 1951, "the strongest contrast is between black and white ... networks of lines intersect and form grids, thus suggesting transitions through variation ... or, to put it differently, superimposed networks, spatially separated, generate the effect of movement which is fascinating above all because the genetic phenomenon is caused by the movement of the eyes."

The constituents of Vasarely's "sculptural alphabet" can also be interpreted as elements of the universe that illustrate the order of the world. The artist was of the conviction that everything is dominated by one "universal law" and that the universe is created by "a constant of all unity". The title *Procion* refers to the eponymous star (Procyon) in the constellation of Canis Minor (small dog), one of the brightest stars in the night sky.

JR

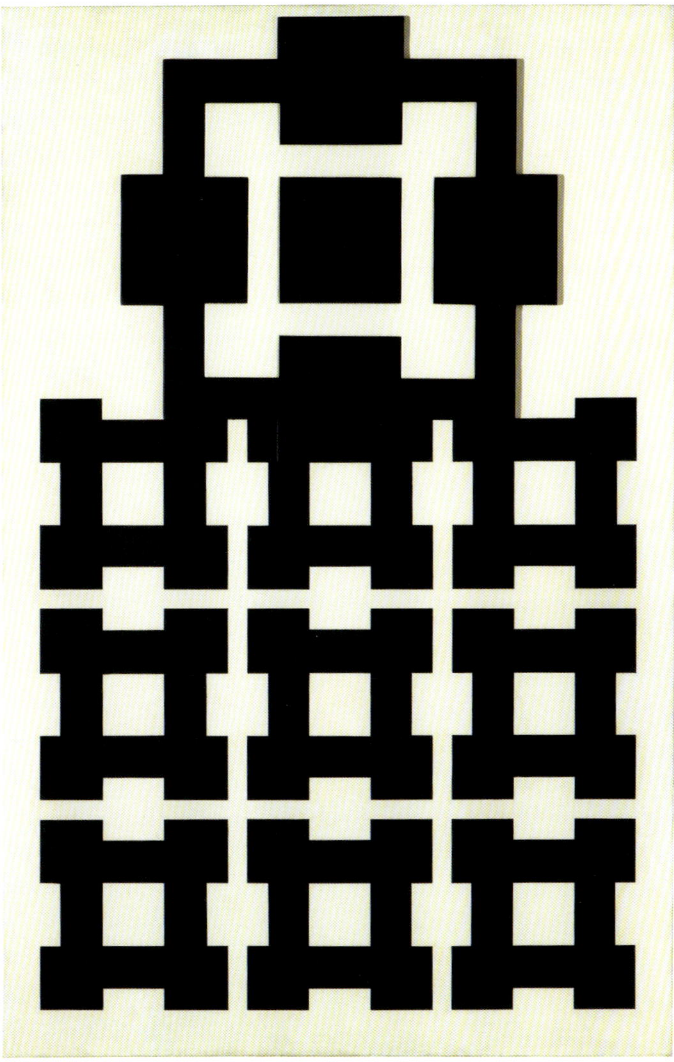

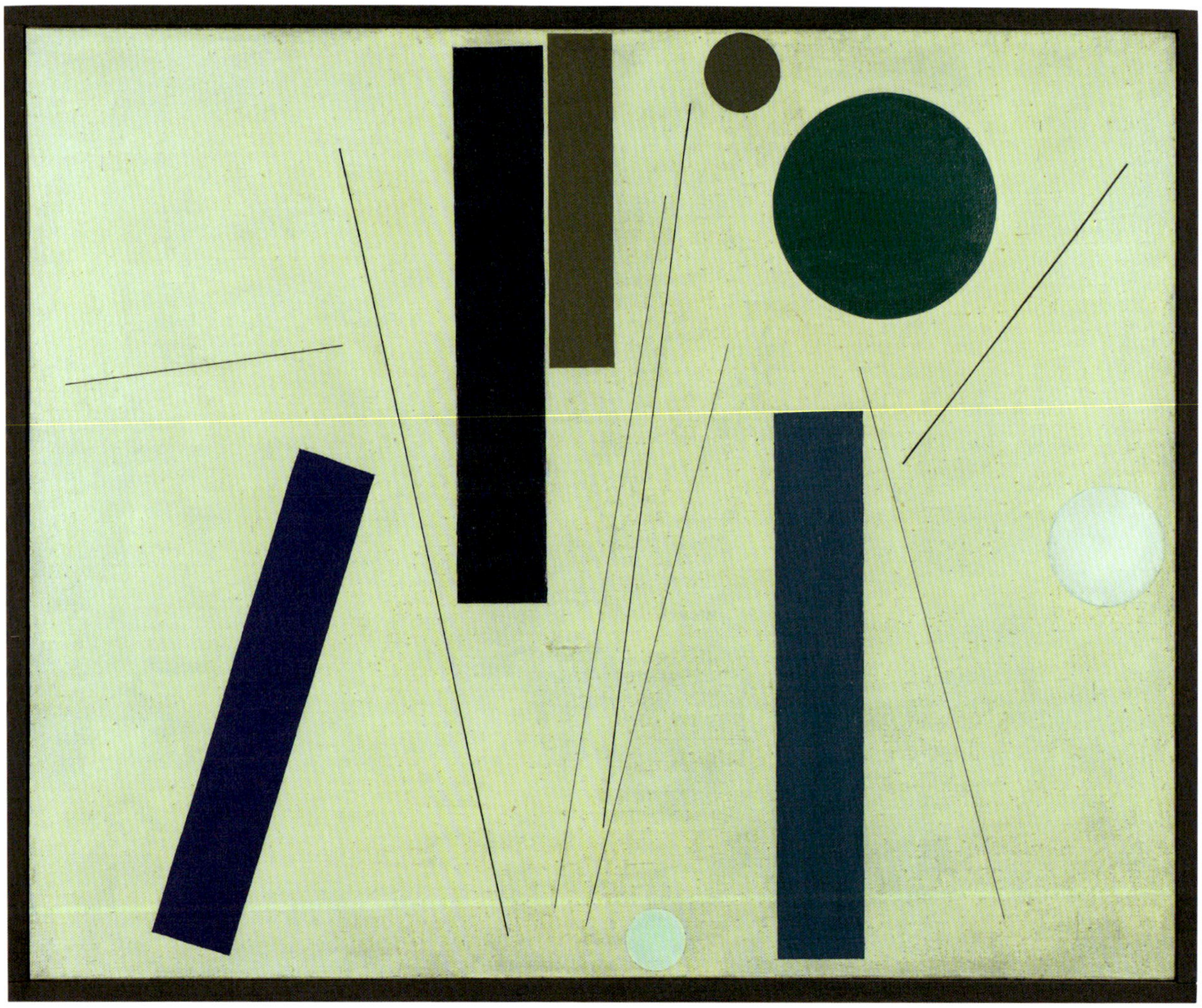

040

Günter Fruhtrunk
Untitled
1956

Günter Fruhtrunk
1923 Munich – 1982 Munich

Oil on burlap
Inscribed, dated and initialled verso:
haut / 1956 / FTK.
130 × 162 cm

Inv. no. P195M / Acquired 2008

Apart from a few late works, Günter Fruhtrunk's paintings feature great constructive precision and vitality. In contrast to what he perceived as the self-absorbed nature of Tachism ("pouring out of the ego"), dominant in the 1950s, Fruhtrunk felt that Fernand Léger, in whose Paris studio he worked in 1952, and also his lifelong friend Hans Arp, refreshingly "minimised the ego for the sake of good work" and "took a rational approach to the matter at hand". These thoughts were uppermost in the artist's mind when he embarked on his artistic career in Paris, where he travelled on a stipend from the state of Baden-Württemberg and the Gouvernement Français in 1954. The city would become his permanent home. Fruhtrunk's paintings – he did not fully endorse them himself until 1954 – testify to his admiration of the Russian painter Kazimir Malevich, whose Suprematist oeuvre aspired to the "liberated nothingness of non-figuration" and whose *Black Square* (1915) ranks among the most radical and influential works of twentieth-century art. Fruhtrunk's *Monument für Malewitsch* of 1954, a composition of circles and polygons in different colours combined with thin lines on a monochrome ground, clearly shows his affinity with Malevich's Suprematist work made between 1915 and 1920. The 1956 painting reproduced here shows the same formal vocabulary and a similar palette, but in contrast to *Monument für Malewitsch*, Fruhtrunk separated the elements of the picture to avoid any suggestion of depth that might be conjured by overlapping. Thus isolated, the composition of circles and rectangles, again complemented by thin lines, yields a delicately balanced whole. Although the elements are separated, the painting still shows a clear distinction between figure and ground, between surface and depth. As the 1960s progressed, Fruhtrunk gradually abandoned this distinction altogether and incorporated the increasingly condensed, rhythmic tectonics into the picture plane.

UW

Günter Fruhtrunk
Diagonale Progression Schwarz-Weiss (Studie II)
c. 1970

Günter Fruhtrunk
1923 Munich – 1982 Munich

Acrylic on canvas
Signed, inscribed and initialled verso
FRUHTRUNK / PARIS / FTK. / STUDIE II / nach BILD / ROSENKRANZ / Ftk
140 × 148.5 cm

Inv. no. P190M / Acquired 2008

By 1963, Fruhtrunk's self-imposed bid to produce "formal structure and tectonic pictures" had become associated with the desire to intensify the rhythm of his tectonic compositions by working exclusively with a visual vocabulary of straight bands of colour arranged horizontally, vertically or diagonally. Irregular variations in their rhythm, direction, length and width in combination with shifts or "cuts", governed only by visual and not mathematical considerations, challenge viewers' sense perception and mental faculties. This is clearly illustrated in the painting *Diagonale Progression Schwarz-Weiss* (Diagonal Progression Black-White).

The dynamics of the diagonal structure in black and white do not abide within the framework of a square but acquire an additional thrust through the slight horizontal elongation of the format. Moreover, the up-and-down of the diagonals prevents the gaze from coming to rest; the irregularity of the rhythm undermines the search for order; and the arrangement of the bands thwarts any attempt to establish a distinction between "figure" and "ground". In addition, the disconcertingly sharp contrast between black and white is heightened by the narrow marginal strips of blue and violet. Significantly, this work is not about the superficial stimulus of the retina in the sense of 1950s and '60s Op Art, nor about the detached playfulness of nonobjective forms in Concrete Art, already dating back to the '30s. Instead Fruhtrunk wanted to find means of intensifying visual experience and, with it, the experience of human existence. In his own words, the image was an inalienable form of "preventing thoughts and feelings from becoming and being machine".
UW

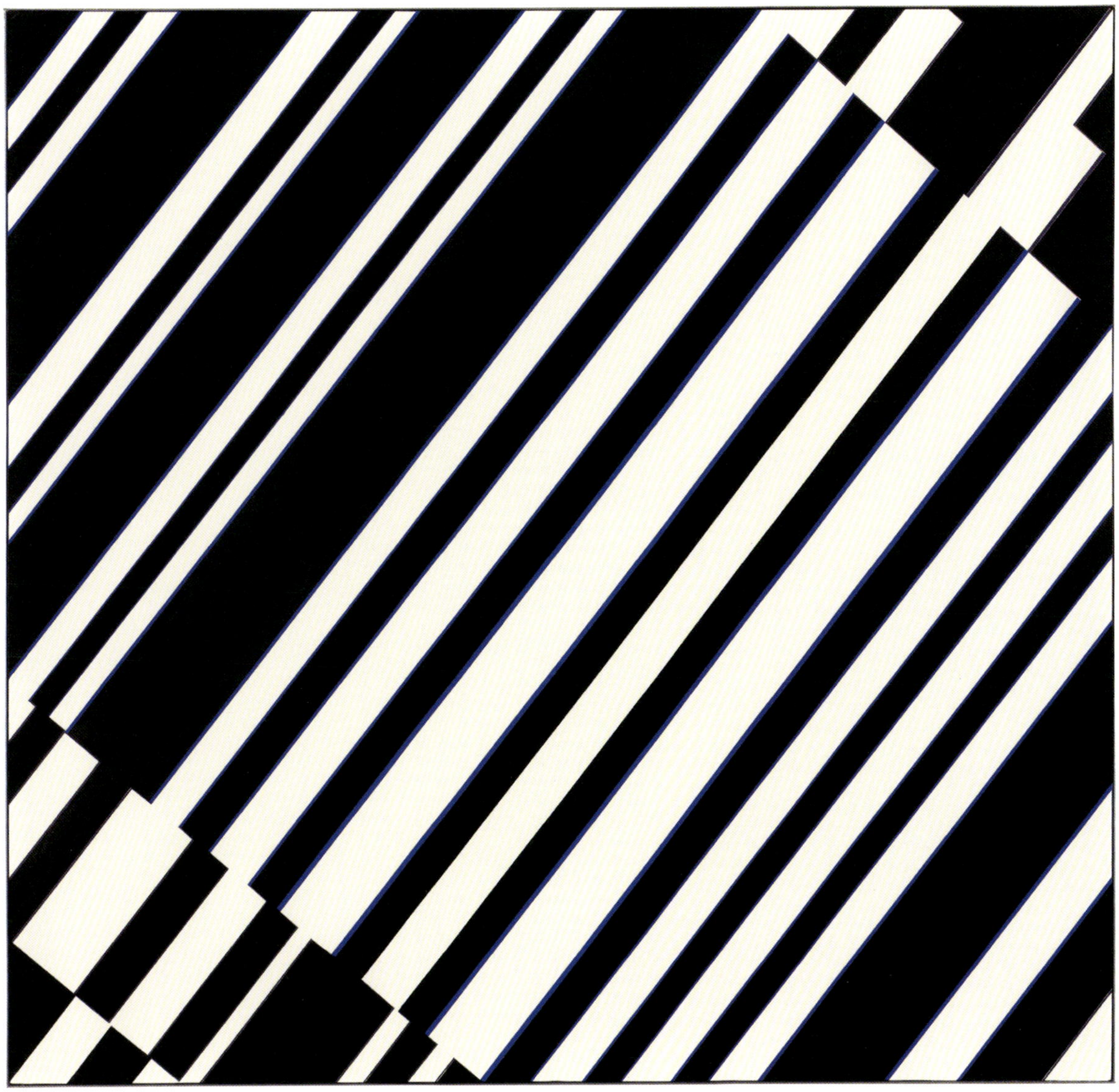

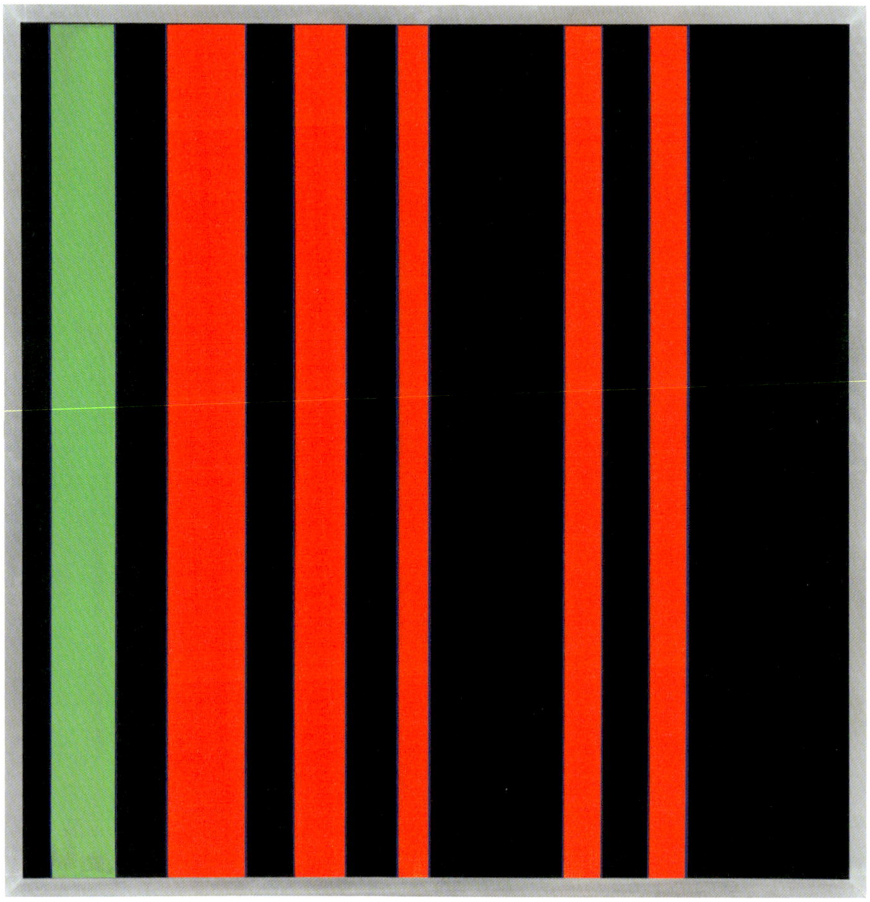

042

Günter Fruhtrunk
1923 Munich – 1982 Munich

Acrylic on canvas
Titled, signed, dated and initialled verso:
Exzentrisches GRÜN / FRUHTRUNK /
1968 / Ftk
90 × 90 cm

Inv. no. P189M / Acquired 2008

Günter Fruhtrunk
Exzentrisches Grün
1968

Günter Fruhtrunk
2 Rot: 1 Rot II
1971

043

Günter Fruhtrunk
1923 Munich – 1982 Munich

Acrylic, casein on canvas
Signed, dated and initialled on canvas verso:
FRUHTRUNK 1971 / Ftk.
Titled on stretcher: 2 ROT: 1 ROT II
231 × 180 cm

Inv. no. P237M / Acquired 2012

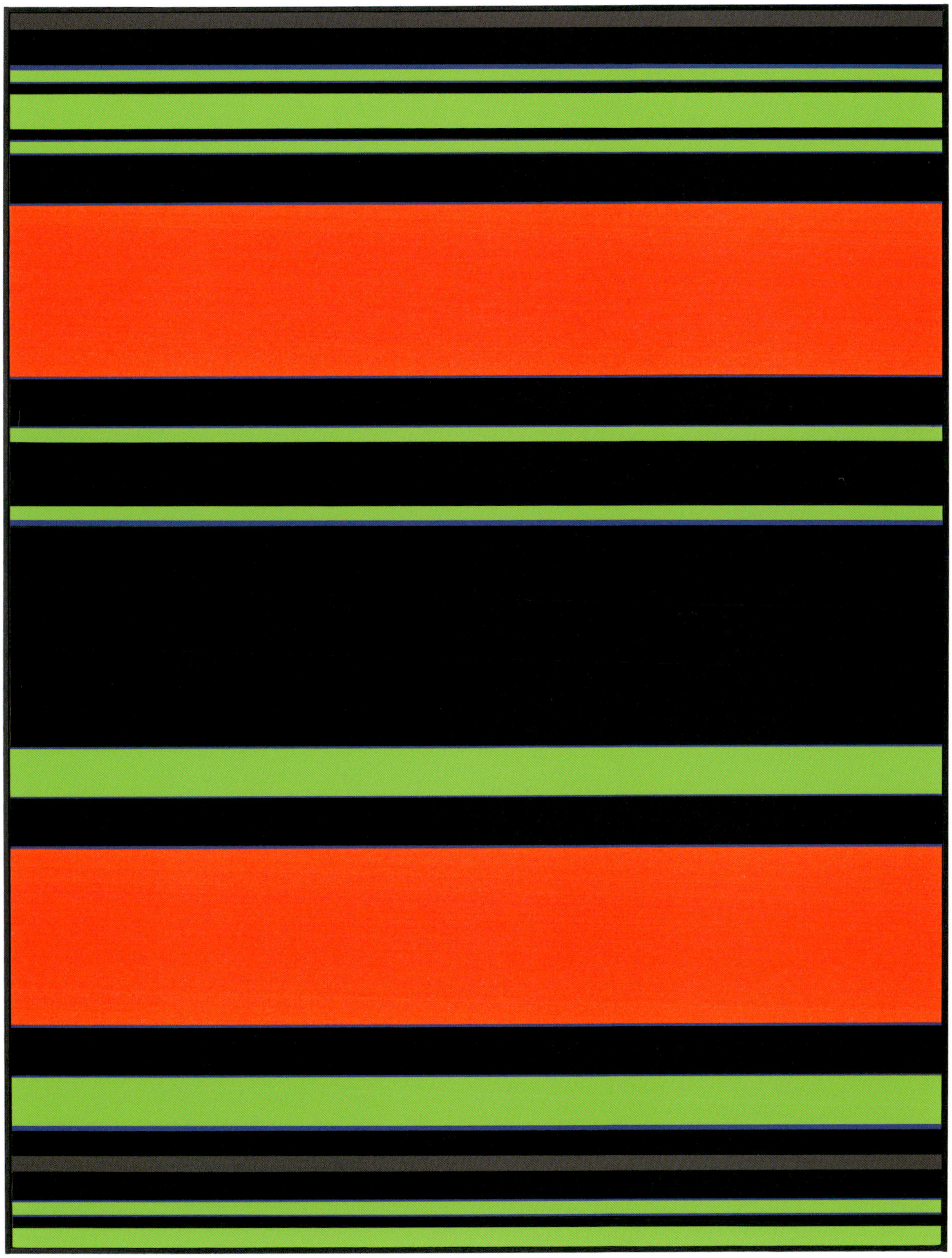

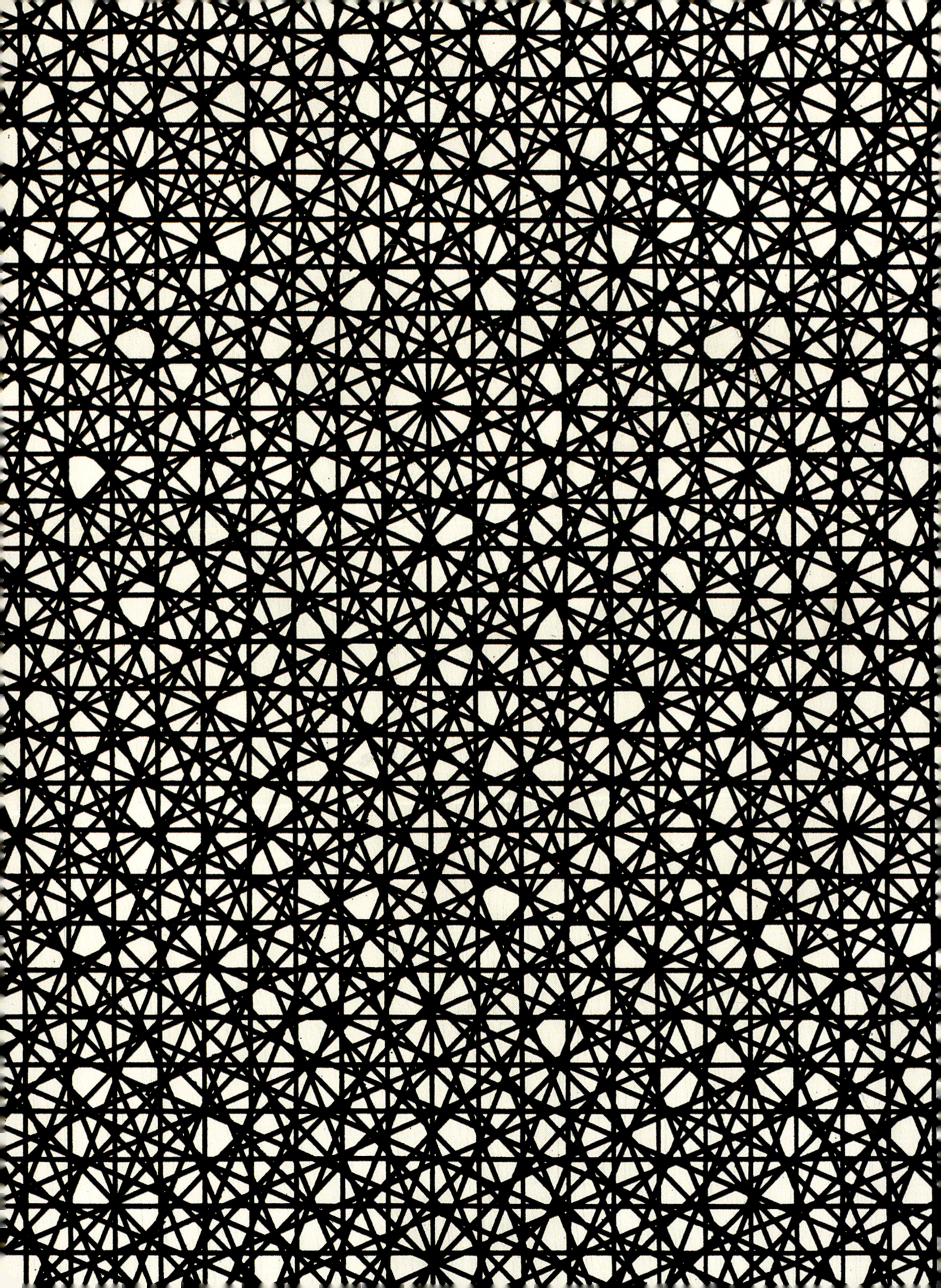

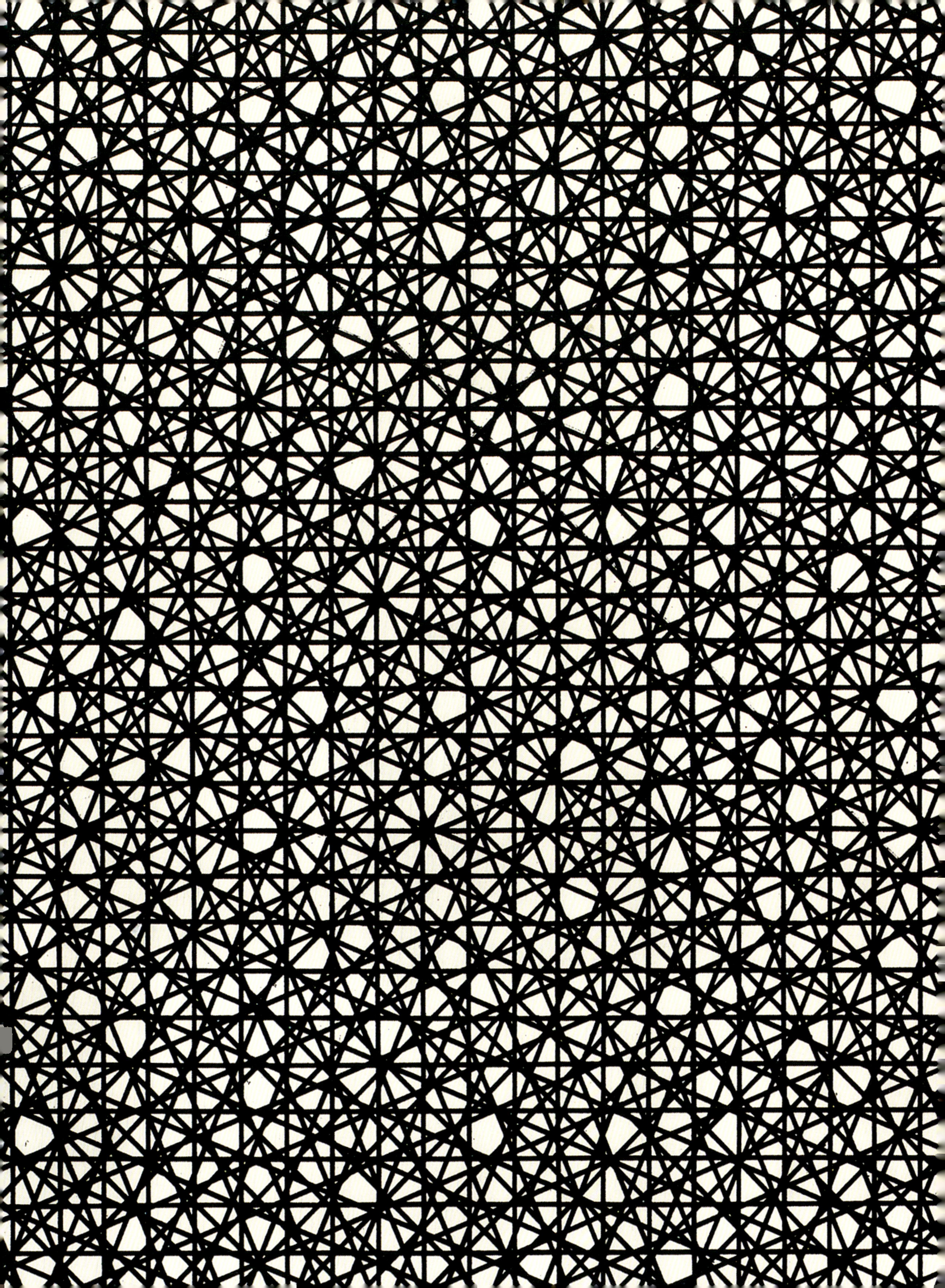

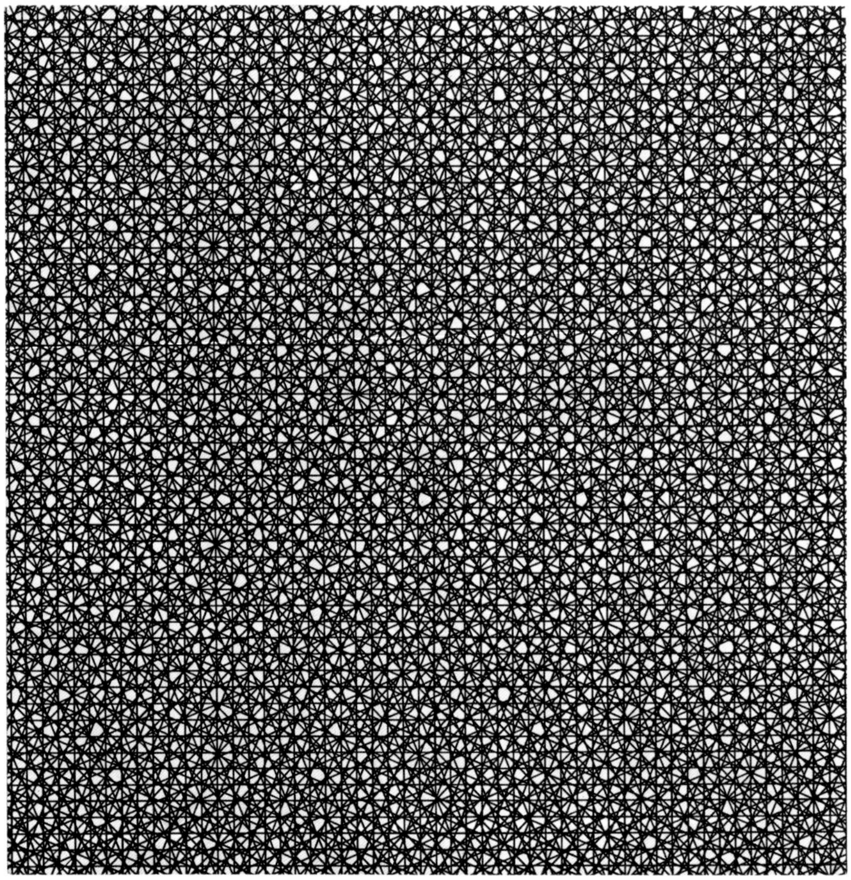

François Morellet
1926 Cholet – 2016 Cholet

Oil on wood
Signed, dated and titled:
Morellet / 1959–69 / 4 trames superposées
80 × 80 cm

Inv. no. P145M / Acquired 2018

François Morellet
4 Trames superposées
1959–1969

When asked about his art in numerous interviews, François Morellet often spoke of his fascination with **systems, their rules and the changes they undergo, for which reason he has often been attributed the role of a game master who stimulates our creative drive.** Morellet never attended an art academy and assisted in managing the family business, a toy factory in Cholet, until the 1970s. However, since the early 1950s, he had consistently taken a stand against the subjective gestural painting of the contemporary École de Paris. He used such terms as *continuous alignment, interference, superimposition* and *chance* to describe the ordering systems that he devised for his configurations of lines running parallel, intersecting or overlapping. They can appear, he says, "as a picture, a wall design or as a sculptural or spatial form." The artist started working with light bulbs and neon in 1962 because, as he says, "I was enthralled by neon lighting, which is the ideal material for me because it is so linear, hard, cold and brutal."

Morellet felt a particular affinity with Max Bill, Concrete Art and the paintings of Piet Mondrian. The wealth of filigree ornament in Granada's Alhambra also made a profound impression when he visited in 1952. *4 Trames superposées* (4 Superimposed Grids) clearly represents nonfigurative European painting. It consists of four superimposed square grids each defined by different angles and evenly laid out on the picture plane. The artist eschews any personal signature or artistic composition. Although the system is intellectually comprehensible, we are confronted with a bewildering structure that offers hardly any visual clues to orientation. The tension between clarity and ambiguity, between rule and chance, evident above all in the irregular interstices, is not merely an artistic principle; it is ultimately nothing less than an abstract description of our lived reality.

Morellet showed an attitude both humorous and entertaining in frequent reflections not only on his own work but on art and its practitioners in general. He wanted to enable his audience to participate in the act of "creation", a goal no doubt more readily achieved by works with simple, neutral structures than clever art that trumpets a message. "Art," he said in an interview of 1972, "must permit viewers to find what they want, that is, what they bring along of their own accord. Works of art are picnic areas, pubs in which to eat what they themselves have brought along."

AS

François Morellet
Négatif n° 14
2011

François Morellet
1926 Cholet – 2016 Cholet

Acrylic on canvas on wood,
neon, wiring, transformer
Titled, signed, dated and num. verso:
"Négatif n° 14" (d'après Steel-Life n° 22) /
Morellet 2011 / 1/3
147 × 147 × 5 cm

Inv. no. P262M / Acquired 2014

Négatif n° 14 of 2011 is a late work, made when the artist was eighty-five years old. As indicated in the title, it refers to *Steel-Life*, a work of 1990, not simply reflecting on it but playfully modifying it. The title's phonetic play on still life is inspired by the thin, black steel frames of the earlier series. These are connected to white squares. *Négatif n° 14* is the negative of this prior work; the white square has become black, the black steel frame has morphed into cold, white neon tubing.

The reference to one of the most famous paintings of the twentieth century is obvious, namely the *Black Square* painted in 1915 on a white ground by the Russian Suprematist Kazimir Malevich. Malevich's painting forms a physical unity that represents the mystic whole of the world. In contrast, *Négatif n° 14* is divided into two parts: the tilted black square and the neon tubes that are open at the bottom.

The uncertain angle at which Morellet has placed his square may have been inspired by the frequently reproduced photograph of the last Futurist exhibition in 1915 in Petrograd (St. Petersburg). It shows the *Black Square* mounted at a diagonal in a corner of the room directly under the ceiling. Morellet's interest in Malevich goes back to the 1980s. In two large works – *Fantôme de Malévitch* (Ghost of Malevich) on the facade of the Musée des Beaux Arts in Chambéry of 1981–82 and *Le naufrage de Malévitch* (The Shipwreck of Malevich) in the Kerguéhennec sculpture park in Brittany of 1987–1990 – Morellet divided the square into four separate triangles. The deconstruction proved to be a definitive consequence of the artist's involvement with Malevich's square. He transposed the art of his predecessor, whom he considered too romantic, too dramatic and perhaps ultimately too personal, to a concrete situation. In the catalogue *Kazimir Malévitch & François Morellet*, 2011, Morellet explicitly expressed his hope that he might still have many years at his disposal to maim and torture the good old square. Nonetheless, viewers of *Négatif n° 14*, cool and aloof as the work may be, may yet discover a hint of the heroic that marks Malevich's square – and, in the final analysis, perhaps realise that Morellet's investigations constitute a tribute to Malevich after all.

AS

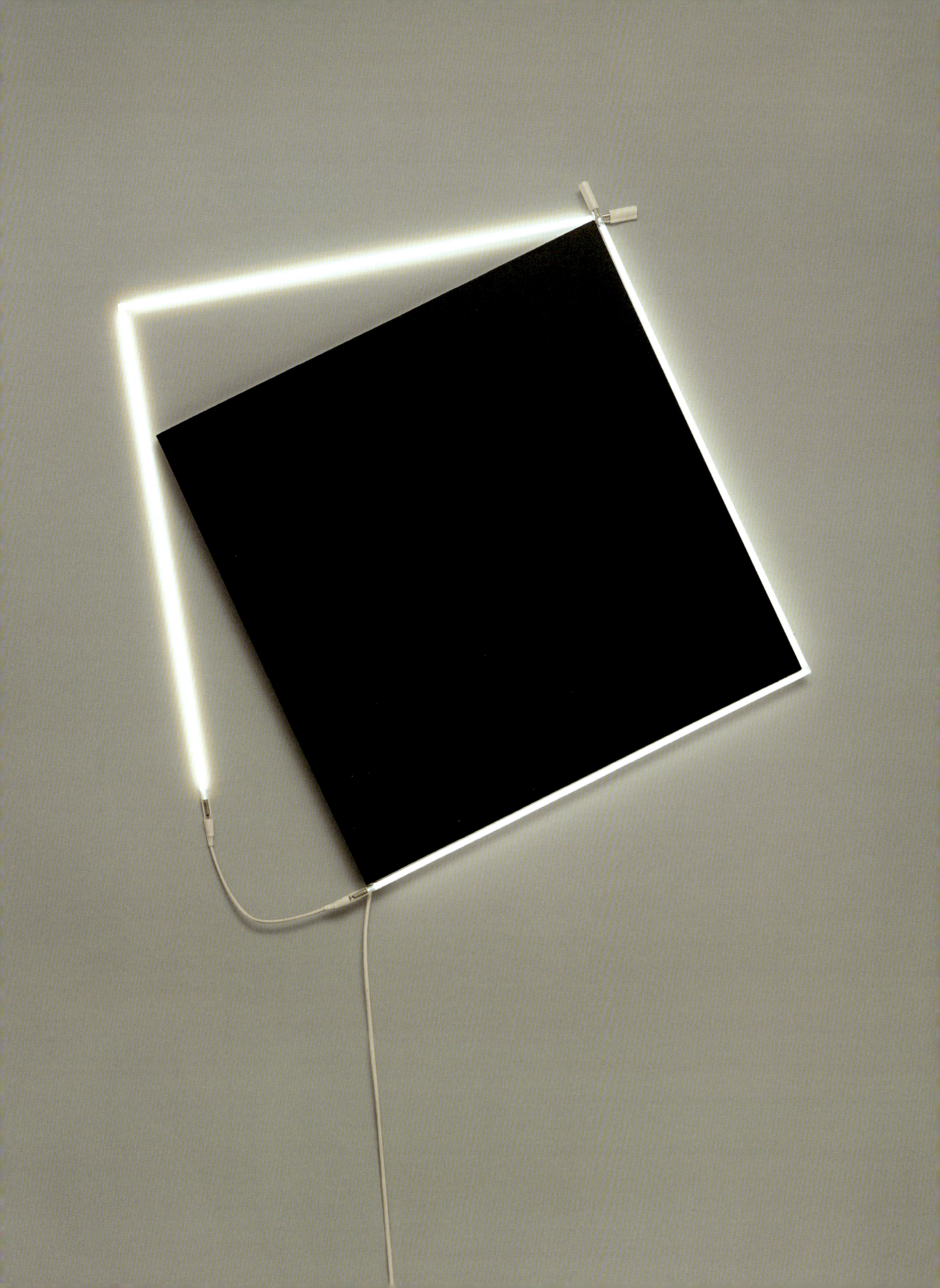

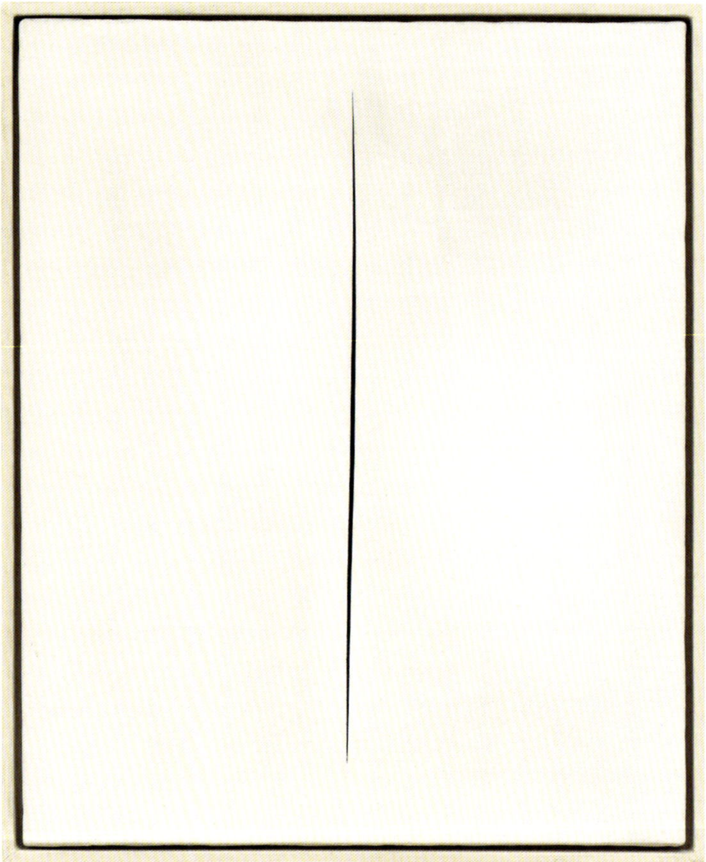

Lucio Fontana
1899 Rosario de Santa Fé –
1968 Comabbio / Varese

Watercolour on canvas
Signed and titled verso: "L. Fontana / Concetto Spaziale / ATTESA / Quante fesserie / sento nella giornata"
55.6 × 46.2 cm

Inv. no. P159M / Acquired 2005

Lucio Fontana
Concetto spaziale, Attesa
1966

In 1958 Lucio Fontana took a knife and slashed the white plane of a canvas, an act of destruction as symbolic as it is real. In so doing, he targeted a medium that artists have used for centuries as a surface of projection for their will to represent and express their ideas. Fontana had already taken a step in this direction nine years earlier when he perforated his paintings with pointed tools. "Iconoclastic" gestures of this kind subvert the secondary function of a canvas as a picture support, drawing attention to its physical reality as an object in and of itself. Slits and holes are, of course, not merely destructive; they are an artistic means of revealing the space behind the canvas and incorporating it into the work of art. Devoted to the realities of surface and plane, this group of works is tellingly entitled *Concetto spaziale* (Spatial Concept). Fontana's *Manifiesto Blanco* of 1946 calls for "an art that is free of all aesthetic artifice" and instead devoted to matter, time and space, as the "primary values of existence", in other words, to all that is "true and natural in man". Heinz Mack dedicated his *Lichtmaschinen* (light machines) to Fontana, his elder by thirty years, astutely noting that his fellow artist's iconoclastic gesture "did not kill the picture" but rather generated a picture in its own right, a picture with one, five or seven slashes on a white, gold or red ground. The slashed canvas has inevitably become a signature feature of the artist's work, but this fact can never eclipse the original radicalism of his message and its profound impact on art in the 1960s, specifically on ZERO and Arte Povera.

UW

Lucio Fontana
Concetto spaziale, Attese
1962

Lucio Fontana
1899 Rosario de Santa Fé –
1968 Comabbio / Varese

Gold paint on canvas
Signed and titled verso: "L. Fontana / Concetto Spaziale / ATTESE / 1+1-UTA7"
82 × 65 cm

Inv. no. P56M / Acquired 1999

Fontana also wielded his knife against the aesthetics of the gold background, widely used from the early Middle Ages until well into the fifteenth century as the incarnation of a metaphysical space suffused with divine light. With five slashes, he "secularised" and removed it to an earthly sphere. He rendered the precious gold leaf of mediaeval art by deftly coating his canvas with gold paint. In his treatise on painting of 1432, Leon Battista Alberti already advocated banning gold backgrounds in painting, arguing that light and space should no longer be represented as transcendental but rather as natural phenomena. It seems, however, that Fontana's destructive act was merely an excuse to revive the gold background of painting.
UW

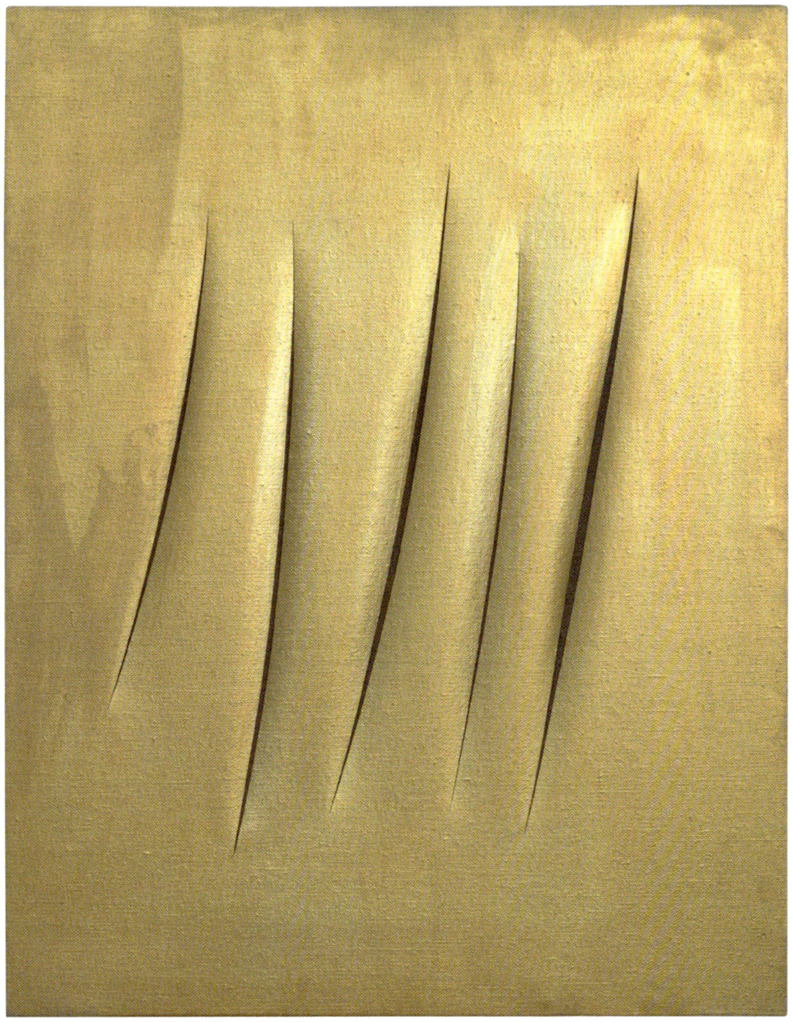

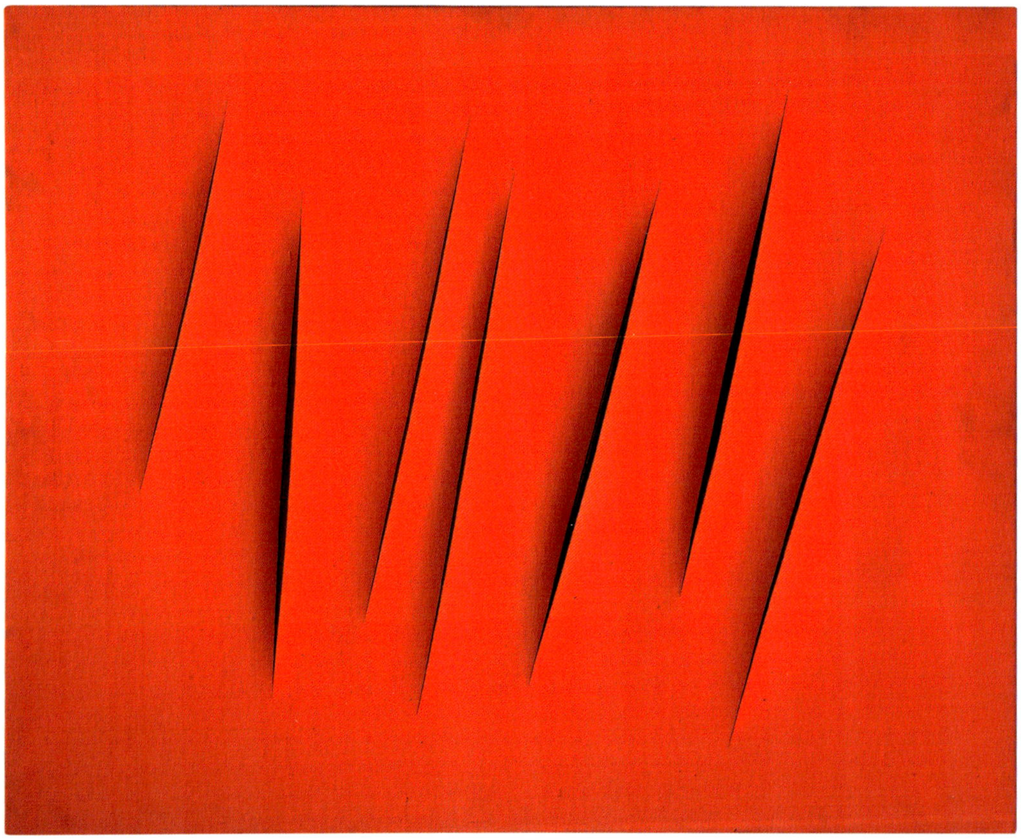

048

Lucio Fontana

Concetto spaziale, Attese

1965

Lucio Fontana
1899 Rosario de Santa Fé –
1968 Comabbio / Varese

Watercolour on canvas
Signed and titled verso:
"L. Fontana / Concetto Spaziale /
ATTESE / oggi / sono stanco e non lavoro"
73 × 92 cm

Inv. no. P57M / Acquired 1999

Yves Klein
Monochrome (IKB 180)
1958

Yves Klein
1928 Nice – 1962 Paris

Pigments in synthetic resin on canvas
Signed verso.: Yves
65 × 54 cm

Inv. no. P18M / Acquired 1995

IKB stands for International Klein Blue, a radiant ultramarine blue. In *Mon Livre* of 1960, Yves Klein writes, "Blue has no dimensions, it is beyond dimensions, whereas the other colours are not." For Klein, blue is the incarnation of cosmic feelings and, like all other pure colours, of unadulterated freedom. He "signed" his first blue painting on the back of the sky while lying on the beach in Nice. Years later he would recall how he hated the birds for flying back and forth and "trying to make holes" in his greatest work.

Klein first attempted to give substance to these poetic sensations of space while working in London in 1949–50 for the frame maker and gilder Robert Savage. Fascinated by the magical luminosity of pure powdered pigments, he created his first *Monochrome*. However, as soon as he added a binder to the powders, they lost their luminosity, and without a binder, they did not adhere to the canvas. In 1955, Klein found a working solution with the help of the Parisian chemist Édouard Adam. Instead of using conventional binders, they suspended the dry pigment in diluted Rhodopas, a petroleum extract ordinarily used to fix paintings. The combination of dry pigment and Rhodopas M60A produced a quick-drying but poisonous paint that Klein applied with a roller, deliberately precluding the possibility of an individual signature. The pigment now adhered to the canvas without losing its luminosity. The picture had come to life; it had become an adequate materialisation of the cosmic sense of space that Klein would call a "cosmic sensibility" and occasionally "pure" or "poetic" energy.

The effect and meaning of that energy or sensibility are not immutably fixed but depend on the disposition of the viewer, as demonstrated in January 1957 at an exhibition at Apollinaire Gallery in Milan. Klein presented eleven works identical in colour, size and composition but different in price. The buyers proved his point; they each paid a different price for their own personal and distinctive experience. His concept had proved effective: "Every one of the blue propositions, all the same in appearance, were nonetheless perceived as being very different by the viewers. The layman simply went from one picture to the next and penetrated the world of blue through spontaneous contemplation. But the blue world of each picture, although of the same blue and presented in the same way as the others, was of an entirely different essence and atmosphere. Not a single one resembled another – no more than painterly or poetic moments resemble each other – although they all possessed the same sublime and subtle nature (of the immaterial)."

AS

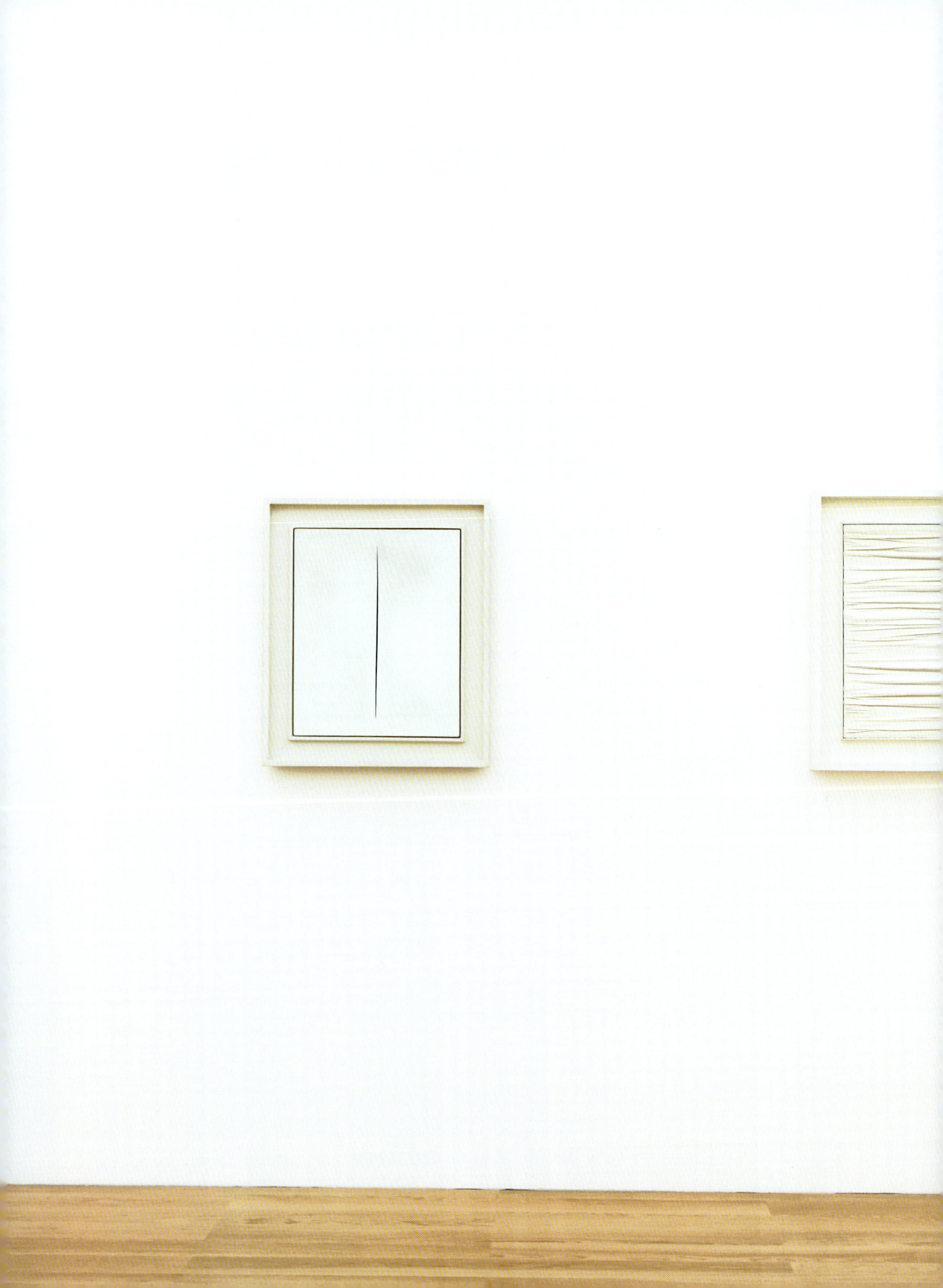

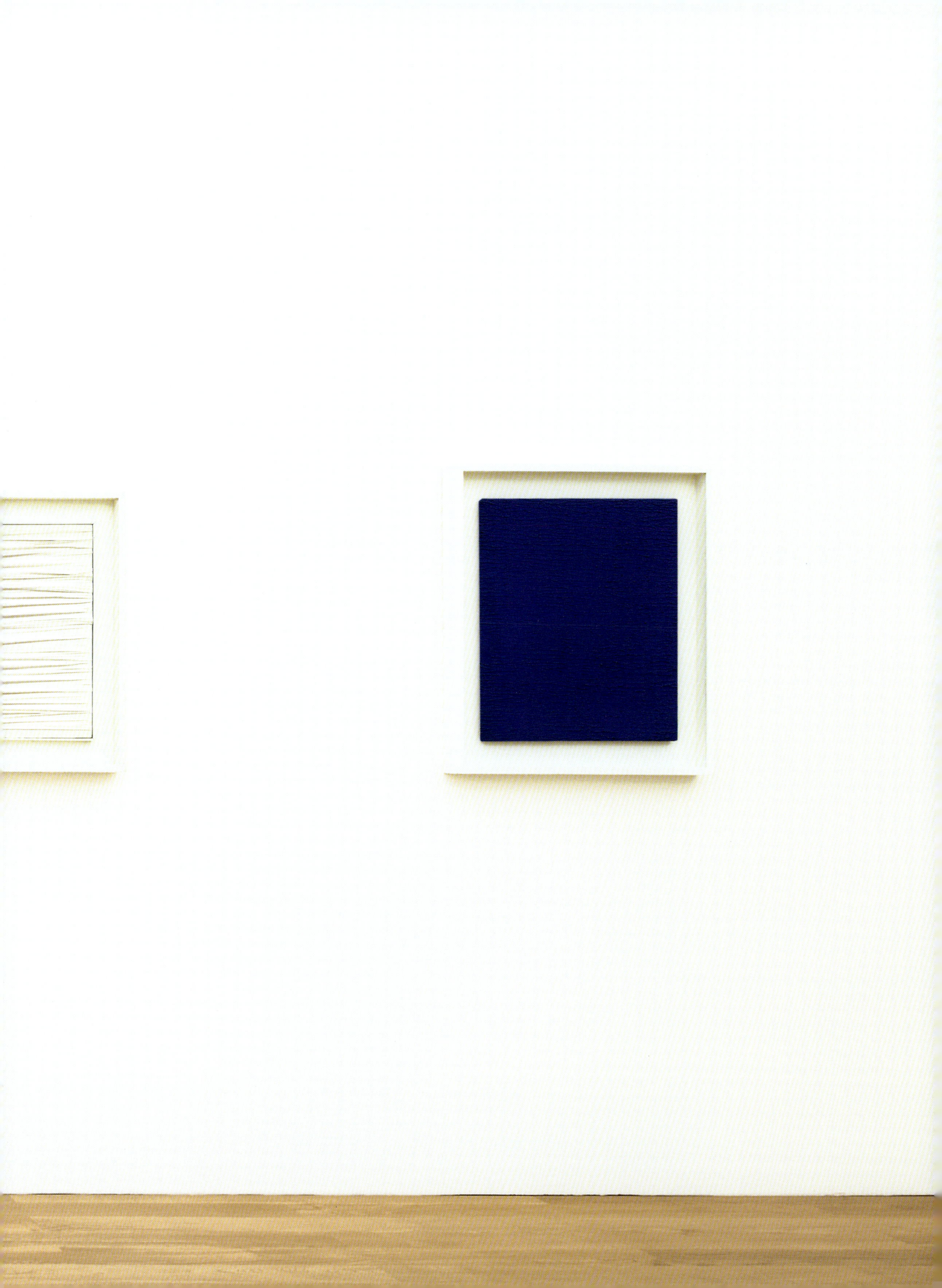

050

Piero Manzoni
1933 Soncino / Milan – 1963 Milan

Kaolin on cotton
57.6 × 73 cm

Inv. no. P82M / Acquired 2001

Piero Manzoni
Achrome
1959–60

Piero Manzoni ranks among Italy's most complex and radical artists after the Second World War. His early oeuvre, indebted to Art Informel, later gave way to an approach between the "Informel gesture and a new bodily concept of reality" (Martin Engler). In only five years, from 1957 until his premature death in February 1963, Manzoni produced a body of work that reduced painting, sculpture, happening and action to absurdity; he dismantled the traditional foundations of these categories, and redefined them. His provocative thrust was meant to abolish art altogether, but proved to have quite the opposite effect, expanding art and even adding a heroic touch. When he breathed his spirit into balloons in *Fiato d'artista* (Artist's Breath, 1959–60), when he signed his *Sculture viventi* (Living Sculptures, 1961), naked women as a rule, or when he produced his now notorious cans of artist's shit, *Merda d'artista*, 1961, these were not simply carnivalesque events, but rather a fundamentally new definition of art. In *Merda d'artista*, Manzoni filled tin cans with 30 grams of his excrement and sealed them off, elevating what the artist excretes to the status of art. We understand the process of production, the artistic gesture and the product but they remain invisible. The contents of the can elude simple, ordinary verification. When a tin can was opened almost thirty years later, in 1989, by the French artist Bernard Bazile as part of an artistic action, it was no longer possible to determine whether the contents were brown sienna soil or excrement.

At first sight Manzoni's white paintings – titled *Achromes* (Uncolour or Colourless), a word he coined in French – appear to be unrelated to the above-described actions. First made in 1957, these works also link the physical gesture – the folding of cotton and pouring kaolin on it – with the visual object. On pulling the cotton taut on the stretcher, Manzoni created a picture plane covered with smaller and larger folds. They are an expression of the artist's extraordinary energy and yet they look relatively neutral, an impression reinforced by the kaolin that he poured on the cotton. Kaolin is extremely fine white clay used primarily in the production of porcelain and paper; it is also a basic ingredient of powder. Its creamy smoothness enhances the quality of the picture as an object, whose solidified surface establishes a mobile and differentiated space of its own.

The *Achromes* vary in structure and material. In the early 1960s Manzoni used cotton, rabbit skin, bread rolls dipped in kaolin, and synthetic fibres, all of which are basically white. As emphasised in the secondary literature, this white does not stand for infinity and purity, as it did for the Suprematists, but for the absence of colour. Despite their neutrality and detachment, Manzoni's *Achromes* still evoke associations. The surface structure of the early works of fabric pulled taut remind the writer and psychoanalyst Dominique Laporte of clinical bandaging. They also look like bed sheets. Bandaging and linens in turn refer to the fragility of our existence between birth and death.

AS

Dadamaino
Volume a moduli sfasati
1960

Dadamaino
1935 Milan – 2004 Milan

Plastic sheets (perforated) in 3 layers
Signed, inscribed, titled and dated verso: DADA MAINO [address] VOLUME A MODULI SFASATI 1960
100 × 70 cm

Inv. no. P91M / Acquired 2001

In 1958 the self-taught artist Dadamaino began making her first series of nonfigurative works, which she presented that same year in her first solo exhibition at Galleria dei Bossi in Milan. Captivated by the ideas advanced by contemporary avant-garde artists in Italy, she took no interest in the conventional parameters of painting, such as composition, spatial illusion or narrative. Instead, the *Volumi*, crucial to her oeuvre, explore such concerns as real space, sculptural volume and form as autonomous pictorial values.

In one of these early works, *Volume a moduli sfasati* of 1960, Dadamaino punctured three sheets of plastic film by hand and superimposed them at varying distances. Not all of the round, see-through holes are congruent; some of them overlap, creating cropped circular openings. The appearance of these openings changes depending on vantage point, infusing the whole with a distinct dynamic and a discreet play of light and shadow. The plastic film replaces the classical canvas and is no longer a vehicle for images and meaning; it becomes a material reality in itself. The Italian avant-garde of the 1960s and the artists of the ZERO and Nul groups showed an avid interest in experimenting with new materials, such as plastic, which acquired increasing popularity at the time. Their use of inexpensive industrial materials signalled a radical departure from the traditional components of painting.

Dadamaino's studies in space and perspective took particular inspiration from the work of Lucio Fontana. She responded in her *Volumi* to his *Concetti spaziali*, which opened up the real space of the picture by perforating or slashing the canvas. The artists of the Galleria Azimut in Milan, such as Piero Manzoni, Enrico Castellani and Agostino Bonalumi, a group she joined in 1959, were also important to the development of her work. They all shared the quest for new, untainted means of artistic expression in the wake of liberating themselves from subject matter. They were looking for a conceptual approach that no longer relied on traditional pictorial means and content.

JR

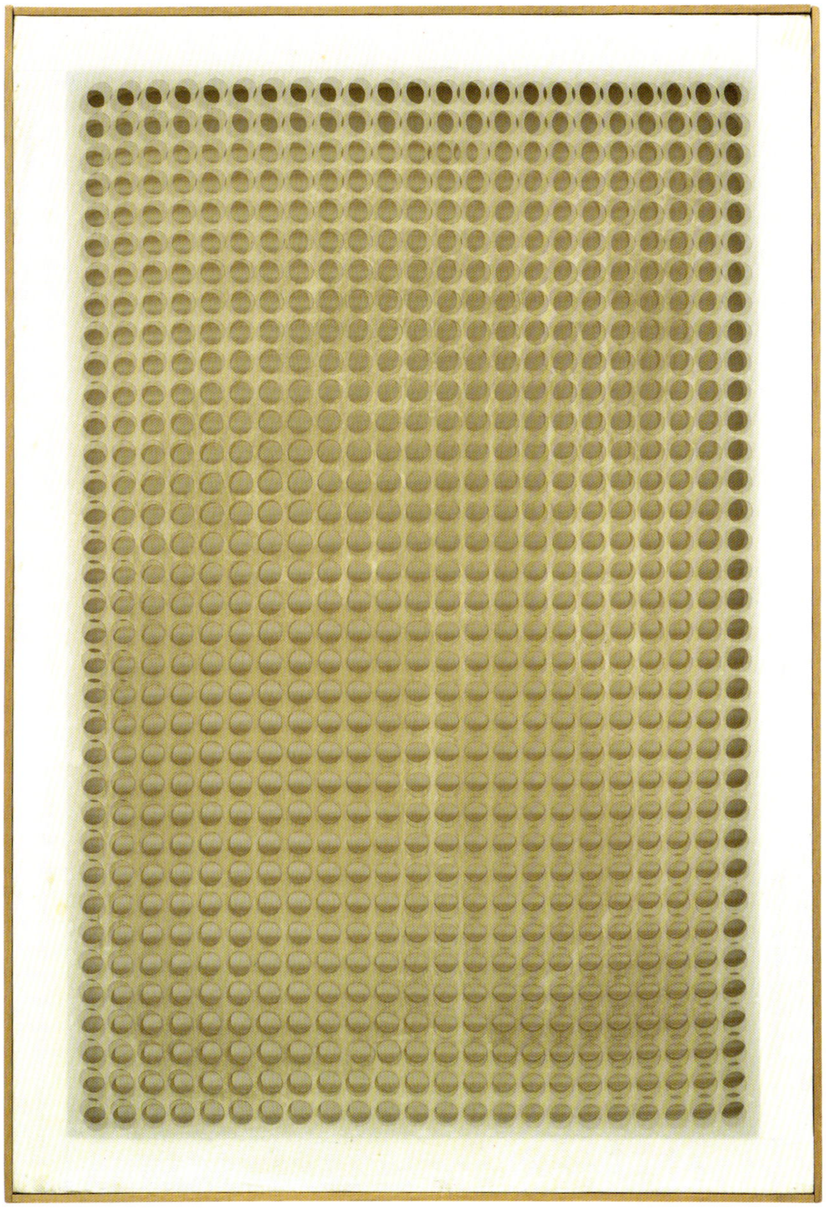

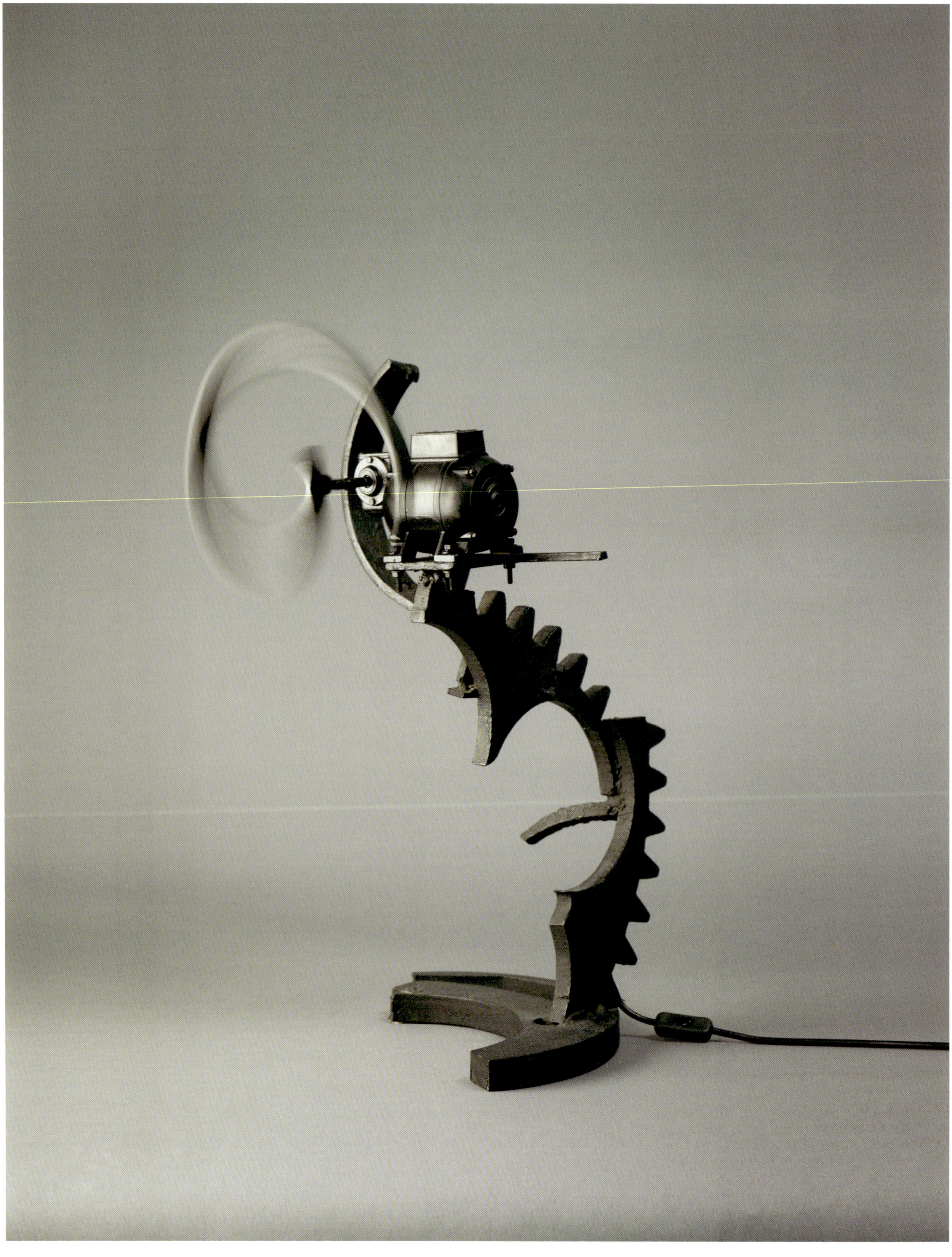

Jean Tinguely
Variation IV
1966

Jean Tinguely
1925 Fribourg – 1991 Bern

Iron, painted black, electric engine
Height: 70 cm

Inv. no. S227M / Acquired 2011

The insight that "everything is in motion, there is no stasis" inspired Jean Tinguely to devote himself to machines. Spearheading kinetic art and Nouveau réalisme, he is known for his movable, machine-like objects and installations. He was particularly interested in how they function, in their technical and aesthetic movement, in the sounds they generate and in the machine as an inherently poetic device. This fascination goes back to Tinguely's lifelong enthusiasm for racing cars, aeroplanes and other high-performance machines.

When Tinguely began painting his machines black in 1963, he temporarily turned his back on the colourful assemblages and junk aesthetics of Nouveau réalisme. The uniformity of colour shifted the priority to sequences of movement. Tinguely created *Heureka*, his first large-scale sculpture and a key work in the series of *Black Sculptures*, for the Swiss National Exposition of 1964 in Lausanne. It now stands at Zürichhorn on the shore of Lake Zurich. In his lifetime, Tinguely already ranked among Switzerland's most successful and important artists internationally, alongside Alberto Giacometti and Max Bill. To make his machines, he used discarded objects, particularly industrial scraps such as iron elements, metal wheels, textiles, animal pelts, feathers and plastic. The creative repurposing of the industrial material gives the parts of the machine a new function, but it is also a critique of the uniformity of industrial processes and the production of useless things.

Tinguely created his black iron sculpture *Variation IV* in Paris in 1966. It is 70 cm tall and presents a welded configuration of solid geometrical iron elements, an abstract whole that evokes the body of a small dragon. Fragments of gears stand for the spinal cord, the spiral is the head, and the electric engine the brain. The sculpture at rest offers no clue to what happens when it is set in motion. Only then can viewers fully appreciate the gusto actively expressed by the movement of the machine. The rotating spiral jutting gently into space generates a virtual volume as an optical phenomenon. The discrete sound of the moving parts underscores the speed. This sculpture undoubtedly embodies the unbridled curiosity, charming humour and, above all, profound love of life generally ascribed to Tinguely. The *Black Sculptures* stimulate viewers to apply the choreographed movement to processes in their own lives.

JR

Gianni Colombo
Spazio elastico
1968

Gianni Colombo
1937 Milan – 1993 Melzo / Milan

Steel, nylon, 2 electric engines
c. 82 × 82 × 100 cm

Inv. no. S196M / Acquired 2008

By the end of the 1950s, Gianni Colombo was already experimenting with both visual and haptic phenomena. He started out working in ceramics and then expanded, incorporating felt, cotton, rubber, polystyrene, cardboard, wood, metal and other materials into his work. He not only gave viewers the opportunity to look and touch the works; he also devised mechanical devices so that they could actually change them. Colombo placed great emphasis on openness, variability and interaction.

In the context of artists' groups like Nouvelle Tendance or Gruppo T, which he cofounded in Milan in 1959, Colombo concentrated on kinetic works in the 1960s, using engines in some cases and reaching out into architectural space. In 1967 he created a suite of works, which he called *spazio elastico* (elastic space) – cubic rooms in darkness that visitors could enter, their stereometry made visible in the form of fluorescent elastic strings, which the artist stretched, contracted and twisted to create disorienting optical effects in space.

The *spazio elastico* (1968) in the collection of the Hilti Art Foundation consists of steel rods suspended from the ceiling, forming eight successively smaller open squares, lined up one behind the other. The squares are tied with nylon thread to a metal frame mounted above them, where two engines slowly and seamlessly transform the squares into parallelograms running in opposite directions, thus generating the impression of a curving space in constant motion.

Gianni Colombo's oeuvre challenges sensual perception. The conventional parameters of daily life no longer prevail; the supposed reliability of assumptions and expectations is undermined. The artist's enquiry into the psychology of perception is buoyed by a playful treatment of material and a poetry of form that lend these works the status of art.

UW

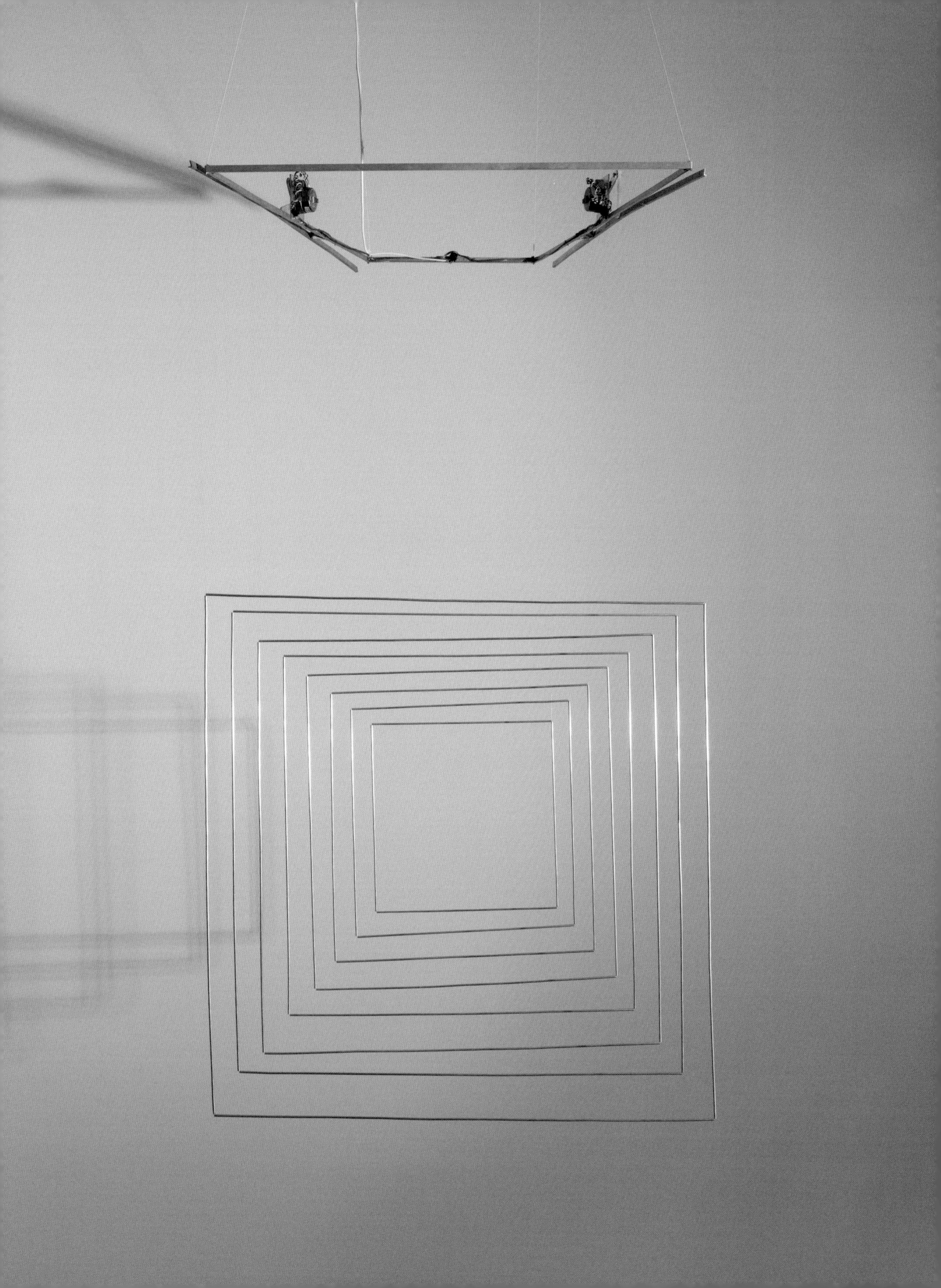

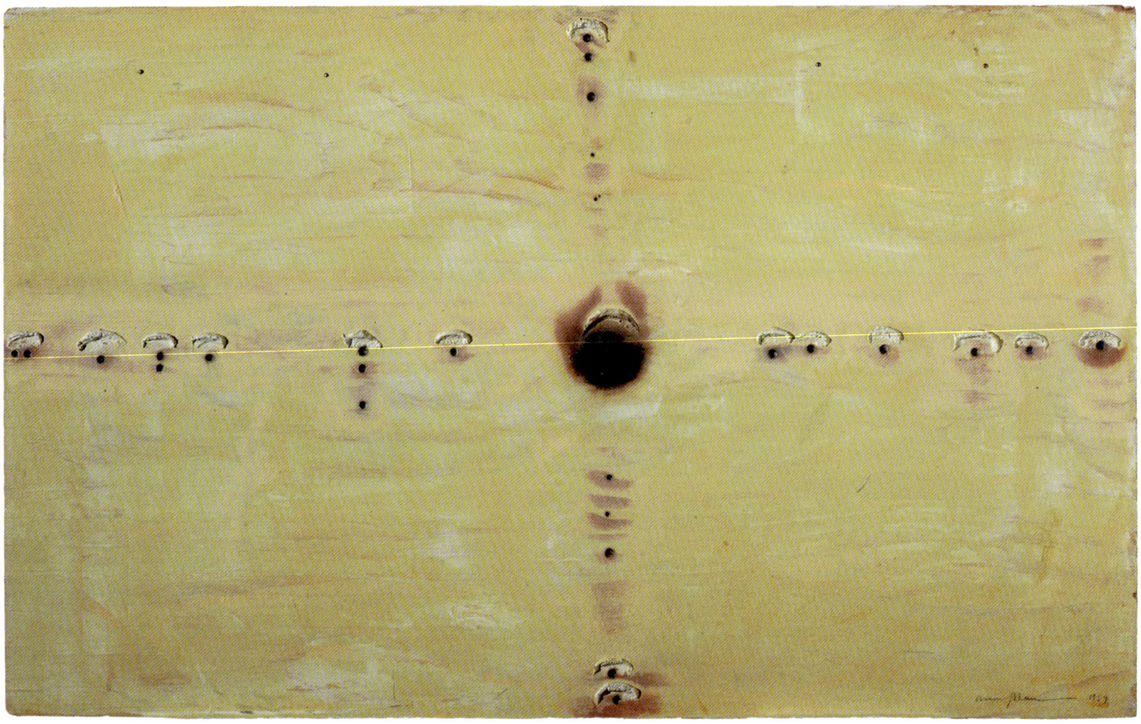

054

Hans Bischoffshausen
1927 Feld am See – 1987 Villach

Lacquer and cellular cement on plywood, fired
Signed lower right: Bischoffshausen 1959
Titled, dated, signed and labelled verso:
"ZUM KREUZ" / 1958 / Bischoffshausen / HVB
60 × 100 cm

Inv. no. P192M / Acquired 2008

Hans Bischoffshausen
Zum Kreuz
1958

Hans Bischoffshausen was among the artists of the avant-garde in Austria who were seeking reorientation in the wake of the Second World War. Bischoffshausen's unfinished architectural studies in Graz led in 1947 to a headlong "plunge into painting", inspired by Classical Modernism, in particular the work of Paul Klee. In 1959, after solo exhibitions at Galleria del Cavallino in Venice in 1957 and a year later at Galerie nächst St. Stephan in Vienna, Bischoffshausen received the Joanneumspreis für zeitgenössische Malerei, a substantial prize for contemporary painting that enabled him to move to Paris where he "spit out hundreds of paintings" despite the precarious circumstances in which he lived. Influenced as of 1958 by the work of the Italian artist Lucio Fontana (cat. 46–48), he abandoned figuration and lyrical abstraction, concentrating instead on the elements that constitute a picture: material, plane, structure, light, paint and space. Thanks among other things to his friendship with Fontana, he became involved in the international ZERO avant-garde, to which not only Fontana belonged but also such artists as Klein, Manzoni, Piene, Schoonhoven, Uecker and Verheyen.

Zum Kreuz (To the Cross) shows an extremely reduced treatment of material, form and colour. The elements all appear sparse, indeed crude, as if the artist were probing the very limits of composition and perception. A row of horizontal and vertical dot-shaped black indentations at irregular intervals form the motif of a cross on a carelessly painted piece of plywood, its slightly off-centre intersection marked by a larger spot burnt into the wood, like a wound or a "stigma". The indentations, which have also been burnt into the wood, are arched over with so-called ribs of intercellular cement, resembling eyebrows above a blind eye. Until well into the 1970s, while Bischoffshausen was living in Austria again, he frequently recurred to the motif of the cross as a symbol, albeit in a broader context that transcends traditional iconography.

By minimalising the means of his art, Hans Bischoffshausen created works of quiet, almost immaterial poetry, in pursuit of his wish to heighten the sensitivity of both sight and touch.
UW

Otto Piene
Untitled
1962

Otto Piene
1928 Laasphe – 2014 Berlin

Oil and soot on canvas
Signed and dated verso: piene 62
68 × 95 cm

Inv. no. P158M / Acquired 2005

"But to praise lightness alone no longer seems enough to me. I tackle darkness itself, I illuminate it, I make it transparent, I take away its terror, I turn it into a volume of power activated by the breath of my body, and I take smoke so that it can fly." Otto Piene, cofounder in 1958 of the Düsseldorf artist group ZERO, pioneered the art of light and fire, creating his first smoke works in 1959 on the basis of smoke drawings made by the traces of soot from a flame. Fire as a natural source of light and energy became the co-author of his works and was thus invested with artistic significance.

The ball of soot with frayed edges in the centre of this work is enshrouded in the honey-coloured aura of an oil-based binder. Piene burned pigments bound in oil, in this case possibly ivory black, directly on the canvas, producing a crusted and bubbled surface. His elemental treatment of fire and soot was motivated by a wish to probe the workings not only of spiritual awareness but equally of physical manipulation. He wanted to enable both the act of making art and the act of becoming in nature to evolve as self-propelled processes. For Piene, the goal of reharmonising the relationship between human and nature was vital.

JR

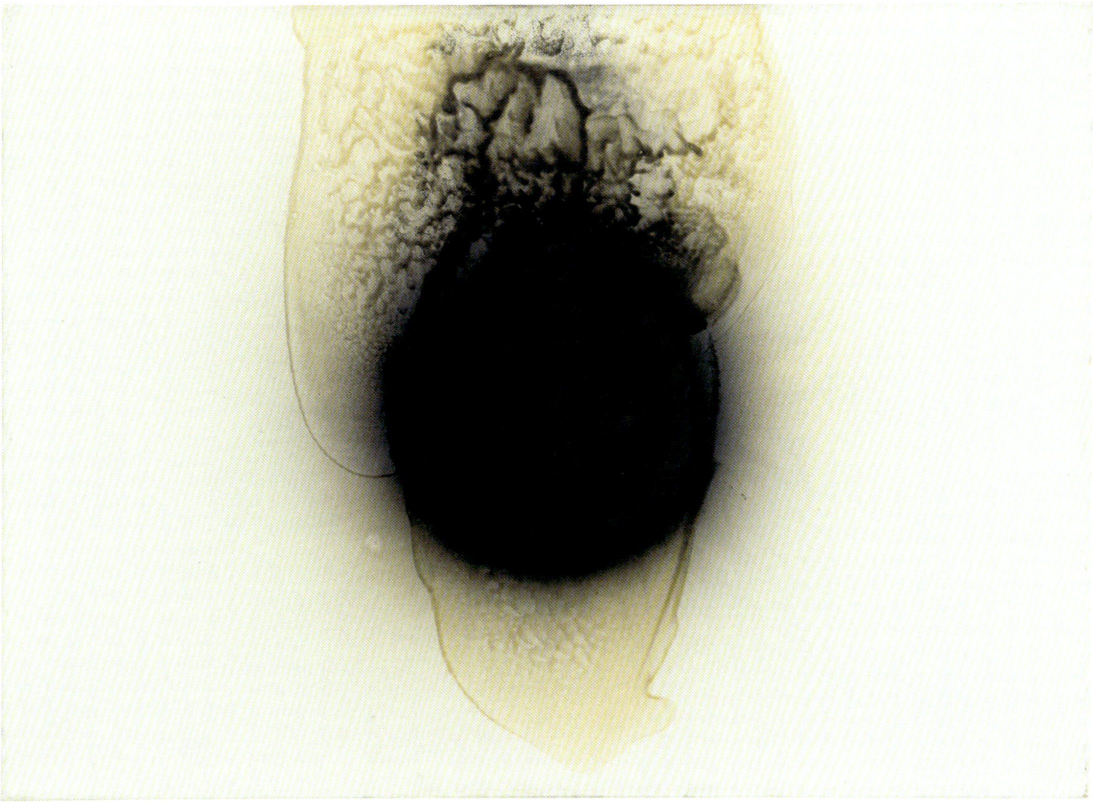

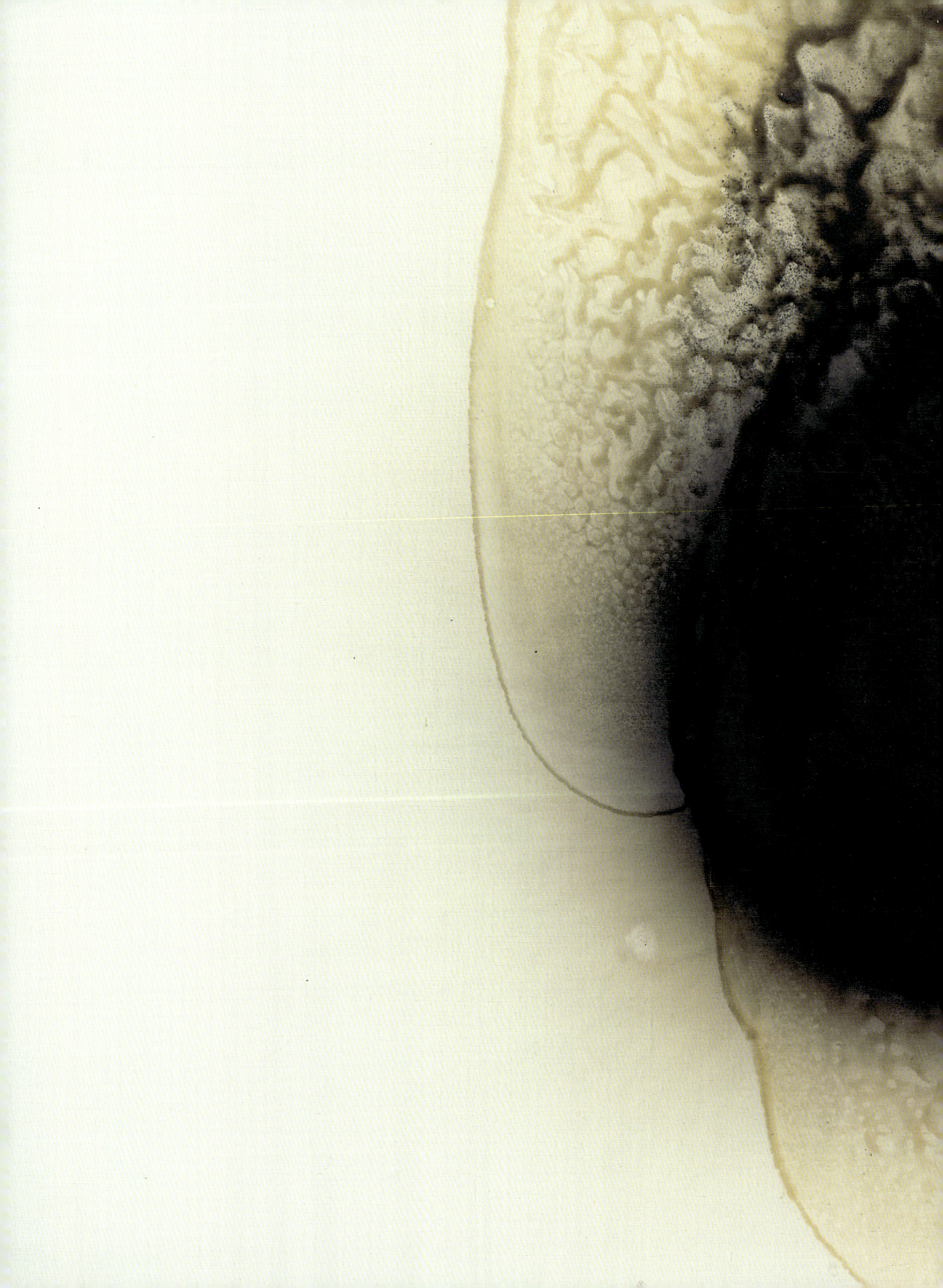

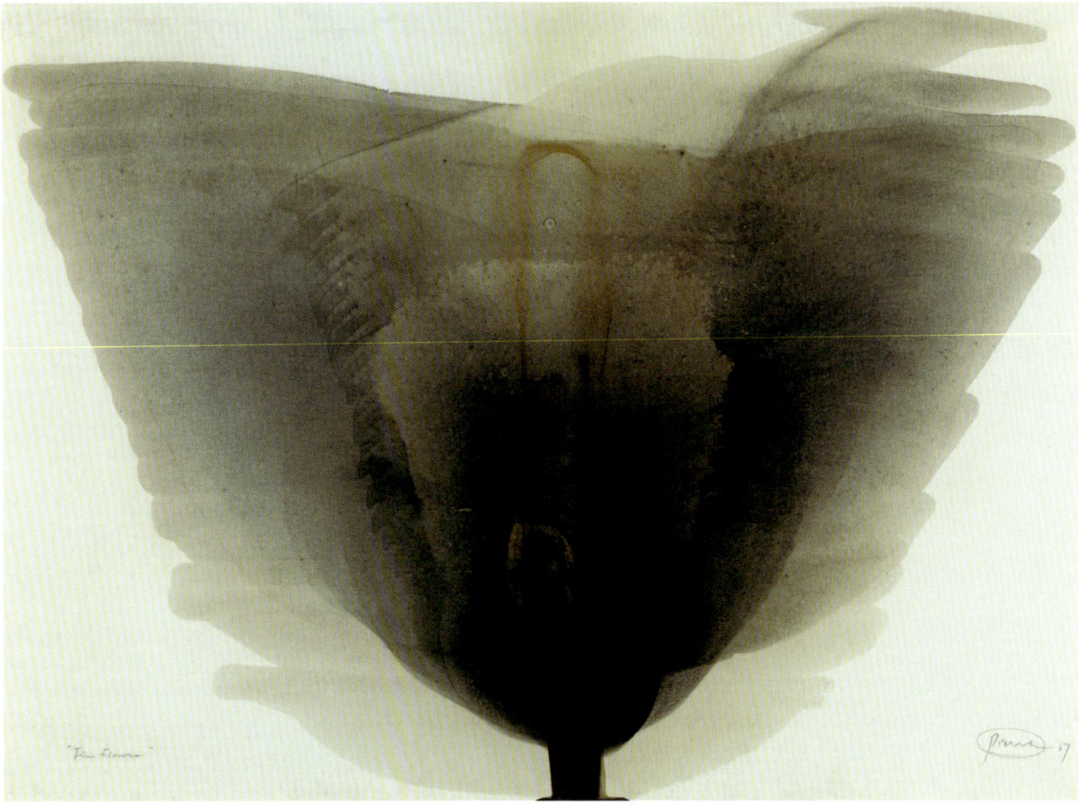

056

Otto Piene
1928 Laasphe – 2014 Berlin

Mixed media and fire gouache on board
Titled, signed and dated: “Fire Flower” / Piene 67
67 × 93 cm

Inv. no. G287M / Acquired 2016

Otto Piene
Fire Flower
1967

Heinz Mack
Untitled (Dynamische Struktur)
1957

057

Heinz Mack
1931 Lollar

Acrylic on canvas
Signature stamp and signed by hand verso: mack 57
101 × 120 cm

Inv. no. P93M / Acquired 2002

Heinz Mack created his first *Dynamische Struktur* (Dynamic Structure) in 1956, two years before founding the artist group ZERO with Otto Piene in Düsseldorf. Inspired by Lucio Fontana and Yves Klein, the ZERO artists wanted to start from scratch in order to set themselves apart from the postwar dominance of Tachism and Art Informel. The group existed until 1966. Mack himself writes that he felt completely unnerved by the anarchistic spontaneity of gestural painting and could not follow it anymore. The overall chaos of disintegration had undermined his artistic confidence and he felt that he could only overcome it by giving up colour. He therefore reduced his palette to the noncolours of black, grey and white. He did use yellow, green, blue and red but mostly in a monochrome context. He not only opposed the eruption of colour and what he considered the destructive formlessness of Tachism; he also abandoned classical composition, introducing structures instead.

Here, in his *Dynamische Struktur* of 1957, Heinz Mack applied black paint to the white ground of the painting with a squeegee, giving it a rhythmic structure and dividing the picture plane into four horizontal bands of almost equal height. The light ground of the picture brings out the nuances of the black, which creates the impression of a dynamic, vibrating surface. The artist writes: "Painting visits our eyes; this visit takes a dynamic turn. Our eyes have the good luck of resting in restlessness ... it is the expression of continuous movement which we call vibration and which our eyes experience aesthetically; its harmony touches our souls, as the breath, the life of the painting."

In addition to using a squeegee, Mack also created his *Dynamic Structures* with light-reflecting aluminium foil. Light, both natural and artificial in origin, plays a dominant role in his oeuvre. He integrated it into his art, giving it shape in reliefs, rotors and stelae of glass and metal. In painting, white is an equivalent for the immaterial phenomenon of light as the sum, so to speak, of the entire spectrum of colours. Speaking metaphorically, as Mack often did, light seeks black as its logical counterpart in order to penetrate it as the dawning day does the night or to illuminate it as snow does the dark earth.

UW

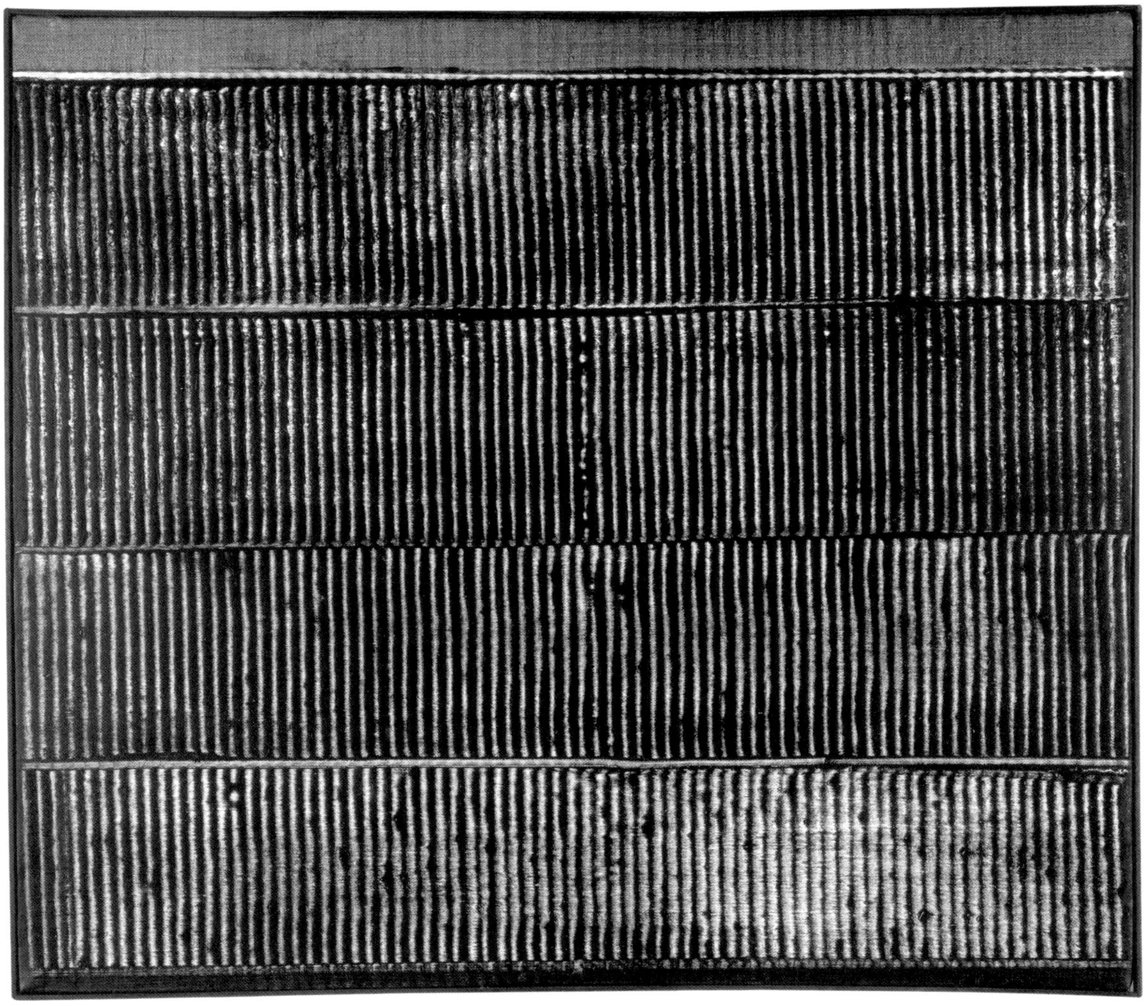

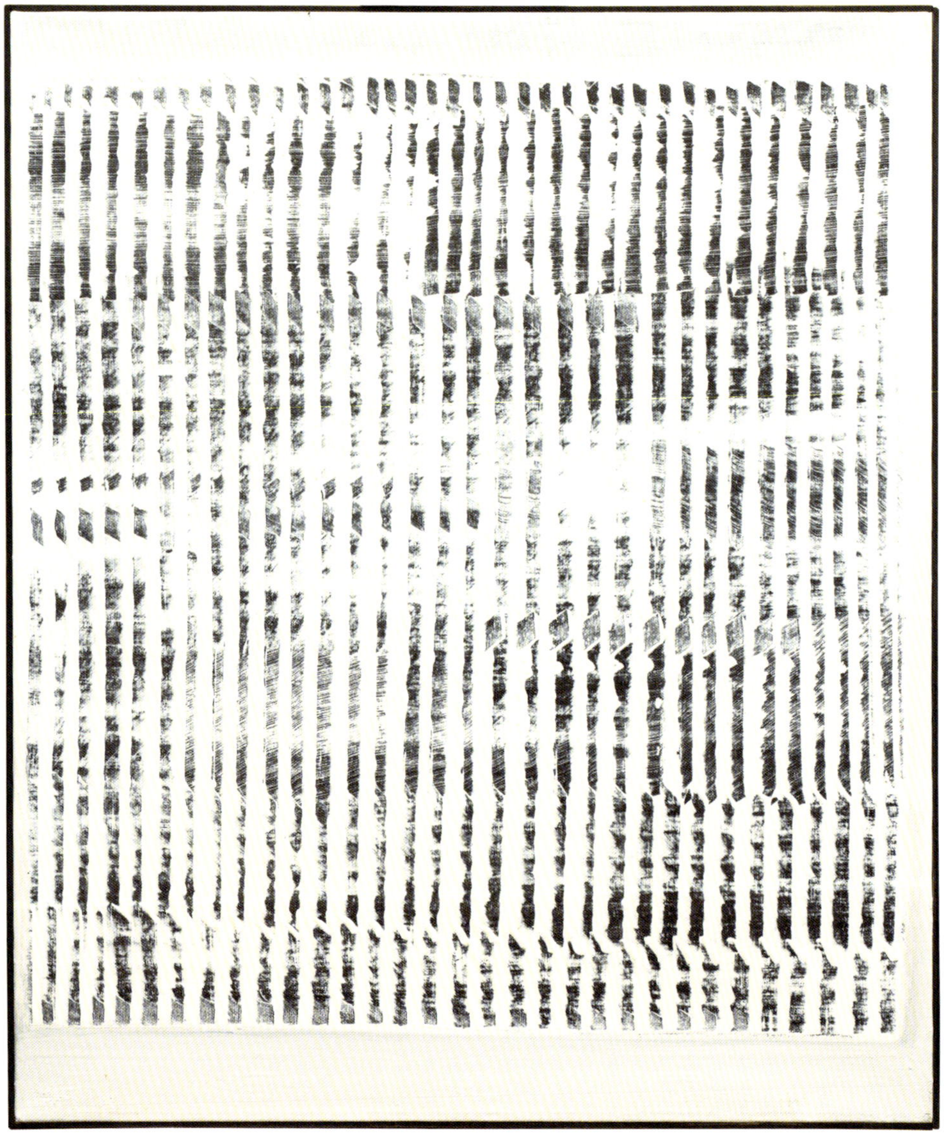

058

Heinz Mack
1931 Lollar

Acrylic on canvas
104 × 89.5 cm

Inv. no. P94M / Acquired 2002

Heinz Mack

Untitled (Dynamische Struktur)

1961

Heinz Mack
Untitled
1964

059

Heinz Mack
1931 Lollar

Silver and black paint on paper
Signed and dated bottom centre: Mack 64
62.5 × 48 cm

Inv. no. G286M / Acquired 2016

For his *Lichtgrafik* (Light Art) Heinz Mack placed sieves or metal nets as stencils on paper (or on metal) and sprayed them with silver aluminium. When he removed the stencils, the negative image of them covered the entire picture plane. Depending on the lighting and angle of view, the pictures look dark grey or bright and silvery.
UW

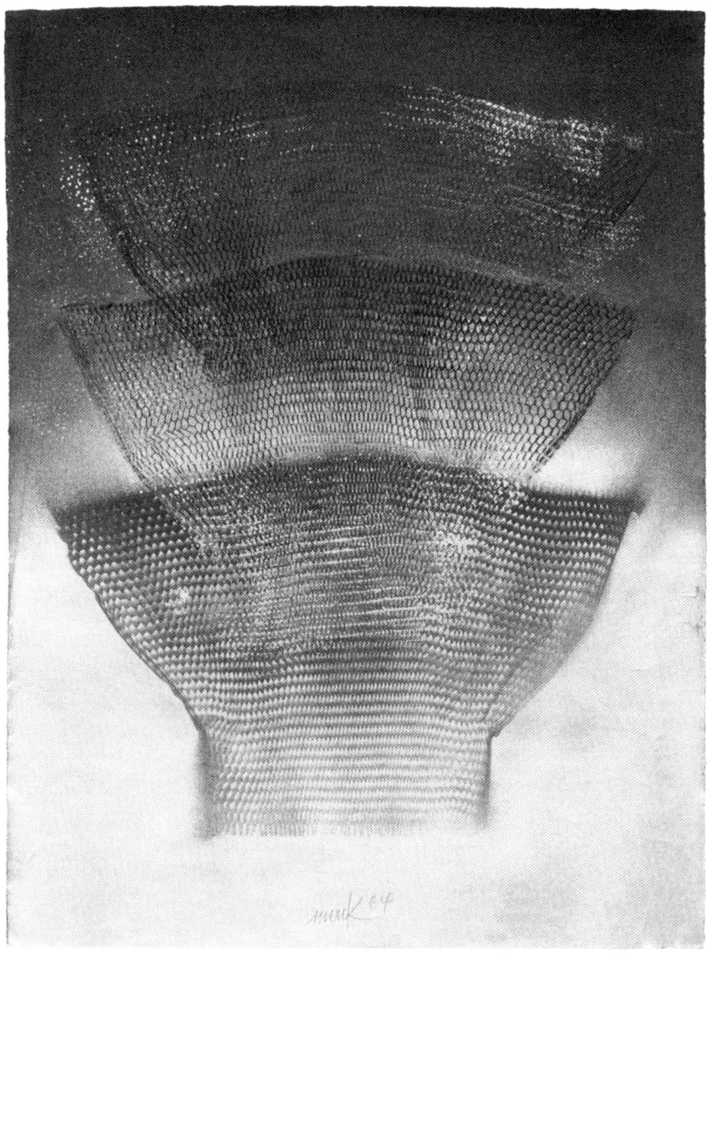

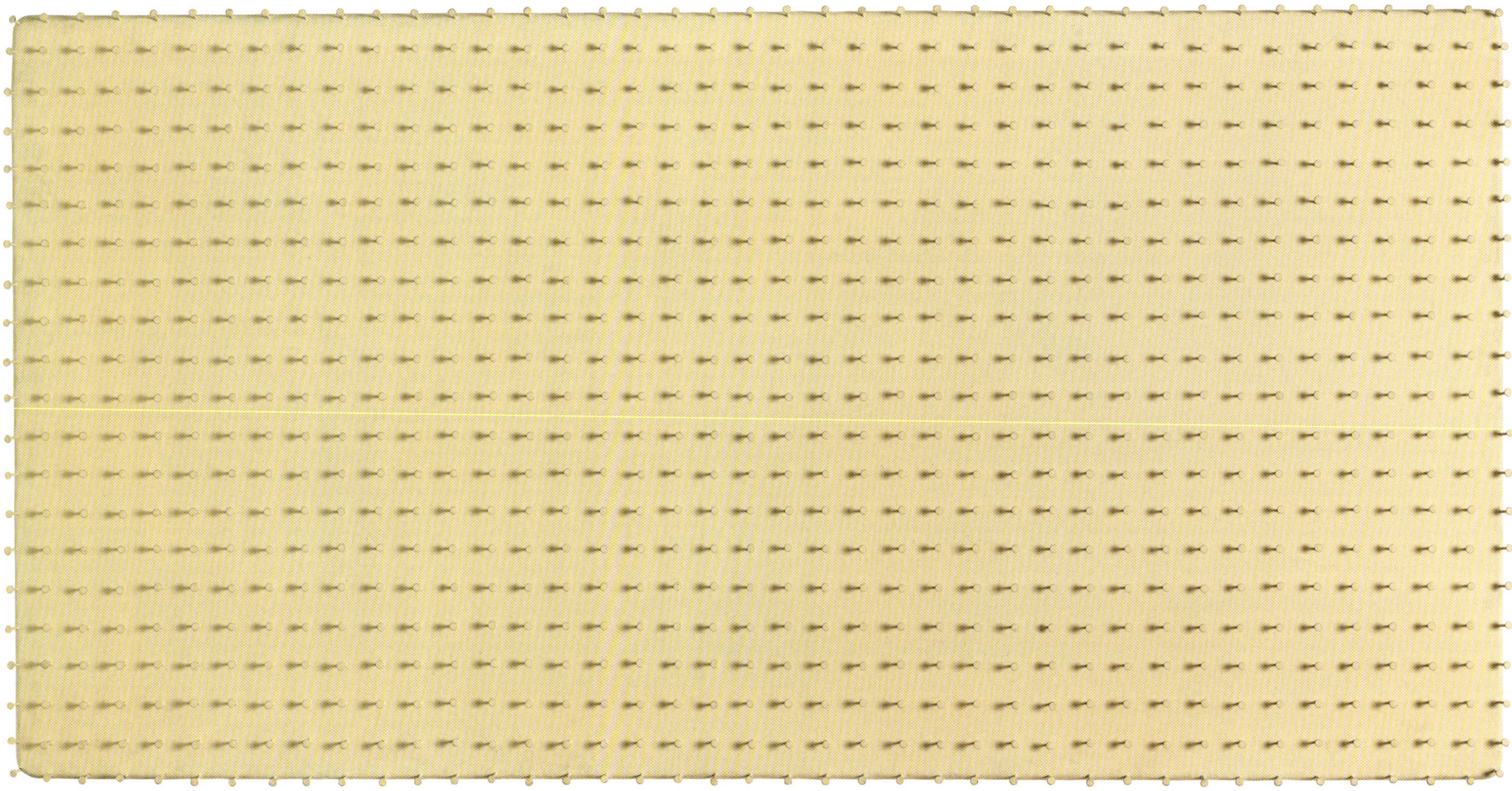

Günther Uecker
Serielle Reihung
1966

Günther Uecker
1930 Wendorf / Mecklenburg

Acrylic, nails, canvas, wood
Inscribed, signed, dated and titled verso:
für Willoughby Sharp / Günther Uecker /
New York 1966 / Serielle Reihung
100 × 200 cm

Inv. no. P331M / Acquired 2019

Uecker made his first nail picture in 1957. Since then, interpretation of his oeuvre has often been biased, confined to his use of this intrinsically nonartistic, everyday item. However, the implications of Uecker's work are much broader. Having experienced the catastrophes of the Second World War as a teenager, he wanted to find a fundamentally new beginning for art beyond Art Informel and Realism, beyond self-display, incitement and propaganda. On moving from East Berlin to Düsseldorf in 1955, he met two like-minded spirits, Otto Piene and Heinz Mack, or, as Piene quite simply wrote, "artists with similar ideas". Calling themselves ZERO, the group established an open and free concept of art not only in Germany but all over Europe (Honisch, 1983). For them, ZERO was an "incommensurable zone in which the old state of things is absorbed into a new one".

Although Uecker did not officially join the group until 1961, the works he created in ZERO's early years, 1957–58, categorically eschewed all forms of traditional painting. As a rule, they consisted of canvases mounted on wood and painted white, into which the artist hammered nails, resulting in structures that range from geometric patterns to impulsive, uncontrolled orders. The act of aggression (hammering) reveals the processual nature involved in making the work and the attendant violation of the canvas. This form of action is crucial to Uecker's art. He made repeated incursions into real life by hammering nails into tables, chairs, a piano and a television set. He would attack what he called the "cultural fetishes" of life until they looked as if their hair was standing on end, thereby putting them up for debate and undermining them as items of consumption.

AS

Günther Uecker
Grosses Feld
1967

Günther Uecker
1930 Wendorf / Mecklenburg

Paint, nails, canvas on plywood
Signed, dated and titled on verso:
Uecker 67 (Grosses Feld)
175.2 × 175.2 cm

Inv. no. P154M / Acquired 2004

Uecker made *Grosses Feld* (Large Field, 1967) the year after ZERO's last exhibition in October 1966. It is a classical work heralding the end of the group. Hundreds of irregularly spaced white nails, hammered into the surface, form gentle undulations. They are, as Uecker once said, "the extension of a point in space". Depending on vantage point and lighting, they cast different and delicate shadows, lending the whole a poetic fragility. Their arrangement on the picture plane generates an impression of potential mobility. The structure looks like an electromagnetic field but it might also be compared to a field of stubble or of sprouting seeds. To quote Otto Piene, the ZERO artists aimed "to reharmonise the relationship between man and nature … The artist is not a fugitive from the 'modern world', no, he uses new technical means as well as the forces of nature."
AS

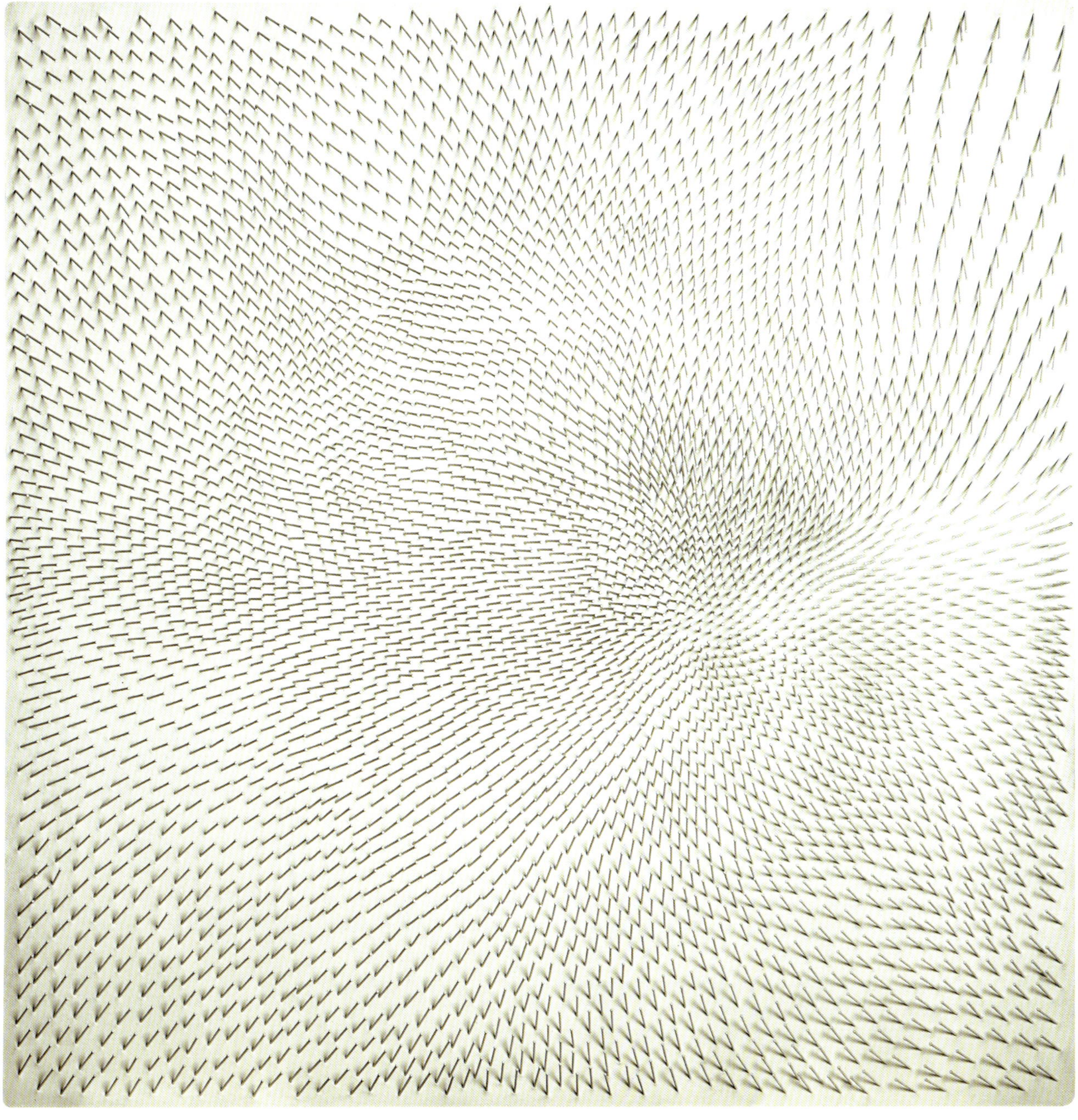

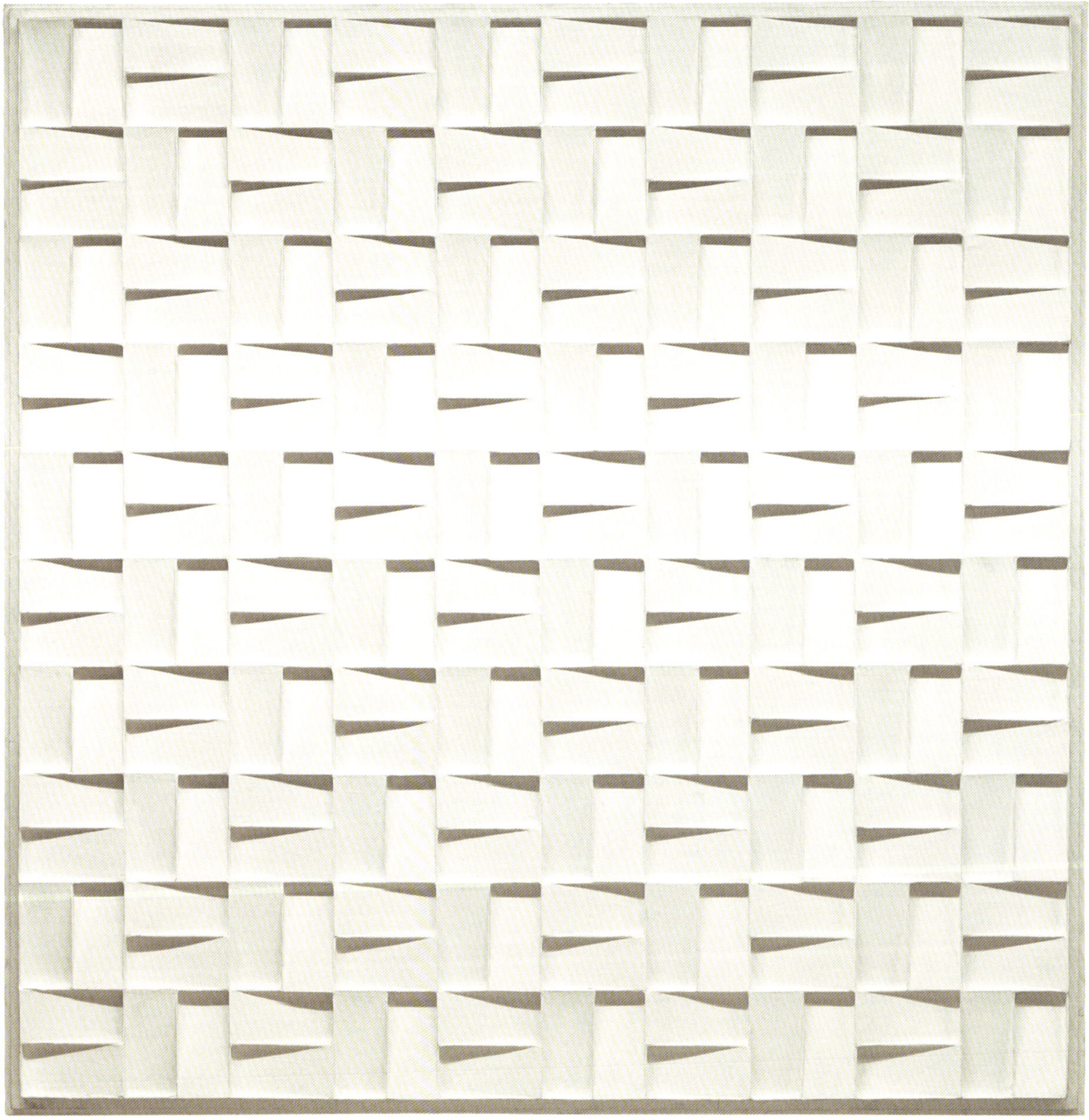

062

Jan Schoonhoven

R 72-25

1972

Jan Schoonhoven
1914 Delft – 1994 Delft

Latex, paper, pasteboard, wood
Signed, dated, inscribed and titled on verso:
Jan Schoonhoven / 23 VII '72 / Delft. / "R72-25"
155.7 × 156.2 cm

Inv. no. P202M / Acquired 2008

Jan Schoonhoven garnered an international reputation with his white reliefs around 1960, the year in which he founded the Nul group (the Dutch equivalent of ZERO) with Armando, Jan Hendrikse and Henk Peeters. Schoonhoven, an employee of the Dutch Postal Service from 1946 until he retired in 1979, was forty-six years old at the time. After studying at the Royal Academy of the Fine Arts in The Hague from 1930 to 1934, he devoted himself almost exclusively to the medium of drawing and created a subtle, sophisticated oeuvre. These drawings and his study, among other things, of the structural aspects of Paul Klee's art formed the basis of his serial reliefs. Both the drawings and reliefs feature geometric structures in rows and repetitions of identical and yet modified forms.

R 72-25 of 1972 belongs to the mature works that he created between 1960 and 1979. They are characterised by a vibrant harmony that rests on the equalisation and traction of verticals and horizontals as well as the play between individual shape and overall image. Like many of the works made during this period, *R 72-25* is square and relatively big. Ten by ten smaller units yield a completely symmetrical whole, based on a perfectly calculated order. Each of the smaller units is divided in half, with the placement of the "flaps" alternating between front and back. Despite the clarity of structure, a labyrinthine impression disrupts the harmony of the whole.
As in most of his work, Schoonhoven used pasteboard (or papier-mâché), which he covered with paper and painted white. Pasteboard is a simple, unspectacular, everyday material that ensures neutrality. Nonetheless the hand of the artist can be detected in the slightly uneven application of the paint and minimal inaccuracies at the interfaces. As Schoonhoven explained in a 1985 interview, "[W]hen I have a rectangle and glue it like that and make a relief out of it, then it should – I think – be a little poetic. So that it's alive. Otherwise I could have a factory produce it." The white plane broken by the alternating direction of the "flaps" becomes an ideal space in which to reflect the light and the delicate shadows that sometimes seem to sink into the darkness. But despite all of these factors, the impression of identical elements dominates. As the art historian Beat Wismer wrote in 1995, "The serial arrangement of identical but individually produced elements no doubt corresponds to an ethical, political conviction that equivalence is an existential prerequisite of individual freedom and individuality per se."
AS

Jan Schoonhoven
R 69-13
1969

063

Jan Schoonhoven
1914 Delft – 1994 Delft

Latex, paper, cardboard, wood
Signed, dated and titled on verso:
J. J. Schoonhoven / 1969 / "R 69-13"
30 × 30 cm

Inv. no. P167M / Acquired 2006

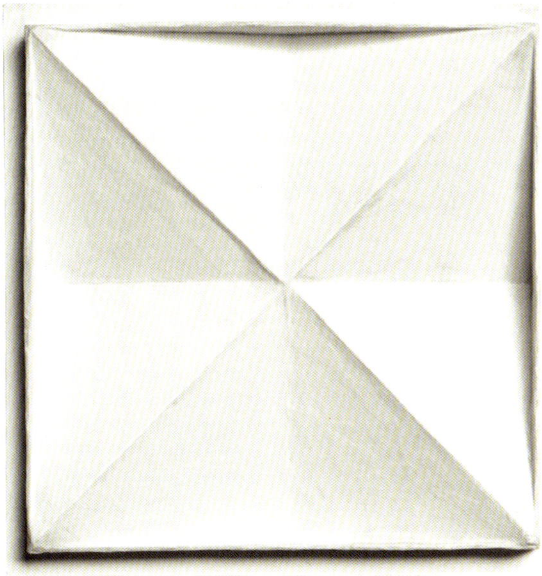

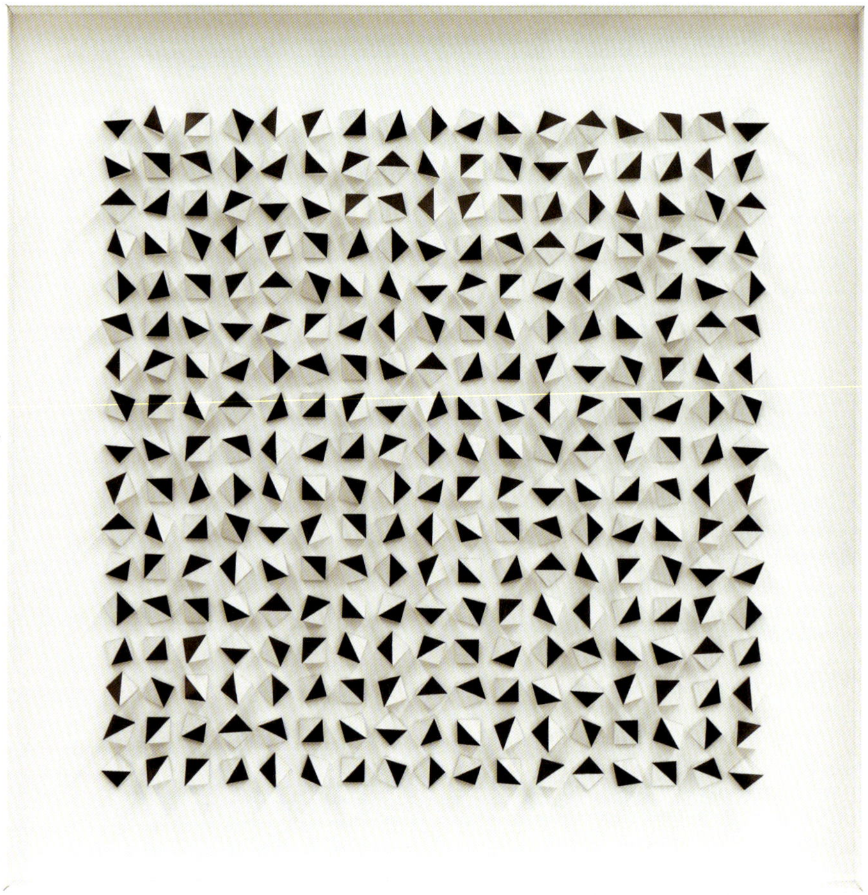

Klaus Staudt
1932 Otterndorf / Niederelbe

Dispersion on wood
Inscribed, dated and signed verso:
1/66 / ohne Titel / 1965 / Klaus Staudt
71.3 × 71.3 × 7 cm

Inv. no. P257M / Acquired 2014

Klaus Staudt
S-W-R 1
1965

Klaus Staudt, whose oeuvre as a whole is indebted to important impulses from the Constructivism of Classical Modernism, as in the work of Josef Albers, Victor Vasarely, Ben Nicholson and most particularly Piet Mondrian, has always shown a preference for the relief, that Janus-headed genre between plane and space, between picture and sculpture. He "confesses" that he also paints, but "with sculptural structures and geometrical elements that capture light". No matter how intensely Staudt works with light and shadow, plane and space, form and colour, in other words with elementary visual parameters, he never does so for their sake alone; his work consistently challenges us to hone our perception. Highly concentrated, focused visual study and thought are indeed indispensable to understanding Staudt's art. Only then do these works become instruments of insight and only then – as he once said about art in general – do they become a genesis and not a product.

The relief *S-W-R 1* consists of 289 square prisms in two sizes, each coming to a peak at a slant. Three of the sides are painted white and the fourth black. They form seventeen by seventeen rows of equal length on a white support. Through variations in height and direction, the figures obscure the right-angled grid and undermine its rigorous order. This impression is reinforced when viewers change their vantage point. The more obtuse the angle of view, the more irregular and even chaotic the whole becomes, for what we then see are arbitrarily overlapping, triangular peaks, pointing in various directions like the quills of a hedgehog, and sharply distinguished by the contrasting black and white. Only when looking at the relief from a centred, middle distance does the optical agitation abide due to the foreshortened view of the prisms on the square of their bases. Staudt has said that it is his aim to stimulate but not overstimulate the eye. And it is indeed stimulating to take up the challenge of exploring the wider implications of an oeuvre that might be read as a "model of perception and thought".
UW

Klaus Staudt
Kreisformation II (FA-RE 5)
1965

Klaus Staudt
1932 Otterndorf / Niederelbe

Dispersion on wood
Titled, signed and dated verso:
Kreisformation II / Klaus Staudt 1965
Ø 60 cm

Inv. no. P242M / Acquired 2013

Klaus Staudt's *Kreisformation* (Circular Formation) looks at first sight as if countless circular yellow cylinders had been randomly scattered on a round, white picture plane. This impression leads to a lively, almost cheerful sensation that prevails even on close, systematic study of the work. We discover that the cylinders are all cut off at an angle and consist of four different sizes and diameters. In addition, the cadmium yellow is divided into four levels of brightness and the cylinders are arranged in equidistant, concentric circles. This pattern is not easily legible since the distribution of the cylinders on the picture plane – their size, their distance from each other and the direction of their slanted ends – is governed not by objective, mathematical laws but by subjective, visceral decisions that preclude formal rigidity.

The density of the yellow cylinders in *Kreisformation* varies, leading to site-dependent variations in light and shadow – two phenomena of great significance for Staudt, despite his love of constructive sculptural design. He combines materiality and immateriality just as he does objectivity and subjectivity or regularity and irregularity. Light and shadow, subtly modulated by form and colour, in particular white and shades of yellow, dematerialise the tangible composition and transcend the immanent.

UW

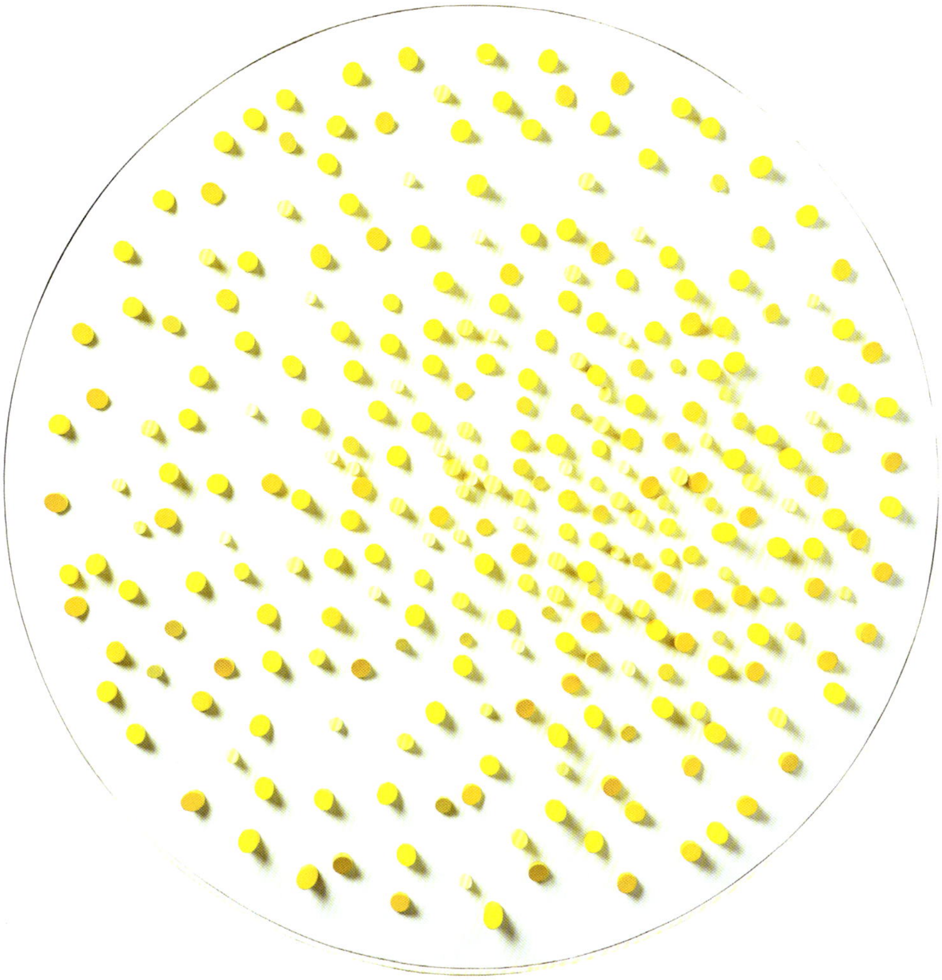

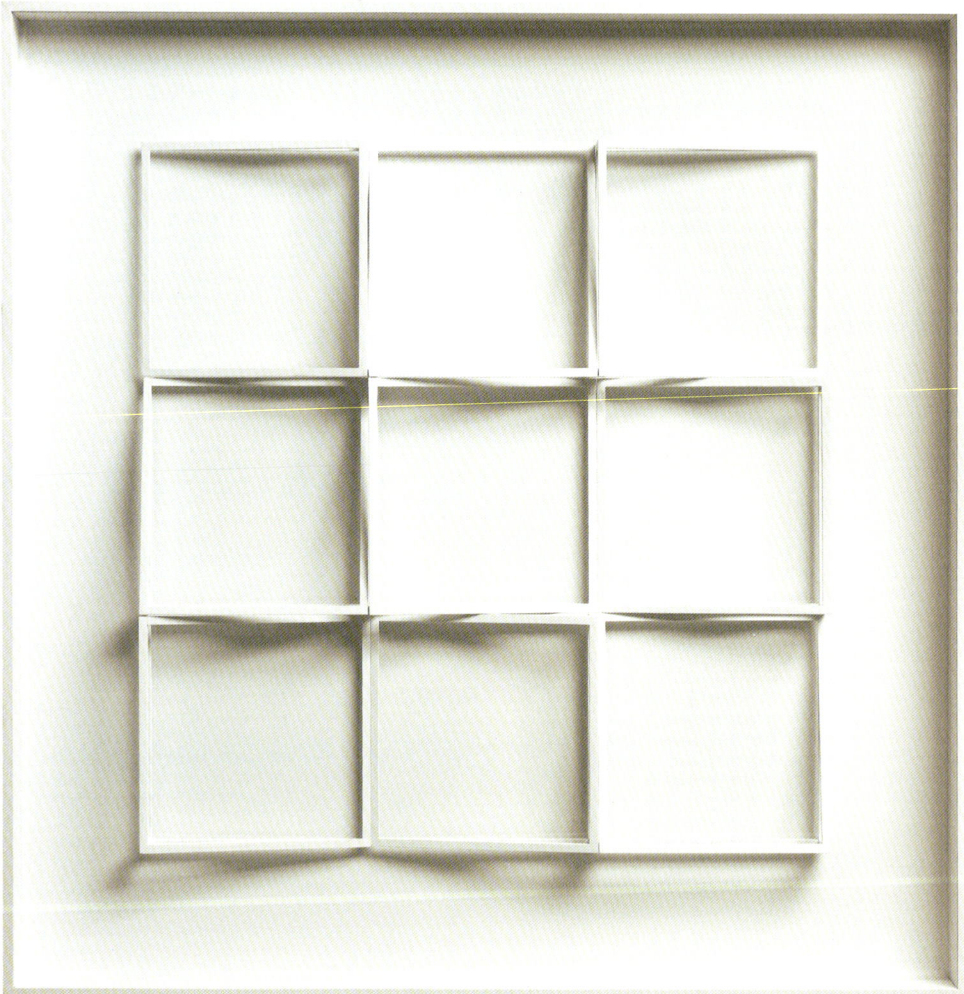

066

Klaus Staudt
1932 Otterndorf / Niederelbe

Dispersion on wood
Inscribed, signed and dated:
1/578 / Klaus Staudt / 1983
100 × 100 × 10 cm

Inv. no. P256M / Acquired 2014

Klaus Staudt
Schattengitter 10 (WR-SG 10)
1983

Klaus Staudt's affinity with Constructivism is particularly explicit in a genre of work produced since the beginning of the 1980s: the *Schattengitter* (Shadow Grids). This particular relief is described in the catalogue raisonné as follows: "3 times 3 slanted, prismatic, square and open elements have been arranged so that there is no horizontal or vertical repetition of the 3 positions." Despite the simple, straightforward description and the squared, prismatic structure of the grid, the work proves to be disconcertingly multilayered. Even when looking head on at the completely white relief, the right-angled structure of the whole is optically distorted by the bars of the grid, which are mounted at a slant in varying positions. As soon as the viewer moves, the change of perspective complicates the overall impression of the prismatic elements with all their connections and slanted variations. Most importantly, as in all of Klaus Staudt's *Schattengitter*, the system of static elements is not aesthetically complete without the complementary, dynamic element of light, which casts shadows on the ground of the relief and undermines the strict but open construction of the work.

UW

Klaus Staudt
Verhaltenes Warm
1988

Klaus Staudt
1932 Otterndorf / Niederelbe

Plexiglas, dispersion (white), coloured pencil (yellow), wood
Signed, dated and titled verso:
Klaus Staudt '88 / "Verhaltenes Warm"
106 × 106 × 4.5 cm

Inv. no. P255M / Acquired 2014

Verhaltenes Warm (Muted Warm) consists of two by nine parallel, vertical strips whose width increases evenly from inside to outside; as a whole, they form an almost perfect square. They are covered with an opaque-transparent pane of plexiglass. Behind it, the rhythmically modulated sequence of slender verticals appears soft and blurred in the flowing transition between light and shadow, while the muted warmth unfolds in the soft white surface of the relief, which radiates a tender touch of yellow. Despite scale, number and order, everything material fades into the immaterial, everything sculptural becomes painterly and all that is tangible becomes pictorial, giving viewers the privilege of appreciating the work in quiet contemplation without changing position.
UW

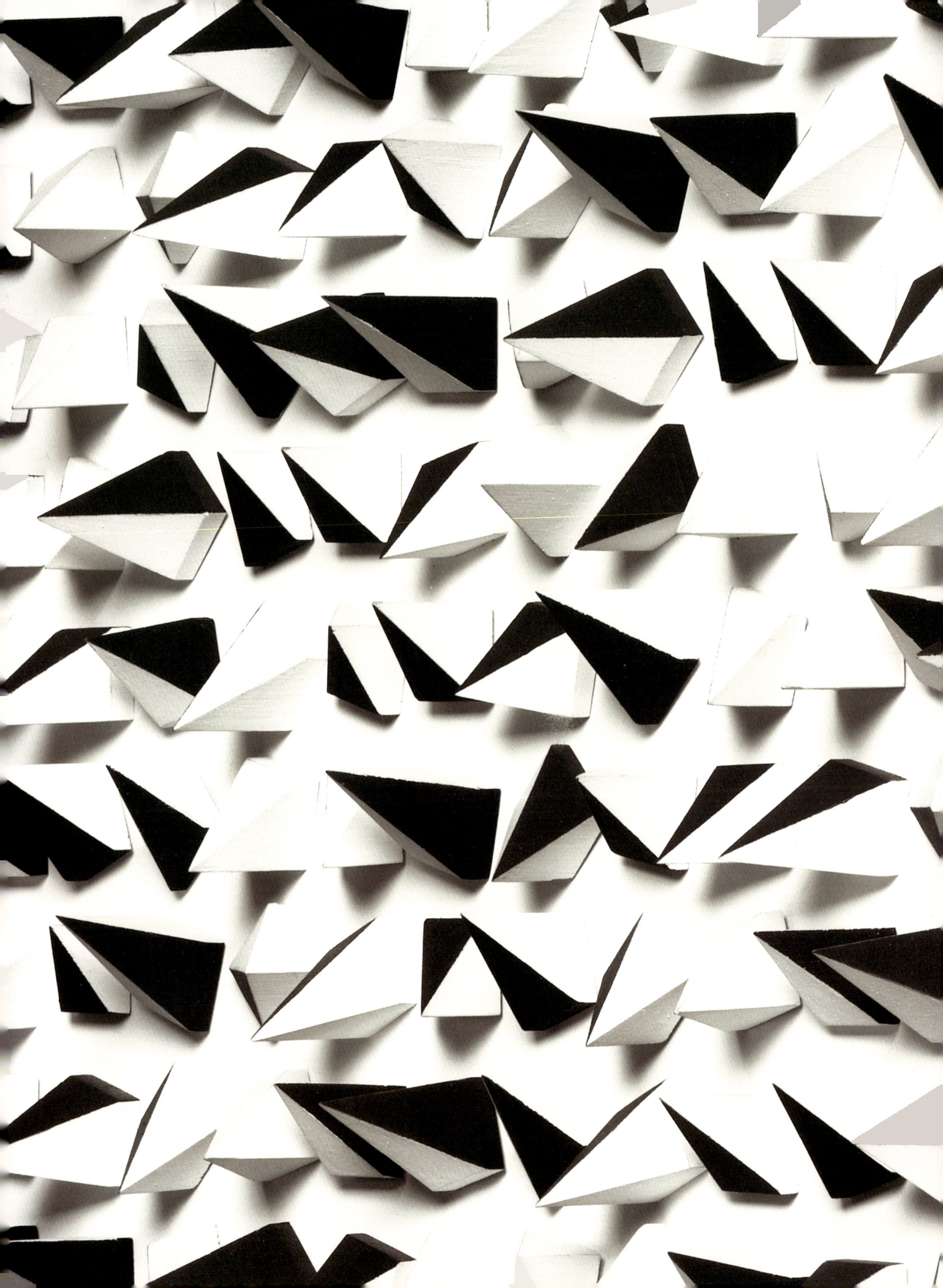

068

Gerhard von Graevenitz
1934 Schilde / Mark Brandenburg –
1983 Traubachtal / Switzerland

Paint, wood
Height: 103.5 cm, Ø 3.6 cm

Inv. no. S258M / Acquired 2014

Gerhard von Graevenitz
Homogene Verteilung (Rundstab), Weisse Struktur
1959

Gerhard von Graevenitz is frequently associated with the ZERO group of artists. He was only slightly younger than its representatives and, with the exception of a few early works, he too concentrated on white structure paintings and white kinetic objects. There are, however, significant differences. Graevenitz was primarily interested in systematic, scientific enquiry into visual imagery, which he specified in June 1961 in the form of an aphorism: "i go on the assumption that words / light / dots / motion / chance / orders / series / say something about my pictures. each of them designates an essential element of / my painting." Referring to the philosopher Ludwig Wittgenstein, he continues: "so i can say / my pictures are / dot-pictures and / dot-light-pictures and / serial-dot-light-pictures and / moving-serial-dot-light-pictures and / ..."

The slender, elegant rod is a neutral object. Unlike Uecker's *Säule* (Column, 1959) with nails hammered into it, it is not charged with meaning. It is more in the nature of a tool; it could, for instance, be an experimental device to blow bubbles. When Graevenitz made it in 1959, he was still officially a student at the Munich Academy of Fine Arts, where he complemented his studies by experimenting with materials. Protruding from the rod, which has been covered with a white primer, are over 1000 evenly spaced white knobs, all of the same size. This all-over structure is based on theoretical study of Jackson Pollock's work and eschews a hierarchical order. Reporting on the summer semester of 1960, Graevenitz wrote, "for some time now, i have been working exclusively with dots. The dot is the simplest and purest sign, rest and movement at once."

The movement in this work is generated by light. Depending on the angle of incidence, the knobs are perceived as protruding bumps or as dimples in shadow. Attempting to trace the course taken by the little white bumps, trying to fix them in place and assess their intervals, the viewer briefly loses sight of the whole, which then consolidates into a single form again. Although – as stated in the title – the rod is a homogeneously distributed white structure, it appears noticeably differentiated, slightly diffuse and individually detailed when seen from a distance. Graevenitz's desire to counteract a personal signature is even more explicit in another *Weisse Struktur* (White Structure, 1960), a cylinder with negative and positive dots. He wanted to liberate art from its cultic context by refusing to prescribe either content or composition. Study and appreciation of the artwork was meant to lead to "a state of freedom".

AS

Gerhard von Graevenitz
Untitled (horizontaler Schnitt)
1959

069

Gerhard von Graevenitz
1934 Schilde / Mark Brandenburg –
1983 Traubachtal / Switzerland

Emulsion, plaster, sand, fibreboard
60 × 50 cm

Inv. no. S259M / Acquired 2014

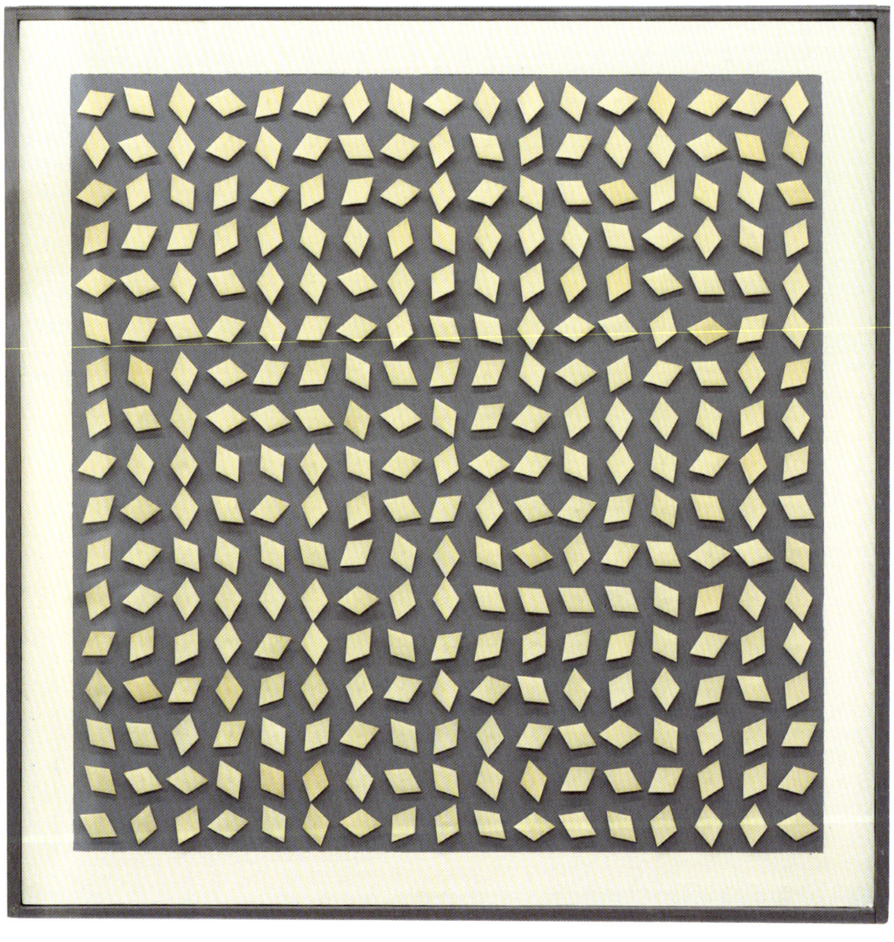

070

Gerhard von Graevenitz
1934 Schilde / Mark Brandenburg –
1983 Traubachtal / Switzerland

Plastic, metal, wood, electric motor
57.5 × 57.5 × 8.5 cm

Inv. no. S187M / Acquired 2007

Gerhard von Graevenitz
Weisse Rhomben auf Grau
1961

Gerhard von Graevenitz
Zwei schwarze Scheiben auf Weiss
1971

Gerhard von Graevenitz
1934 Schilde / Mark Brandenburg –
1983 Traubachtal / Switzerland

Metal, wood, electric motor
Ø 120 cm

Inv. no. S218M / Acquired 2010

Gerhard von Graevenitz won international acclaim for his kinetic objects, for the most part square, white panels with motorised movable parts, such as slats, bars and rhombuses (see cat. 70). He also made circular works: movable disks mounted on larger circular panels.

Art that moves, such as water features known as *jeux d'eau*, already adorned gardens in the Baroque period, but kinetic art as we know it today was not introduced until the twentieth century. This led to an expanded definition of the role of the artist, who was now no longer merely an ingenious creator but also a scientist, technician and communicator. In 1920, Naum Gabo and Antoine Pevsner issued their *Realistic Manifesto* in Moscow, affirming "in these arts a new element, the kinetic rhythms, as the basic forms of our perception of real time." Marcel Duchamp worked on his entertaining and appealing Rotoreliefs from 1926 to 1930: colourful discs, rotating in opposite directions, so that their movement seems to expand and articulate space; in 1929, Alexander Calder created his first movable wire constructions, which Graevenitz saw in Munich in 1959; and over a period of eight years from 1922 to 1930, László Moholy-Nagy produced his famous light-space modulator, engineered to combine movement, time and light. However, it was not until the 1960s that kinetic art came into its own, represented, for instance, by Gianni Colombo (see cat. 53), Jesús Rafael Soto, Jean Tinguely (see cat. 52), Yaacov Agam and Günther Uecker.

In 1961 Graevenitz built his first kinetic object in Munich, where he also had it patented. The two black discs on a white ground might be read at first sight as the cool, abstract rendition of a technical device. In art history, particularly in the Renaissance, the perfectly circular tondo was considered an ideal format of sacrosanct perfection, used by such artists as Botticelli, Raphael and Michelangelo as a vehicle for their Madonna paintings.

Graevenitz defined his circular discs as independent fields, presenting viewers with an entirely new visual experience, for the unpredictable, accidental movement of the parts unsettles and obstructs perception. No specific rhythm can be identified in these works, as they ceaselessly yield new visual combinations. In the present work, the two black discs slowly rotate in all directions on the white tondo, which in turn circles around its own axis. Two different, mutually independent sequences of movement are combined, showing a harmony that does not, however, preclude exceptionally surprising encounters, much like those between celestial bodies. We are faced with a visual and intellectual challenge since the movement gives us no "insight into the control system".
AS

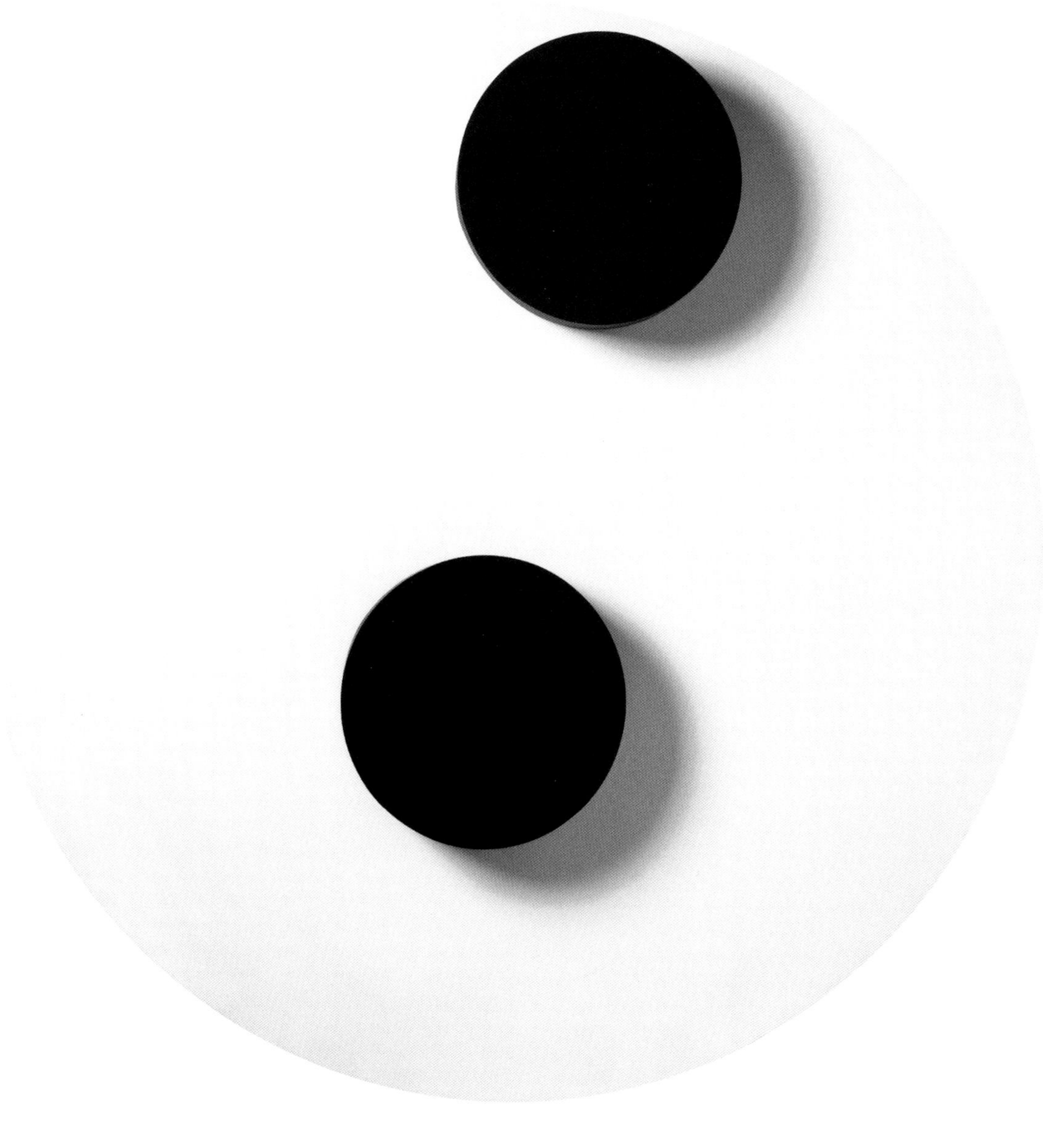

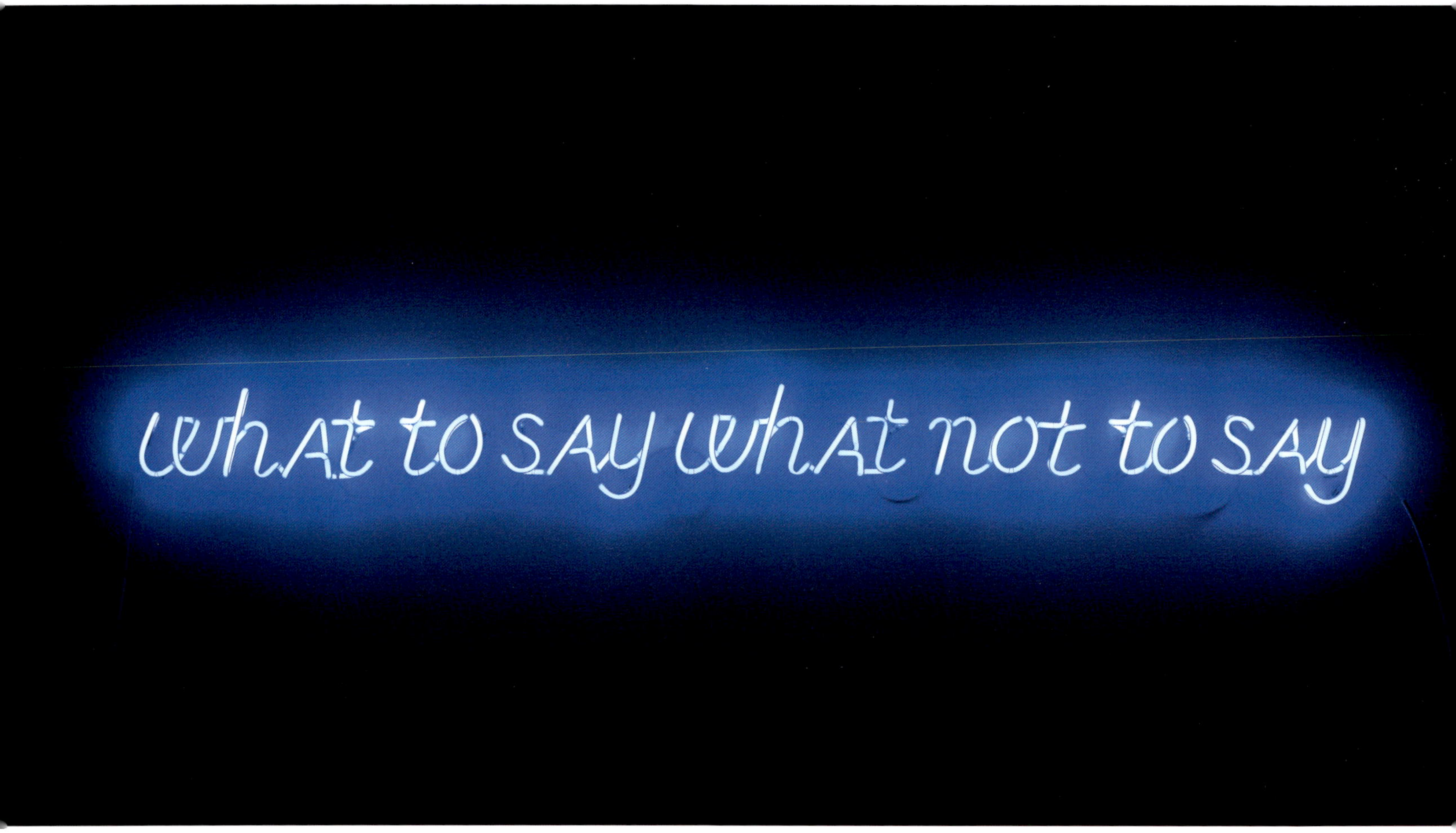
what to say what not to say

072

Maurizio Nannucci
1939 Florence

Neon, wiring, transformer
15 × 180 cm

Inv. no. S240M / Acquired 2012

Maurizio Nannucci
what to say what not to say
1979

Maurizio Nannucci's initial interest was colour. However, it is the word that is at the heart of his work. As the artist, still based in Florence, puts it: "The medium is word." And since the 1960s it has been his subject matter in every shape and form: spoken, drawn, written, out of neon, in isolation or in sentences. In prints, multiples, vinyl records and art books, he has explored the iridescent relations and capricious meanings that emerge when word, image, space, colour and light interact in the context of concrete and visual poetry. In 1969 he started working in neon, mostly in his preferred colours of red, blue, yellow, white and green.

The seven words of *what to say what not to say were* mouth blown by a local glassmaker near Verona. The letters are lined up forming a narrow, luminous band; the words composed as a harmonious whole. Upper and lowercase letters are even in height except for the ascenders and descenders of lowercase h, y and t. Placed at a slight slant, the "colour words" (Domesle, 1998) look like someone's handwriting. Although constructed, the subtly rhythmic lettering flows, unfolding in space and time.

what to say what not to say has been on view in several places, including Nice in 1992 and Rouen in 1993, each time in a different spatial context and in combination with other neon words, also in blue. The relatively small letters were quite legible despite their diffuse light. They gradually produce thoughts while reading, in a variation on Heinrich von Kleist's renowned essay *On the Gradual Production of Thoughts Whilst Speaking*. Nannucci has explicitly stated that his work is not meant to convey concrete messages but to stimulate thought.

Interpretation of the blue light of the neon tubes can vary substantially depending on the situation, place and mood of the viewer. According to Nannucci, "One single interpretation of a colour sign is difficult." He refers to the blue of a night sky, two electric sources of light, but also to the blue in Van Gogh's paintings and Yves Klein's IKB (cat. 49). International Klein Blue is a deep ultramarine powder and the incarnation of a cosmic sense of space, usually described as cosmic sensitivity by Klein.

what to say what not to say is a challenge, a casual saying, a statement and also the opposite of that. It eludes concrete determination and encourages mental caprice. It describes forms of human communication both political and personal and, in a larger sense, it is a definition of human existence per se. After all, the ability to speak distinguishes human beings from all other living creatures. As St John says in the Scriptures: In the beginning was the word.

AS

Peter Roehr
PR FO-34 (Untitled)
1965

Peter Roehr
1944 Lauen / Pommern –
1968 Frankfurt am Main

Paper on pasteboard
Signed on verso: PETER ROEHR
(stamp of the estate)
91 × 91 cm

Inv. no. G213M / Acquired 2009

Despite his untimely death, Peter Roehr produced an oeuvre of unique significance. Having trained in the field of neon advertising and signage, followed by studies at the School of Applied Arts in Wiesbaden, he culled his subject matter from the world of goods and standardisation. Roehr presented industrial, mass-produced items such as stickers, buttons, beer caps or clippings from newspapers, magazines and brochures, in repetitive, stringently precise series. In 1965 the artist wrote, "I put together things of the same kind. These might be photographs, freestanding shapes like letters, tones and sounds, film footage, etc. I call the result *montages*." He doggedly avoided composition and subjective staging: "... the choice of object and determining the quantity is the only arbitrary work of the maker." Roehr deliberately eschewed the least hint of authorship in his artistic endeavour.

PR FO-34 consists of six by six rows of thirty-six identical eyeballs in black and white, their gaze directed to the lower right. The highlight seen on the iris just barely touches the pupil, in the centre of which the date 1966 is printed. The picture confronts us with the artist's optical tool. Its bald representation, repeated thirty-six times, has the character of an entirely neutral object that could potentially produce an unlimited number of pictures. Florian Illies observed that Roehr takes Walter Benjamin's notion of "the work of art in the age of its technological reproducibliity" to extremes by endlessly reproducing pictures that are themselves technical reproductions. Illies also notes that the aesthetic method of constant repetition echoes a conviction expressed by Gottfried Benn, an author Roehr is known to have read. According to Benn, only something repeatable can lead to art; style can be achieved only by being compelled to repeat. Peter Roehr embraced that compulsion, creating pictures of striking clarity and objectivity in an oeuvre that gave vital impetus to Minimal and Conceptual Art.

JR

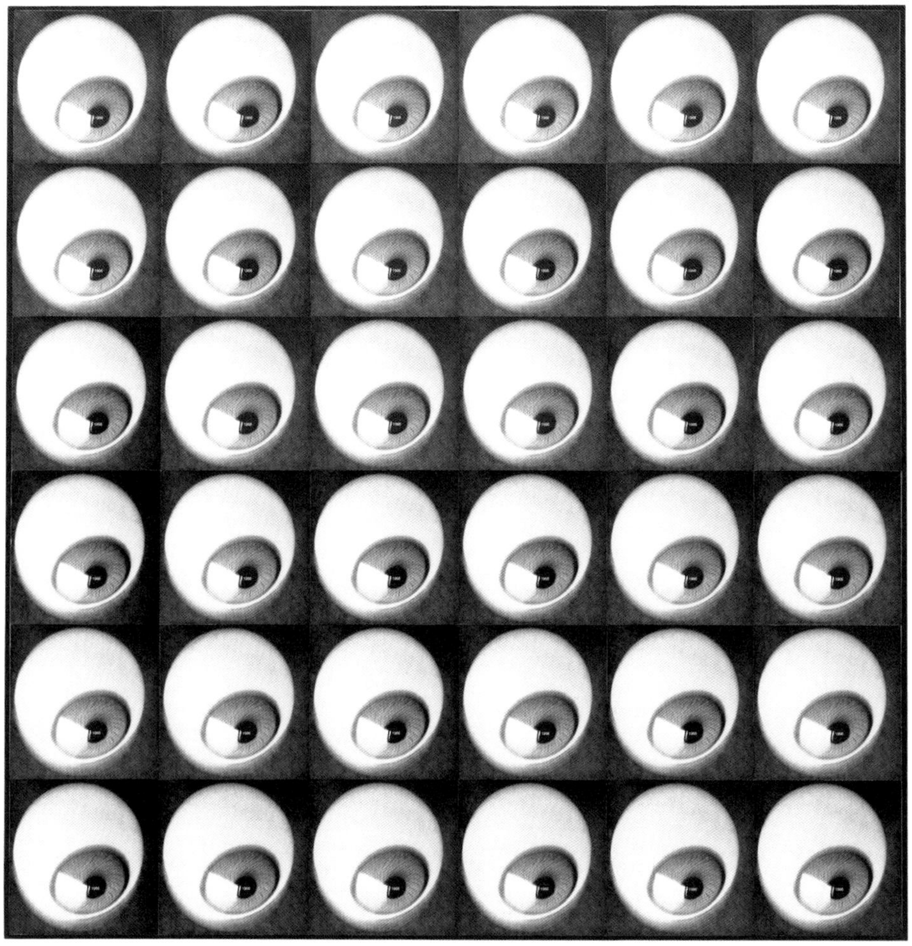

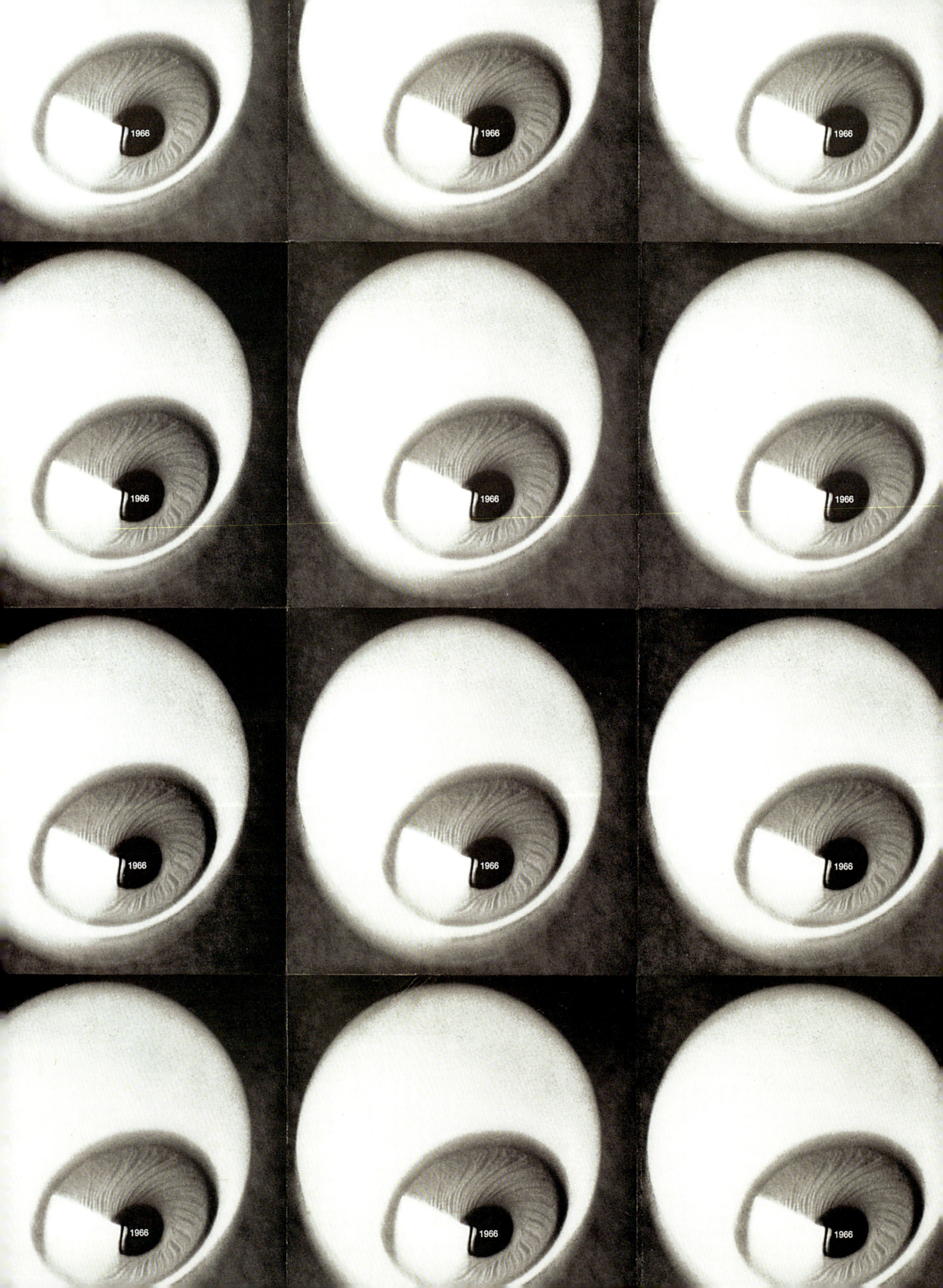
1966
1966
1966
1966
1966
1966
1966
1966
1966
1966
1966
1966

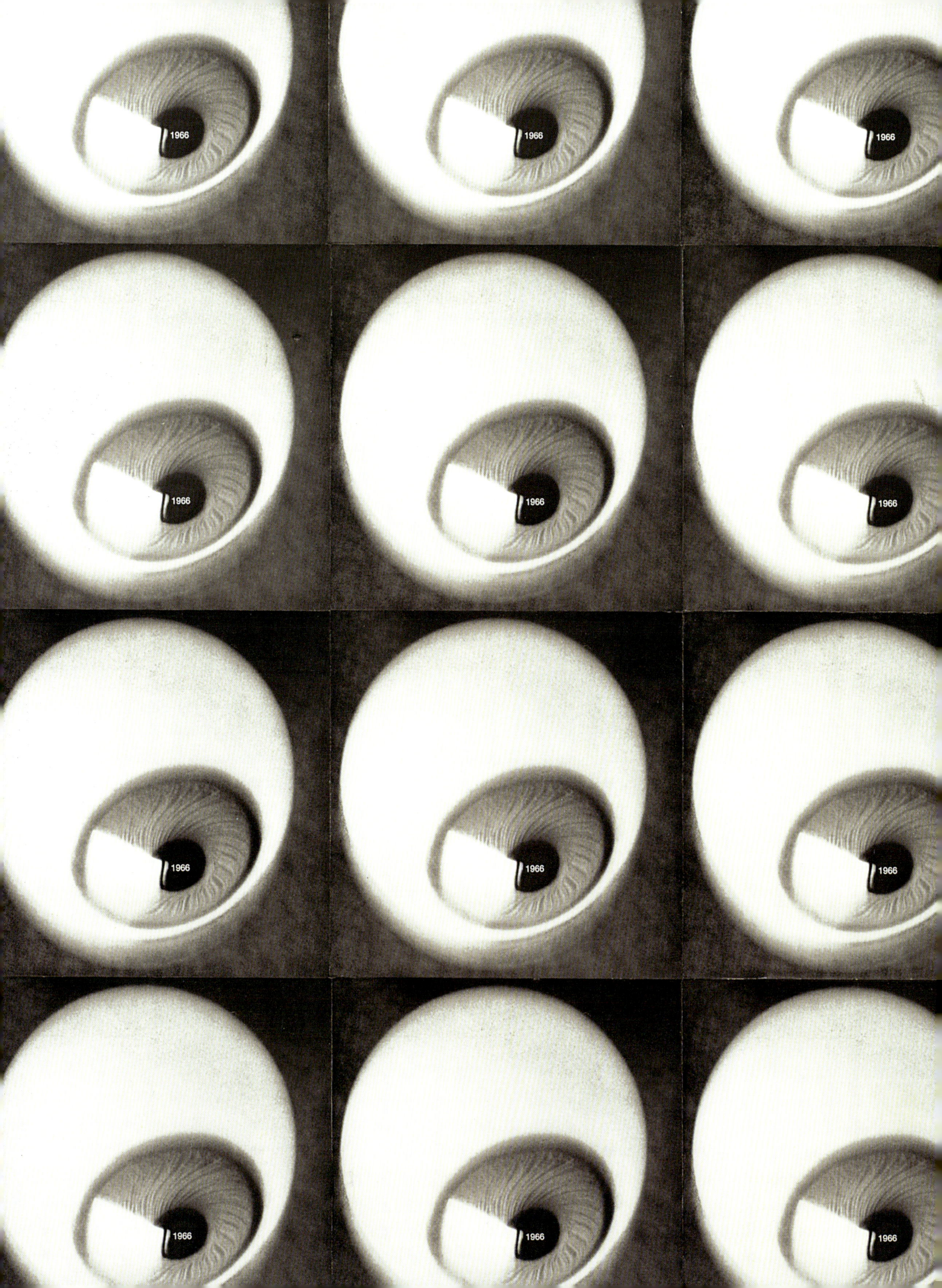
1966
1966
1966
1966
1966
1966
1966
1966
1966
1966
1966
1966

The Düsseldorf Academy

Norbert Kricke
Raumplastik Gelb-Weiss-Schwarz
1952

Norbert Kricke
1922 Düsseldorf – 1984 Düsseldorf

Painted steel
44 × 52 × 45 cm

Inv. no. S175M / Acquired 2006

In the early 1940s, in the midst of the war, a young Norbert Kricke discovered sculpture as a personal calling, as the "sublime joy of creation". He did not carve his human figures out of stone or wood but moulded them out of clay. Professional guidance fostered his skills, but it was not until after the war that he was able to enjoy a formal education at the Academy of the Arts in Berlin. He continued making figures in natural and classical poses, some of which reflect his admiration of such artists as Rodin or Lehmbruck. The year 1950 was a radical turning point. Kricke abandoned figuration and stopped working in clay, plaster and bronze, choosing instead to make intricate constructs of wire and steel with architectural leanings. He called them "space sculptures". They explicitly addressed contemporary sculptural concerns regarding material, form and subject matter. In 1954 Kricke wrote, "My problem is not the mass, it is not the figure, it is space and it is movement – space and time."

By the 1920s, such artists as Naum Gabo, Rodchenko and Moholy-Nagy had already abandoned figure and mass, the time-honoured properties of conventional sculpture. That same decade Picasso and Calder experimented with works made of wire, although in a more playful and anthropomorphic mode than the constructivist, architectural approach cultivated by artists from Eastern Europe. Kricke's *Raumplastik Gelb-Weiss-Schwarz* (Space Sculpture Yellow-White-Black, 1952) is a prime example of his wish to visualise space and movement instead of focusing on figure and mass. It consists of a straight steel wire that he has bent ten times at variously sharp and rounded angles, following a course that takes several intersecting directions until finally returning to its starting point. The artist has thus created a shape without plane and volume through the exclusive use of line and contour. Although the stand suggests four privileged vantage points, it is only by walking around it that one can fully appreciate the asymmetrical, intricately balanced views. These testify to the unerring sense of scale and proportion that Kricke acquired in the course of studying the human figure. The sculpture is actually small enough to be taken in at a single glance, but viewers cannot fully appreciate the rhythm, dynamic and sensuality of the line without visually tracing its path from yellow to white to black, for only then will they experience the sculpture's movement in space and through time.

The "space sculptures" play a singular role in art history of the latter twentieth century and have met with international acclaim. They underwent countless metamorphoses in the course of Kricke's life. He multiplied, stretched, bundled, knotted and bent his linear constructions until they became positively chaotic, only to morph back into the clarity of playfully light "curves", gliding, as if aimlessly, through space and time. The works give an insight into what Kricke meant when he wrote, "Away from measurable reality – it is the stiff corpse in our space – and towards imagined, transformed reality – then we will be saved."

UW

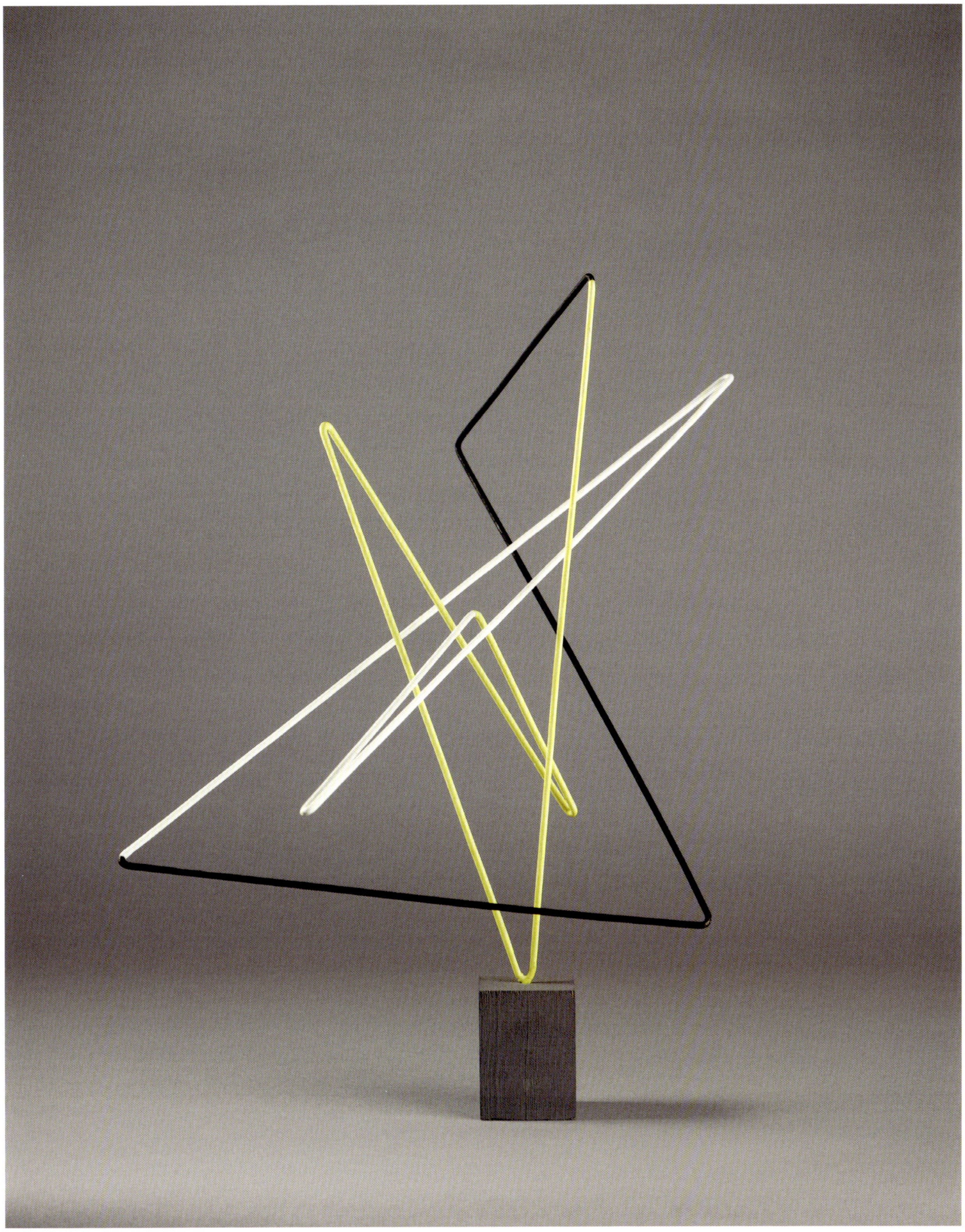

075

Gotthard Graubner
1930 Erlbach – 2013 Düsseldorf

Foam cushion on canvas,
covered with Perlon and painted
Signed, dated and titled verso:
Gotth. Graubner / 68 / "lichter körper"
100 × 100 × 12 cm

Inv. no. P191M / Acquired 2008

Gotthard Graubner
Lichter Körper
1968

Gotthard Graubner's artistic interests were focused primarily on organic life processes. When he did take note of subject matter, for instance, of a tree or a human figure, he focused not on contour or shape but rather on the sense of movement and space that emanates from within the organism. As he noted himself, we cannot apprehend a tree unless we begin with the roots, for the meaning of a tree lies not in its shape but in its growth. Growth, as such, is of course invisible and therefore beyond representation. It finds a correspondence only in the course of the artistic process, through which it is revealed sensually and conceptually in each single work. Graubner's emphasis on the nature of becoming rather than being derives from his focus on the genetic origins of organic life, that is, his interest in probing life from inside out.

Graubner's choice of materials – paper and cardboard, taffeta and nylon, sponge and cotton, fleece and canvas, pigment and binder – reflects the perception of organic life that he wished to render in his art. His investigations led to watercolours and gouaches, to his *Cushion Paintings* and *Paint Bodies* as well as the *Paint-Space-Bodies* that he made from the early 1970s until his death, giving physically tangible, visual shape, through abstraction and reduction, to his understanding of organic nature and especially the human body.

Lichter Körper (Luminous Body) is a pictorial object of tender materiality, a "cell", protected by a thin membrane, under which the artist has created a barely visible bipolar aura, hinting at the division of a still compact "cell body" and thus implying growth. Light, which might be said to be the primary cause of this growth, weaves in and out of the membrane, which is as vulnerable as it is protective, producing on and beyond its surface gradations of white so fragile and delicate that they fade into immateriality.
UW

Gotthard Graubner
Takyre I / Farbraumkörper
1974

Gotthard Graubner
1930 Erlbach – 2013 Düsseldorf

Oil on Perlon on synthetic cotton
Signed, dated and titled verso:
Graubner 74 / "Farbraumkörper" /
"TAKYRE I" / Gross
200 × 130 × 9.5 cm

Inv. no. P320M / Acquired 2018

Gotthard Graubner's interest in organic life processes led in the early 1970s to a genre that he designated *Farbraumkörper* (Paint-Space-Body), which gives sculptural, spatial shape, in the form of abstraction and reduction, to his understanding of organic nature, particularly the human body. At the same time, paint became both the medium and content of his paintings, as described in a formula of his own devising: paint = condensation into an organism = painting.

What does the condensation of paint into an organism actually mean? To begin with, Graubner's painting process involves the steady layering of bound pigments applied to a support, such as Perlon or canvas. The resulting condensation remains visible because the single layers are not opaque but essentially translucent and see-through. As in *Takyre*, the thin paint seeps through the soft layer of Perlon and the thick padding of cotton underneath, so that its effect rises up out of the depths and unfolds on the surface. The appearance of the paint is neither hermetic nor homogeneous; its application is unconstrained and differentiated.

In addition, the condensation of paint into an organism refers explicitly to the perception of colour, as influenced by such properties as the contrast between warm and cold or simultaneous contrasts. Graubner transforms colour into a pulsating, breathing medium by conjuring such a copious array of nuances that any hint of monochrome treatment is definitively undermined. The coexistence of these factors and their interplay generates the organism to which the artist aspires. The greatest significance of painting lies in the paint itself that forms a unity with the material that is its support and which it has saturated. This yields a condensed body, to wit, a *Farbraumkörper* that resonates with viewers, eliciting both a sensory and spiritual response.

UW

077

Gotthard Graubner
1930 Erlbach – 2013 Düsseldorf

Acrylic (mixed media) on canvas
on synthetic cotton on canvas
Signed and dated verso: Graubner 1990/91
255 × 255 × 18 cm

Inv. no. P181M / Acquired 2007

Gotthard Graubner
Herbstnacht
1990–91

A great, all-embracing serenity emanates from Gotthard Graubner's work despite the pulsating intensity of the colours and the painting. The visible outcome of a creative, often arduous and lengthy process becomes an object of contemplation, culminating in an utterly absorbing and immersive aesthetic phenomenon. Graubner consistently mounted his works low on the wall to foster the calming effect of looking down. Immersion in these paintings can lead to a sense of oblivion, a feeling of slipping into uncertainty. On the other hand, the physical presence of the *Farbraumkörper* makes viewers aware of their own physical presence, wrenching them out of oblivion and uncertainty. The organic condensation of paint, space and body in Graubner's paintings facilitates a synthesis of contemplation and self-awareness. Viewers are invited to abandon themselves to their sense perceptions, to become absorbed in the painting and the never-ending variations in this artist's universe of colour. No prior knowledge is required to appreciate these works, to lose and find oneself again in their appearances, and, ultimately, to realise that the sphere of colour is the sphere of human life and, indeed, of life per se between pure light and pure darkness.

UW

Gotthard Graubner
Le vent du soleil I (atmo)
1996

078

Gotthard Graubner
1930 Erlbach – 2013 Düsseldorf

Acrylic (mixed media) on canvas
on synthetic cotton on canvas
Signed, dated and titled verso:
Graubner 96 / "atmo"
280 × 360 × 25 cm

Inv. no. P182M / Acquired 2007

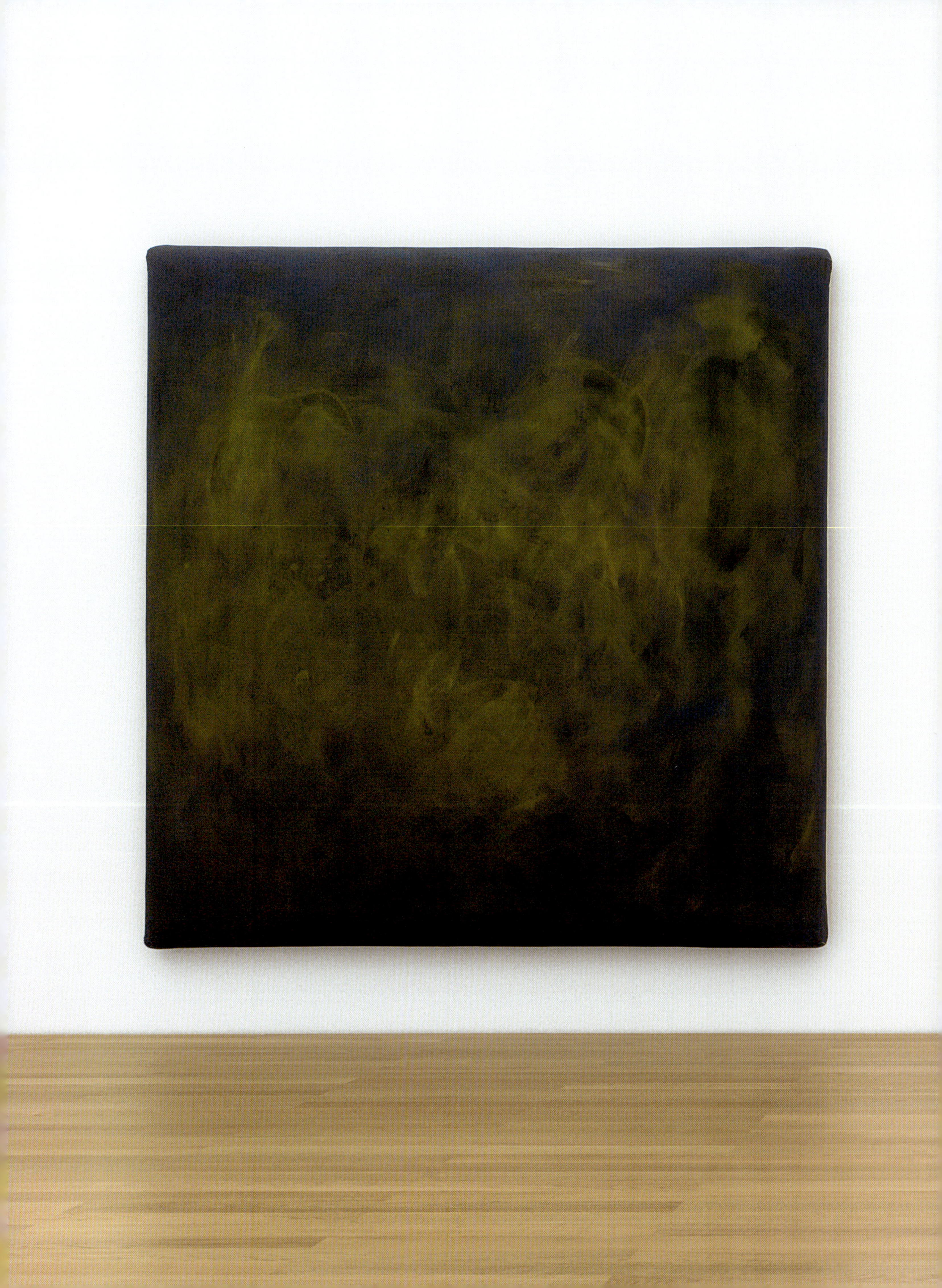

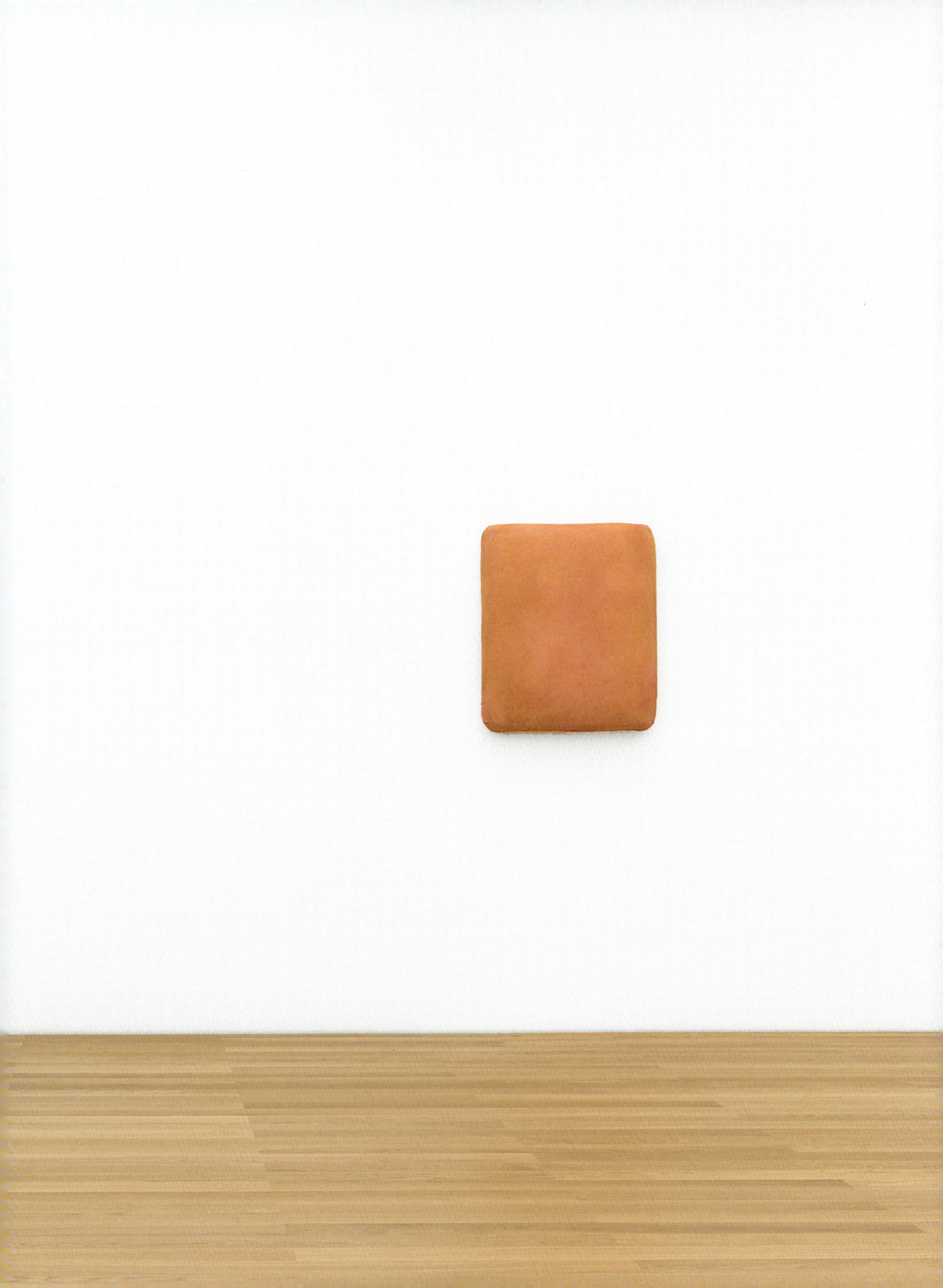

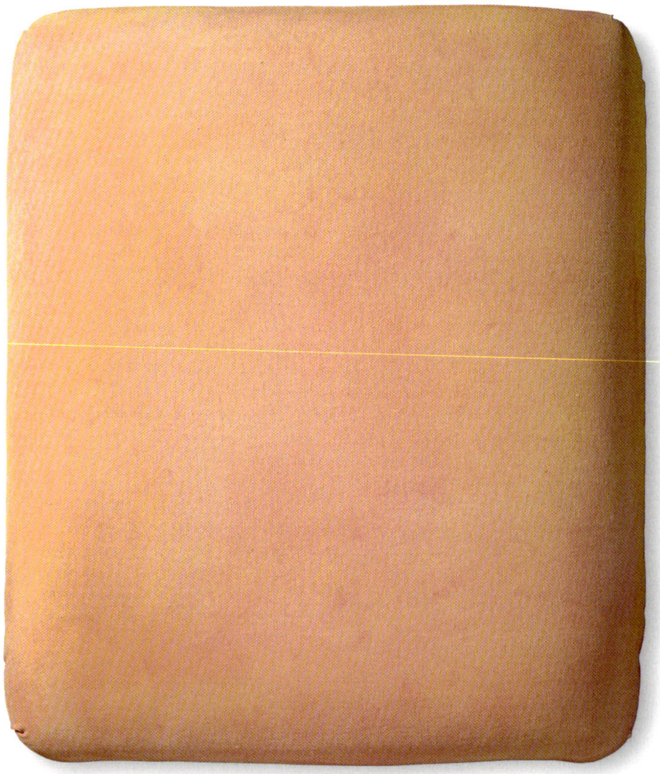

079

Gotthard Graubner
1930 Erlbach – 2013 Düsseldorf

Acrylic (mixed media) on canvas on synthetic cotton on canvas
Signed, dated and titled verso:
G. Graubner / 010, / "haut"
74 × 64 × 11 cm

Inv. no. P232M / Acquired 2011

Gotthard Graubner
Haut
2010

Gerhard Richter
Vesuv
1976

080

Gerhard Richter
1932 Dresden

Oil on wood
Numbered, signed and dated verso:
Nr. 407 / Richter / 1976
66 × 95 cm

Inv. no. P214M / Acquired 2009

Gerhard Richter started out painting stage sets and subsequently studied art at the Academy in Dresden from 1951 to 1956. He left the GDR in 1961 and pursued his studies at the Düsseldorf Academy. Initially, he focused on older artists such as Giacometti, Dubuffet and Fautrier (see vol. 1, cat. 75 and 79), although his peers and friends at the Academy were younger artists like Konrad Lueg, Sigmar Polke and Blinky Palermo. Richter made his first paintings based on photographs in 1962, the year that also marks the beginning of his ongoing catalogue raisonné.

The motif that gives the painting its title, Mount Vesuvius in the Gulf of Naples, cannot be readily identified at first sight. In the long history of representations from William Turner to Andy Warhol, the mountain ordinarily dominates as an active volcano, a threat to nature and civilisation, spewing fire, smoke and molten lava, while yet a source of painterly beauty. Richter's painting does not abide in this tradition. In his painterly landscape, Mount Vesuvius itself has almost vanished in the haze of the distant, barely visible coast of the Gulf. This description fits six other paintings of the same title, all created not on site but from a series of different photographs the artist had taken. In the present work, we look northeast beyond the hills of Capri at the ocean, the mainland with volcano and the expanses of sky overhead.

The landscape looks romantic, almost meditative. The *Vesuv* paintings clearly testify to Richter's frequent and appreciative reference to Caspar David Friedrich, arguably the most famous painter of German Romanticism. They do not render the location in the sunlight of the Mediterranean but, rather, in atmospheric, delicate shades of colour. The two figures on the terrace pictured at the bottom of the painting evoke those occasionally shown silently contemplating the landscape in Friedrich's work, though larger in scale. However, despite expanses of cosmic proportions, the works in Richter's series do not share the spirituality of his predecessor; they are more physical than divine in nature.

Gerhard Richter commits to painting fully aware that it is literally "questionable", having also been written off as a supposedly obsolete genre in the wake of contemporary polemical debate and criticism. Can we attain a view of the world with the help of painting that does not congeal into a worldview? The current of scepticism that runs through his paintings in both form and content derives from the artist's personal experience with ideologically informed worldviews. The use of everyday photographs taken with little ambition by himself or others, from family albums or magazines, enables Richter to render characteristic aspects of reality. These aspects undergo critical review for their pictorial viability and comprise a wide-ranging panorama of our human, historical and physical, natural universe. In his paintings, the artist dignifies "unartistic" photography, creating works that he considers more faithful to reality. At the same time, as in his *Vesuv* paintings, the blurred subject matter echoes a specifically photographic property, indebted not to handcrafted incompetence but rather to the spectral quality of all things visible and ultimately to our fundamentally blurred perception of reality.

UW

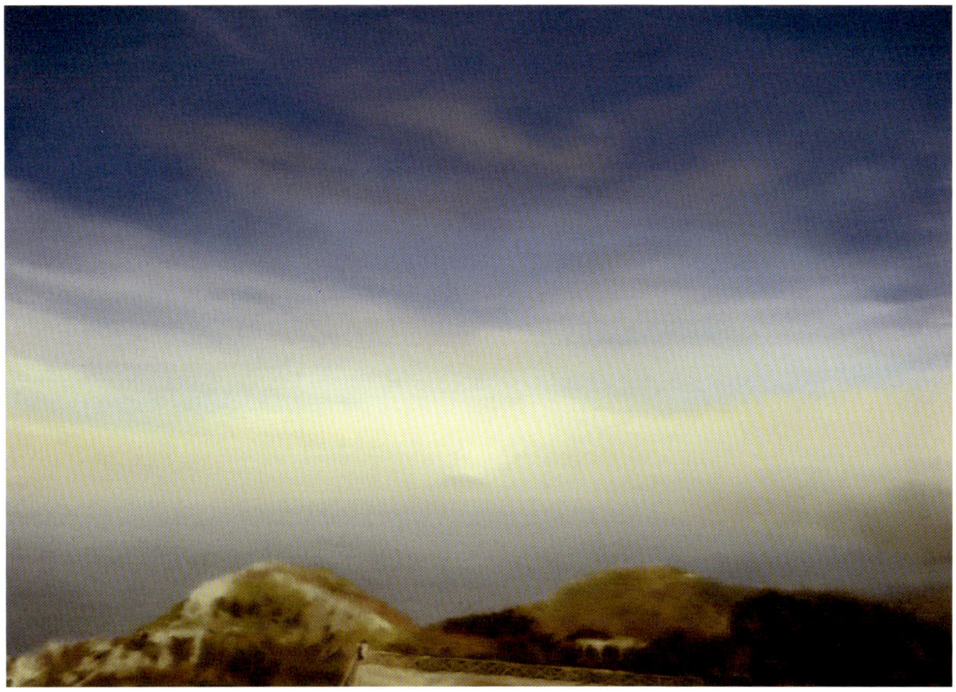

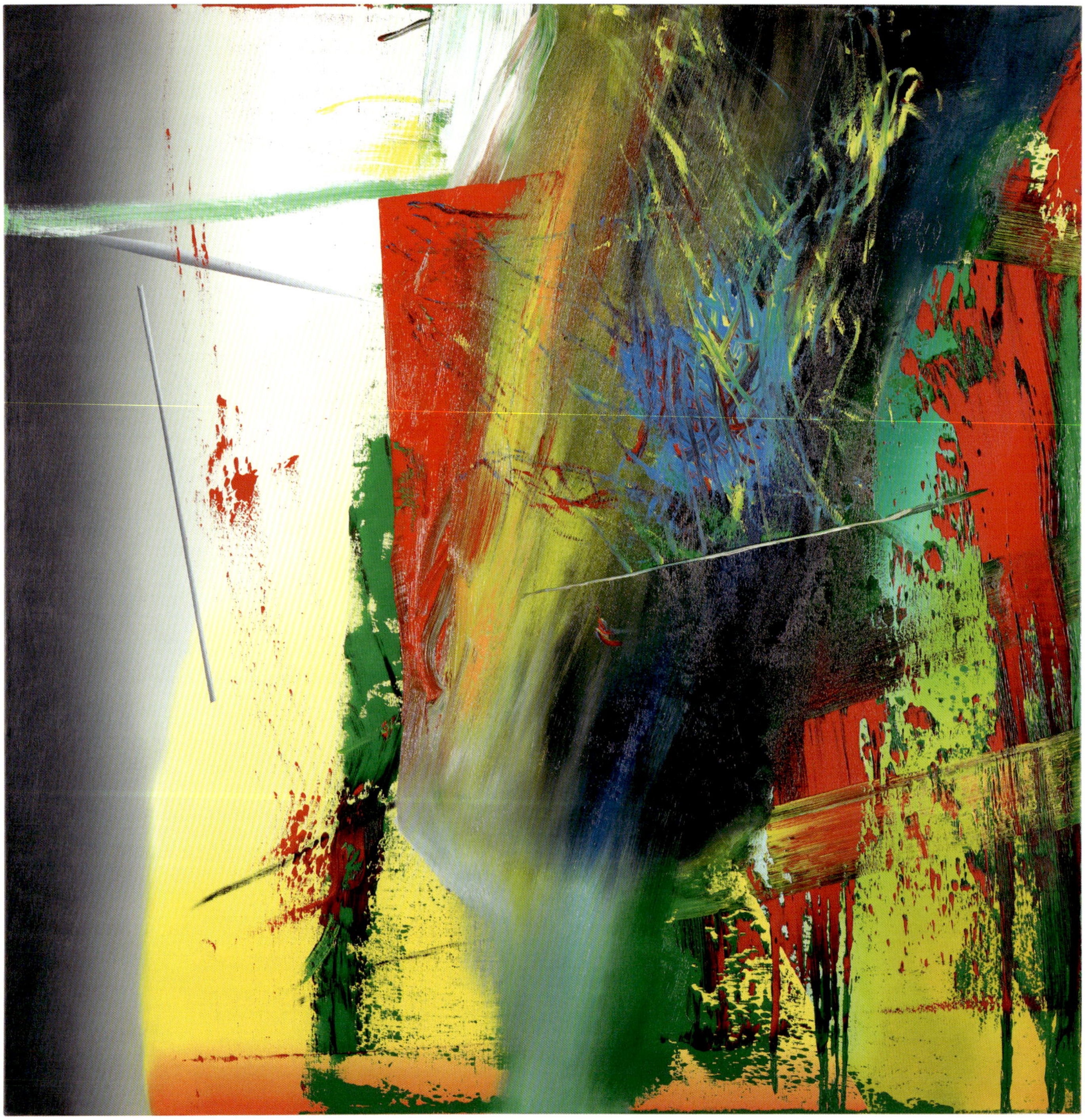

081

Gerhard Richter
D.G.
1985

Gerhard Richter
1932 Dresden

Oil on canvas
Numbered, signed, titled and dated verso:
575-1 / Richter / "D.G." / 1985
200 × 200 cm

Inv. no. P206M / Acquired 2009

Gerhard Richter takes an interest in both figurative and nonfigurative forms of expression, that is, in the pictorial and autonomous qualities of painting. In 1976, at the same time as the *Vesuv* (see cat. 80), *Grau* (Grey) and *Wolke* (Cloud) series, the artist turned his attention to the largest corpus in his oeuvre, the so-called *Abstracts*. *D.G.*, painted in 1985, is a case in point; it is named after Dieter Giesing, a theatre director from Hamburg and the painting's first owner. *D.G.* rests neither on deliberately defined composition nor on uncontrolled gestural action. As in all of his *Abstract Pictures*, Richter seeks to create "something ... I don't know, wouldn't be able to plan, something better, cleverer than I am." In a constructive-deconstructive process of painting, he lets the pictures emerge by stepping out of themselves, as it were, although he does not act with indifferent detachment but, rather, sensitive deliberation, stopping now and then to work on other paintings at the same time. His aim is not to produce a psychogram or self-contained work but, rather, an open-ended model that one might even call a visual parable "of the possibility of living together in society. ... Seen in this light, all I attempt to achieve in a painting is to unite difference and contradiction in the most vibrant and viable way and with the greatest possible freedom. No paradises."

D.G. also holds the potential of contradictory readings: initially, the paint is perceived as the purely physical medium of nonfigurative art. Unbridled colours spread out across two-thirds of the canvas, in paintwork both explosive and viscous. A third of the picture plane to the left stands in contrast; the paint follows a homogeneous course from grey to white and from white to yellow in an oddly illusionist pictorial depth with an enigmatic rod afloat on the surface, entirely objective and nonetheless beyond grasp. Richter worked the surface with both paintbrush and scraper to spread the paint on the canvas or to scrape it off again where several layers were applied and the paint had not dried yet, a technique that leads to unpredictable structures and chromatic effects of surprising beauty.

By comparing his *Abstracts* to human society, Richter rules out a purely aesthetic approach to appreciation although he clearly draws on aesthetic means to generate a powerful image of freedom under conditions of heterogeneity and contradiction.

UW

Gerhard Richter
25 Farben
2007

Gerhard Richter
1932 Dresden

Lacquer on Alu-Dibond
Numbered, signed and dated verso:
902-30 / Richter 2007
902-46 / Richter 2007
Each 48.5 × 48.5 cm

Inv. nos. P198M / P199M
Both acquired 2008

In 1966 Gerhard Richter came across colour charts in a Düsseldorf art supply store that inspired a new form of work which he calls *Farben* (Colours) or *Farbtafeln* (Colour Charts). One of the first of this kind consists of sixteen by twelve squares of colour separated by narrow white spaces. The colours are each individually defined and distributed unsystematically within the grid. Titled *192 Farben*, Richter painted this large-format work (200 × 150 cm) in oil on canvas. In the ensuing works, however, he chose to use enamel paint, which produces a more neutral effect. The conventional idea of pictures having a theme, composition or personal signature no longer applies to the form and content of these works. Nor does the "indifferent" arrangement of the colours, laid out like samples, offer viewers anything specifically sensual or, even less, symbolic.

When Richter returned to this work category in the early 1970s, he neutralised the subjective factor even more by systematising the colours and arranging them on the picture plane by lot. In 1974, he produced *4096 Farben* in enamel on canvas (254 × 254 cm) and in 2007, *4900 Farben* (680 × 680 cm), now using the unstructured, smooth surface of Alu Dibond as his picture support. *4900 Farben* is directly related to Richter's commission to design the window in the south transept of Cologne Cathedral (see cat. 102), consisting of 11,500 squares of colour, their layout randomly generated by computer as in *4900 Farben*. The latter comprises 196 squares measuring 48.5 by 48.5 cm, each in turn containing 25 single squares (196 × 25 = 4900) as the smallest unit.

The two paintings presented here belong to the 2007 series of *25 Farben* and correspond in scale and form to the 196 elements of *4900 Farben*. As stated in the title, they are limited to 25 different colours, the familiar spectrum arranged in even gradations from colour to colour and light to dark to ensure that no colour dominates. The colours have been spray-painted in enamel on small panels of Alu Dibond (97 × 97 × 2 mm). They are numbered and placed on the picture support by lot. Richter distinguishes three ways of drawing lots: simple (A), multiplied (B) and endless (C). The first, A, yields homogeneous pictures since each colour can only be drawn once per lot, while B and C yield extremely heterogeneous results since each colour can be drawn repeatedly or endlessly. Richter chose to use the third, endless system so that every painting is different in combination and individual number of colours. He has thus undermined the monotony of sameness because the two pictures would consist of the same colours had they been painted on the basis of the A principle. Richter logically concludes that a society based on the B and C principles will be superior to one based on the A principle, since the former ensure greater diversity in consequence of a calculated chance based on agreed rules of play.

UW

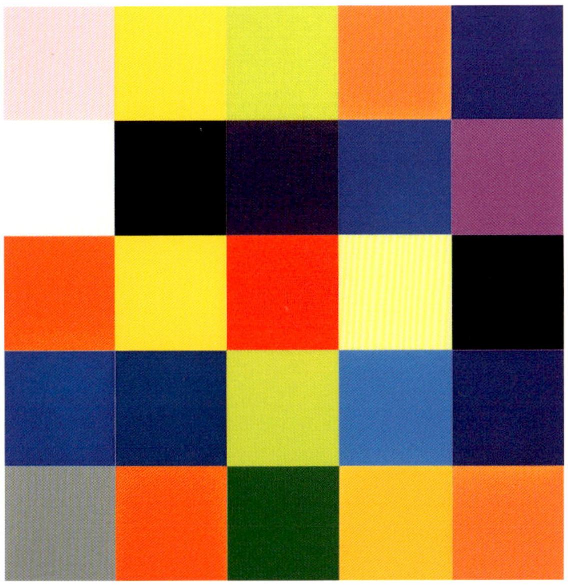

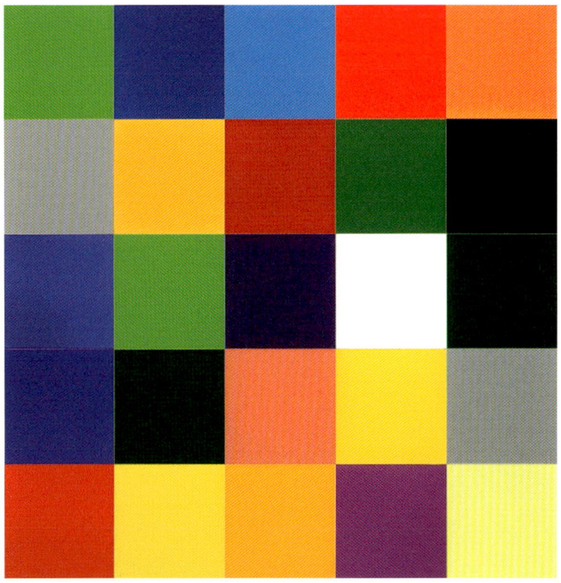

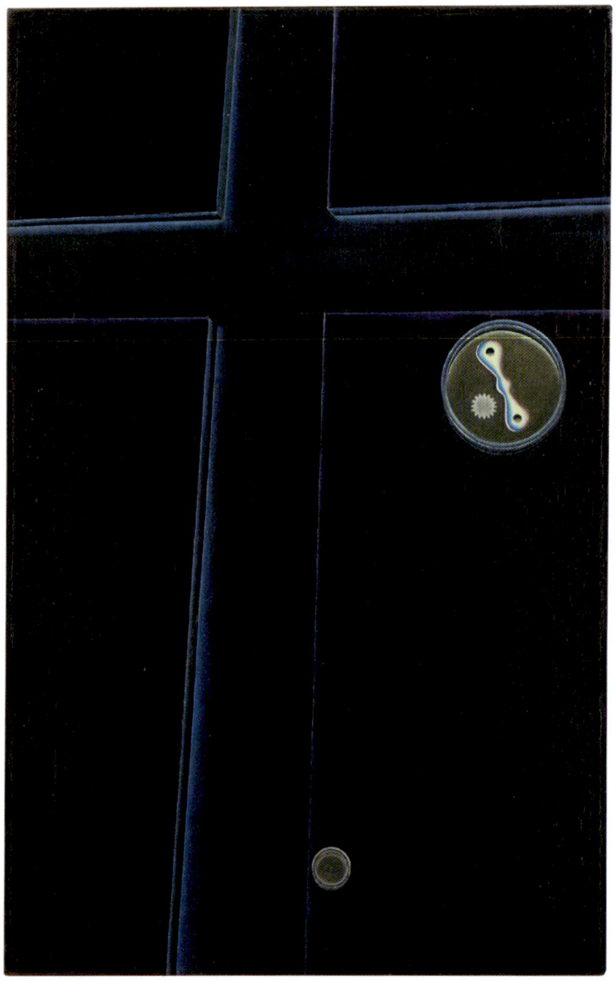

083

Konrad Klapheck
1935 Düsseldorf

Oil on canvas
Signed on canvas verso: Klapheck
Signed and titled on stretcher:
Klapheck / traurige Mama
62.5 × 40 cm

Inv. no. P273M / Acquired 2015

Konrad Klapheck
Traurige Mama
1959

Konrad Klapheck already showed a strong interest in Surrealism while studying with Bruno Goller at the Düsseldorf Art Academy in the 1950s. His subject matter includes such devices and utilitarian objects as typewriters, sewing machines, telephones, irons, shoe trees, clocks and bicycle bells. Rendered in a cool, precise realism, these objects appear curiously detached and estranged, a style much appreciated not only by Goller but also by the Paris Surrealists, with whom Klapheck became personally acquainted in 1961 through the art critic José Pierre. He knew Max Ernst, and later met André Breton, writer, poet and foremost theoretician of Surrealism, who wrote the catalogue essay for Klapheck's 1965 solo exhibition at the Sonnabend Gallery in Paris.

The painting *Traurige Mama* (Sad Mama) of 1958 features a window crossbar against a deep purple to pitch-black background. It is inclined slightly to the right with bluish highlighting along the edges. Circular parts of a bicycle bell are "floating" in space. One of the two parts shows the inner life of the bell with gear and propeller. The other is presumably the lid, painted farther away in the imaginary space and hence much smaller. Bicycle bells make a frequent appearance in Klapheck's paintings because, as he writes, "The bicycle bell is a point of departure for especially free variations. In the gear, we encounter the tooth of a saw; the rotating propeller evokes fans and aeroplanes. The smallest things are a reflection of the greatest." His fascination with this object may well have originated from a childhood experience. "I unscrewed the cover of the bell and was surprised that it didn't ring any more. Silent and helpless, the propeller rotated around its own axis. It was as if it had come from the same workshop as the winged maple seeds that we used to stick on our noses."

The whimsical titles are the product, Klapheck writes, of free association in the process of painting or after finishing the work; they are not descriptive but rather complementary and independent in nature, since the pictures come first. Even so, they do offer important, if not always explicit, allusions to the content and interpretation of the paintings. *Traurige Mama*, for instance, refers to the artist's close relationship with his mother. Konrad was an only child and four years old when his father died, and he and his mother, Anna, witnessed his grandparents' home going up in flames in an air raid. Could the two parts of the bicycle bell be interpreted as a symbol of mother and child physically separated in the nocturnal depths of the universe? And could the crossbar have familial implications as well, perhaps the cross on the grave of father and husband? All interpretation of the painting must inevitably remain vague, fading into the darkness of its mysterious and magical atmosphere.

JR

Konrad Klapheck
Familienleben
1961

084

Konrad Klapheck
1935 Düsseldorf

Oil on canvas
Signed on canvas verso: Klapheck
90 × 100 cm

Inv. no. P176M / Acquired 2006

Familienleben (Family Life) by Konrad Klapheck of 1961 shows a seemingly technical configuration of pipes in different shapes, set off almost in relief against a light ground. Although physically intertwined, the parts do not appear to be governed by any perceivable function, a conclusion quickly drawn since there is no indication whatsoever of how the whole might be operated or set in motion. The configuration hovers over an invisible ground, showing an enigmatic solidity without any definable material properties.

Were it not for the title, the painting could be read as a critique or an ironic take on technology and machines. Machines, in all their alienating inaccessibility, play a dominant role in the artist's oeuvre. However, the title invites a broader interpretation, transforming the subject matter of the painting into an allegory in technical disguise. The pipes might be read as embodiments of human beings in a state of mutual dependence that is as inescapable as it is oppressive.

JR

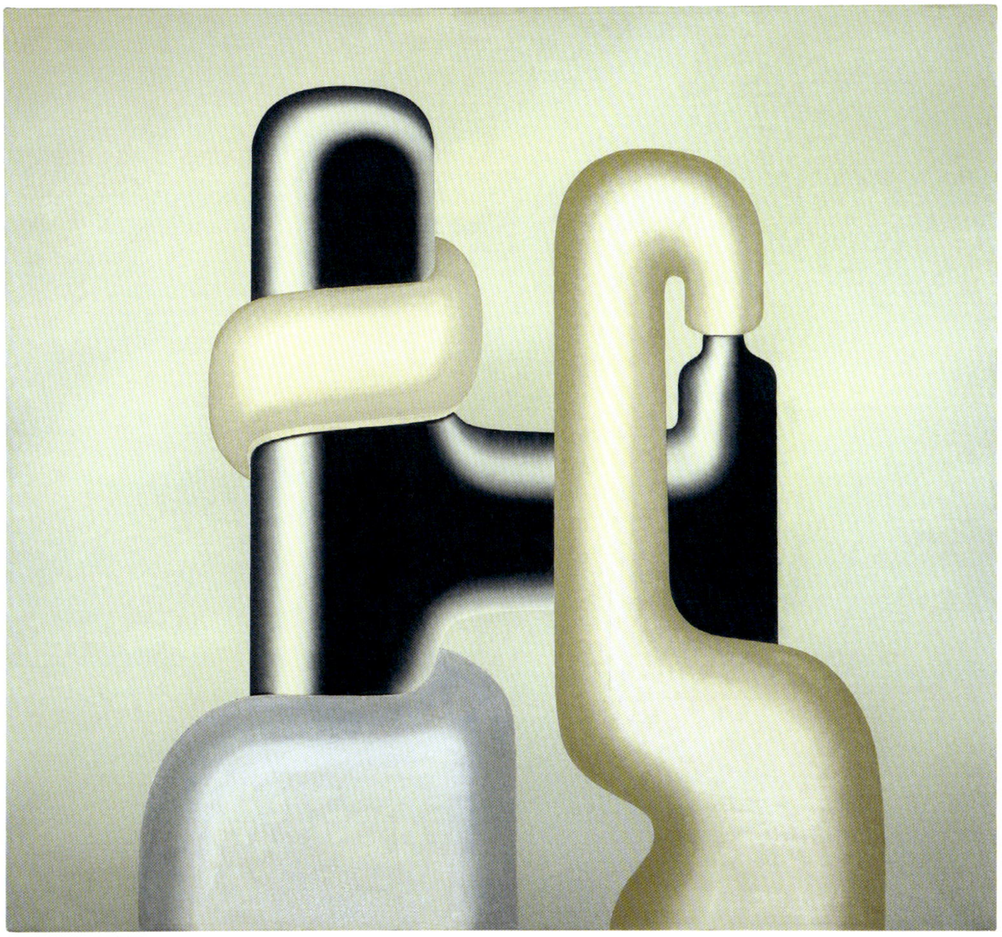

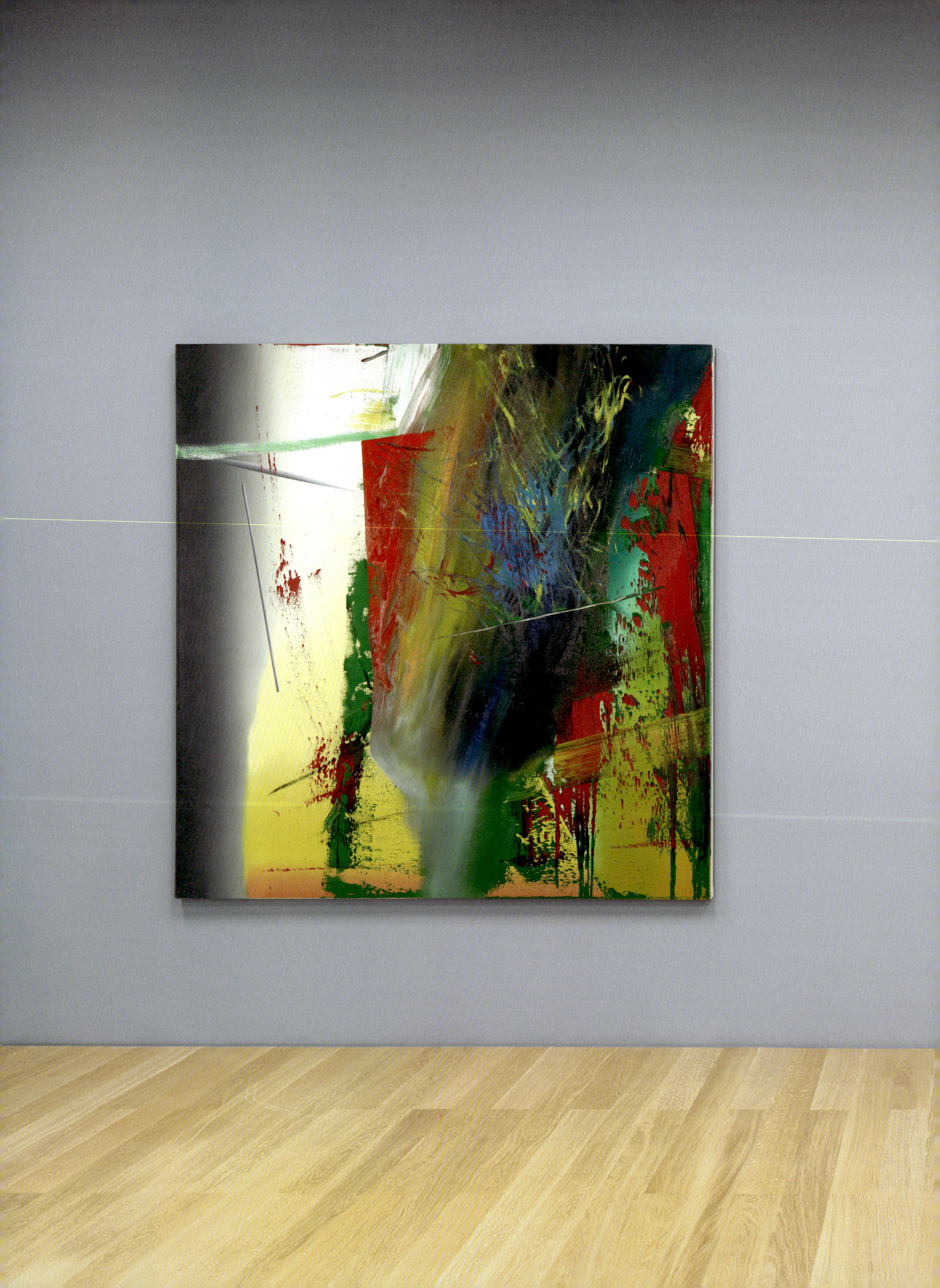

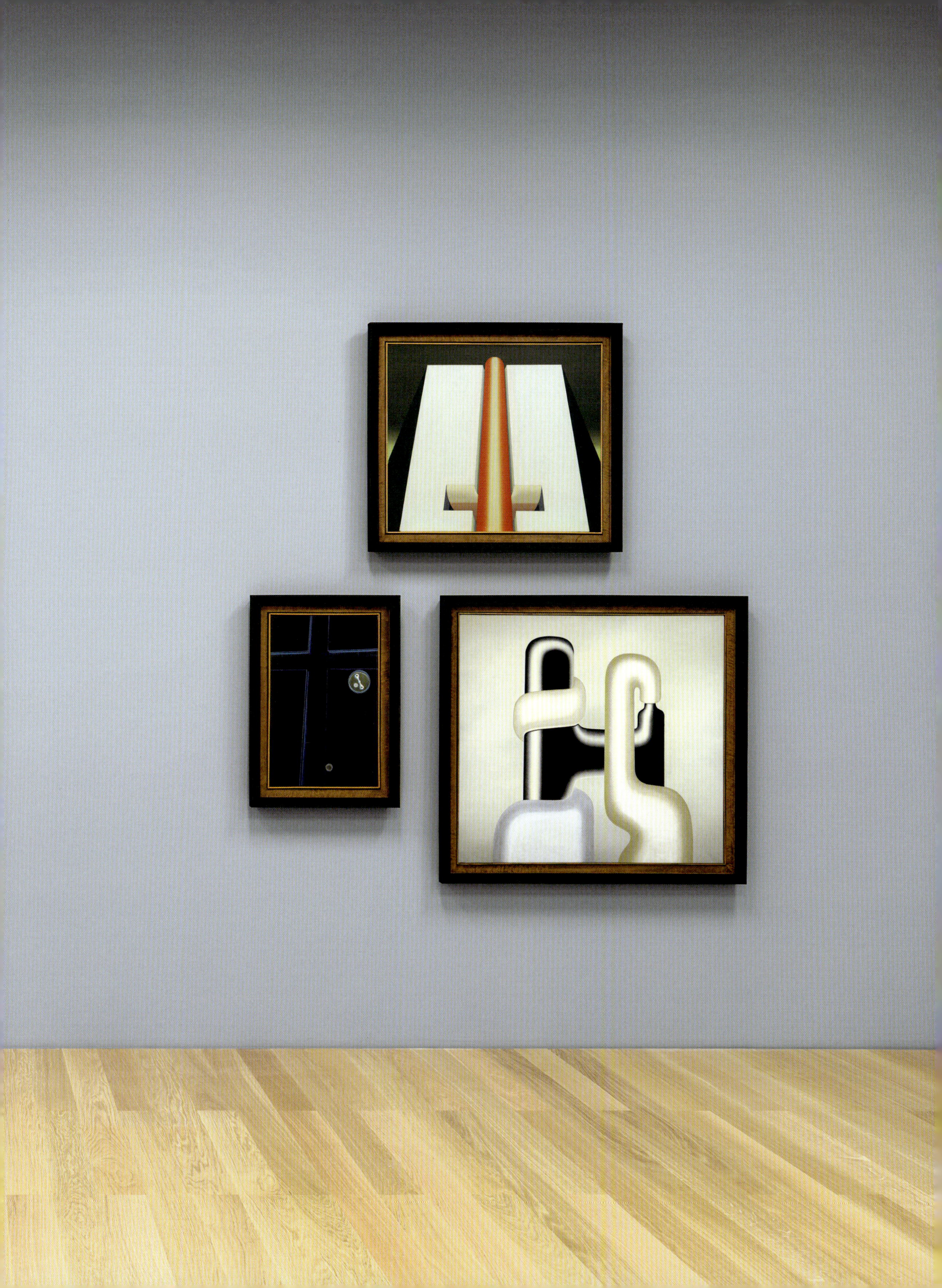

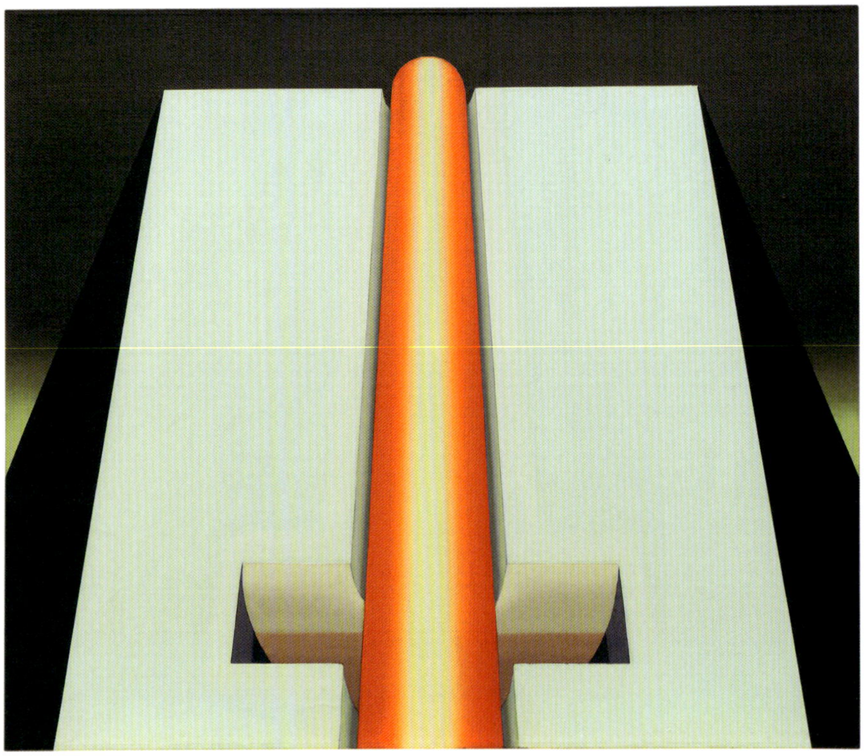

085

Konrad Klapheck
Am Ziel der Wünsche
1963

Konrad Klapheck
1935 Düsseldorf

Oil on canvas
Signed on canvas verso: Klapheck
Titled on stretcher: ("l'aboutissement des désirs") am Ziel der Wünsche of desires
69 × 81 cm

Inv. no. P272M / Acquired 2015

Konrad Klapheck personally dedicated this painting to André Breton in gratitude for his contribution to the catalogue published in conjunction with Klapheck's solo exhibition at the Sonnabend Gallery, Paris, in 1965. Breton was a writer and poet and, as the foremost theoretician of Surrealism, penned the Surrealist Manifestoes of 1924 and 1930. Klapheck first met the Frenchman, born in 1896, in 1961, and Breton kindly invited him to join the daily evening get-togethers of the Paris Surrealists at the café La Promenade de Venus. Breton owned three paintings by Klapheck.

Am Ziel der Wünsche (Wishes Come True) of 1963 is a largely abstract composition although everything in it seems to be objective. A slender pipe lies centred in a groove in a cubic body, perceived as a trapezoid in foreshortened perspective and almost filling the entire picture plane against a background that suggests depth. What does this represent? The barrel of a canon plus mount? A machine? A flue? A drainpipe? The difficulty of interpreting the painting is compounded by the fact that one can barely distinguish whether the representation is from a bird's- or worm's-eye view. The mysterious objects, the smoothness and lack of texture, and the fanciful colours lend the work a clearly Surrealist character, inviting free association. Nonetheless, Klapheck notes that perhaps Breton did not appreciate this work since he never saw it in the Surrealist's studio.

JR

Imi Knoebel

s 0,6 w 1,0

1967

Imi Knoebel
1940 Dessau

Dispersion on linen on fibreboard
160.5 × 130.3 cm

Inv. no. P264M / Acquired 2015

From 1966 to 1968, even before completing his studies at the Düsseldorf Academy with Joseph Beuys, Imi Knoebel produced a series of ninety *Linienbilder* (Line Paintings), launching an oeuvre whose artistic development would be independent from that of his teacher. The series includes eleven portrait-format white paintings with vertical black lines at intervals gradually declining from 20 to 10 millimetres. Knoebel used a ruling pen, drawing the lines with great precision on white primed linen mounted on fibreboard. The number of lines increases at uneven intervals from 65 to 130. Nine other paintings are related to this suite: not only do they show a steady, similarly irregular increase in the number of lines but also an increase in width from 2 to 10 millimetres. The paintings thus become darker and darker until they appear to be white lines against a black ground. Only in their totality can we perceive the serial logic of these twenty almost equally sized *Linienbilder*.

Yet, even individually, they reveal the central issue that has motivated Knoebel from the beginning of his artistic career: the feasibility of relating elementary forms of composition to geometry. Knoebel also considered the larger debate regarding the function and content of painting in general, which propelled artistic discourse in the 1960s. It seemed that Kazimir Malevich had already found the absolute answer in 1915 when he painted his black square on a white ground, a work that seminally influenced Knoebel. Liberated from any reference to nature, it offered the experience of unadulterated non-objectivity. This icon of Modernism was a cornerstone of geometric abstraction in the fine arts – and of Imi Knoebel's oeuvre as well. However, the purity and rigour of his black-and-white *Linienbilder* did not share the pathos of the philosophy championed by the pioneers of Classical Modernism; they were quite the opposite in their quest for a possible beginning. And indeed, the meticulous, handcrafted drawing of lines on the surface of a traditional rectangular painting was a beginning that proved to be viable.

Throughout his career as an artist, Knoebel has incorporated the universal vocabulary of geometry into his work. But unlike Malevich and Mondrian, the trailblazers of geometric abstraction, Knoebel's works oscillate between analysis and synthesis, gravity and irony, production and playfulness, so much so that they not only elude a formal dogmatism; they also leave room for enquiry into the aesthetic and substantial meaning of a picture as picture and ultimately of art as art.
UW

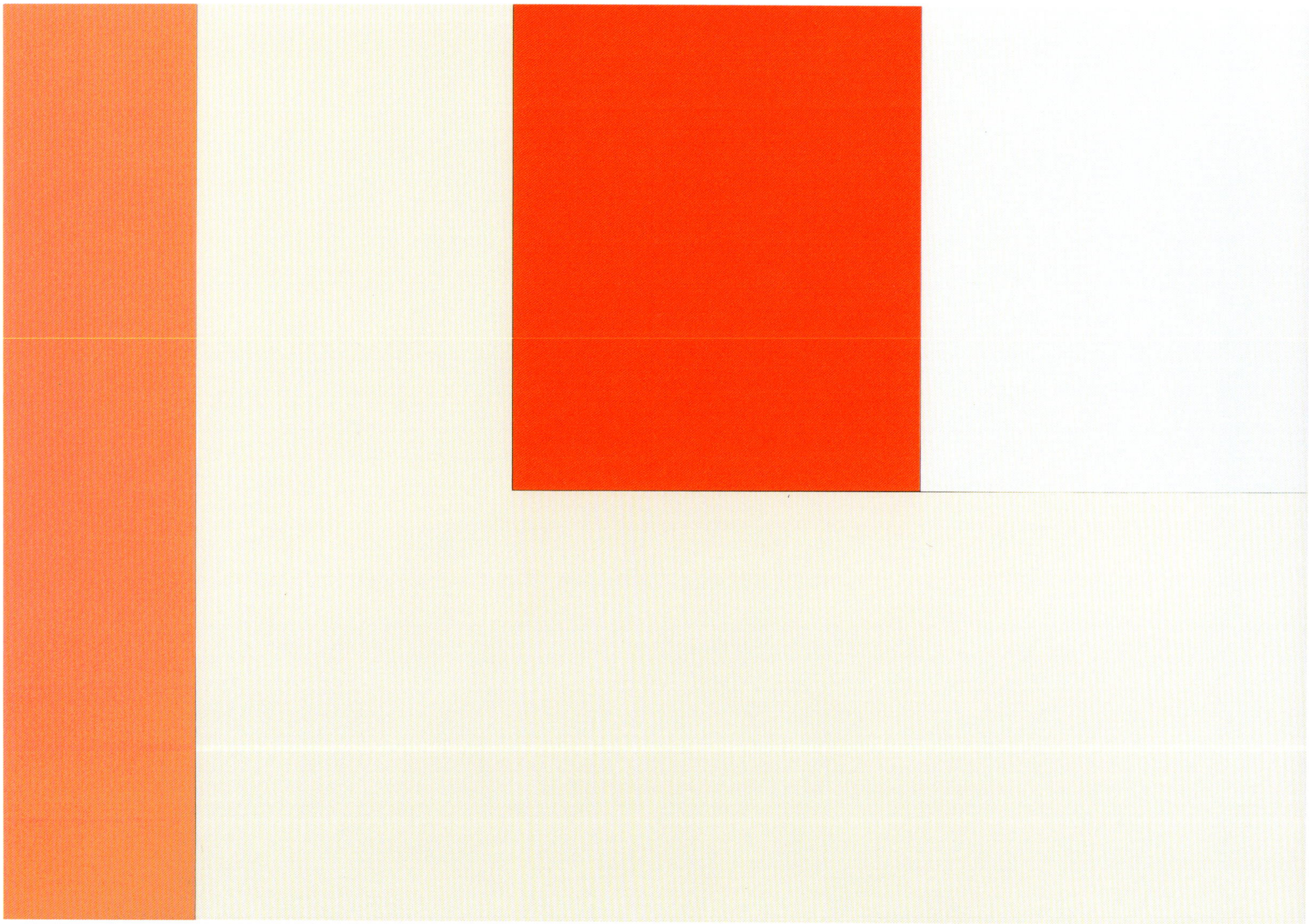

Imi Knoebel
1940 Dessau

Acrylic on wood
Signed and dated verso: imi 88
170 × 250 cm

Inv. no. P169M / Acquired 2006

Imi Knoebel
Figur 49
1988

In the late 1960s, when painting and the image were subject to widespread scepticism, Imi Knoebel succeeded in charting an artistic path to painting by embracing non-figurative forms closely aligned with geometry. He had found an initial sense of direction in the practical answers to questions of function and content provided by Kazimir Malevich and Piet Mondrian in the teens of the twentieth century. Despite the seminal influence of Malevich's *Black Square* of 1915 and the attendant experience of pure nonobjectivity, Knoebel has consistently countered the aesthetic stringency and pathos underlying the weltanschauung of Classical Modernism's pioneers with playfully refractory experimentation.

Knoebel created his so-called *Figurenbilder* (Figure Paintings) between 1985 and 1991, prior to which his work had oscillated between painting, object and installation in a nonobjective approach ranging from the geometric to Art Informel. In his *Figurenbilder*, he confined himself to strictly wall-related, horizontally or vertically oriented, rectangular wooden planes. He painted free compositions of physically distinct pictorial components within the rectangular framework to suggest combinations of tin, tiles or other building materials. The point of departure for his first *Figurenbilder* were the balconies in what was then still the German Democratic Republic. They had attracted the artist's attention as the most authentic places in the tenants' flats, for they had not undergone deliberate modification. This also explains the improvisational, constructive character of the paintings.

As the series progressed, concrete reference to a reality beyond the art context faded. The *Figurenbilder* that followed consist of several distinct rectangular and monochrome components. *Figur 49* is a large rectangular assemblage of four elements, each different in format. An almost square, luminous red plane, placed just slightly off centre, dominates the upper half of the composition with two white fields on either side, each distinguished by size, hue and surface texture. A salmon-coloured field marks the left margin of the painting, forming an appealing counterpoint to the red plane. Visible brushstrokes in the application of the paint testify to the freedom of the artist's hand. The asymmetrical composition underscores the finely calibrated overall balance of the painting.

In his *Figurenbilder*, it seems that Knoebel has finally vanquished his scepticism and indeed aversion to the traditional painting. He has not only reinvigorated the form and colour of the geometric abstraction cultivated by Classical Modernism, he has also established a beautiful and harmonious congruence between them. Even so, a look at other paintings made at the same time reveals that Knoebel's contrary spirit consistently applies to his own work as well.

UW

Imi Knoebel
Untitled (Schwarzes Bild No. 9 [of 24], Schlachtenbild)
1990

Imi Knoebel
1940 Dessau

Lacquer on fibreboard
Signed and dated verso: IMI 90
209.5 × 150 cm

Inv. no. P229M / Acquired 2011

The high esteem in which Knoebel holds the visual syntax of Malevich and Mondrian, the two great representatives of Classical Modernism, does not prevent him from taking an undogmatic, playfully creative approach to their substantial and formal rigour. At times, he even jettisons the geometric syntax altogether, subjecting his work to intense treatment not only using paintbrush and paint but also a variety of tools that violate the picture plane. This is seen not only in the series of *Schwarze Bilder* (*Schlachtenbilder*) (Black Paintings [Battle Paintings]), but is prefigured in earlier works, such as the *Drachenzeichnungen* (Kite Drawings, 1980–81) and the suite of works titled *Im Sommer 84* (In Summer 84, 1984). He created the latter in France during a period of unremitting rain. His analogue reflection of an elemental experience of nature is recorded on the fibreboard support not simply in the form of the painterly gesture but scored and perforated, in other words, also subjected to sculptural treatment. Johannes Stüttgen writes that in the *Schwarze Bilder* (1990–91) this violent and violating gesture was "dramatically heightened, acquiring a shape of its own". Knoebel gouged, scored or cut linear traces of varying width into the picture plane, covering almost the entire surface and even perforating it completely in several places. But despite the severe violation of the support, the black lacquer, with which he has coated the panel, lends it great aesthetic nobility. Depending on the angle of the lighting, the dark surface radiates a lustrous splendour, with flashes of light sparkling in the furrows, grooves and incisions that occasionally reveal the reddish-brown of the fibreboard.

What appears, metaphorically speaking, to be a battle on the picture plane could also be interpreted as a sense impression that has erupted on the surface, as in the *Im Sommer 84* series. However, here it seems that the work does not render a personal experience, but is, rather, a gestural event deliberately intended to lend visibility to material, surface, space and paint per se. Lucio Fontana (cat. 46) already pierced or slashed his canvases in a radical gesture that draws unfiltered attention to the actual components of a painting – its material, surface and space. But Knoebel's *Schlachtenbilder* do not share the serene elegance of a precisely placed hole or slash; the vibrancy and energy of his chaotic confusion of lines may, in fact, be understood as resolute artistic opposition to any kind of formalism.

UW

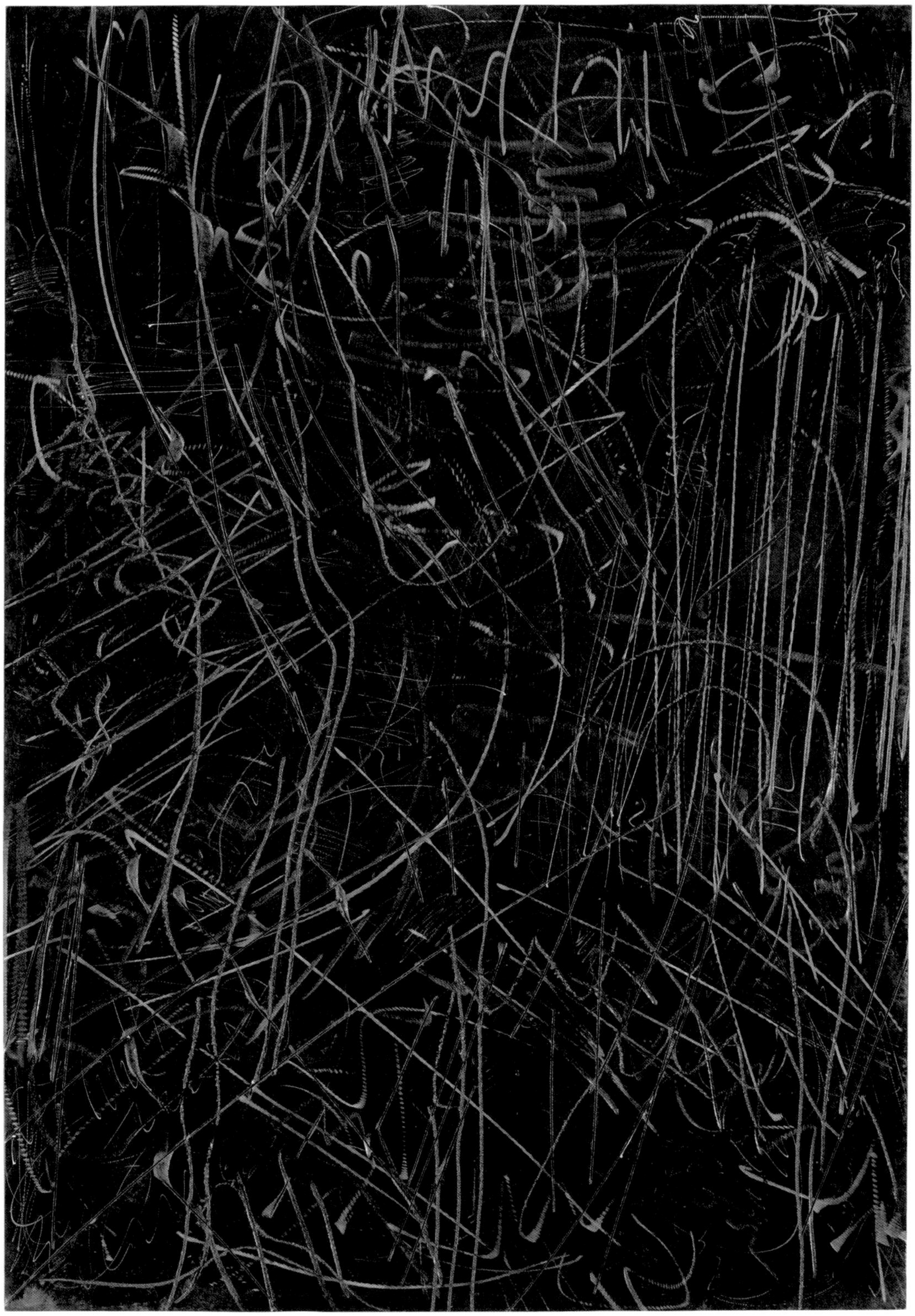

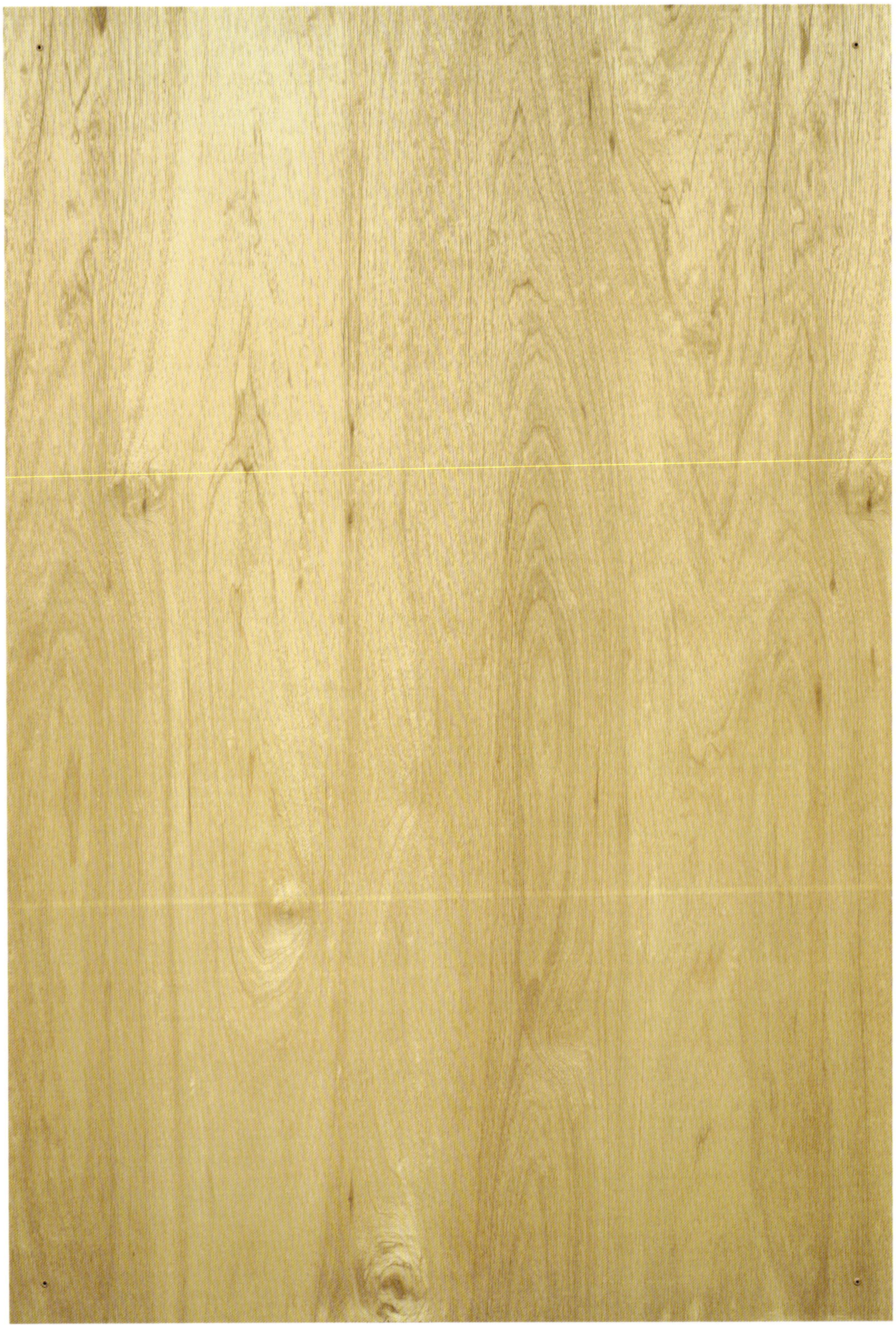

Imi Knoebel
Sandwich Blau-Rot-Rot-Gelb
1993

Imi Knoebel
1940 Dessau

Acrylic on plywood
Signed and dated verso: IMI 93
210 × 146 × 1.8 cm

Inv. no. P251M / Acquired 2014

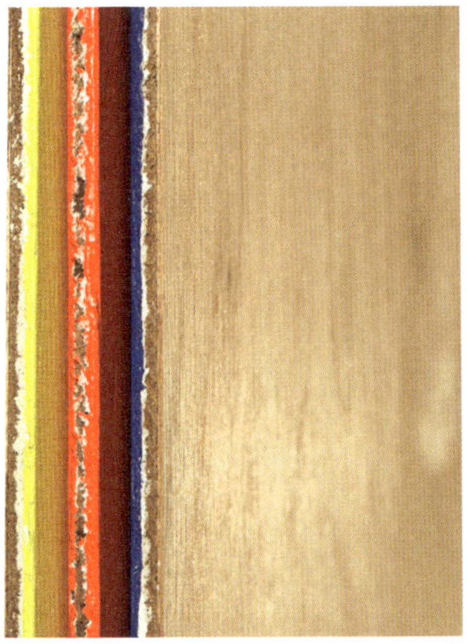

In his "sandwich pictures" dating from the early 1990s and based on the two-layered prototype in horizontal format of 1982, Imi Knoebel returns once again to his ceaseless enquiry into the value of pictures as pictures, and their form of presentation. His choice of raw plywood indicates that their value does not lie in the specific quality of the material. Nor does it lie in what we see on the support, since the front of the three loosely layered plywood panels, attached at the corners, shows nothing but the wood itself. Moreover, the work is not about the presentation of plywood as plywood, although the grain is no doubt pleasing to the eye, as demonstrated by a look at the edges of the panels, which reveals they have been painted: blue on the back of the front panel, red on the front and back of the panel in the middle, and yellow on the front of the panel at the back. Although these layers of paint, primed in white, completely coat their respective supports, they are all three covered up, so that the work loses its conventional character as a picture, that is, as visible material on a surface, even if monochromatic. Knoebel's paint faces inwards; it is invisible and is thus not only liberated from its conventional pictorial and representative function; it also escapes the visual appropriation of the viewer. The picture confronts us as a non-picture, or, to put it differently, as an optical zone of rest. That said, however, the implied critique of pictures threatening to flood the world cannot be formulated without a picture.

The colour combination of yellow, red and blue, Knoebel's palette since the end of the 1970s, has played a crucial role in painting from the early seventeenth century to the present day. Writers from François d'Aguilon (1613) to Johannes Itten (1961) have theorised on the so-called trio of primary colours, while artists from Peter Paul Rubens to Barnett Newman have explored them in practice. Knoebel's "sandwich pictures" elude complete visibility; we are offered the liberating freedom of meditating on picture and colour in theory and practice.

UW

Imi Knoebel
Odyshape C4
1995

Imi Knoebel
1940 Dessau

Acrylic on aluminium
Signed and dated verso: imi 95
121.3 × 121 × 13.7 cm

Inv. no. P216M / Acquired 2010

Imi Knoebel's playful, experimental approach to material, form and colour led in the early 1990s to his first aluminium reliefs, based on meticulous designs made out of coloured strips of paper and then transferred to the new material. As in the prototypes, Knoebel coated every element of the actual relief with a colour of its own. In the case of *Odyshape C4*, a square panel or plane in luminous yellow (90 × 90 cm) dominates the whole and forms the top level of the relief. Behind it, six layers of white, yellow, red and blue slats or strips can be seen protruding every which way since they are slightly longer (100 cm) than the uppermost panel. The light-reflecting aluminium heightens the intensity of the pure, unmixed layers of paint, both translucent washes and solid coats, in which traces of the paintbrush and thus the artist's hand are clearly visible.

Red, yellow and blue – established both theoretically and practically as primary colours in the early Baroque – have featured in Knoebel's work since the end of the 1970s. In combination with white, they evoke the work of Piet Mondrian, to whom Knoebel has often made appreciative reference (e.g., *Für Piet, Kasimir und Carmen*, 1981, and *Little Piet*, 1993). Mondrian's rigorous compositions of horizontals and verticals that even dominate his late work in New York (1940–1944), although now without the black dividing lines, have given way in Knoebel's painting to a constructive but less rigid arrangement of pictorial elements. The contemporary artist's perfectly level yellow square is thus pitted against a disorderly placement of diagonal slats protruding from underneath and playfully subverting the sublime substance of the self-contained geometrical shape which has been brought to bear with such gravity since the early twentieth century, not least because of Kazimir Malevich.

The title *Odyshape*, a play on body shape and odyssey, is identical to that of the album released in June 1981 by the British all-female band The Raincoats, the recording of which was photographed by the artist's wife, Carmen Knoebel. In the titles of his works, in particular the aluminium pictures, Knoebel has repeatedly referenced music, sound and rhythm.

UW

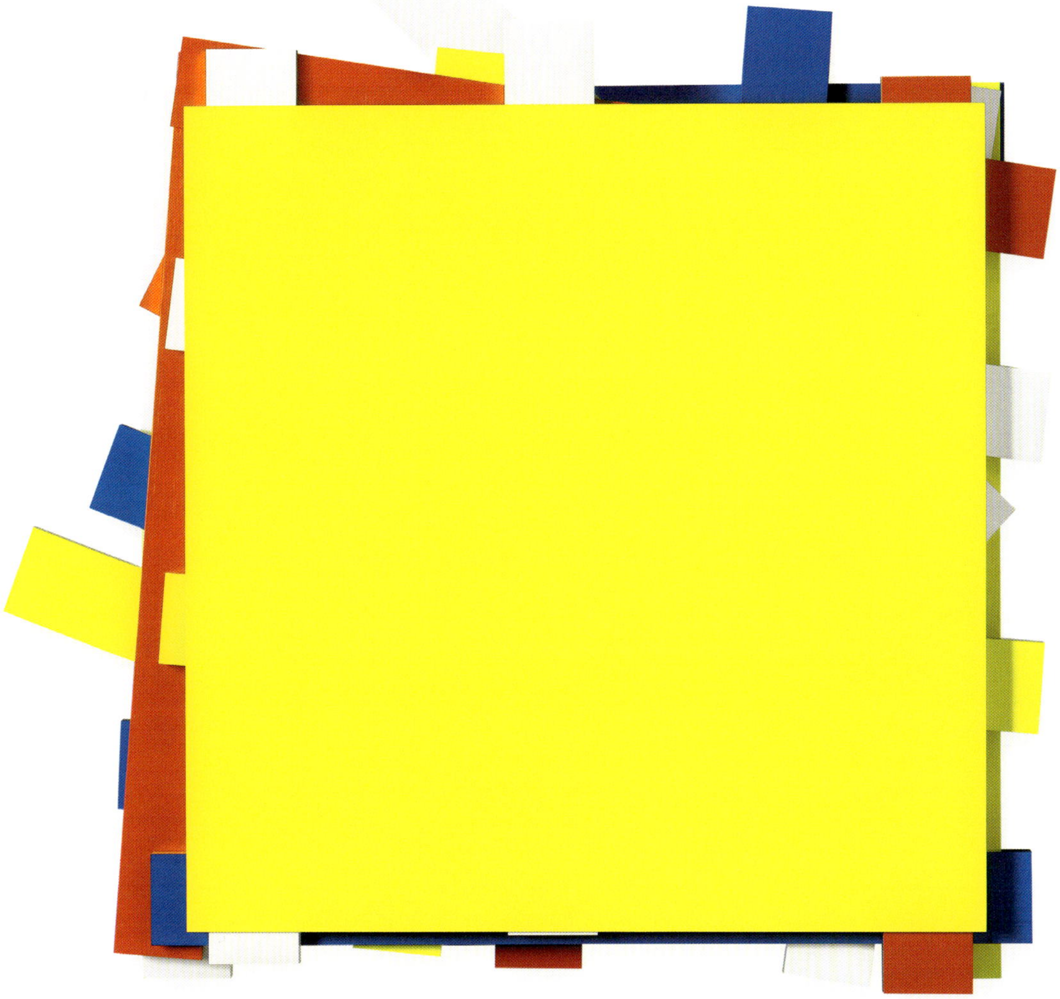

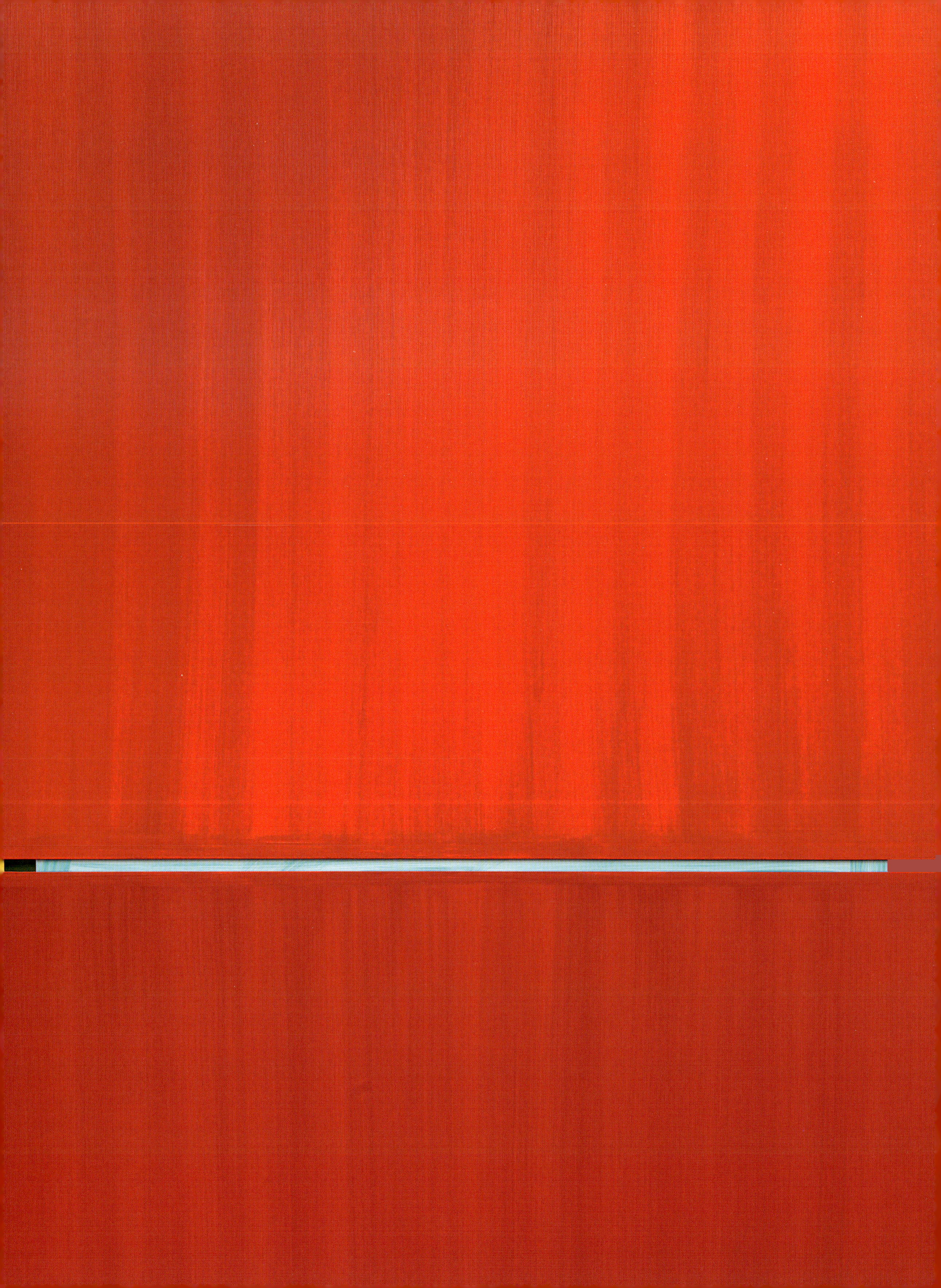

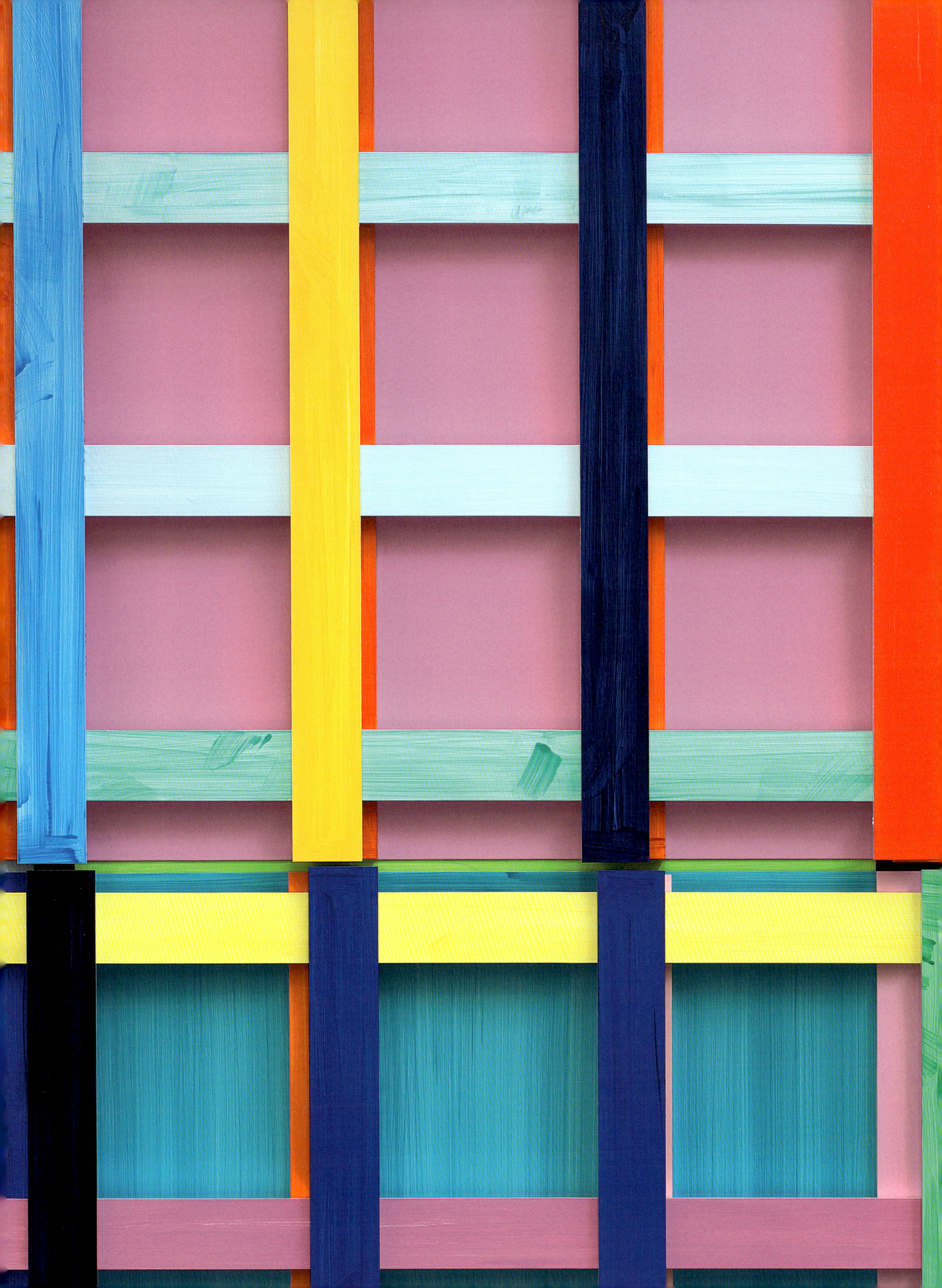

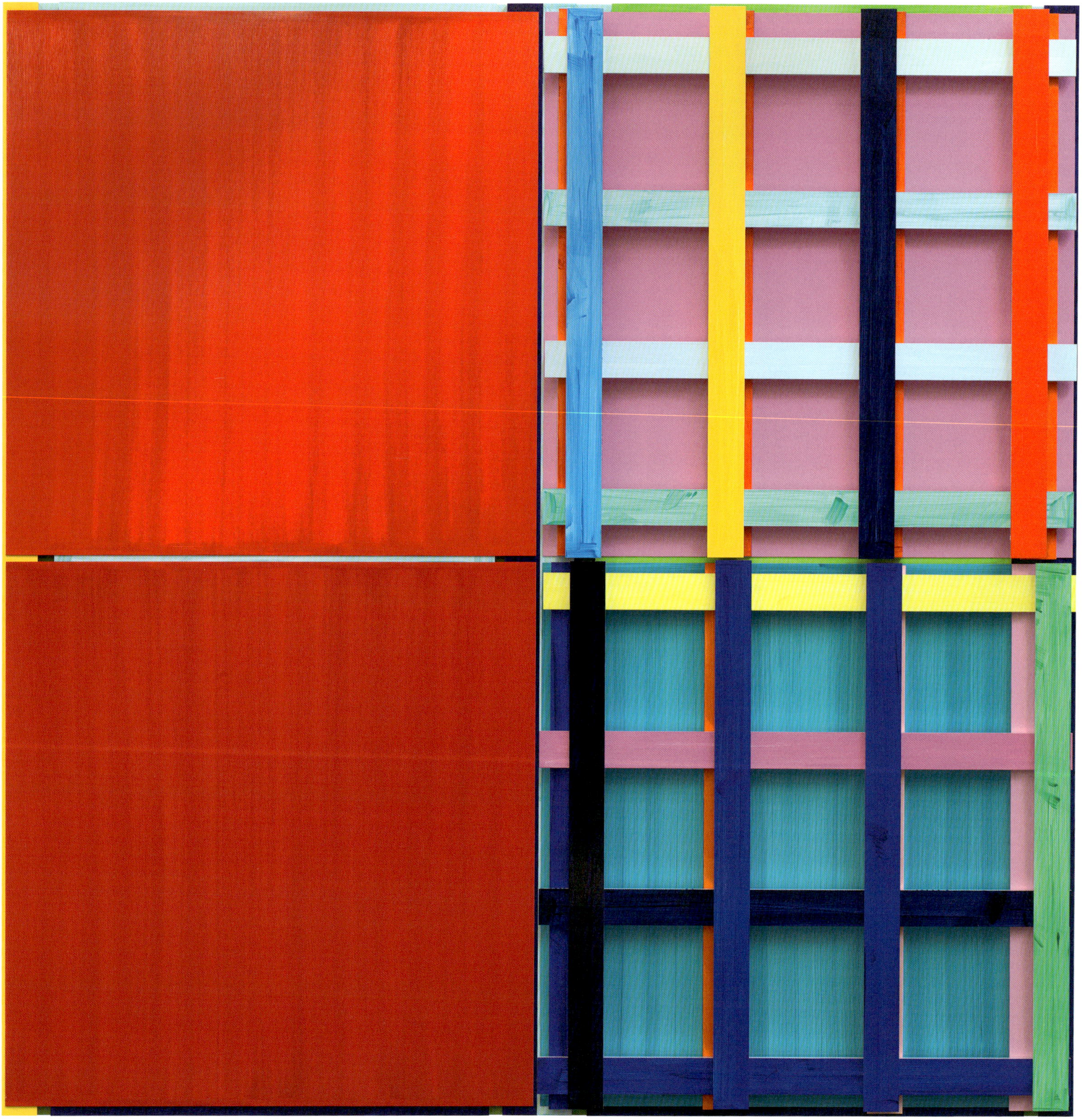

091

Imi Knoebel
1940 Dessau

Acrylic on aluminium
Signed and dated verso: imi 2003
307.5 × 305.1 × 10.8 cm

Inv. no. P108M / Acquired 2003

Imi Knoebel

LILLI

2003

Imi Knoebel
Blaue Schokolade
2004

092

Imi Knoebel
1940 Dessau

Acrylic on aluminium
Signed and dated verso: imi 2004
253 × 222.3 × 7.4 cm

Inv. no. P153M / Acquired 2004

Imi Knoebel's works in aluminium may be strictly orthogonal or an irregular composition of panels and slats, each bearing a single colour, creating the impression respectively of a constructively planned or chaotic and even accidental arrangement. The notion of a picture as an intentionally composed entity may thus be reinforced and undermined. Since the work consists of several superimposed layers, it is also an object, that is, a relief that stands out from the wall to which it is related. Depending on whether the panels (i.e., planes) or slats (i.e., strips) dominate, the work may be perceived primarily as a picture or as a relief.

In *Blaue Schokolade* (Blue Chocolate), Imi Knoebel has placed a strictly parallel arrangement of slats around the margins of the up-ended rectangle of four panels, restricting their visibility to the narrowest of strips not only around the edges but in the joints between them as well. In this work, the uniformly dark-blue panels or planes are clearly dominant, defining the character of the whole and subtly enhanced by the coloured accentuation of the edges. A dark blue is presented to the viewer in painterly luminosity and depth.

UW

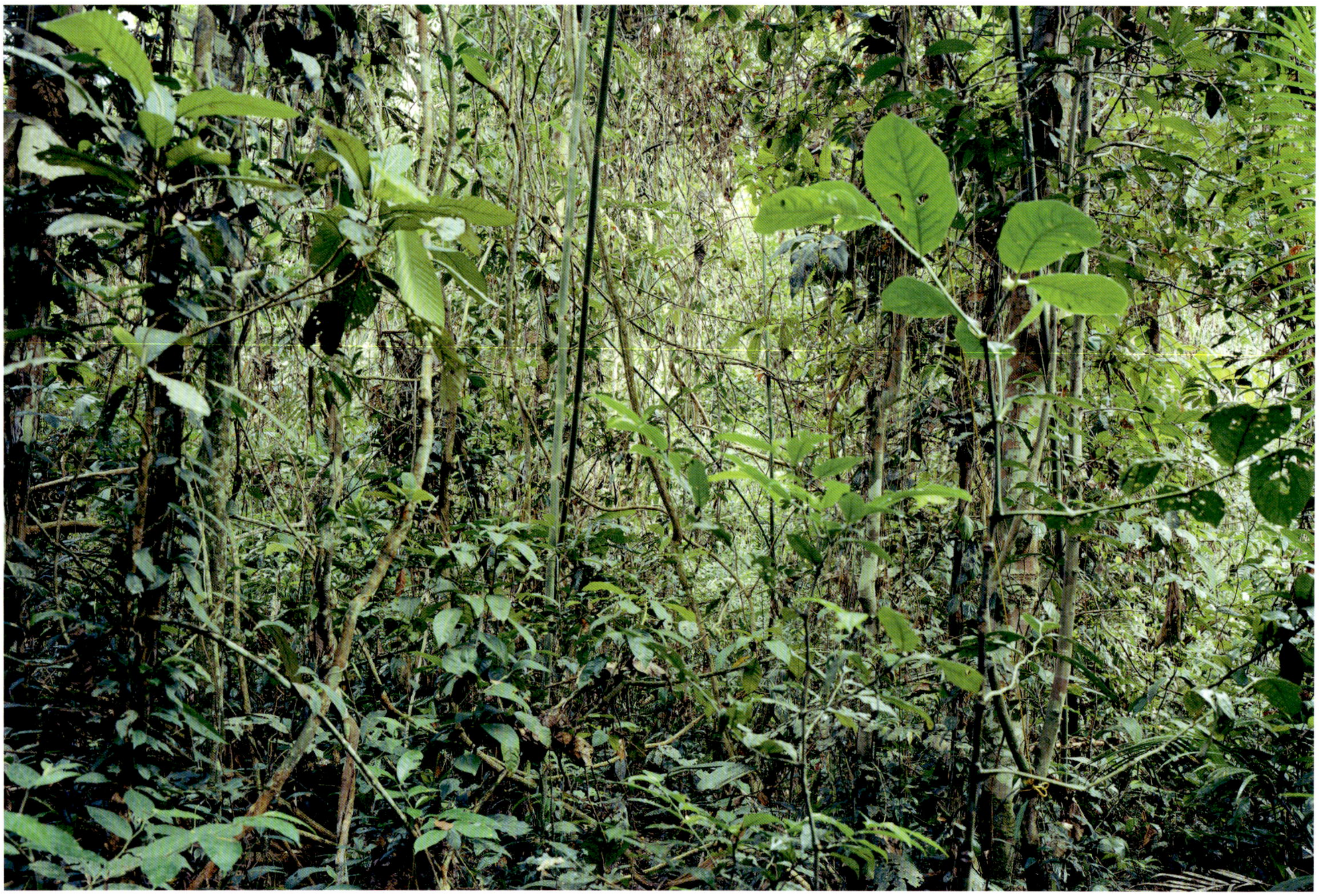

093

Thomas Struth
1954 Geldern

Chromogenic print (9/10)
Titled, dated, numbered and signed verso
Framed 165.7 × 255.4 cm

Inv. no. PH265M / Acquired 2015

Thomas Struth

Paradise 29, Rio Madre de Dios, Peru 2005

2005

Thomas Struth attended the Düsseldorf Academy of Art from 1973 to 1980. Having studied painting with Gerhard Richter until 1976, he decided to switch to the medium of photography and spent the next four years under the tutelage of Bernd Becher. He proved to observe with exacting precision, taking a detached stand even when zeroing in on his subject matter with unmitigated fascination. It is this detachment in conjunction with the unity of place, time and subject matter, as well as the authenticity of representation, that lends his work such compelling truthfulness. Despite the documentary value of Struth's photographs and their unmistakable indebtedness to the oeuvre of Bernd and Hilla Becher, they are not documents but, rather, autonomous works of art.

Struth has divided his photographs into series, with such titles as *Unbewusste Orte* (Unconscious Places), *Familienportraits* (Family Portraits), *Kultstätten* (Sanctuaries), *Museum Photographs* and *New Pictures from Paradise*. On a global scale, he looks closely at streets, squares and buildings, at people, at sacred architecture and museums, at museum visitors or at nature and vegetation. Since about 2007, he has focused increasingly on the complexity of industry, technology and research. The series *New Pictures from Paradise*, begun in 1999, consists of thirty-six large-format photographs. For Struth, this series (see also cat. 94) is not about documenting botanical properties or ecological processes in the primeval forest, or about the dwindling presence of untouched nature. His interest is primarily phenomenological with a focus on the perception of visible reality amid a surfeit of visual information in the form of nonhierarchically organised natural detail.

Paradise 29 was taken at the Rio Madre de Dios, a river that flows through the jungle of Peru and Bolivia. This picture of rampant, indiscriminate vegetation does not focus on the foreground but on the middle ground, where viewers are almost literally drawn into the impenetrable vegetation. Confronted with such overwhelmingly dense growth, we lose our sense of orientation; we are thrown back on ourselves, becoming keenly aware of our physical isolation – an effect that is dramatically heightened upon being completely surrounded by vegetation in a room-sized installation of the kind Struth envisions for the *Paradise* series. As "modern" denizens, the product of a civilisation of our own making, we find ourselves immersed in the atmosphere of a natural environment where we aliens no longer belong.

UW

Thomas Struth
Paradise 30, Rio Madre de Dios, Peru 2005
2005

094

Thomas Struth
1954 Geldern

Chromogenic print (4/10)
Titled, dated, numbered and signed verso
Framed 222 × 280.7 cm

Inv. no. PH296M / Acquired 2016

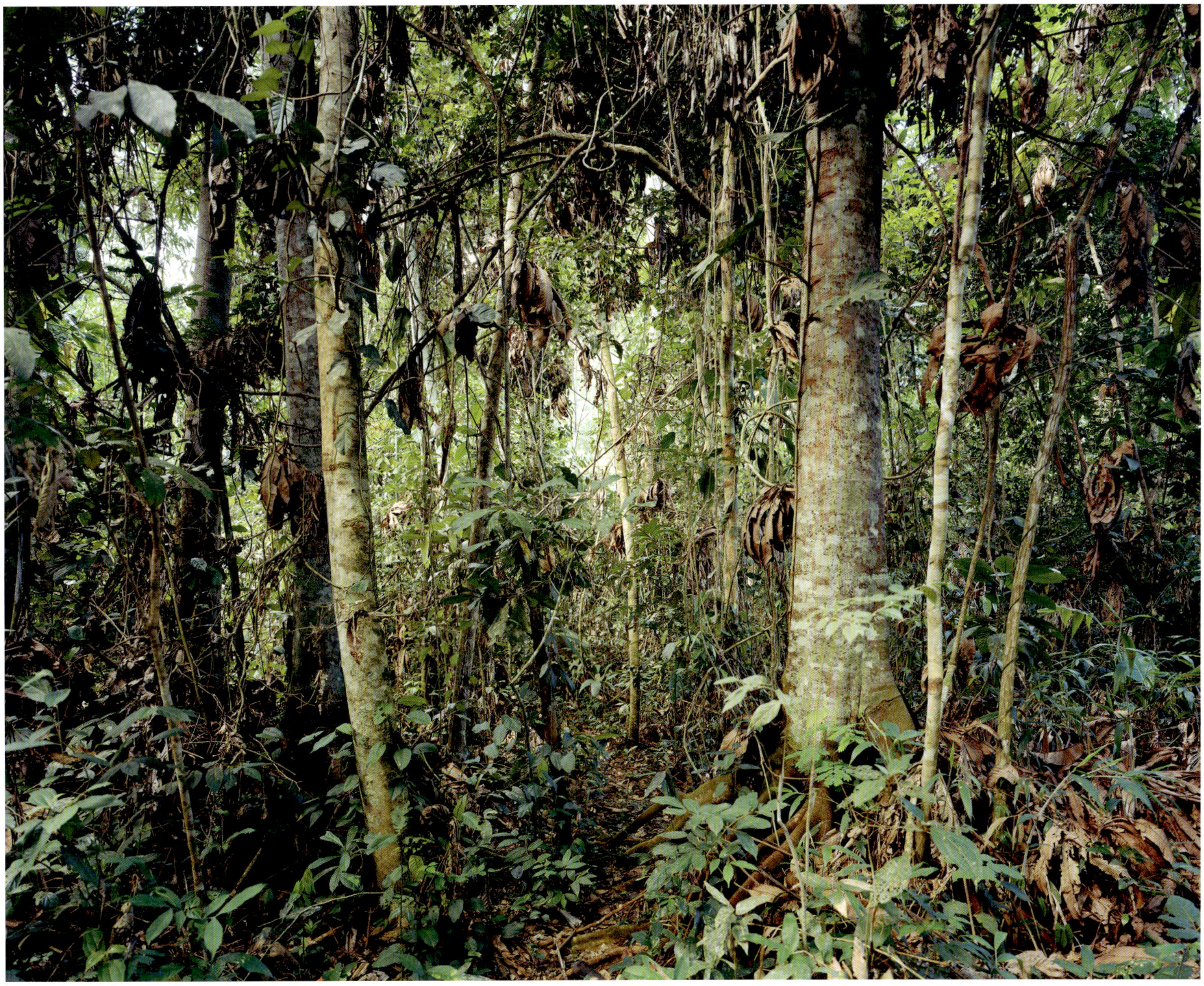

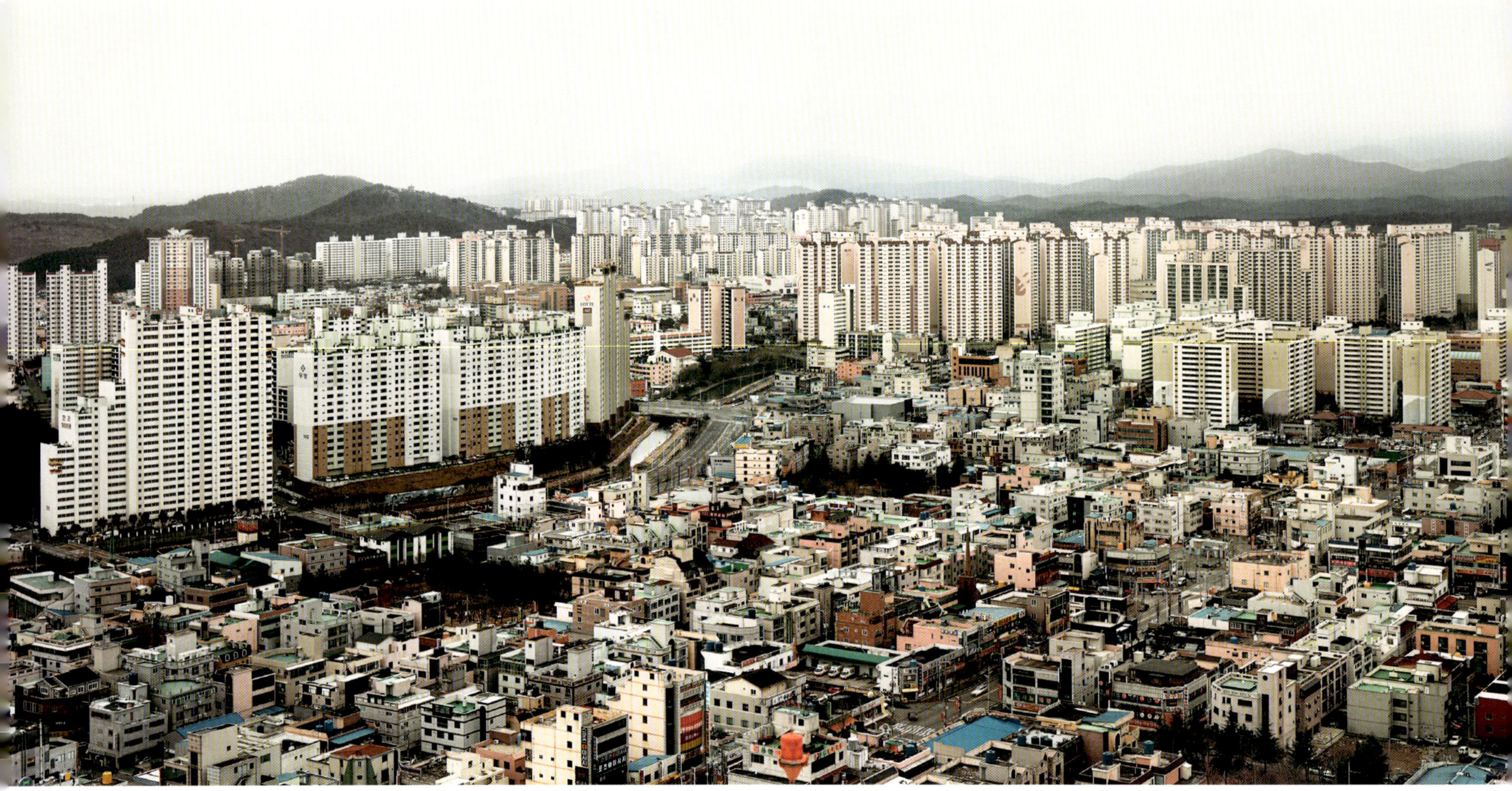

095

Thomas Struth
1954 Geldern

Chromogenic print (2/6)
Titled, dated, numbered and signed verso
Framed 159.5 × 323.7 cm

Inv. no. PH267M / Acquired 2015

Thomas Struth
Ulsan 2, Ulsan 2010
2010

Struth has taken this large, landscape-format photograph of the South Korean city of Ulsan from an elevated vantage point. The picture shows a dense fabric of houses and buildings where several hundred thousand people live and work. They are barely visible and essentially not of interest. The artist focuses primarily on the forms and structures created by human endeavour and bearing witness to the lives people lead. Three quarters of the picture plane, starting at the lower edge, are teeming with buildings. Above the city skyline of Ulsan, showing a uniform phalanx of high-rises, the mountains of the hinterland fade into the haze of the atmosphere beneath grey skies. It is only a matter of time, the picture suggests, until the remaining bits of landscape vanish as well. Referring to modern urban development in his native town of Aix, the French painter Paul Cézanne lamented in the early years of the twentieth century, “There’s this mania to make everything straight and destroy the harmony of the past. ... You have to hurry if you want to see the little that is left.” Modernism, whether in France or in South Korea, has been relentlessly inscribed on the face of the planet. The view of Ulsan clearly illustrates what prompted the Dutch atmospheric chemist Paul J. Crutzen, in the year 2000, to describe our age as the Anthropocene.
UW

Thomas Struth
Hanjin Gamman, Port Busan 2007
2007

096

Thomas Struth
1954 Geldern

Chromogenic print (6/10)
Titled, dated, numbered and signed verso
Framed 172 × 241 cm

Inv. no. PH335M / Acquired 2019

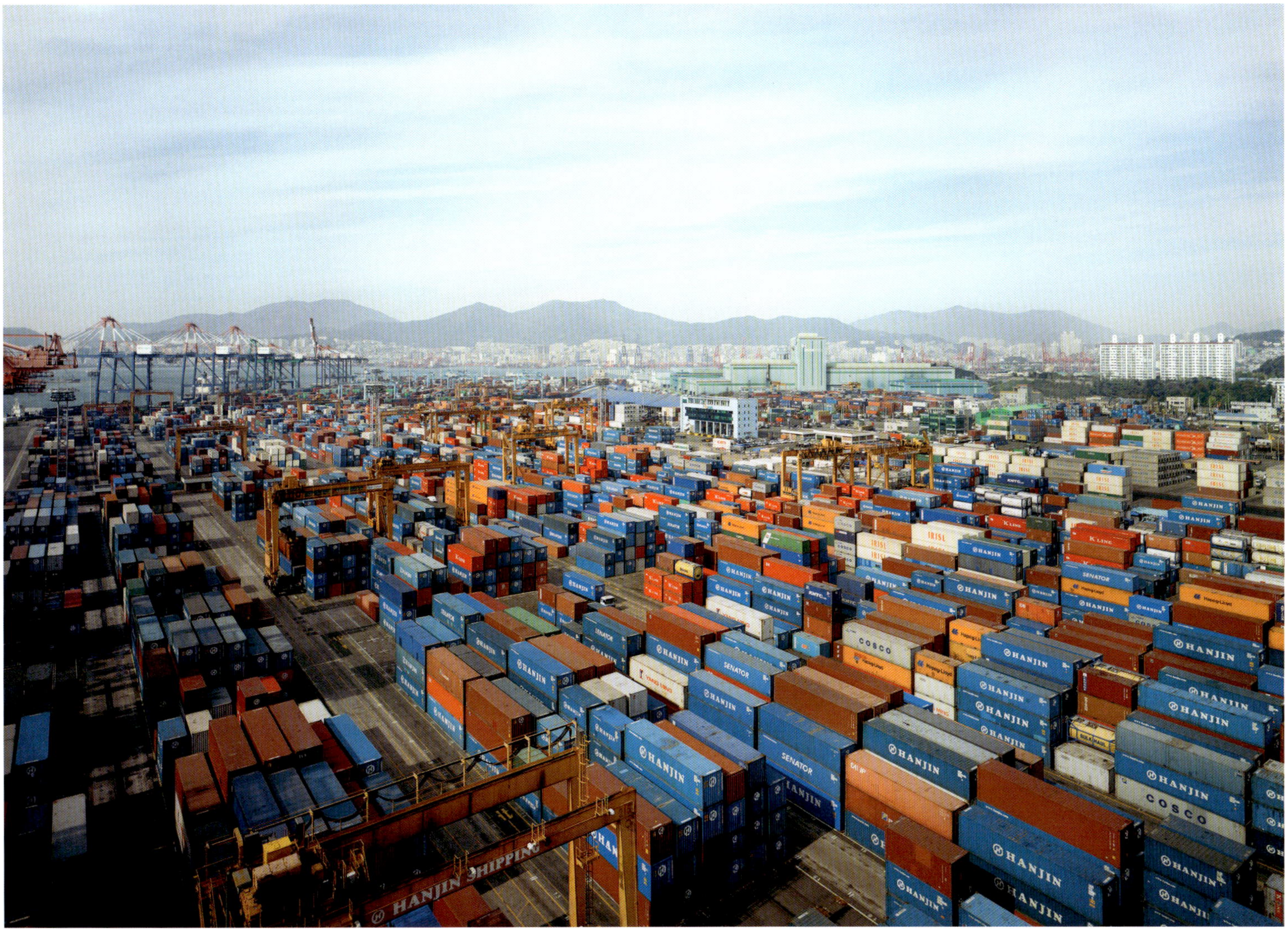
HANJIN SHIPPING
HANJIN
COSCO
SENATOR
IRISL

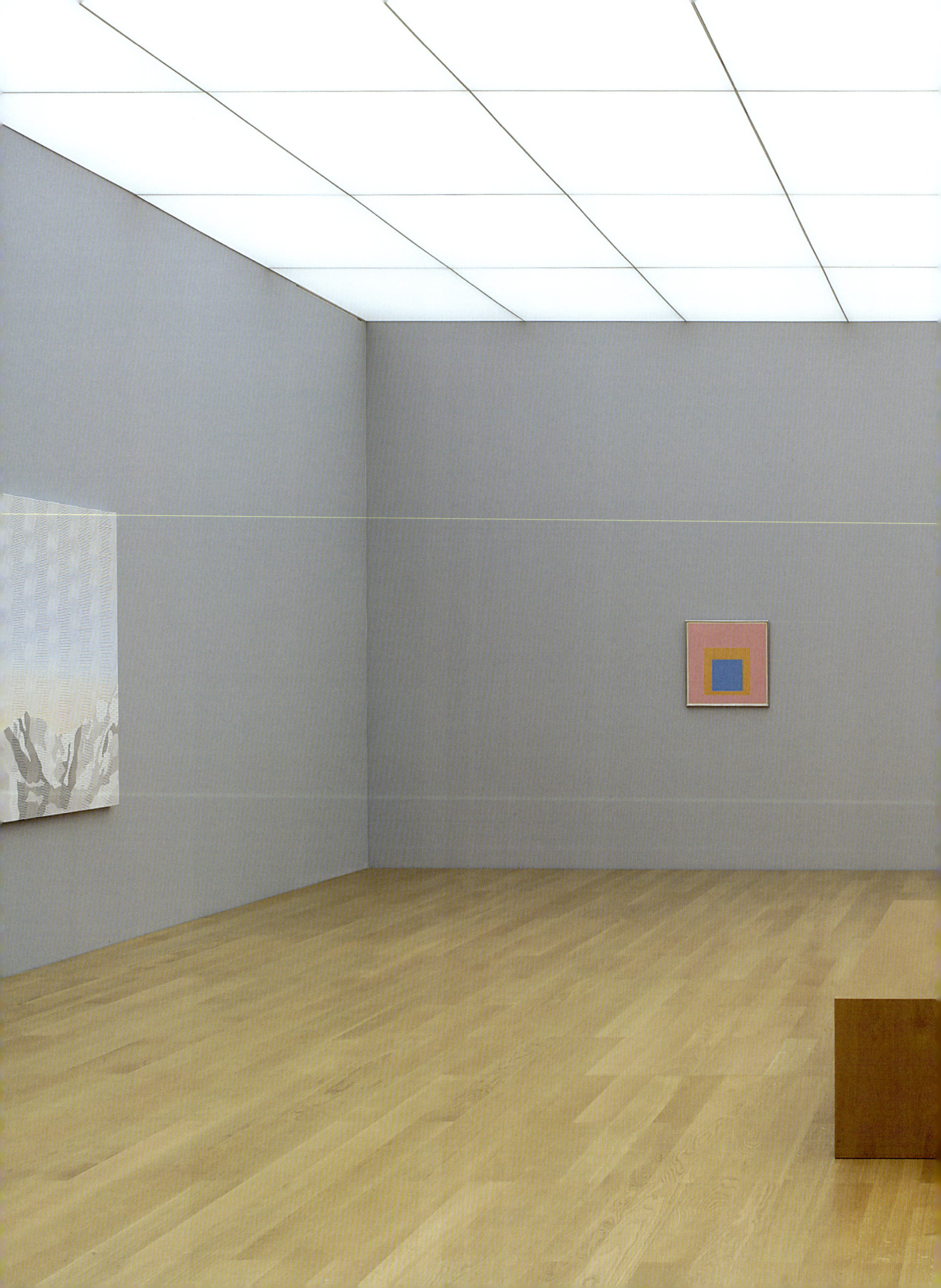

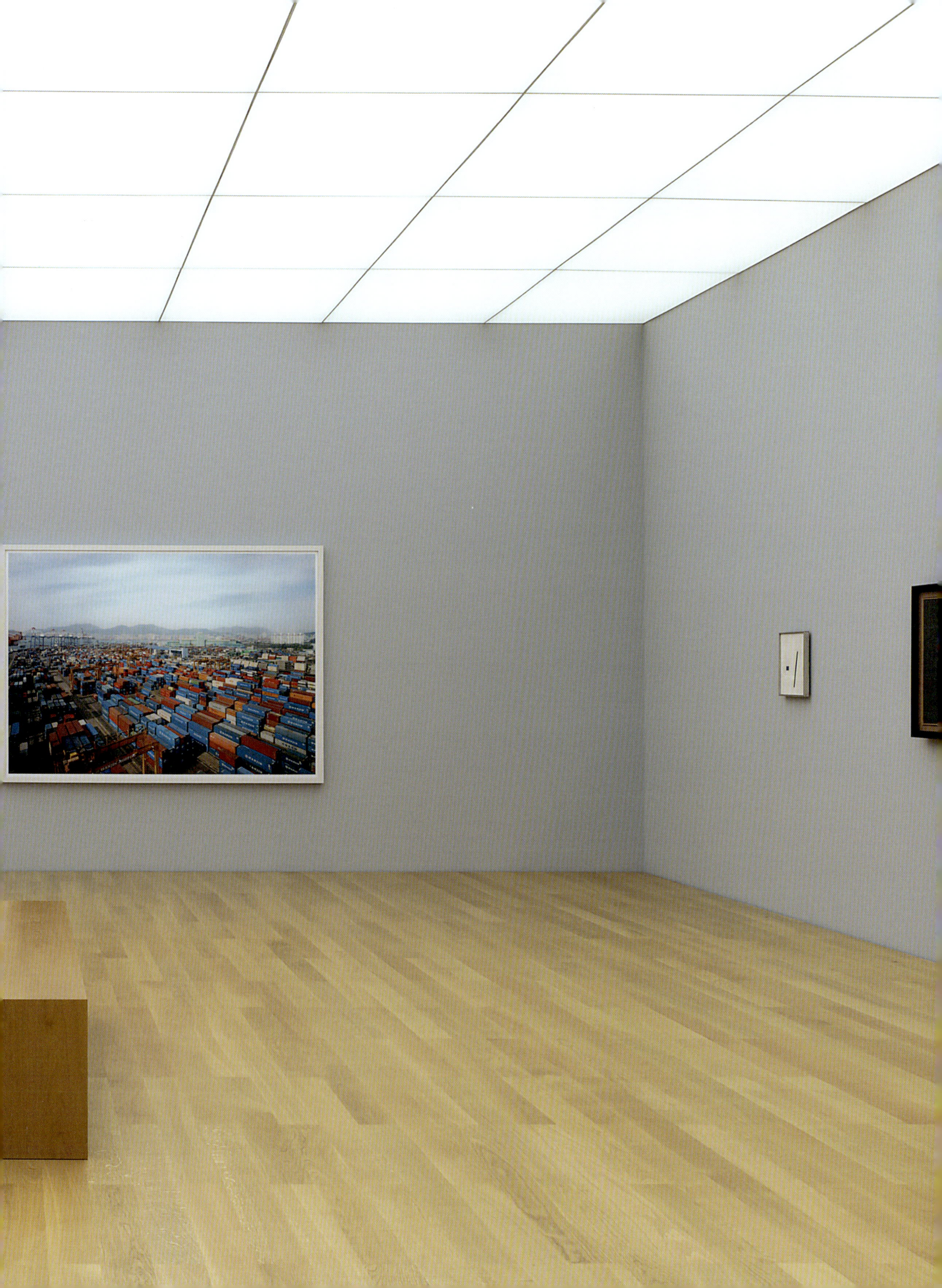

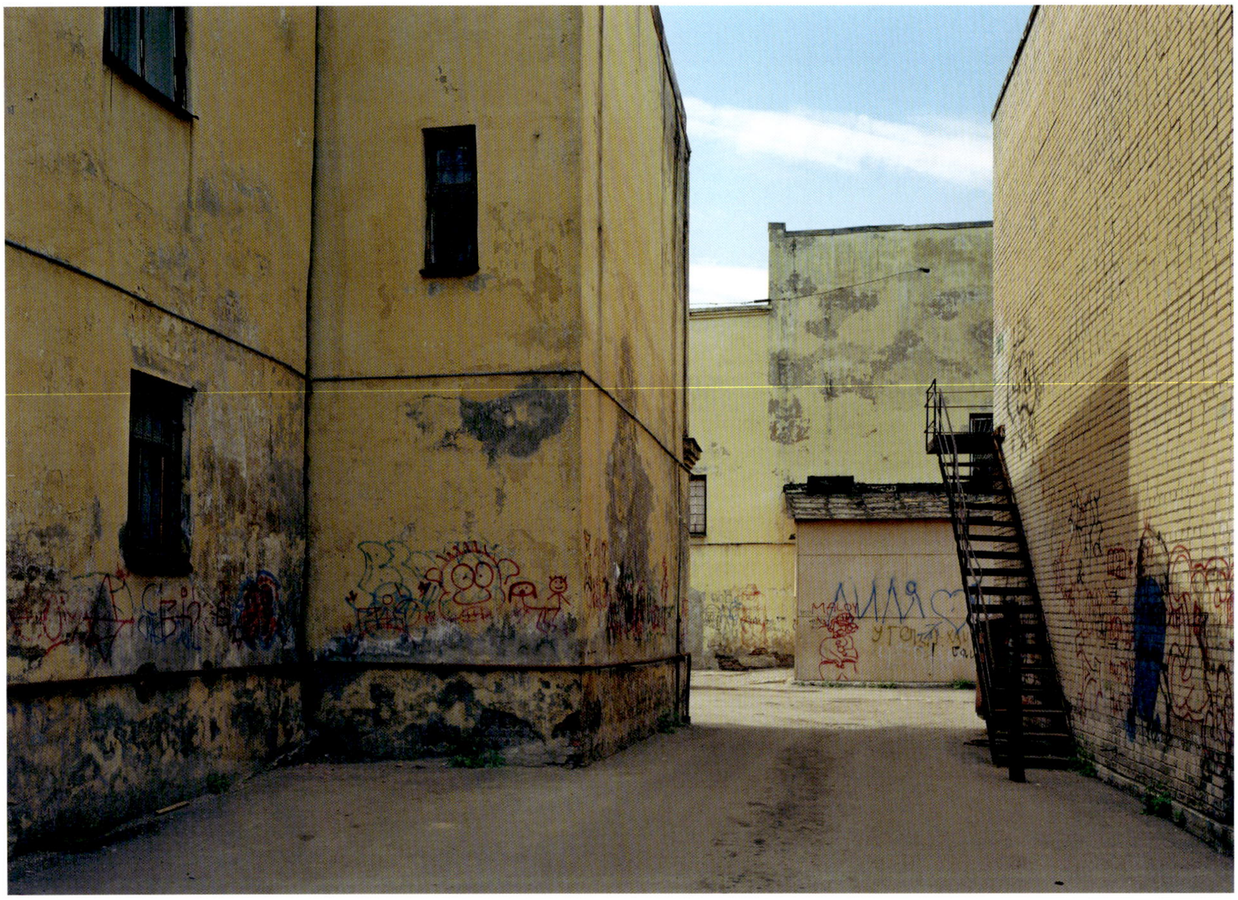

097

Thomas Struth
1954 Geldern

Chromogener Abzug (2/10)
Titled, dated, numbered and signed verso
Framed 145.3 × 204.9 cm

Inv. no. PH299M / Acquired 2016

Thomas Struth

Kovenskij Pereulok, St. Petersburg 2005

2005

Thomas Struth

Blowout Preventer, Mountrail County, North Dakota 2010

2010

Thomas Struth
1954 Geldern

Chromogenic print (6/10)
Titled, dated, numbered and signed verso
Framed 169.5 × 204.7 cm

Inv. no. PH253M / Acquired 2014

In his photographs of technical plants and facilities, Thomas Struth penetrates a field of human endeavour that requires exceptional expertise well beyond the realm of common knowledge. Struth's pictures give us a direct insight into this technology and the bewildering multiplicity of a physiognomy whose appearance is dictated exclusively by function and use. It is an expression of the single-minded pursuit of here-and-now success, in which logic is subject solely to the present moment, showing history, not as a lived experience of timeless value, but as a process of erosion, of outmoded topicality and ultimately of no value at all. Yet, at the same time, it is this logic, aimed exclusively at gratifying everyday needs, and the tools it spawns, that makes technology so fascinating.

The blowout preventer in Struth's photograph is part of a fracking plant in North Dakota, USA. Blowout preventers are designed to prevent the uncontrolled release of oil or gas from a well. If the device fails, as it did on the offshore drilling rig Deepwater Horizon in the Gulf of Mexico on 20 April 2010, the resulting blowout can lead to catastrophic environmental damage. The use of fracking to extract gas and oil in the first decade of the twenty-first century has made the United States largely independent of the OPEC countries in the Near and Middle East and, according to the Energy Information Administration (2013), the world's largest producer of crude oil.

Both the colours and composition in Struth's photograph of the blowout preventer are extremely appealing, but their aesthetic cannot gloss over the knowledge of the device's physical and technical fragility. Behind it looms a second, almost symbolic image of humankind, unscrupulously exploiting natural resources, guzzling energy and ceaselessly pursuing the necessary means to do so.
UW

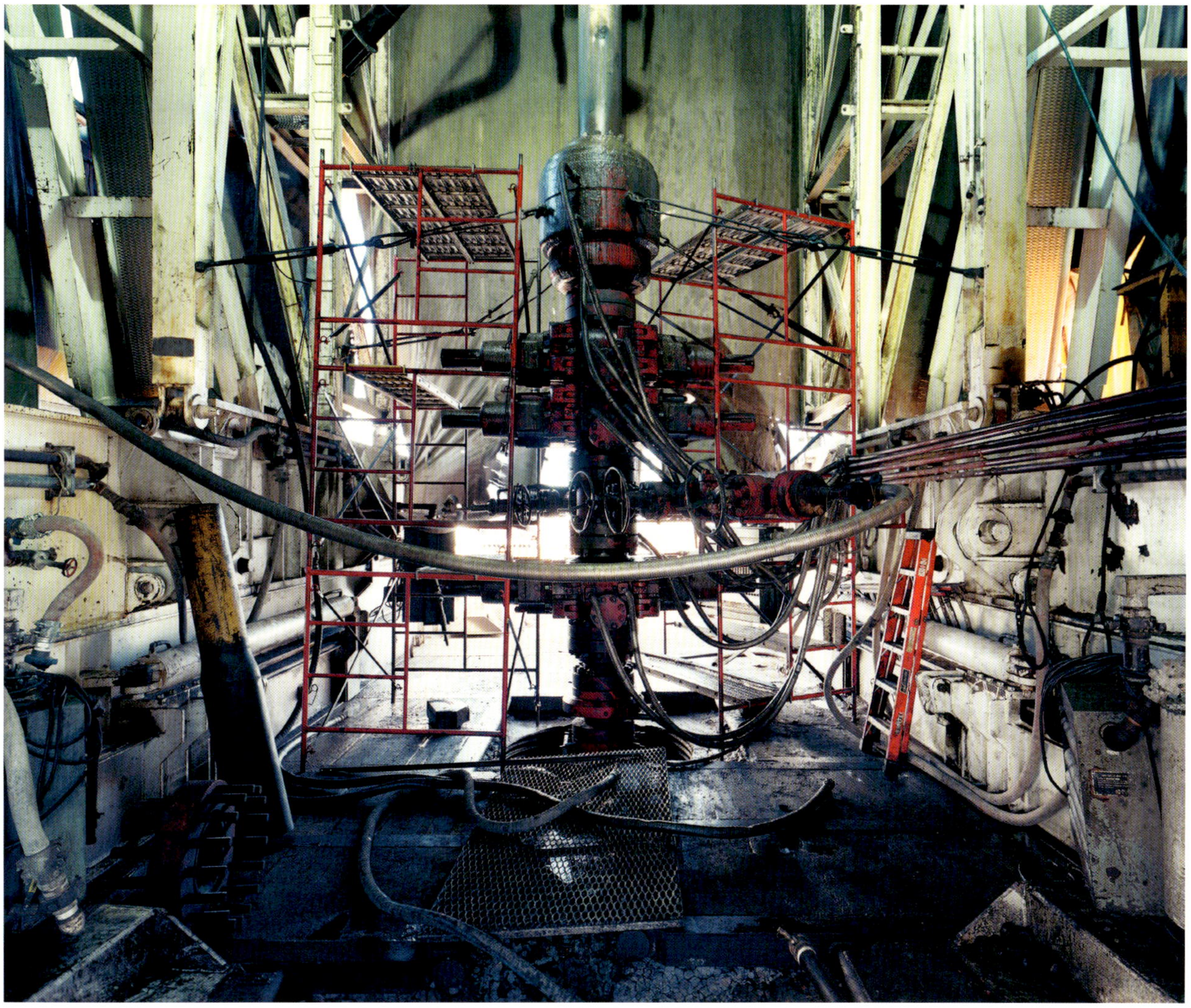

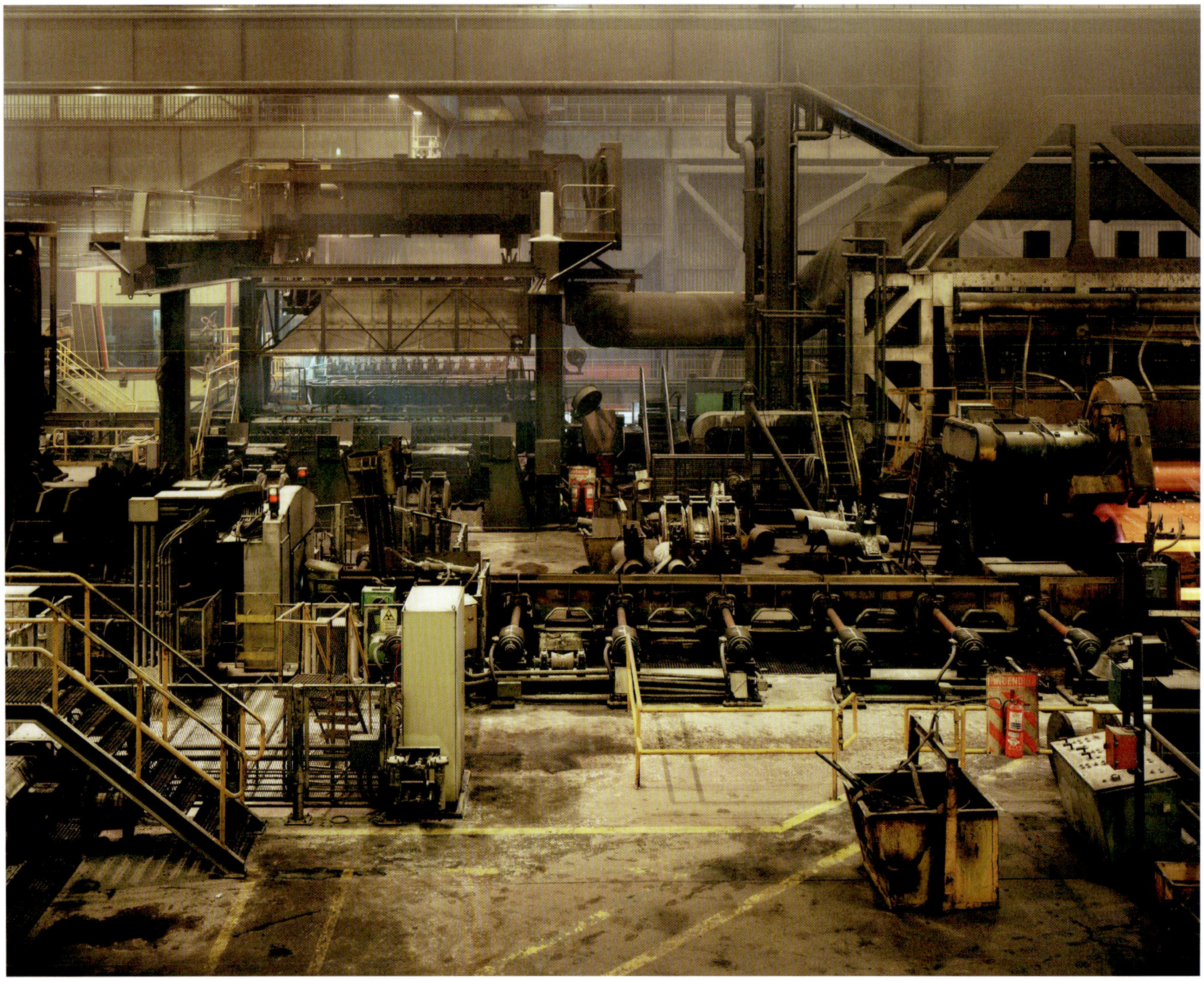

099

Thomas Struth
1954 Geldern

Chromogenic print (6/10)
Titled, dated, numbered and signed verso
Framed 172.2 × 215.6 cm

Inv. no. PH334M / Acquired 2019

Thomas Struth

Seamless Tube Production, Buenos Aires 2009

2009

Thomas Struth
Museo del Prado 2, Madrid 2005
2005

Thomas Struth
1954 Geldern

Chromogenic print (5/10)
Titled, dated, numbered and signed verso
Framed 180 × 214 cm

Inv. no. PH297M / Acquired 2016

This photograph, part of the *Museo del Prado* series begun in 2005, shows two visitors to the Prado in Madrid. Founded in 1819 as the Royal Museum of Painting and Sculpture, the museum is renowned for its world-class art of European origin. The two young women seen in profile are gazing in concentration at a painting out of frame. They are unknown tourists but clearly from East Asia, dressed in casual Western wear and carrying whatever they deem necessary for a tour of the city and the museum. The woman standing at the central axis of the picture is holding an audio guide, an almost indispensable item for contemporary museum visitors. Although barely visible, it marks the exact intersection of the lines between the corner of the room and the wall panelling. At the same time, it marks the point of maximum focus, so that the lettering on the technical device becomes legible: MUSEO NACIONAL DEL PRADO.

Behind the women we see two paintings by the Spanish artist Diego Velázquez (1599–1660), showing full-length portraits of dignified grandeur, to the left the Greek fabulist Aesop (probably sixth century BC), of whom no actual likeness survives, and to the right King Philip IV of Spain (1605–1665) from the house of Habsburg, who had appointed Velázquez his court painter. The attire and attributes of the two figures reflect their social and intellectual standing. The hoary, melancholy poet is portrayed with threadbare cloak and book; the young king is shown in dashing hunting garb with gun. Struth set up his camera in advance, pointing the lens at these two paintings and the corner of the room, which is accentuated by a motion detector. The two young women enter the frame by chance and take no notice of the camera. Unwittingly, they inspire the artist to release the shutter at the decisive moment. The simultaneous observation of individuals from such widely divergent places and times in Struth's photograph invites anthropological reflection on cultural differences and global mobility.

UW

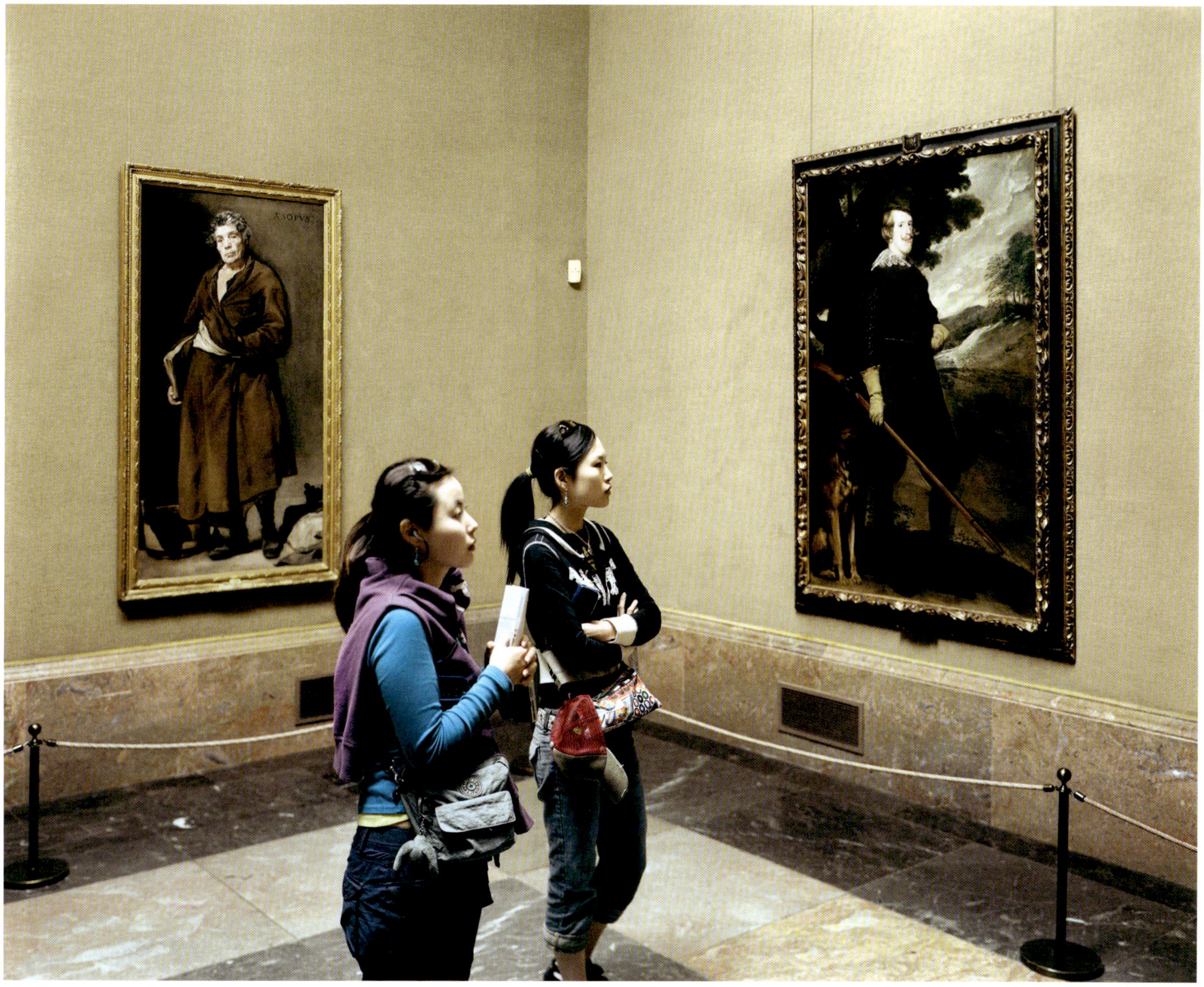

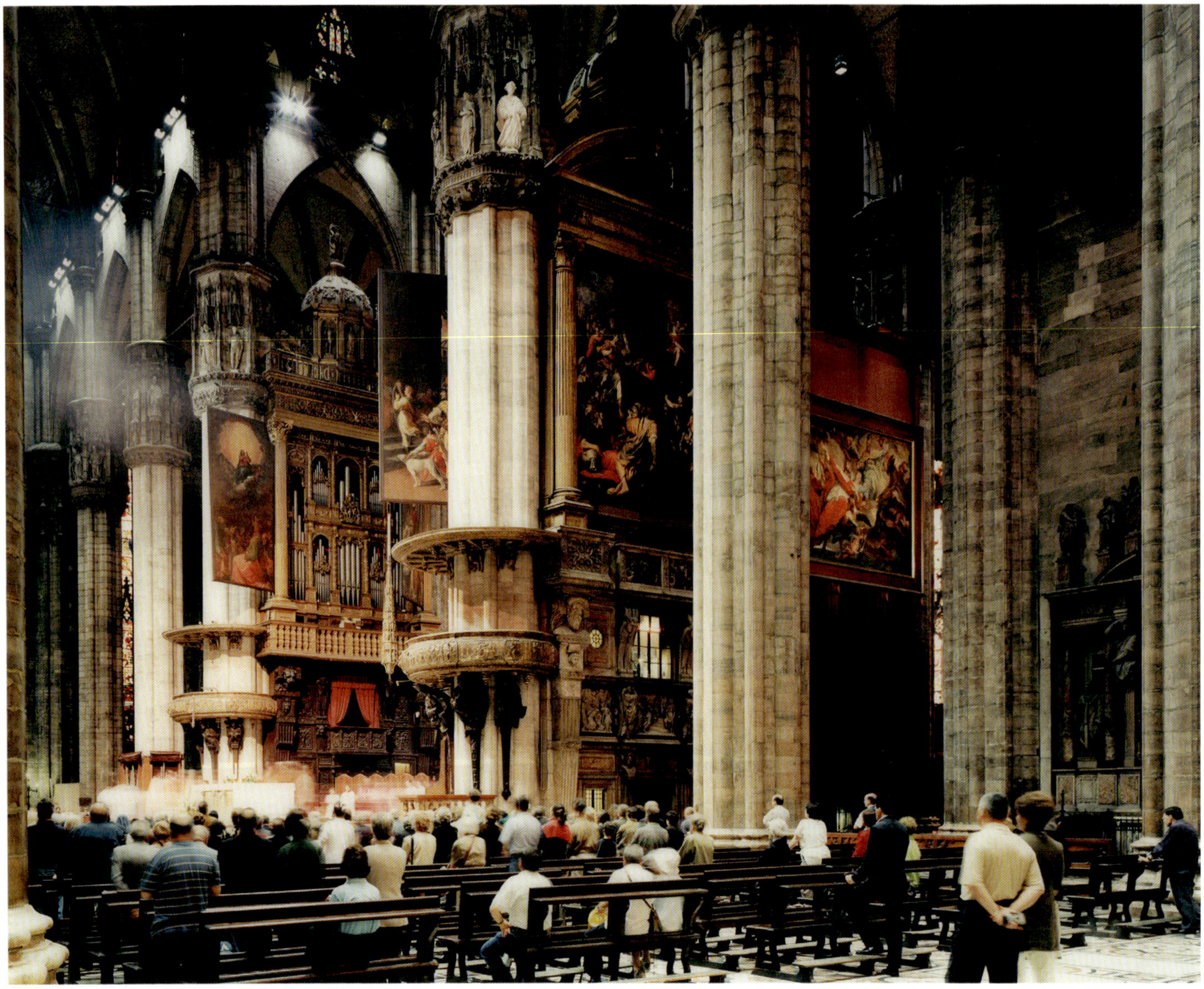

101

Thomas Struth
Mailänder Dom (innen), Mailand 1998
1998

Thomas Struth
1954 Geldern

Chromogenic print (7/10)
Titled, dated, numbered and signed verso
Framed 178.8 × 224.2 cm

Inv. no. PH332M / Acquired 2019

While the Prado Museum (cat. 100) is a secular structure housing art that has been divorced from its original context, the Milan Cathedral, one of the most magnificent examples of Gothic architecture in Europe, contains a host of altars and tombstones, of paintings and sculptures, commissioned and created specifically for the location, as seen in Thomas Struth's photograph. Although they do not all date from the same period as the cathedral, whose foundation stone was laid by Gian Galeazzo Visconti, the Duke of Milan, in 1386, they have always, since their creation, served the purpose of directing the thoughts and attention of the faithful to the mysteries of the Christian faith and the legends of the saints.

For this interior view of the cathedral, Struth has not photographed the longitudinal axis of the nave in symmetrical vanishing point perspective but, rather, an asymmetrical view from the southern transept to the left into the northern transept and past the four crossing piers flanking the choir with canopied pulpits. The brightly illuminated altar is seen in the crossing itself but only upon closer study do we distinguish the blurred outlines of several priests celebrating Mass. The faithful are sitting or kneeling in quiet devotion in the pews facing this altar. There may also be tourists among them, a permanent fixture nowadays in monuments of such significance. Here, everyone bows to the hierarchical order that has prevailed for millennia, going back in Milan to the very beginnings of Christianity and the Catholic Church under Milan's first bishop and later church father, Ambrosius († 397). In contrast, Struth's seemingly casual vantage point inside the cathedral circumvents the hierarchical order of the Catholic liturgy and draws attention to the art, to the truly marvellous unity of architecture, sculpture and painting that still prevails in this place.
UW

Thomas Struth
Kölner Dom, Köln 2007
2007

Thomas Struth
1954 Geldern

Chromogenic print (7/10)
Titled, dated, numbered and signed verso
Framed 209 × 168 cm

Inv. no. PH266M / Acquired 2015

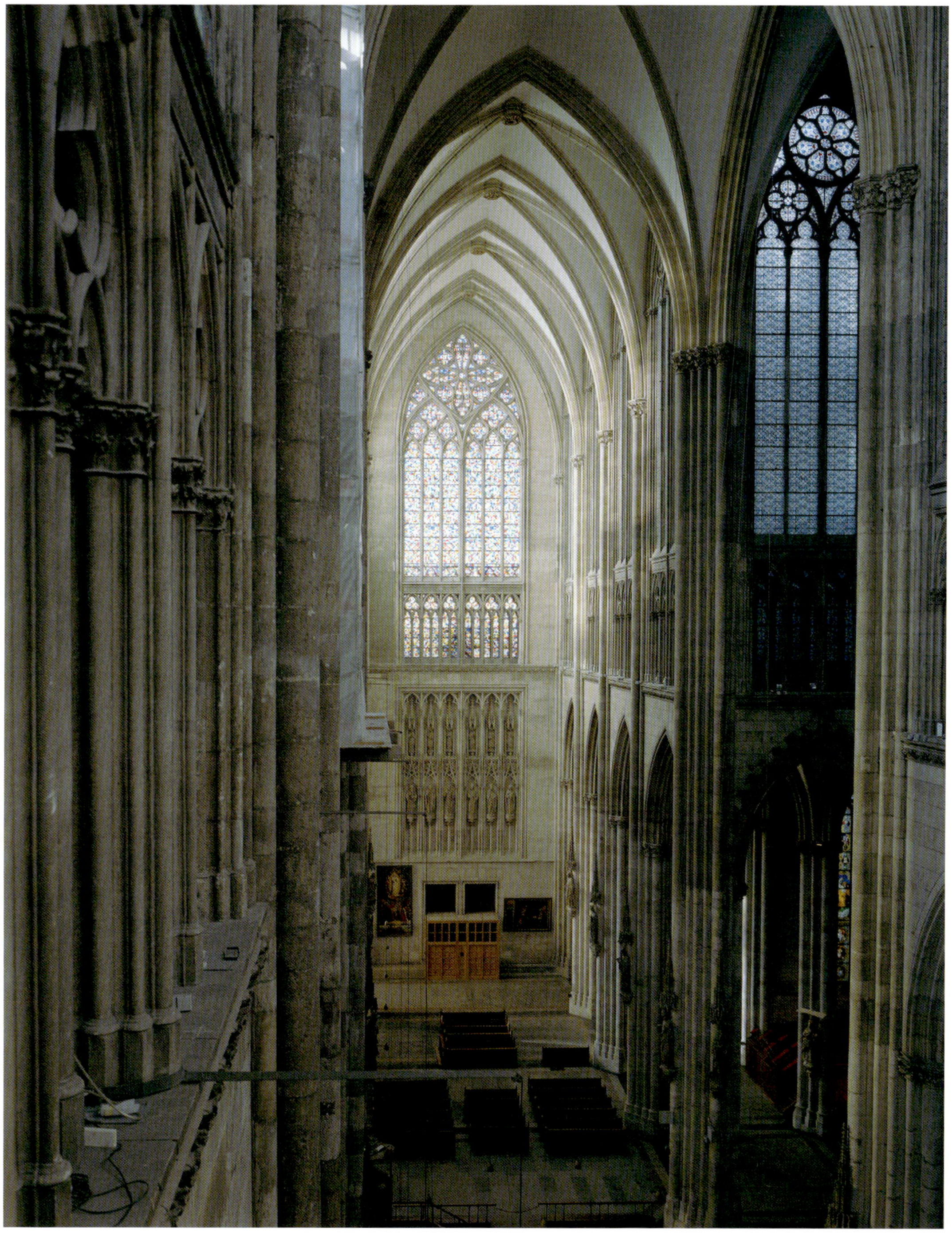

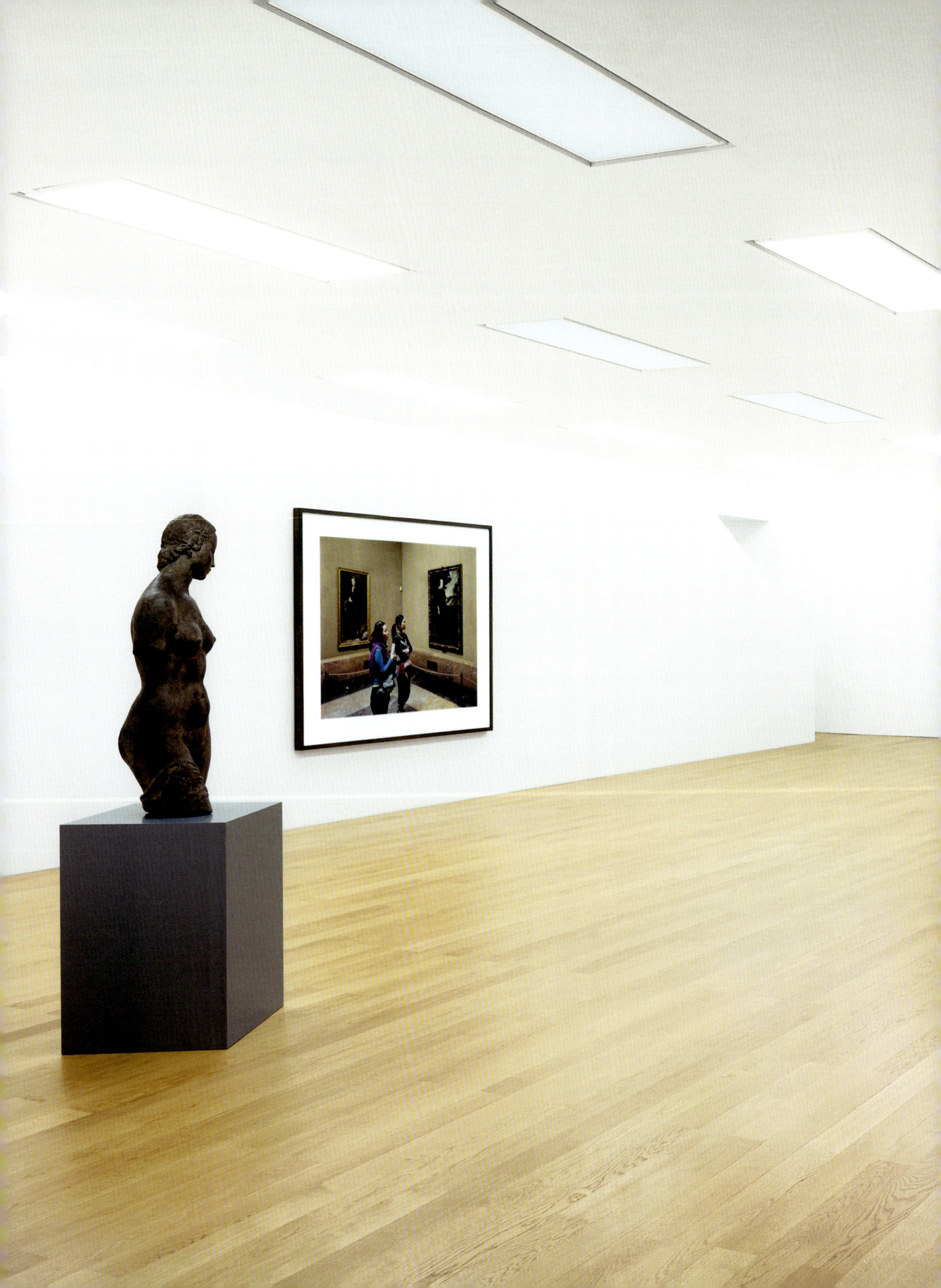

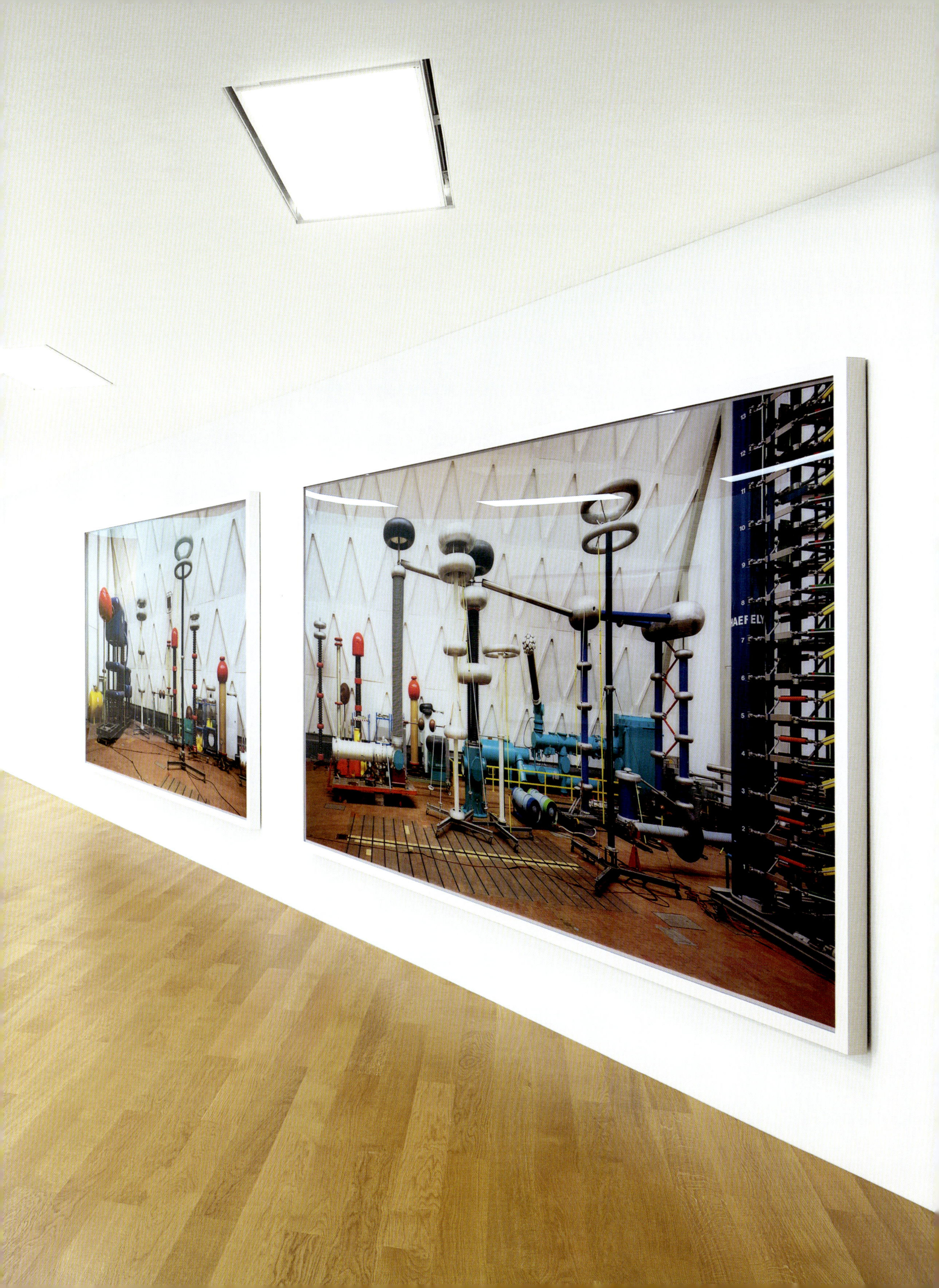

Works after 1990

Willi Kopf
Random Raster 2
1986

Willi Kopf
1949 Röthis / Austria

Particleboard
Signed and dated verso: Willi Kopf / 1986
63.5 × 63.9 × 8 cm

Inv. no. S204M / Acquired 2009

After training in the building of altars and attending a school of arts and crafts, Willi Kopf studied with the sculptor Fritz Wotruba at the Academy of Fine Arts in Vienna from 1970 to 1976. His interest in Cubism, Constructivism and Minimalism led, as of 1985, to his characteristic wall and floor sculptures out of particleboard, such as *Random Raster 2* of 1986 and *Red Square* of 2003 (cat. 104).

At first sight, these works would seem to be industrial products assembled out of the simplest geometric elements, namely, rectangular panels. Closer study reveals that the artist's handcrafted works are extremely complex objects, both sculptural and pictorial in nature when mounted on the wall. Their construction yields a composition consisting of planes with edges marked in irregular horizontals and verticals, with variations in texture and colour, depending on the qualities of the particleboard.

One cannot get to the bottom of Kopf's Minimalist works of art because, as the artist says, they are too convoluted, too nested, and thus informed with "a certain magical substance". An ambivalent exchange ensues between that sense of mystery and the simplicity of their shape and material. Viewers see themselves facing hermetically closed objects with no personal signature whatsoever. The works seem utterly self-contained in the neutrality of their presence, regardless of whether they are placed on the floor or mounted on the wall. And yet, being both fulfilled and consumed in the very simplicity of that presence, they draw attention to the subtlety of their construction and generate a beauty as understated as it is timeless.

JR

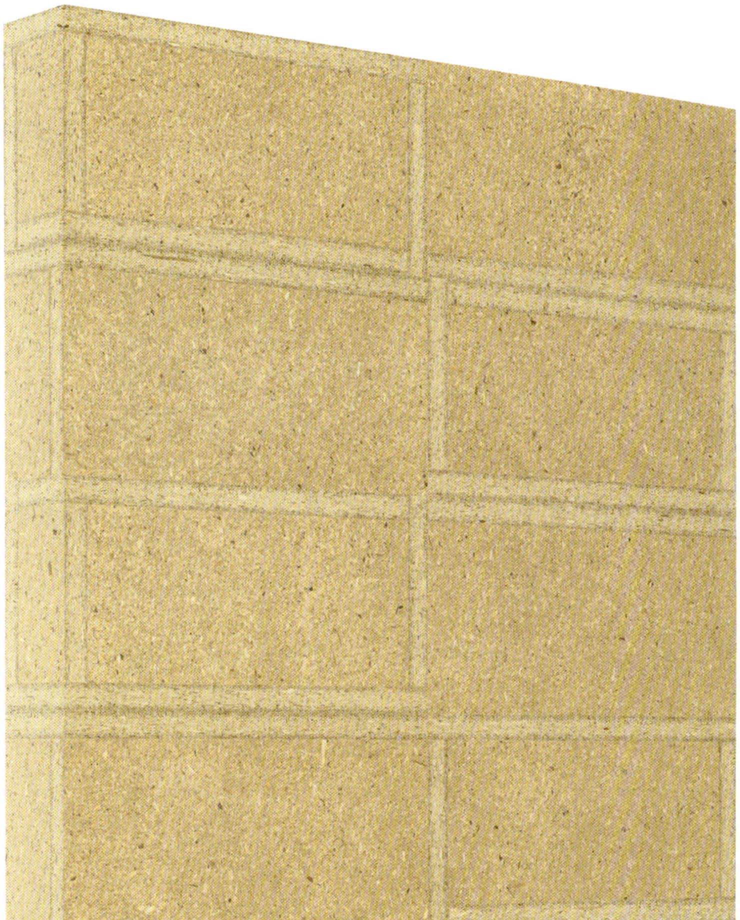

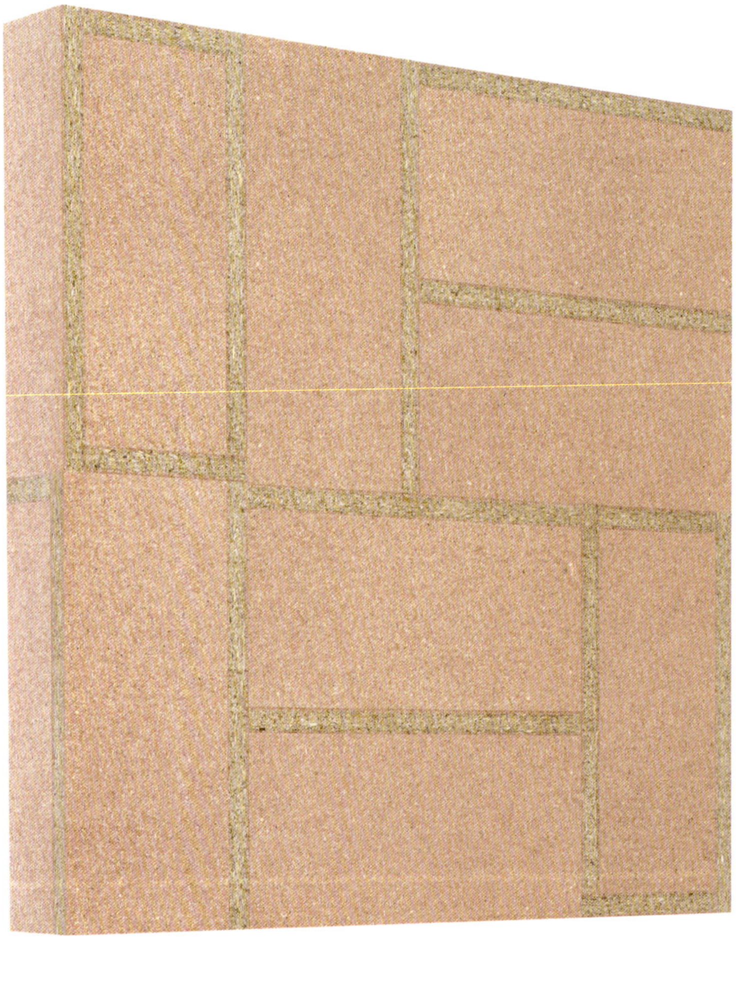

104

Willi Kopf
1949 Röthis / Austria

Plywood
Signed and dated verso: Willi Kopf / 2003
64.1 × 64 × 8 cm

Inv. no. S208M / Acquired 2009

Willi Kopf
Red Square (Wandstück)
2003

Hanna Roeckle
Xoana H, Chikin
2002

Hanna Roeckle
1950 Vaduz

Mixed media on birch
Signed and dated verso: Hanna Roeckle 2002
100 × 260 cm

Inv. no. P103M / Acquired 2003

In her oeuvre, the Liechtenstein artist Hannah Roeckle explores system and order as well as the variable and open boundaries between genres. *Xoana H, Chikin* consists of eighteen panels, all of equal size: they function like a module, which, even when multiplied or rearranged, can always be identified as the basic constituent of the whole. The modules are clearly distinct in colour and structure, echoing the artist's painterly practice of working each panel separately. Her brushstroke is not free and gestural but, rather, calm, serene and in horizontal harmony with the landscape format. *Xoana H, Chikin* can thus be described as a "composite" of eighteen individual works whose arrangement is flexible and variable.

The title comprises two terms from Greek and Mayan respectively: *Xoana* refers to the structure of the painting and *Chikin* to its sensuous quality. The singular Xoanon designates a divine image carved out of wood; Hanna Roeckle has adopted Michel de Certeau's interpretation that the Greeks used it as a portable boundary marker. *Chikin* in Mayan means the west, sunset and night, and is associated with the colour black; the east is associated with red, the north with white and the south with yellow. Accordingly, *Xoana H, Chikin* is a "west picture" based on change and dominated by dark colours, its palette ranging from blue, chestnut brown and purple to black. In between, a luminous yellow, a pale purple and a watery blue render the waning light of evening skies.

Hanna Roeckle invites contemplation for she has found a charmed balance in her paintings between rationalism and sensuality.

UW

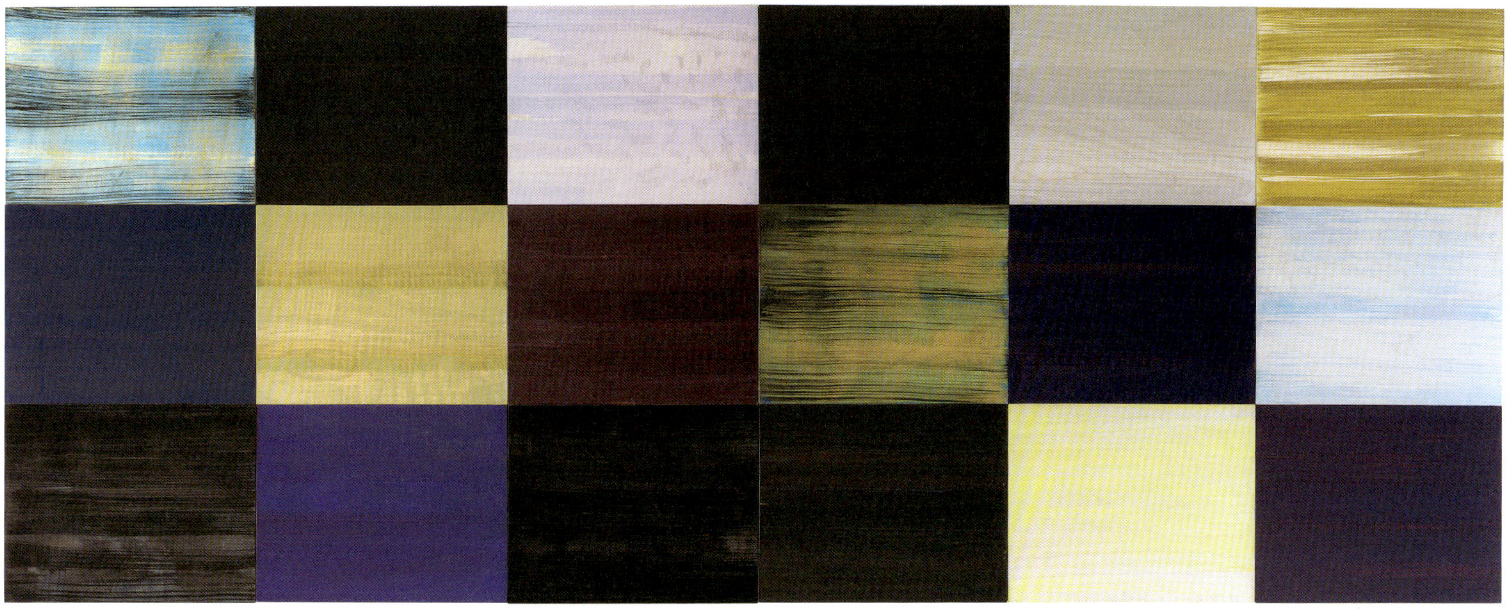

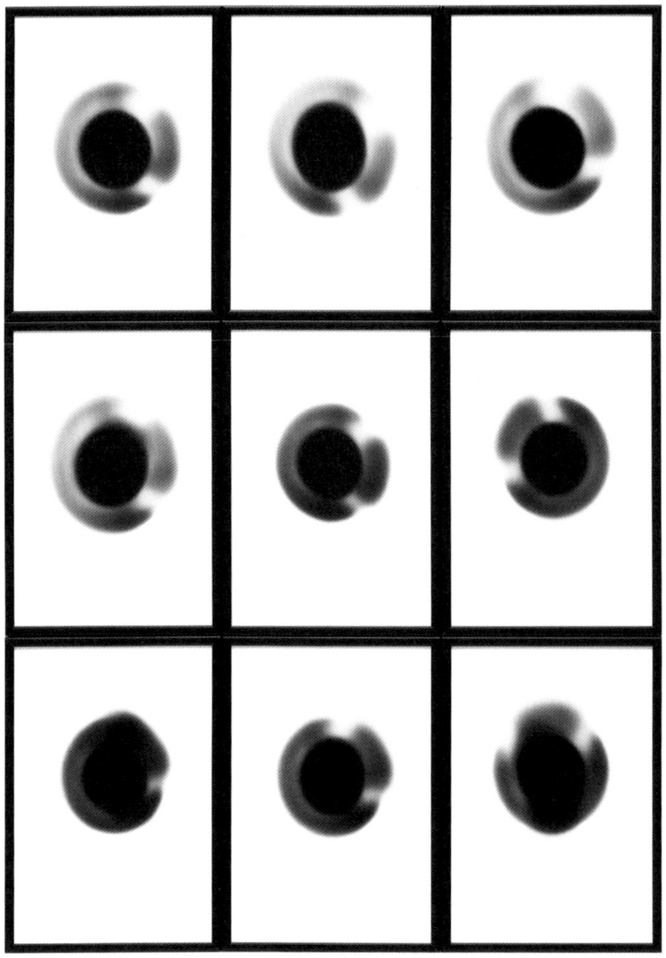

Giovanni Di Stefano
Punti Laser
2002

Giovanni Di Stefano
1958 Rome

Laser beam on photographic paper
Numbered, dated, inscribed and signed verso:
1–9 / 29.12.2002 / 10" / G. Di Stefano
91.5 × 66 cm (9 parts)

Inv. no. G193M / Acquired 2008

As a young exponent of Eventualismo, a movement founded in the late 1970s by Sergio Lombardo (*1939), Giovanni Di Stefano first presented artistic actions at the Galeria Jartrakor in Rome in the early 1980s. These actions did not aim to produce a finished work with a personal signature; instead, the content of the work was the action itself or the *evento*, as it was called in Italian. The events, carried out both by himself and by others under his direction, were based on precisely defined tasks, for example, briefly looking at a square outlined on a piece of paper, then being blindfolded and subsequently painting the square completely black without crossing the boundaries. The practical execution of the events varied depending on the complexity of the task. Thus, it is much more demanding to perceive and remember an irregular shape than a square or a circle. The performative character of Eventualismo activates participants' faculties of perception and memory and their physical and mental reactions to the task at hand. According to Di Stefano, these spontaneously activated reactions, the prelude, as it were, to artistic work, are themselves a creative act and, in fact, the work of art itself. What remains when the event is over, a picture or a text, is merely a record of the actual artwork. In this respect, Eventualismo is related to comparable ideas advanced by performance and action art since the early 1960s. That said, the underlying substance and meaning of Di Stefano's art lies not in the spectacular gesture but in the intimacy of quiet and simple acts of great mental concentration.

In *Punti Laser*, the artist stood in a dark room holding a laser and, from a fixed distance, pointed a brief ray of light freehand at the centre of a sheet of photographic paper. Despite extreme concentration, the artist was unable to produce two identical "pictures". Variations in the exposure to light on all nine sheets of photographic paper yield irregular black circles surrounded by a grey-white "aura", creating the impression of irises suspended in isolation against a light ground. The mental and physical constitution of human beings does not permit the task to be carried out as precisely defined, neither once nor in constant repetition. Inevitably there are deviations and differences caused by chance, tonicity and the momentary mood of the agent, variations that can only be precluded by a machine. Difference – between theory and practice as well – is thus intrinsically metaphorical, signifying, as it does, the "imperfection" or, more importantly, the uniqueness of human action. This implication has become a concrete image in *Punti Laser* and, as such, possesses aesthetic quality despite the fact that it is only meant to be the record of an action.
UW

Giovanni Di Stefano
dArts a colori
2018

Giovanni Di Stefano
1958 Rome

Acrylic on wood, dart
Titled, dated, inscribed, numbered and initialled: "dArts a colori" / 6.6.2018 / OPERA IN 16 PARTI / 16 / Colori collocati per estrazione a sorte / G.D. St.
80 × 80 × 6 cm

Inv. no. G336M / Acquired 2019

dArts a colori represents a type of picture that Giovanni Di Stefano already experimented with over a decade ago. It, too, is based on a predefined concept as set forth by the principles of Eventualismo (see cat. 106). From a predefined, larger distance, the artist throws a dart at a wooden panel measuring 20 × 20 cm and, if he hits his target, draws straight lines from the point of entry to the corners of the panel, thus dividing it into four triangles of different sizes and shapes. He does the same to each panel and then combines them into a larger whole, producing a network of irregular lines. If the artist were to fulfil his impossible goal of hitting the exact centre of each panel, the combined image would show a completely regular net of continuous straight lines.

In another work (2008) that also belongs to the Hilti Art Foundation, Giovanni Di Stefano drew the lines in white on a black ground. Here, in this work of 2018, he has painted the triangles in white, yellow, blue and black. Both pictures communicate an impression of space and perspective: the first more graphic in nature, the second suggesting crystalline depth. The composition of the sixteen panels is flexible and can be changed as desired, but since the lines drawn from the dart's point of entry always meet at the corners of the adjoining panels, the grid of squares remains a constant visual factor. Viewers see a concrete picture that is no longer just a record of an "eventualist" action but also an aesthetic object that is tantamount to an autonomous work.

UW

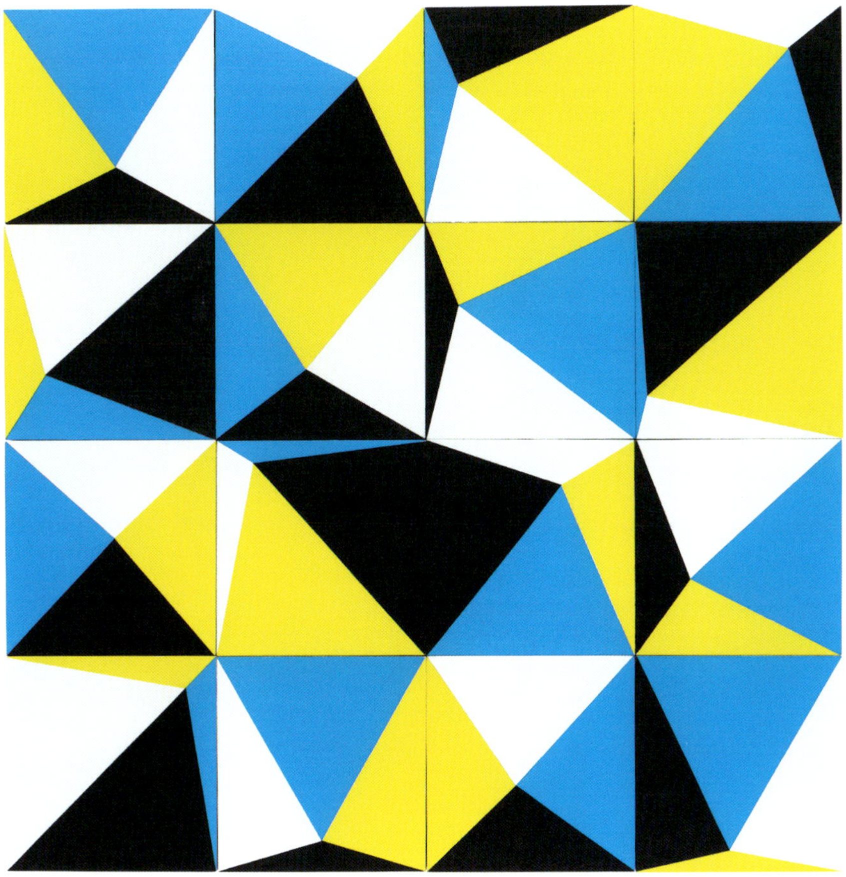

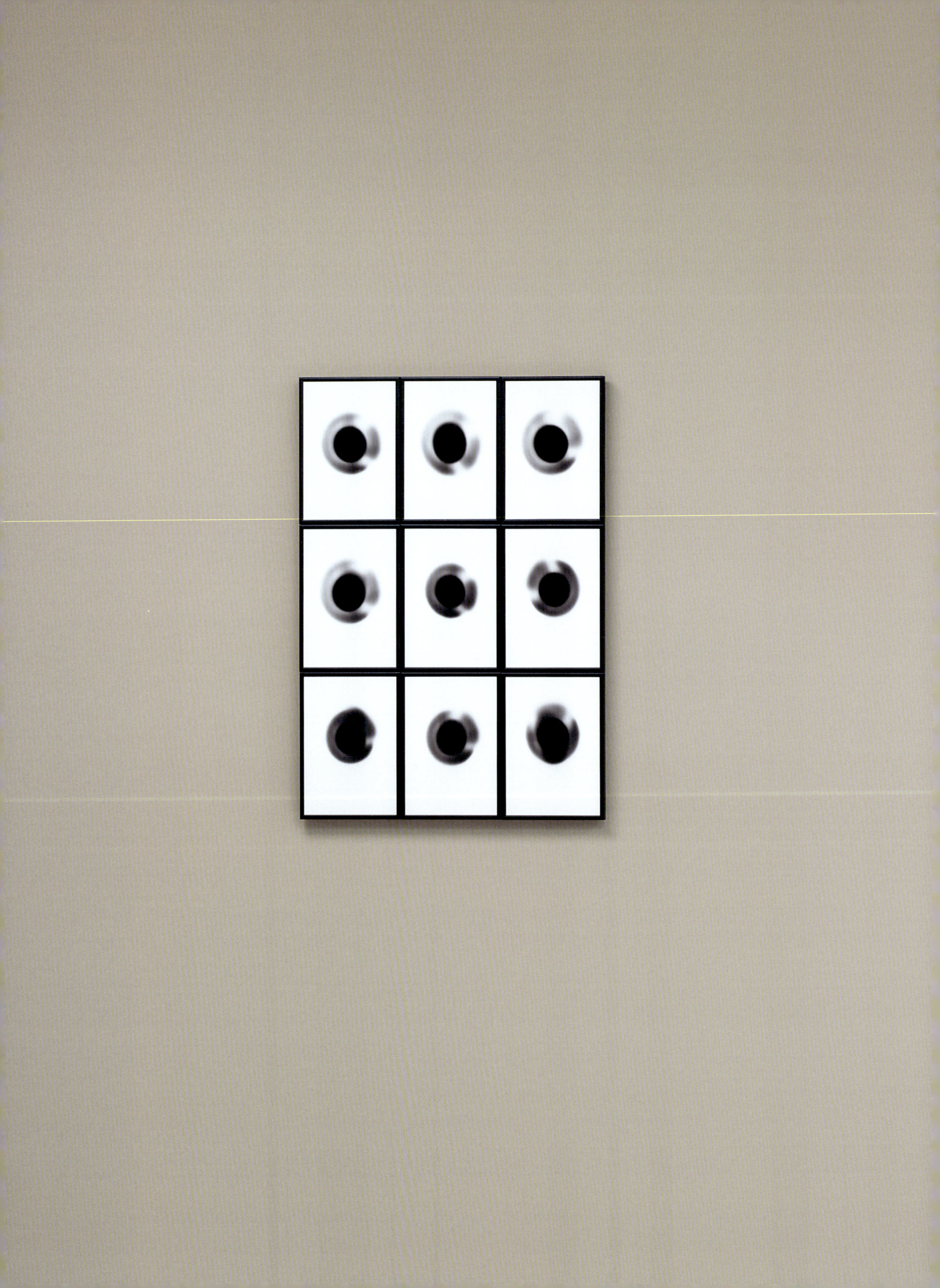

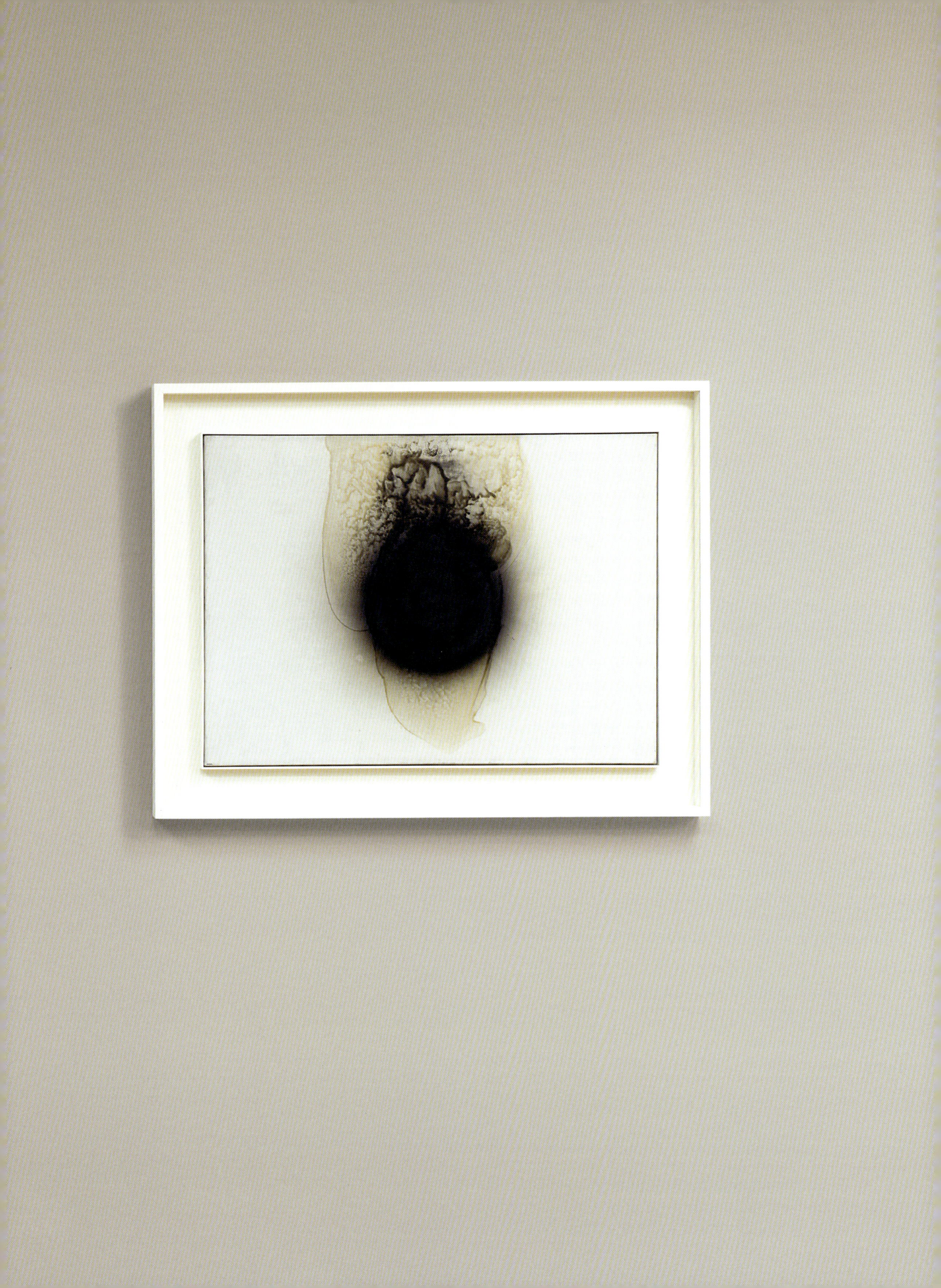

108

Karol Broniatowski
1945 Łodż

Gouache on paper
Signed lower right: Karol Broniatowski 97
110 × 194 cm

Inv. no. G123M / Acquired 2003

Karol Broniatowski
Drei schwarze Figuren
1997

While Karol Broniatowski has chosen to devote himself almost exclusively to the human figure, whether in isolation or in groups, on paper or in bronze, in small format or large, his commitment to a form that reaches back into ancient Greece and Egypt does not ignore the achievements of modern times. Ultimately, the human image that underpins his work is timeless and unconstrained.

Broniatowski takes a sculptural approach, starting with an amorphous substance like clay, which he kneads, presses, squeezes, flattens, smooths or cuts. Even when working in two dimensions on paper, he begins with a sculptural process instead of resorting to the drawing or painting tools of the artist. His figures in black or red gouache are the coloured imprint of a form he has created out of clay, poured in silicone, pressed onto the paper and subsequently pulled off again. The work thus has the character of a monotype made in several steps and using several shapes; it exists only once. Corrections are not possible. Either the figure works and is placed in the right spot, or the picture is ruined.

The three black figures captured here show the traces and smears typical of the printing process. The application of the black paint on the white paper is uneven, creating vibrant, cartilaginous planes and contours that are feathery and fragile but also compact. The sculptural effect of the armless figures is a consequence of the sculptural process. With teetering, probing, unsteady steps, they pace off the space that is, of course, of their own making, for one cannot escape realising how inconceivable it is to envision a figure, and a human one at that, without space. Our vision instantly adds depth to the plane of the paper.

A direct look at the figures makes the direction in which they are moving oddly indeterminate. Are they moving towards or away from us? The first impression is deceptive. Prolonged study generates an optical illusion: if they are facing us and walking towards us, the imagined space becomes smaller; if they are walking away with their backs turned to us, it becomes larger. Clothing and gender cannot be identified although one might interpret the figures as a meeting between one man and two women. But we cannot be certain. Even the notion of encounter is an assumption, for we could as easily read a chance encounter into the delicately balanced placement of the figures on the paper.

Broniatowski's gouache is a snapshot of humans as a species, who make an immediate, unfiltered appearance, beings in isolation, with no context and no specific identity. Only the interpreting viewer can invest them with a role and a route – can, in fact, give them qualities and orientation, and ultimately existence, in which our own may "temporarily" be reflected.

UW

Karol Broniatowski
Rote Figur
2009

109

Karol Broniatowski
1945 Łodź

Gouache on paper
Signed lower right: K Broniatowski 2009
c. 170 × 114 cm

Inv. no. G220M / Acquired 2010

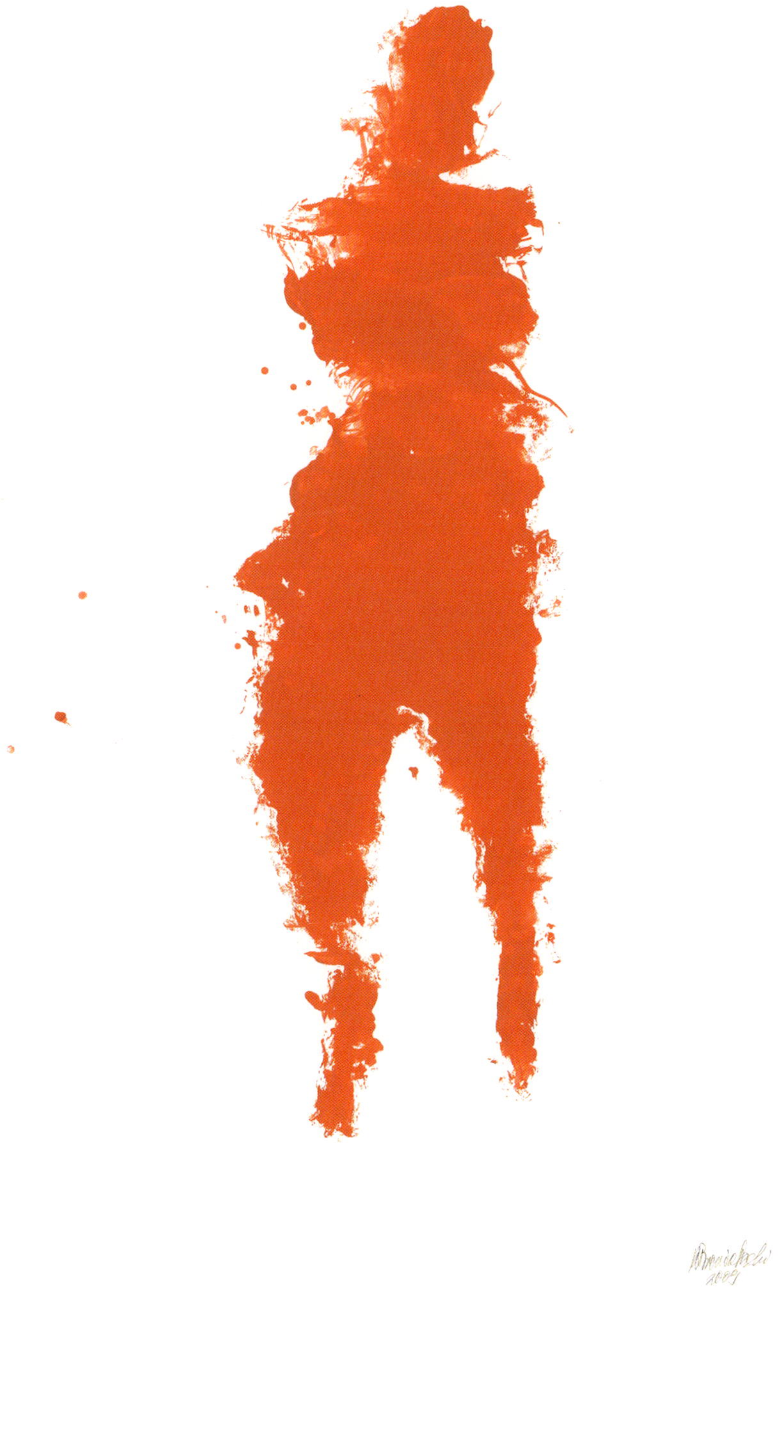

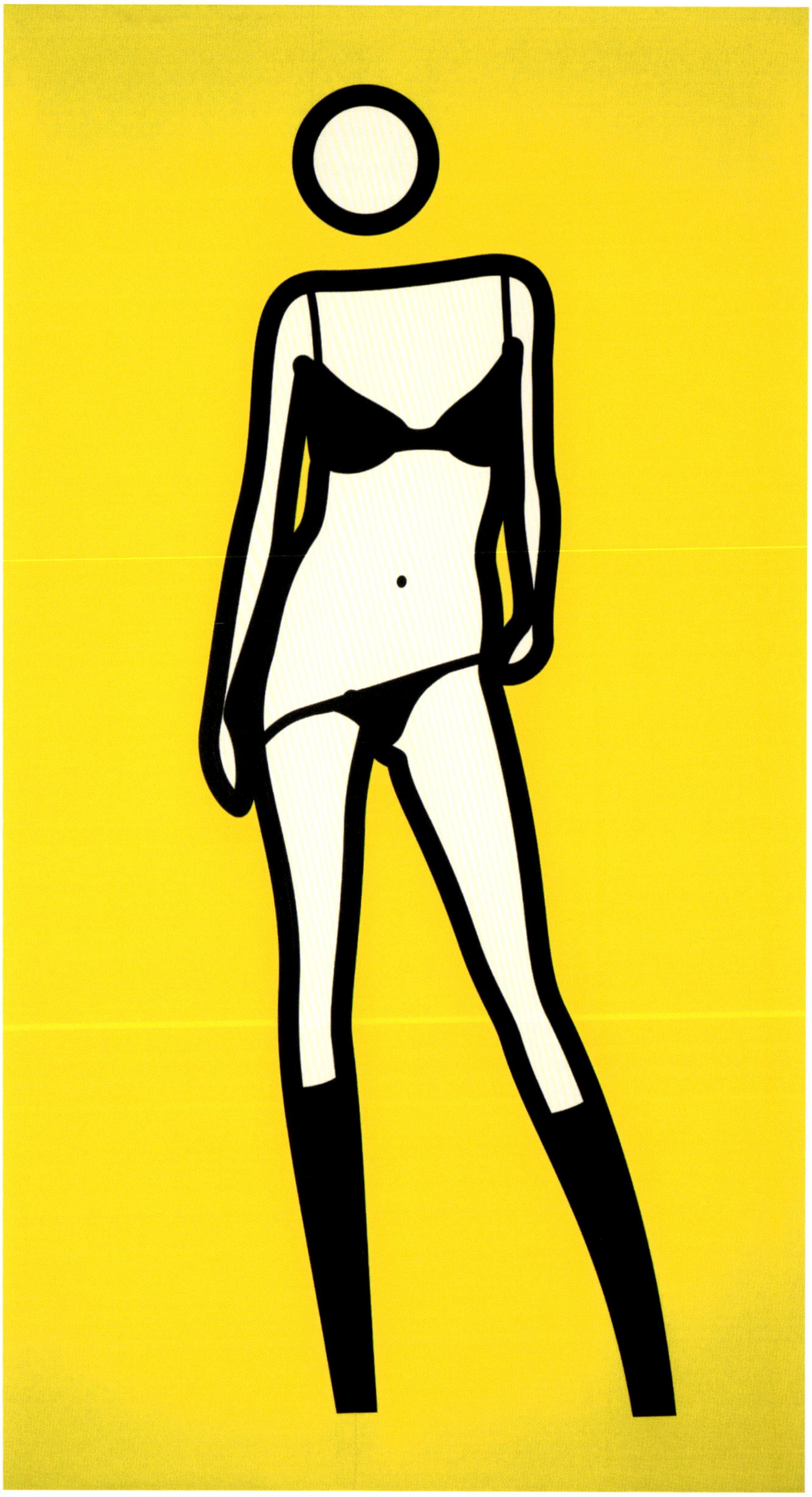

Julian Opie
Sara Gets Undressed
2003

Julian Opie
1958 London

Vinyl
Signed on verso: Julian Opie
239 × 137 cm

Inv. no. P224M / Acquired 2010

Like many artists of his generation, Julian Opie studied at Goldsmiths College in London from 1979 to 1982. Goldsmiths, an influential and innovative art school in the 1980s, was known for giving students the opportunity to work across disciplines in pursuit of their artistic ideas and for taking them seriously as artists. One of the leading tutors, Michael Craig Martin, a conceptual artist from Ireland who had studied in Paris and at Yale, passed on his international experience to younger artists, among them, Tracey Emin, Damien Hirst, Fiona Rae and Thomas Demand.

Like his teacher, Opie also drew on the heritage of Pop Art and Minimalism. For Opie, the former did not feel like history; it was modern and that made it attractive. It allowed him to look at the world with a fresh perspective, to appropriate and substantiate it without preconceived notions. The subject matter could be “anything that jumps out at me and captures my attention”. Animals, landscapes, cars, buildings and streets figure in his early work. Their simplicity and significance recall illustrations in children’s books, whose aim is speedy, holistic comprehension while at the same time depicting subject matter that invites contemplation.

Julian Opie garnered international acclaim in the late 1990s with his portraits and pictures of people that often resemble pictograms or road signs. He is still frequently identified primarily with such subject matter. He painted *Sara Gets Undressed* in 2003 as one of twenty-four versions of this motif. The larger-than-life figure, wearing only a bra, panties and knee socks, is pictured on yellow vinyl, a material commonly used for flooring. She was designed at the computer, cut out in vinyl and then transferred as a flat relief against a radiant yellow background. The white figure outlined in black with a circular “empty” head seems to be floating in undefined space. Advertising, perhaps for underwear, instantly reverberates, as does the erotic ambivalence of dressing and undressing. Although Opie’s figure could not be more anonymous, his title clearly refers to a specific person named Sara, a model and dancer that Opie hired through a London agency. On the one hand, the artist is investigating the relationship between singular and generic, and on the other, the impact of signs.
AS

Julian Opie
Lily
2013

Julian Opie
1958 London

Computer animation, media player,
55" LCD screen
Signed on label verso: Julian Opie
122 × 69.5 × 12 cm

Inv. no. P263M / Acquired 2015

The oversized portrait of *Lily* shows a young woman who lives in Julian Opie's neighbourhood and occasionally babysat for him. In addition to appearing on-screen as a computer animation, her head is also seen on inkjet paintings, on a mosaic and in the form of a large sculpture. Representations are based on photographs taken by the artist and processed at the computer. In the animated version, evoking billboards, Lily's eyes rhythmically alternate between looking at and past the viewer. Opie benefits from new techniques, linking them with the characteristics of his models and creating a new form of portraiture that incorporates both the attributes of "timeless" representation and the vibrancy of the experienced moment.

In contrast to *Sara Gets Undressed* (cat. 110), Lily's face, though simple in line, is clearly that of an individual. The composition as a whole, half in shadow and half in the light, features a classical characteristic of portraiture. In an interview, Opie expressed his interest in art of the past, the study of which inspired him to become a collector: "I think learning from art is an essential part of making it." A clear-cut model for *Lily* from older art cannot be identified but there are similarities with Anthony van Dyck and English portrait painting of the eighteenth century, particularly the work of George Romney. Romney selected a variety of angles for his numerous likenesses of Lady Emma Hamilton, renowned as the most beautiful woman of her time.

Opie demonstrates that a person cannot be captured in one single "picture": he changes and moves Lily, has her appear and disappear, removes her from conventional picture supports and makes her accessible.
AS

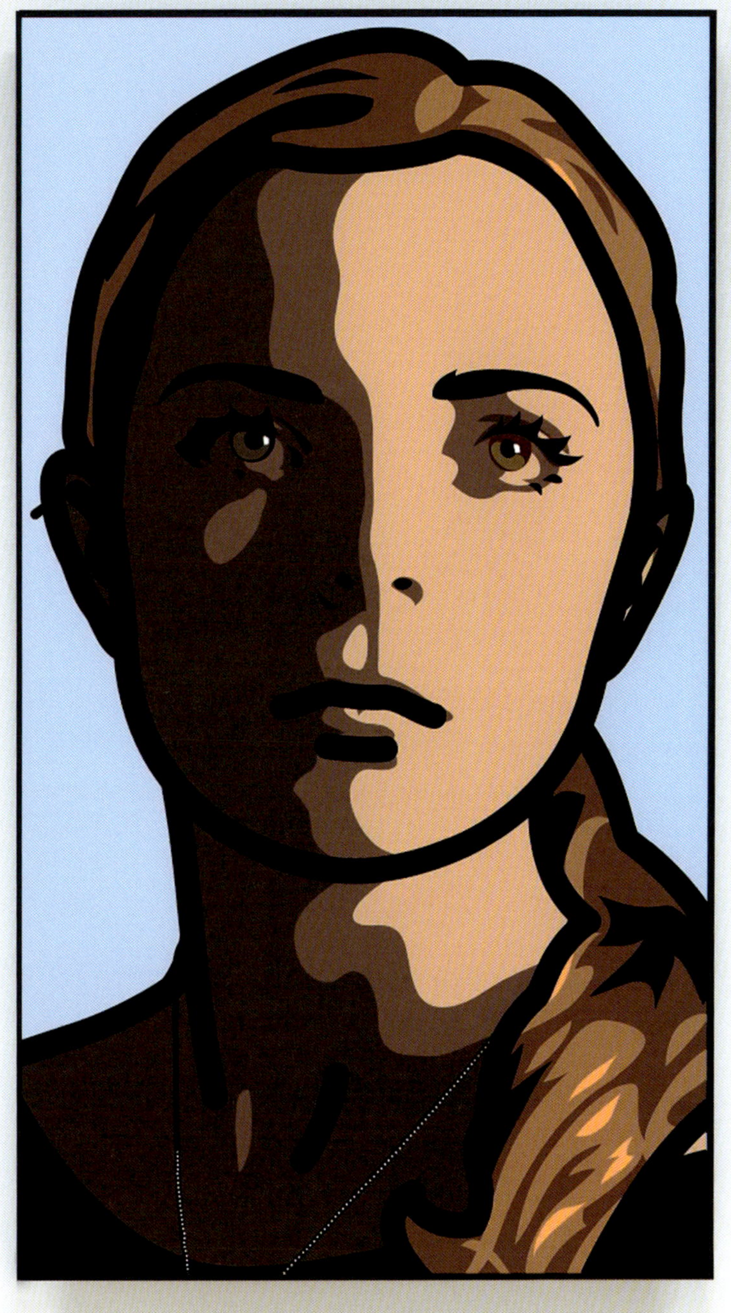

112

Callum Innes
Exposed Painting Delft Blue
2018

Callum Innes
1962 Edinburgh

Oil on linen
Initialled and dated verso: CI C 14 2018
235 × 230 cm

Inv. no. P342M / Acquired 2019

A concept as simple as it is subtle underlies the *Exposed Paintings* Scottish painter Callum Innes has produced in particular since the mid-1990s. Using a broad paintbrush, he applies exclusively horizontal swathes of paint, flush left and right, to a plane of predefined height, and leaves the top and bottom margins of the canvas empty except for a white primer. After applying several layers of paint to produce an extremely dense plane of colour, he divides it vertically and, as in this painting, applies turpentine to the right half. Again using horizontal strokes of the brush, Innes dilutes the paint until it becomes transparent enough to reveal its original blue. Working rapidly, he makes the paint, now mixed with turpentine, so thin that it flows down, also colouring the once-white area of canvas to the lower right. Occasionally, Innes will add horizontal swathes of a second colour such as orange to the already diluted paint, once again working it with turpentine until it flows down as well. In this way, he achieves extremely intricate chromatic nuances.

Upon completion, the painting appears as a five-part, slightly asymmetrical and finely proportioned composition. The planes of colour now differ widely in quality. Saturated and glossy, the black to the left asserts its homogeneous density, generated exclusively by paint actively applied. The adjoining plane to the right now consists only of thin transparent layers, originally applied horizontally, but now clearly showing vertical traces of flowing, diluted paint. In contrast, the structure of the lower right portion of the work is exclusively vertical, the result of turpentine copiously applied and becoming mixed with pigment in a process dictated by gravity. The white portions of the canvas remain unchanged. They enhance both the contrast and the luminosity of the colours.

Callum Innes presents painting as a concentrated process in the course of which material and immaterial factors of bound and diluted paint, of gravity and light, leave specific traces behind and become physically perceptible.
UW

Callum Innes
Exposed Painting Crimson Red
2014

Callum Innes
1962 Edinburgh

Oil on linen
Signed and dated verso: Innes 14
160 × 156 cm

Inv. no. P324M / Acquired 2018

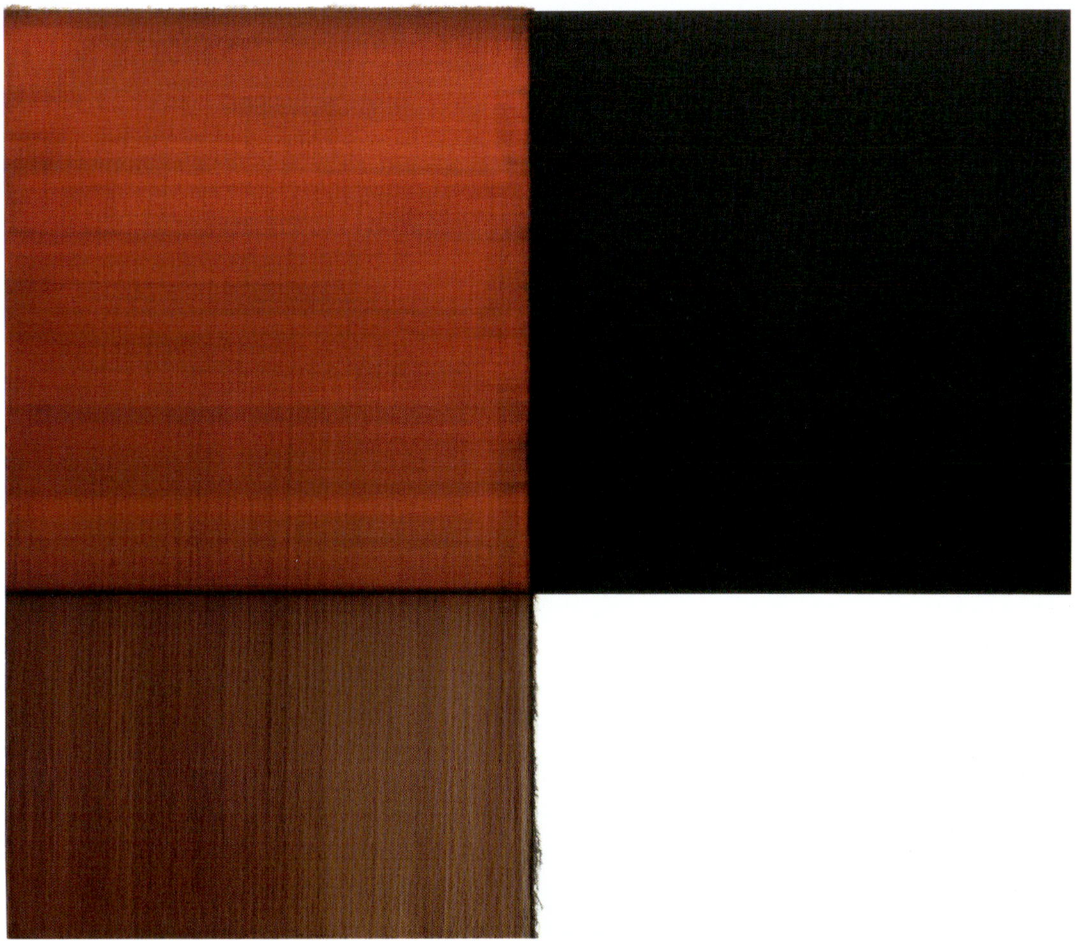

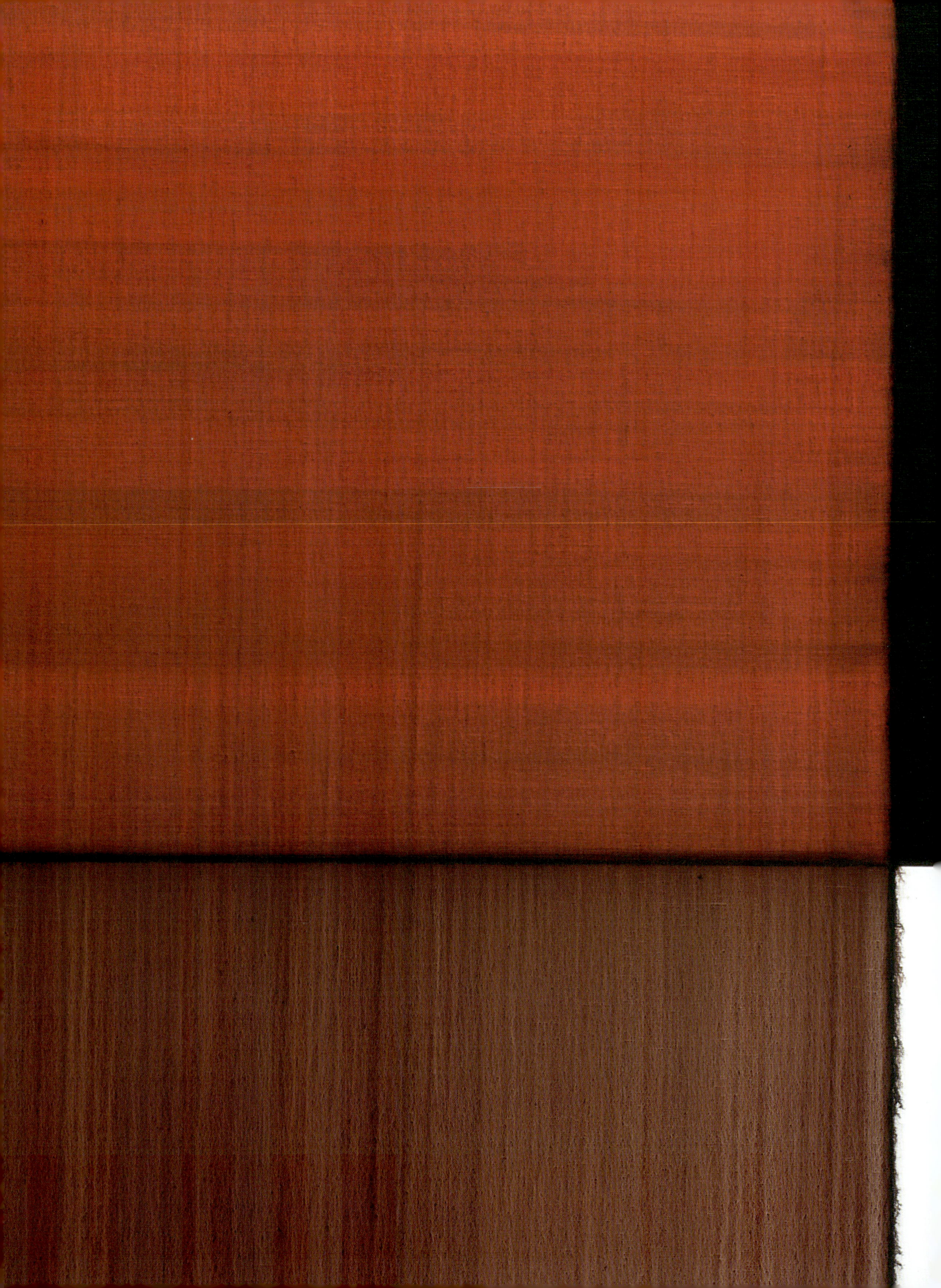

Hanns Kunitzberger
1. Hälfte 2017 früher
2017

Hanns Kunitzberger
1955 Salzburg

Oil on molino fabric
Initialled, titled, inscribed and signed verso:
HK / "1. HÄLFTE 2017 FRÜHER" /
225 × 150 cm / Hanns Kunitzberger
225 × 150 cm

Inv. no. P314M / Acquired 2017

Hanns Kunitzberger studied widely across several disciplines at the Mozarteum University of Salzburg. In addition to working in theatre and film, designing stage sets and directing, he devoted himself increasingly to painting as of 1980 and by 1991 it had become his sole occupation. He turned to purely nonrepresentational art at an early stage. A look at Kunitzberger's work might evoke Claude Monet's water lilies, Gotthard Graubner's *Paint-Space-Bodies* or paintings by Mark Rothko, but these associations fade on closer study.

The vertical, rusty red field of colour floats weightlessly in the centre of the picture, its diffuse edges melting into space, the whole becoming an almost immaterial presence. The red intensifies the longer we look at it. As nuances and contrasts slowly rise up out of the depths, the two-dimensional field of colour, a homogeneous plane at first sight, evolves into a vibrant, animated patch of misty red in an imaginary space, perceived as a delicate emergence, a becoming of colour as colour.

Kunitzberger achieves this effect by working from the depths of the pictorial ground, applying the thinnest of layers, washes of oils in different colours, step by step until the whole acquires a meditative and yet immanent dynamic. This time-consuming process is reflected in the titles of the paintings.

Colour as space, space as picture and the relationship between work, space and viewer are crucial concerns for Kunitzberger. This explains why the artist chooses not to frame his paintings. Only without the confinement of framing can the works reverberate in space, inviting beholders to participate actively, discovering how perception changes as they move about, modifying their angle of view. The space between picture and viewer becomes part of the work.

JR

Hanns Kunitzberger
1. Hälfte 2017 später
2017

115

Hanns Kunitzberger
1955 Salzburg

Oil on molino fabric
Initialled, titled, inscribed and signed verso:
HK / "1. HÄLFTE 2017 SPÄTER" /
225 × 150 cm / Hanns Kunitzberger
225 × 150 cm

Inv. no. P315M / Acquired 2017

116

Hanns Kunitzberger
1955 Salzburg

Oil on linen
Initialled, titled, inscribed and signed verso:
HK / "2. HÄLFTE 2018 SPÄTER" /
180 × 130 cm / Hanns Kunitzberger
180 × 130 cm

Inv. no. P340M / Acquired 2019

Hanns Kunitzberger
2. Hälfte 2018 später
2018

Frank Thiel
Perito Moreno #16
2014

Frank Thiel
1966 Kleinmachnow / Berlin

Chromogenic print
Titled, dated, inscribed, signed and dated verso: Perito Moreno # 16 / 2012/13 / 160 × 299.5 cm / Frank Thiel '2014
Framed 160 × 299.5 cm

Inv. no. PH254M / Acquired 2014

The large photographs at Checkpoint Charlie in the centre of Berlin, the former border between East and West Berlin, put Frank Thiel on the map. Mounted in a light box, connected back to back, they show portraits of a Soviet soldier looking out over the western sector of the city and an American soldier gazing at the eastern sector. The work is a monument, entirely without pathos, to the historical interface between two different "world systems", where there is now a steady rush of traffic and thousands of Berliners and tourists stroll about day after day, looking around and engaging in animated conversation.

"The depiction of process has always been more important to me than disseminating immutable, crystal-clear or simply valid statements or truths." Thiel's profound and crucial interest in transience and change as a link between past and future, near and far, stasis and movement, takes shape in a wide range of subject matter from photographs of construction sites in Berlin to large-format pictures of the glaciers in Patagonia.

Thiel has travelled to South America several times to the unique, stunningly wild glaciers in Los Glaciares National Park. On visiting the region in 1832–33, Charles Darwin wrote, "it is scarcely possible to imagine anything more beautiful than the beryl-like blue of these glaciers." Thiel was equally spellbound. In his photographs, he has concentrated primarily on the Perito Moreno glacier of 254 km², a UNESCO World Heritage Site, a glacier whose tongue reaches into the immense Lago Argentino.

In Thiel's photographs, the walls of ice, towering up to 70 metres in height, are pictured head-on and appear to extend infinitely beyond the frame of the picture. They are overwhelming in size and inner structure, their crevices shaped not only by wind and weather but by the drama of breaks, by horizontal and vertical carving. The choreography of the shapes suggests movement but also instability, an impression reinforced by the fact that the glaciers are subject to ceaseless change so they never look the same from day to day. Thiel took these pictures during the Arctic summer in the months of January and February 2012. Since he was standing in a rocking boat, he used a digital camera for the first time to ensure precise images undisturbed by movement. The panorama photograph is assembled out of many single pictures, processed where necessary to match his emotional and visual memory. Although this is a hotspot of tourism, Thiel shows no people. The empty space and the inaccessibility of nature recall the paintings of Caspar David Friedrich. The bright, even lighting does not describe a moment but, rather, a frozen eternity.
AS

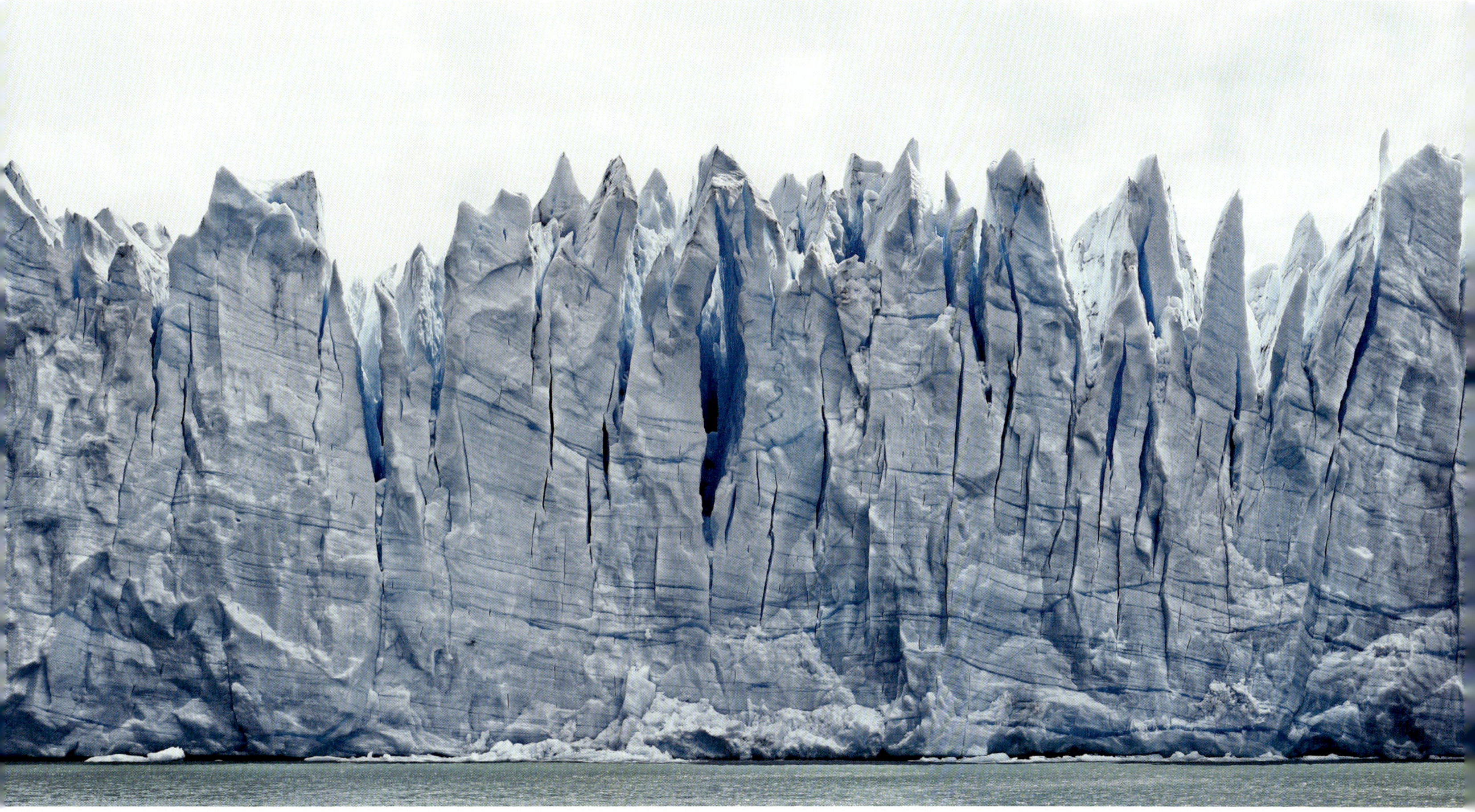

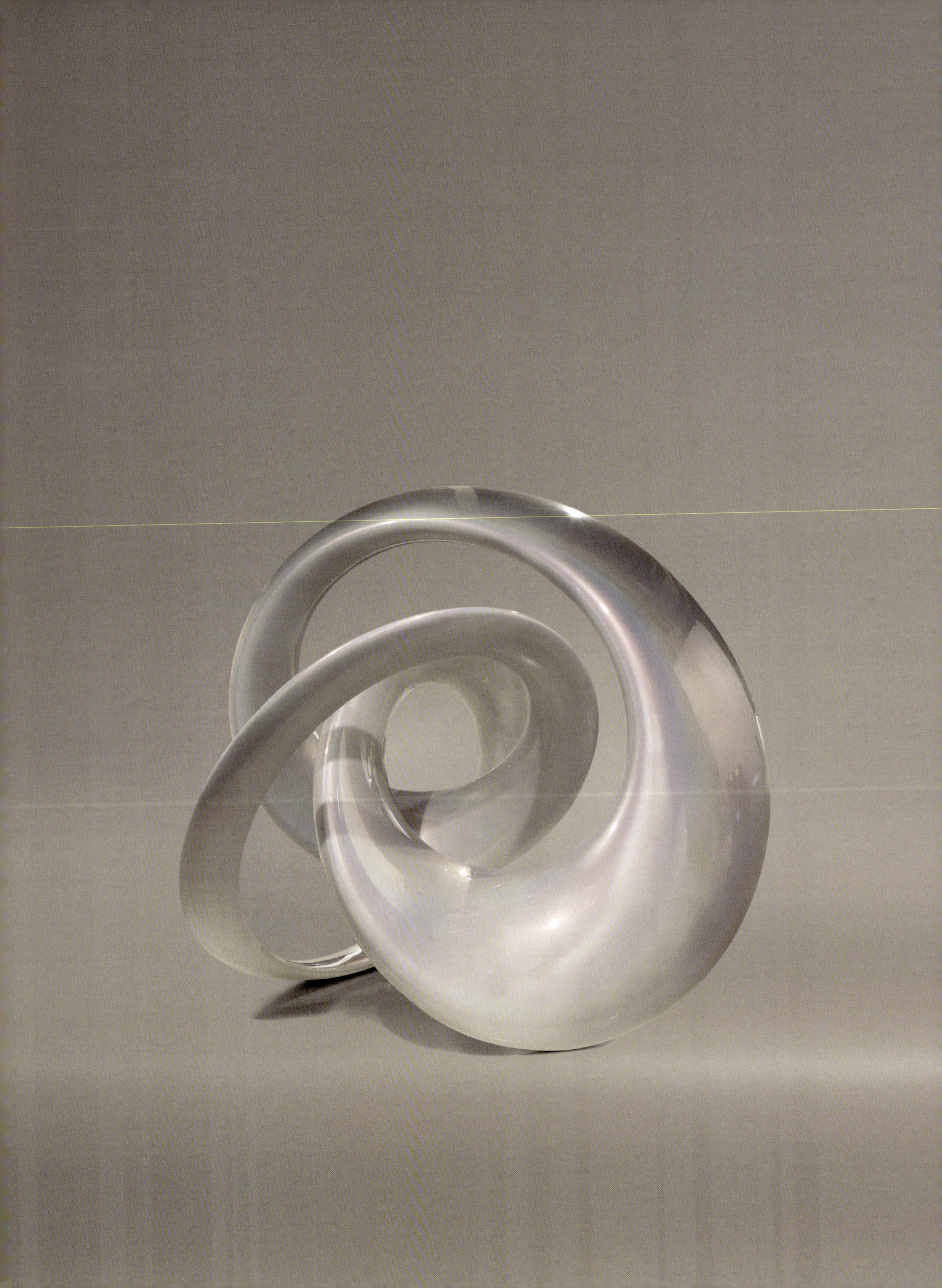

Mariko Mori
1967 Tokyo

Aluminium, hologram coating (3/5)
200.9 × 248.6 × 178.9 cm

Inv. no. S63T / Acquired 2014

Mariko Mori
Cyclic I
2014

Mariko Mori studied at Bunka Fashion College in Tokyo before transferring in 1988 to London's Chelsea College of Art and Design, and thereafter enrolling in the Whitney Museum's Independent Study Program in New York. She has worked as a model, a photographer and a performer in her videos, and also makes sculptures. She has appeared in extravagant costumes of her own design as a manga figure, shaman, Shinto priestess, cyborg and in other roles, and also transposes herself into a wide variety of mental and artificial contexts. She is as fascinated with global spirituality, from Buddhism to Mayan religion, as she is with state-of-the-art technology. Her growing interest in cosmic processes and global ideas in the late 1990s is reflected in *Cyclic*. The title of these sculptures made in 2014 references the theory of conformal cycling cosmology advanced by British physicist Sir Roger Penrose. In very simplified terms, Penrose holds that the universe is subject to an endless series of big bangs signalling the end of one universe and the beginning of another. The convoluted bands of Mori's large sculpture unfold dynamically in space, with no distinguishable beginning or end, suggesting infinite repetition, much like the so-called Möbius strip. *Cyclic I* is based on a small 3D model, an aluminium sculpture with a hologram coating of the kind often used in advertising. It makes the sculpture iridescent and multicoloured, with the surrounding space reflected in it. The real space mirrored in the surface produces a second virtual space.

Cyclic I embodies the approach to body, space and movement that informs sculptural innovation in the twentieth century, but it also recalls models of celestial globes from the Baroque to the present day, which bear witness to ever more scientific enquiry into the universe. The work has such lightness that it could almost take flight, and it is infused with a subtle elegance that is entirely un-European. Japanese art resonates here, for instance, the woodcuts of Katsushika Hokusai (1760–1849) and Ando Hiroshige (1797–1858), both ukiyo-e artists who created images of the "floating world". The twists and turns of Mori's undulating bands clearly bear comparison with the extremely stylised, virtuoso depiction of rounded mountain hills and dramatically breaking waves. The mother-of-pearl sheen and the snaking bands of this sculpture refer to nature and its attendant myths. Molluscs and oysters have iridescent shells. The religions of the world consider snakes, millions of years old, divine or devilish, ultimately seductive, erotic and enigmatic and, in ancient Greece, they are even endowed with immortality for their youth is repeatedly restored as they shed their skin.

AS

Leiko Ikemura
Ozean I–III
2000–01

Leiko Ikemura
1951 Tsu, Mie Prefecture, Japan

Oil on burlap
Signed, titled, dated and inscribed verso:
Leiko Ikemura / Ozean I–III, 2000/01,
Inv. no. M-00/01-302
120 × 160 cm ("Ozean I" and "III")
130 × 160 cm ("Ozean II")

Inv. no. P102M / Acquired 2002

Leiko Ikemura has always inhabited two worlds. She is part of two cultures, and, as such, she is equally alienated from both specifically Japanese and from European traditions. The critical, authentic observations attendant upon being a stranger in the world are central points of reference in both her life and her art. "A stranger I arrived, a stranger I depart." Thus begins Franz Schubert's *Winter Journey* of 1827. Ikemura grew up in Tsu, south of Nagoya on the Pacific coast of Japan, and studied Spanish at the University of Osaka, before transferring to Salamanca in 1972 and studying art in Seville in 1973, followed by several years in Switzerland. In 1984 she went to Cologne and in 1991 became a professor at what is now the University of Art in Berlin. Since then she has been commuting between her two studios and has also taken on a professorship in Japan.

The triptych *Ozean I–III* dates from the beginning of the new millennium. The central panel, 10 cm taller than those to the left and right, shows overlapping, light, dark and partly transparent bands, views in and onto endless sea that cannot always be distinguished from the sky. The ocean was the lifeblood of Ikemura's youth, a site of hope and of horror, where light and shadow merged; it has remained a crucial theme in her art. The empty space in the central panel is kept in check by figures piled up like monuments in the side panels. These spectral girls are of a different order and have appeared in Ikemura's work since the mid-1990s. They look like dolls, artificial and yet true to nature; almost floating, transparent beings and at the same time shadows of themselves.

The artist mounts the three panels far apart. Although they are a triptych, they call to mind Edvard Munch's *Reinhardt Frieze* of 1907, now at the Neue Nationalgalerie in Berlin, and Yves Klein's *Anthropometries* (imprints of bodies) of the early 1960s. All the artists do without a primer and work the canvas, burlap or fabric directly so that the figures dig into the fabric, melting into it. Although distinct in shape, colour and design, these are all visions of human fate. Munch described his frieze as "a poem of life, of love and death …"; Klein's shadow figures allude to atomic death in Hiroshima, which he visited in 1953; and Ikemura's figures with their poisonous green hair and blank faces with just bare hints of eye sockets refer to the catastrophes in Hiroshima and Nagasaki. In an interview of 2011, Ikemura speaks of the two atom bombs, and, in another context, of her pictures as subversive memento mori.

AS

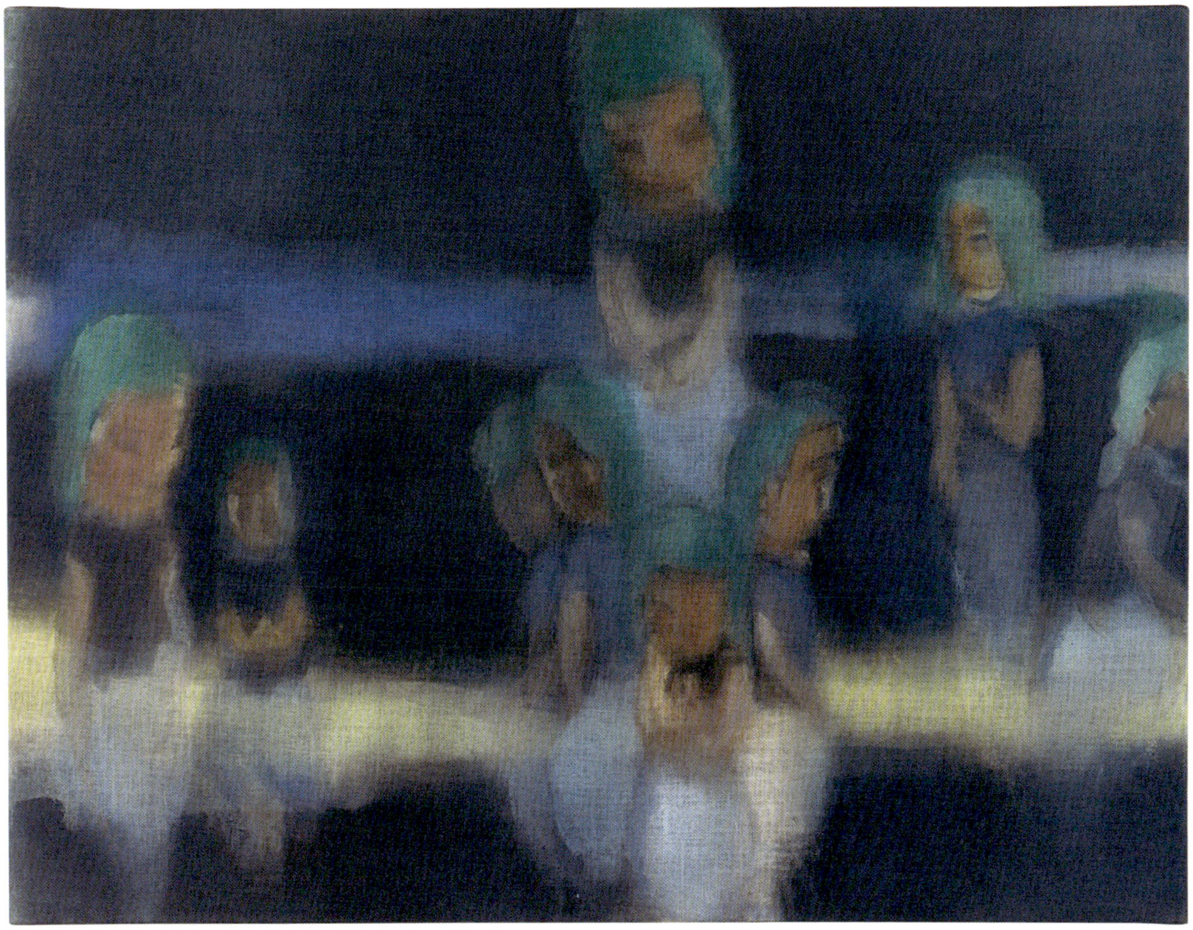

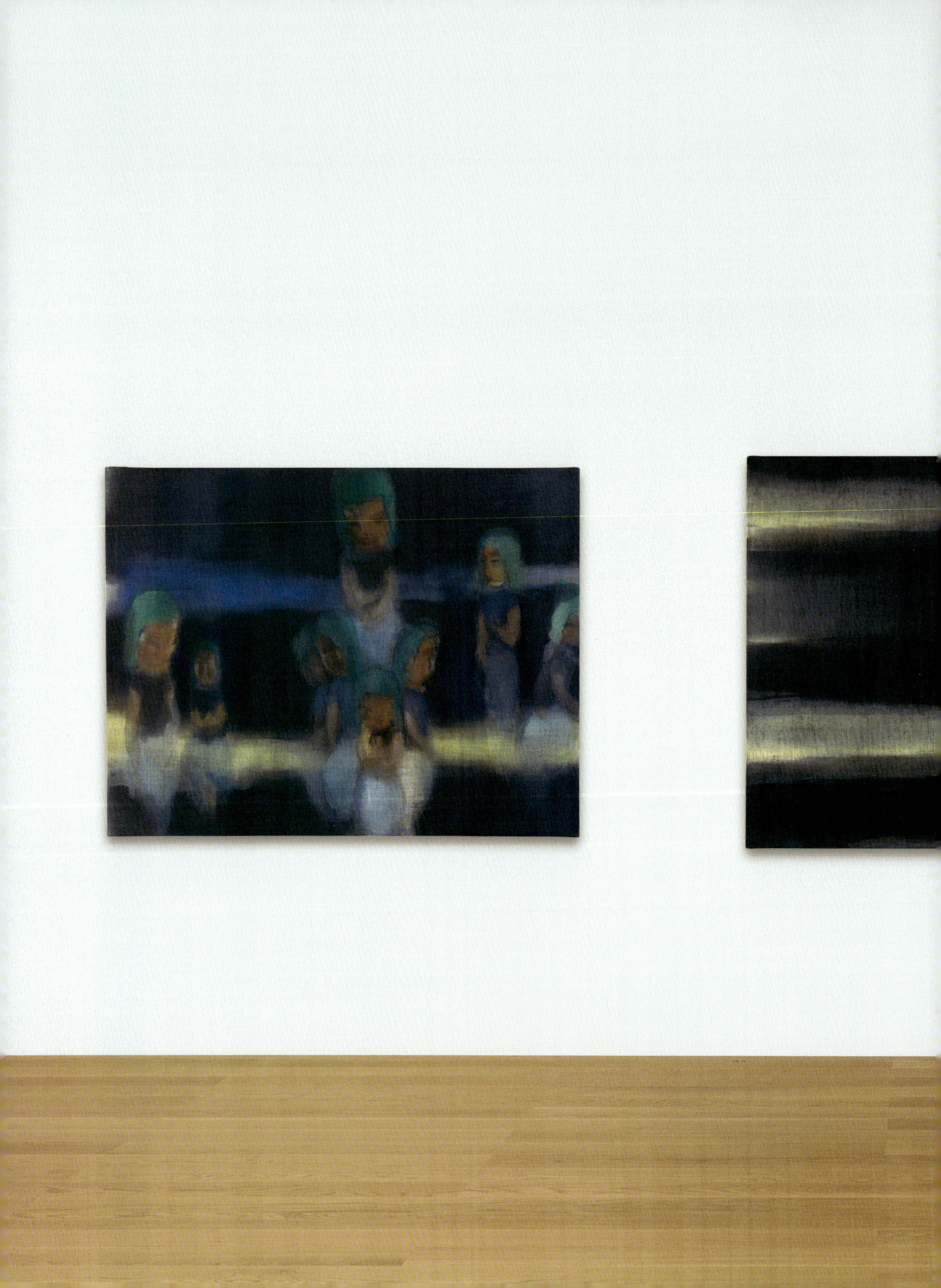

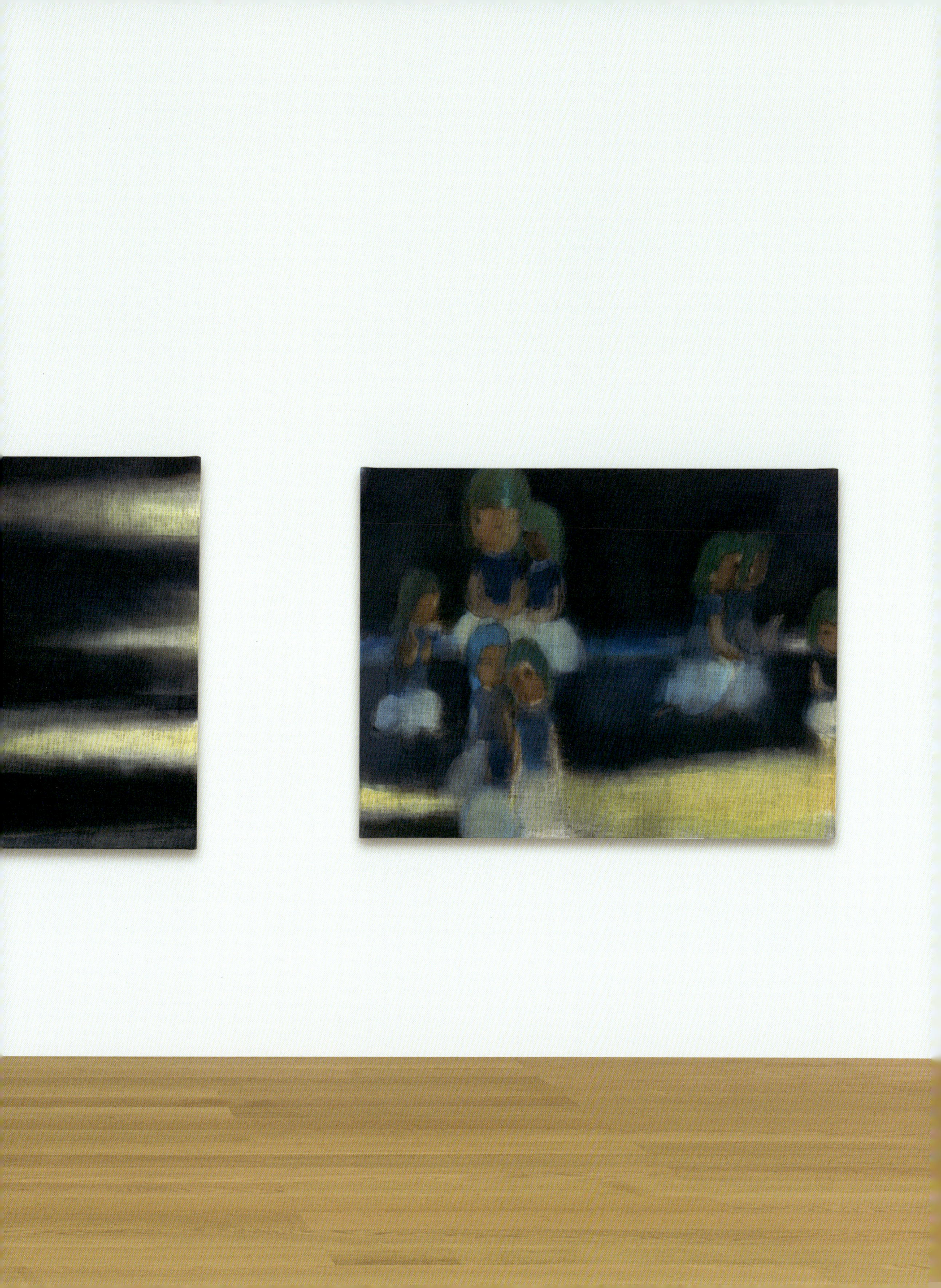

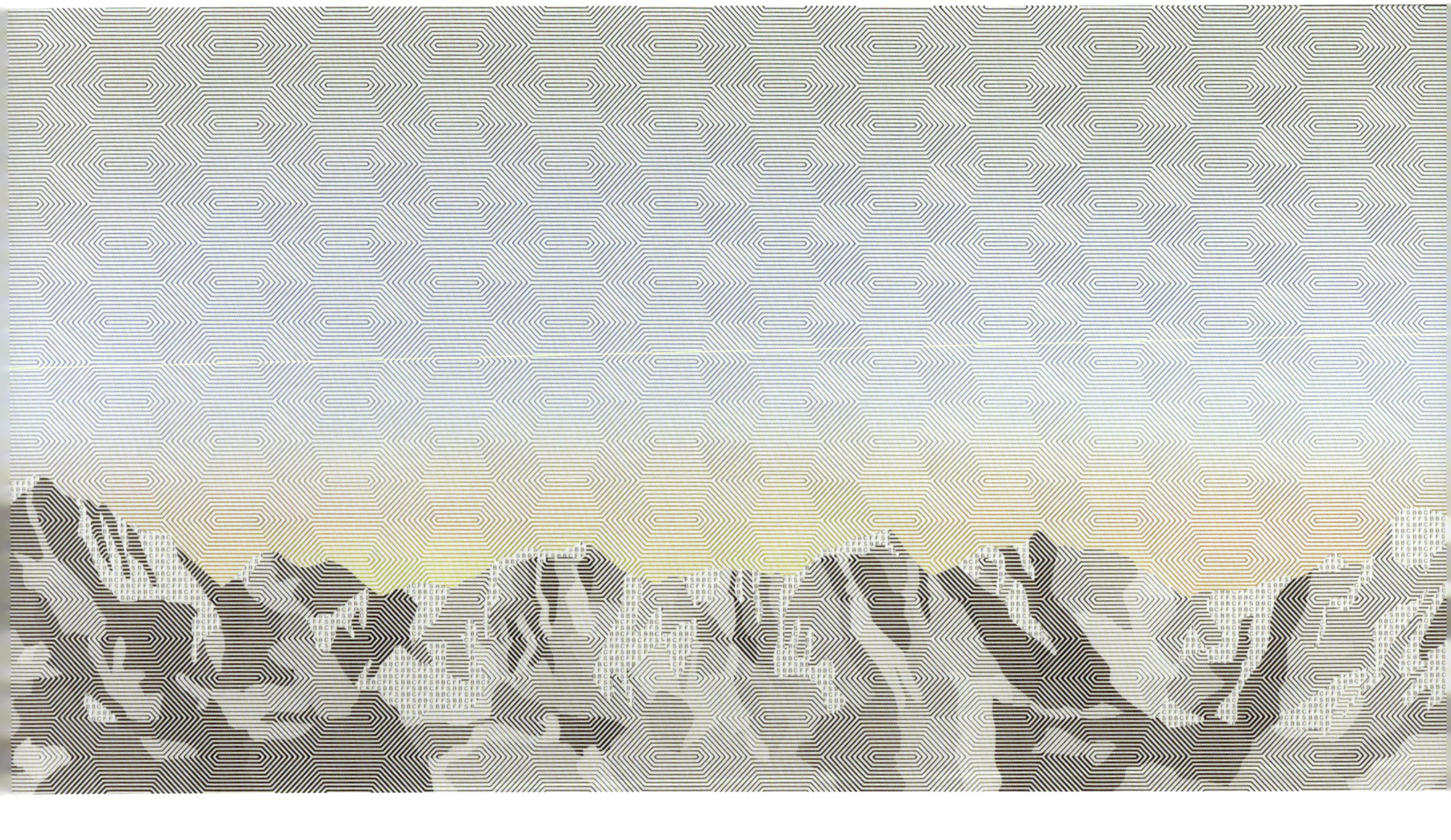

120

Stéphane Kropf
1979 Lausanne

Acrylic on canvas
Signed, titled and dated verso:
S. Kropf / SANS TITRE (TUILIERE) 2012
152 × 305 cm

Inv. no. P146M / Acquired 2013

Stéphane Kropf
Untitled (Tuilière)
2012

Stéphane Kropf has created the present work in the traditional style and horizontal format of landscape painting. It is subtitled *Tuilière*, after the town in which the French-speaking Swiss artist's studio is located on Lake Geneva near Lausanne. But on comparing this picture with Ferdinand Hodler's 1915 painting (vol. 1, cat. 24), we discover that Kropf was not looking at a Swiss mountainscape. He was not standing before nature, like Hodler did, but instead used a source that was itself a picture: a diagrammatic panorama of mountains in Switzerland, produced in an endless loop on rolls of paper as a motif for Swiss railway tickets. Kropf computerised the design and transferred it with a plotter to self-sticking film that in turn served as a template on the canvas. After painting the canvas with spray gun and paintbrush, he removed the film. The result is a synthesis of computer graphics and painting.

The point of departure for Kropf's series of mountain pictures is a train ticket dated 11 October 2009. *Tuilière* is the first picture in the series; the collection of the Hilti Art Foundation also holds a second work from the same series. Although the mountain panorama has a distinctive profile, it does not give the impression of depicting specifically identifiable mountains. It looks more like a stereotype, to which one of the most striking features of Swiss topography has been reduced. In addition, Swiss Federal Railways has inscribed its logo (SBB/CFF) in the design, transforming the landscape into a marketing product.

In his mountain pictures, Stéphane Kropf has extracted the landscape from its purpose-oriented context and reclaimed it as the subject matter of art, rendered in large scale but without modifying the design of the source image. The stereotypical image of landscape in the narrower sense and nature in the broader sense are thus both open to view. In this way, Kropf draws attention to the train ticket both as documentary indication of a concrete journey to a concrete place and metaphorical indication of our journey through life.
In the course of studying the pictures, we cannot help wondering whether travelling and the experiences and impressions acquired in the process are turning into stereotypes as well.
UW

Provenance
Exhibitions
Literature

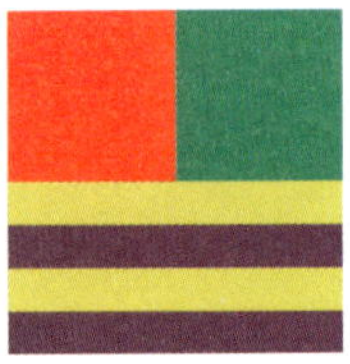

001

Camille Graeser
Doppelte Komplementär-Relation
1965

Provenance
Camille Graeser-Stiftung, Zurich
Galerie am Lindenplatz, Vaduz

Exhibitions
1966 Esslingen, (op)art galerie, *Camille Graeser*, no. 3
1966 Krefeld, Galerie 123, *Camille Graeser*, no. 2
1967 Basel, Kunsthalle, *Camille Graeser, Friedrich Vordemberge-Gildewart, Frans Danksin*, no. 57
1976–77 Münster, Westfälisches Landesmuseum; Düsseldorf, Kunstmuseum, *Camille Graeser: Gemälde, Zeichnungen*, no. 52
1979 Zurich, Kunsthaus; Ludwigshafen am Rhein, Wilhelm-Hack-Museum, *Camille Graeser*, no. 37
1981 Bottrop, Moderne Galerie Quadrat; Hanover, Kunstmuseum, *Camille Graeser*, no. 37
1994 Lugano, Studio d'arte contemporanea Dabbeni, *Camille Graeser*
1997 Zug, Galerie am See, *Camille Graeser. Bilder, Zeichnungen, Grafiken*

Literature
Koella 1995, p. 221 (B 1965.20)

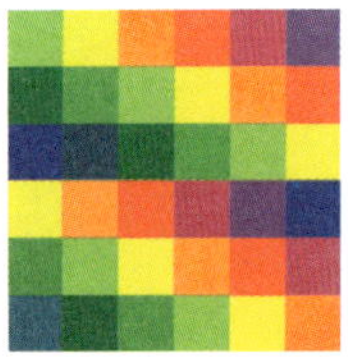

002

Richard Paul Lohse
6 systematische Farbreihen von blau zu blau
1955/1965

Provenance
Richard Paul Lohse-Stiftung, Zurich
Edith Wahlandt Galerie, Stuttgart

Exhibitions
1969 Zurich, Galerie Renée Ziegler, *Richard P. Lohse, Serielle und Modulare Ordnungen*
1972 Venice Biennale, Swiss Pavilion, *Richard Paul Lohse, Willy Weber*
1975 Düsseldorf, Kunsthalle, *Richard Paul Lohse*, no. 63
1976 Zurich, Kunsthalle, *Richard Paul Lohse*
1997 London, Annely Juda Fine Art, *Richard Paul Lohse*
2000 Zurich, Galerie Renée Ziegler, *Richard P. Lohse*

Literature
Lynton 1996, p. 41

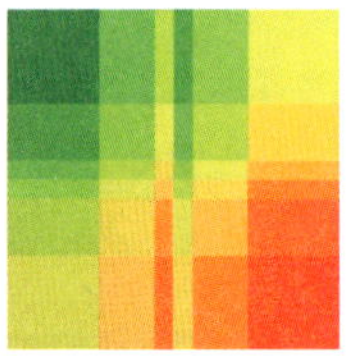

003

Richard Paul Lohse
6 systematische Reihen in rot und grün mit Verdichtung nach innen
1955/1971

Provenance
Richard Paul Lohse-Stiftung, Zurich
Edith Wahlandt Galerie, Stuttgart

Exhibitions
1971 Olten, Kunstverein, *Zürcher Konkrete, Max Bill, Camille Graeser, Verena Loewensberg, Richard Paul Lohse*, no. 44
1980 Berlin, Galerie Bossin, *Richard Paul Lohse*

Literature
Lohse 1984, p. 263

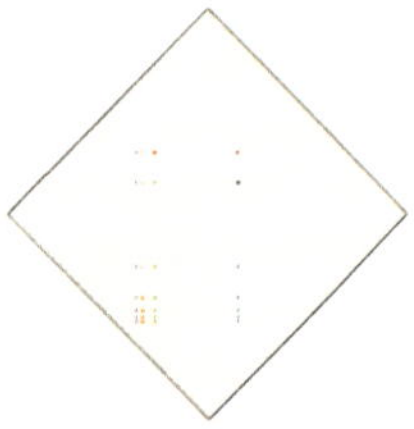

004

Max Bill
geordnete spannungen
1948

Provenance
Private collection, Austria
Galerie am Lindenplatz, Vaduz

Exhibitions
2005 Vaduz, Kunstmuseum Liechtenstein, *Werke aus der Hilti Art Foundation. Von Paul Gauguin bis Imi Knoebel*, p. 78, no. 31
2008 Winterthur, Kunstmuseum / Gewerbemuseum, *Max Bill: Aspekte seines Werks*, p. 137
2008 Zurich, Haus Konstruktiv, *Max Bill* 100

Literature
Wieczorek 2005, p. 78, no. 31

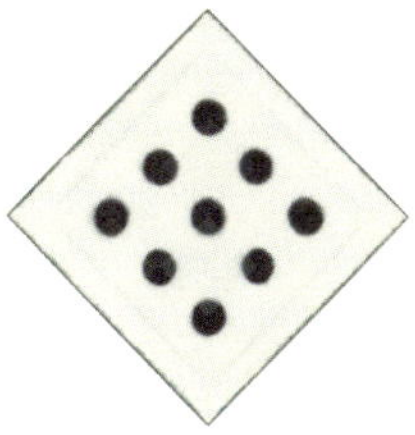

005

Max Bill
neun akzente aus quadratischem feld
1949–1951

Provenance
Galerie am Lindenplatz, Vaduz

Exhibitions
1958 Winterthur, Kunstmuseum, *Ungegenständliche Malerei in der Schweiz*
1991 Locarno, Pinacoteca Comunale Casa Rusca, *Max Bill*
2005 Vaduz, Kunstmuseum Liechtenstein, *Werke aus der Hilti Art Foundation. Von Paul Gauguin bis Imi Knoebel*

Literature
Caramel / Thomas 1991
Hüttinger 1978
Thomas 1993, pp. 98–119

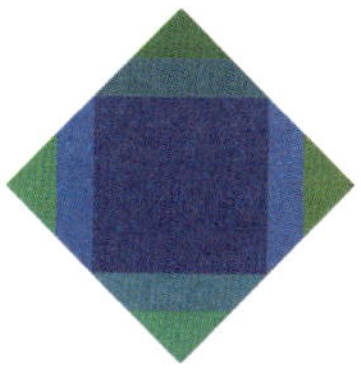

006

Max Bill
zerstrahlung von blau
1972–1974

Provenance
Art & Editions Haas, Dornbirn
Galerie am Lindenplatz, Vaduz

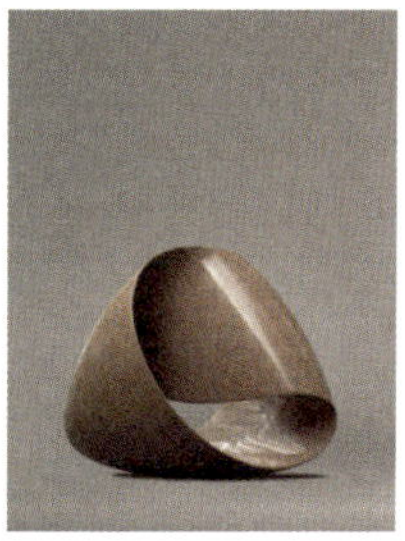

007

Max Bill
unendliche schleife
1994–95

Provenance
Jakob Bill, Switzerland
Galerie am Lindenplatz, Vaduz

Exhibitions
2005 Vaduz, Kunstmuseum Liechtenstein, *Werke aus der Hilti Art Foundation. Von Paul Gauguin bis Imi Knoebel*, p. 110, no. 49

Literature
Bill 2000, pp. 71 ff.
Wieczorek 2005, p. 110, no. 49
Brüderlin 2005, pp. 198–99

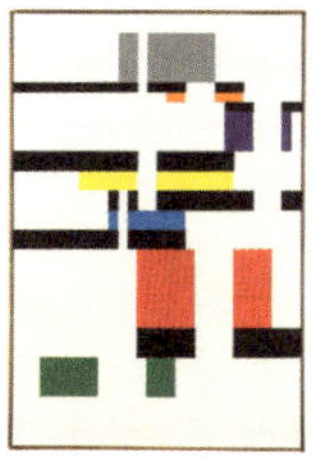

008

Verena Loewensberg
Untitled
1948
(WVZ 34)

Provenance
Henriette Coray Loewensberg, Zurich

Exhibitions
1950 Zurich, Galerie 16, *Verena Loewensberg, Hans Coray*
1960 Zurich, Galerie Suzanne Bollag, *Contrastes II*

Literature
Coray Loewensberg 2012, p. 142, no. 25

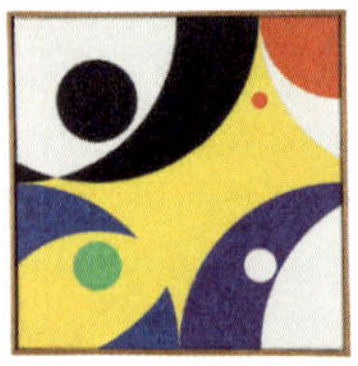

009

Verena Loewensberg
Untitled
1947
(WVZ 25)

Provenance
Henriette Coray Loewensberg, Zurich

Exhibitions
1950 Zurich, Galerie 16, *Allianz. H. Aeschbacher, M. Bill, H. Eichmann, H. Fischli, H. Gantenbein, R. S. Gessner, C. Graeser, Oe. Koch, L. Leuppi, V. Loewensberg, R. P. Lohse*
2012 Winterthur, Kunstmuseum, *Verena Loewensberg*

Literature
Coray Loewensberg 2012, p. 142, no. 25

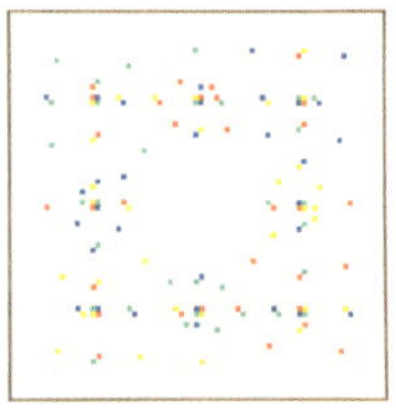

010

Verena Loewensberg
Untitled
1977
(WVZ 481)

Provenance
Henriette Coray Loewensberg, Zurich

Exhibitions
1977–78 Basel / Chur, Galerie Beyeler Basel, Bündner Kunstmuseum Chur, *bill, glarner, graeser, loewensberg*, no. 126
1978 Zurich, Galerie du Carrois, *verena loewensberg*
1981 Ludwigshafen, Wilhelm-Hack-Museum, *Verena Loewensberg*, no. 126
1981 Zurich, Kunsthaus, *Verena Loewensberg*, no. 126
1992 Aarau, Aargauer Kunsthaus Aarau, *Verena Loewensberg 1912–1986. Retrospektive*, no. 62
2006–07 Zurich, Haus Konstruktiv, *Verena Loewensberg. Unendliche Folgen*, p. 39

Literature
Kappeler 1980, p. 115
Coray Loewensberg 2012, p. 218, no. 481

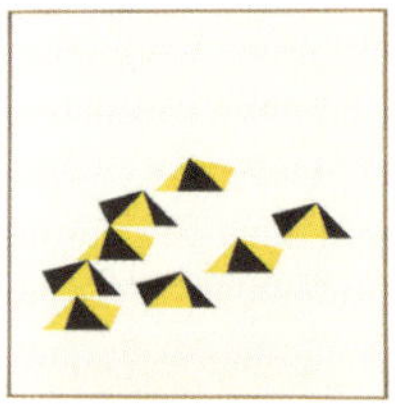

011

Verena Loewensberg
Untitled
1981
(WVZ 541)

Provenance
Henriette Coray Loewensberg, Zurich

Exhibitions
1982 Bottrop, Moderne Galerie Bottrop, *Verena Loewensberg*, no. 71
2006–07 Zurich, Haus Konstruktiv, *Verena Loewensberg. Unendliche Folgen*
2012 Winterthur, Kunstmuseum, *Verena Loewensberg*

Literature
Coray Loewensberg 2012, p. 228, no. 541

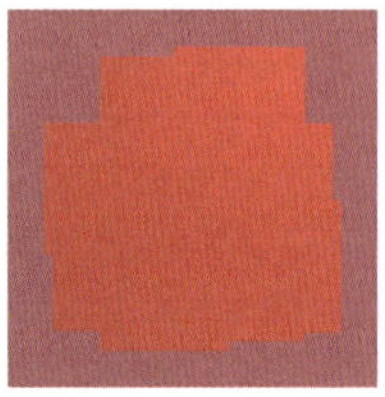

012

Verena Loewensberg
Untitled
1984
(WVZ 600)

Provenance
Henriette Coray Loewensberg, Zurich

Exhibitions
1992 Aarau, Aargauer Kunsthaus Aarau, *Verena Loewensberg 1912–1986. Retrospektive*, no. 125
1998 Frankfurt am main, Frankfurter Kunstverein, *Regel und Abweichung. 40 Jahre konstruktive Kunst in der Schweiz*
1998 Neuenburg, Musée d'art et d'histoire, *Règle et déviance. Constructivisme en Suisse 1960–1997*
1998–99 Zurich, Haus für konstruktive und konkrete Kunst, *Verena Loewensberg Retrospektive*, p. 60
1999 Otterndorf, Museum moderner Kunst Landkreis Cuxhafen, *verena loewensberg, zürich 1912–1986*
2012 Winterthur, Kunstmuseum Winterthur, *Verena Loewensberg*

Literature
Coray Loewensberg 2012, p. 238, no. 600
Grossmann 2012, pp. 124 ff. and fig., p. 129, no. 157

013

Verena Loewensberg
Untitled
1984–85
(WVZ 612)

Provenance
Henriette Coray Loewensberg, Zurich

Exhibitions
1986 Zurich, Galerie Jamileh Weber, *verena loewensberg bei jamileh weber*
1993–94 Zurich, Haus für konstruktive und konkrete Kunst, *Thematische Veränderungen: Bill–Graeser–Loewensberg–Lohse*
2015 Vaduz, Hilti Art Foundation / Kunstmuseum Liechtenstein, *Hilti Art Foundation – Painting and Sculpture. From Classical Modernism to the Present Day*, p. 160, no. 48

Literature
Coray Loewensberg 2012, p. 240, no. 612
Grossmann 2012, pp. 124 ff.
Wieczorek 2015, p. 160, no. 48

014

Verena Loewensberg
Untitled
1985
(WVZ 632)

Provenance
Henriette Coray Loewensberg, Zurich

Exhibitions
2015 Vaduz, Hilti Art Foundation / Kunstmuseum Liechtenstein, *Hilti Art Foundation – Painting and Sculpture. From Classical Modernism to the Present Day*, p. 162, no. 49

Literature
Coray Loewensberg 2012, p. 243, no. 632
Grossmann 2012, pp. 124 ff. and fig., p. 132, no. 160
Wieczorek 2015, p. 162, no. 49

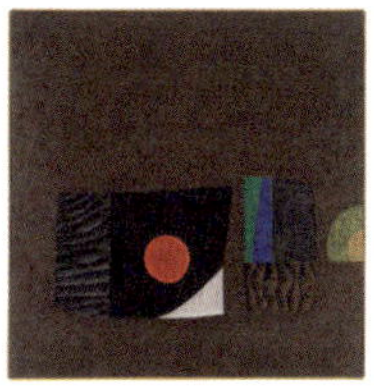

015

Gottfried Honegger
Gestern
1957–58

Provenance
The artist's studio

Courtesy Fondation Gottfried Honegger, Zurich

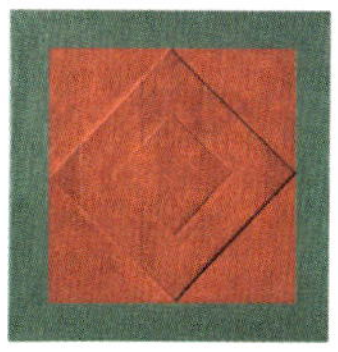

016

Gottfried Honegger
Untitled
1957

Provenance
The artist's studio

Exhibitions
2005 Vaduz, Kunstmuseum Liechtenstein, *Werke aus der Hilti Art Foundation. Von Paul Gauguin bis Imi Knoebel*, p. 100, no. 42

Literature
Wieczorek 2005, p. 100, no. 42

Courtesy Fondation Gottfried Honegger, Zurich

017

Gottfried Honegger
Waria
1960

Provenance
Sam Francis, New York
Galerie Proarta AG, Zurich

Exhibitions
1960 New York, Martha Jackson Gallery, *Gottfried Honegger: Swiss Purist*

Courtesy Fondation Gottfried Honegger, Zurich

018

Gottfried Honegger
Tableau-Relief Z.825.1
1979

Provenance
The artist's studio
Private collection, Switzerland

Exhibitions
2010 Freiburg-Zähringen, Stiftung für Konkrete Kunst Roland Phleps, *Gottfried Honegger. Die Poesie der Geometrie. Gemälde, Plastiken, Grafik*
2015 Vaduz, Hilti Art Foundation / Kunstmuseum Liechtenstein, *Hilti Art Foundation – Painting and Sculpture. From Classical Modernism to the Present Day*, p. 156, no. 47

Literature
Forster 1972
Lemoine 1983
Wieczorek 2015, p. 156, no. 47

Courtesy Fondation Gottfried Honegger, Zurich

019

Gottfried Honegger
Tableau-Relief P 725
1973

Provenance
The artist's studio

Exhibitions
2005 Vaduz, Kunstmuseum Liechtenstein, *Werke aus der Hilti Art Foundation. Von Paul Gauguin bis Imi Knoebel*, p. 100 and p. 105, no. 45

Literature
Wieczorek 2005, p. 100 and p. 105, no. 45

Courtesy Fondation Gottfried Honegger, Zurich

020

Gottfried Honegger
Tableau-Relief Z 629
1971

Provenance
The artist's studio

Exhibitions
2010 Freiburg-Zähringen, Stiftung für Konkrete Kunst Roland Phleps, *Gottfried Honegger. Die Poesie der Geometrie. Gemälde, Plastiken, Grafik*

Courtesy Fondation Gottfried Honegger, Zurich

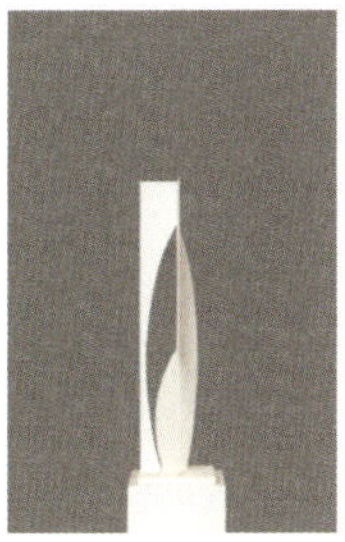

021

Gottfried Honegger
Pliagen (1–16)
2002–2004

Provenance
The artist's studio

Exhibitions
2005 Vaduz, Kunstmuseum Liechtenstein, *Werke aus der Hilti Art Foundation. Von Paul Gauguin bis Imi Knoebel*, p. 108, no. 48
2010 Freiburg-Zähringen, Stiftung für Konkrete Kunst Roland Phleps, *Gottfried Honegger. Die Poesie der Geometrie. Gemälde, Plastiken, Grafik*

Literature
Wieczorek 2005, p. 108, no. 48

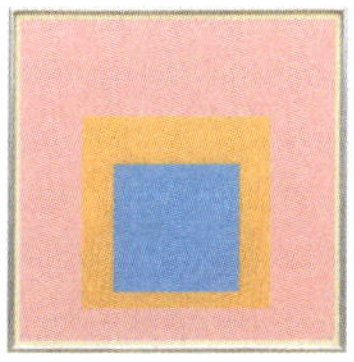

022

Josef Albers
Homage to the Square (Early Diary A)
1954

Provenance
Sidney Janis Gallery, New York
Private collection, New York
Private collection, New York
Sotheby's, New York, 11 May 2006, lot 175

Exhibitions
2019–20 Vaduz, Hilti Art Foundation / Kunstmuseum Liechtenstein, *Epidermis – Conditio humana – Kosmos*, no. 28

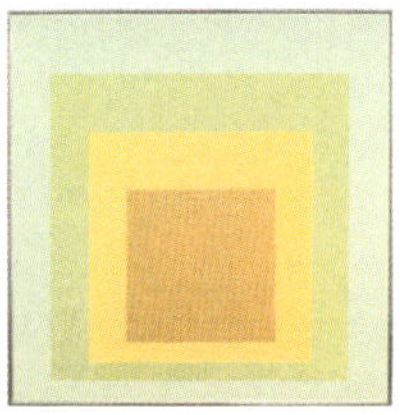

023

Josef Albers
Homage to the Square
1959
(JAF 0916)

Provenance
André Emmerich, New York, Zurich
Karsten Greve, Cologne
Private collection, Switzerland

Exhibitions
2015 Vaduz, Hilti Art Foundation / Kunstmuseum Liechtenstein, *Hilti Art Foundation – Painting and Sculpture. From Classical Modernism to the Present Day*, p. 124, no. 35

Literature
Wieczorek 2015, p. 124, no. 35

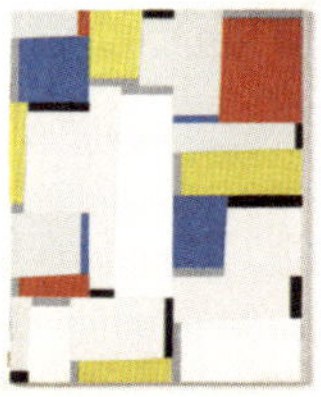

024

Fritz Glarner
Relational Painting No. 58
1952

Provenance
Galerie Louis Carré, Paris
Galerie Barbara Mathes, New York
Private collection, Switzerland
Galerie von Bartha, Basel

Literature
Staber 1976, p. 131

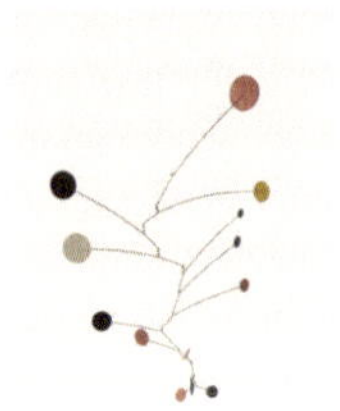

025

Alexander Calder
Untitled
1947
(A26562)

Provenance
Samuel Berenger, Connecticut, USA
Sotheby's, Paris, 3 December 2014, lot 4
Fernando Mignoni Gallery, New York

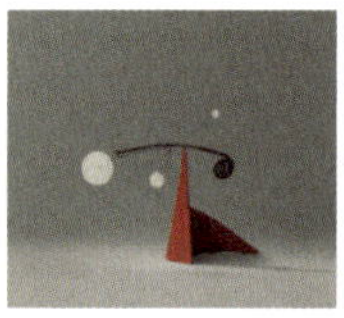

026

Alexander Calder
Untitled
1960

Provenance
Private collection, New Mexico, USA
(gift of the artist)
Achim Moeller Fine Art, New York

Exhibitions
2005 Vaduz, Kunstmuseum Liechtenstein, *Werke aus der Hilti Art Foundation. Von Paul Gauguin bis Imi Knoebel*, p. 68, no. 26

Literature
Wieczorek 2005, p. 68, no. 26

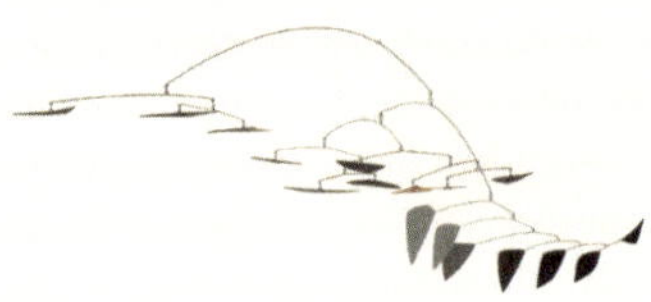

027

Alexander Calder
Lone Red Among Blacks
1961
(A07589)

Provenance
Fairweather-Hardin Gallery, Chicago
Edwin and Grace Hokin, Chicago
Galerie Thomas, Munich

Exhibitions
2003 Bilbao, Guggenheim Museum; 2003–04 Madrid, Museo Nacional Centro de Arte Reina Sofía, *Calder. Gravity and Grace*, no. 63

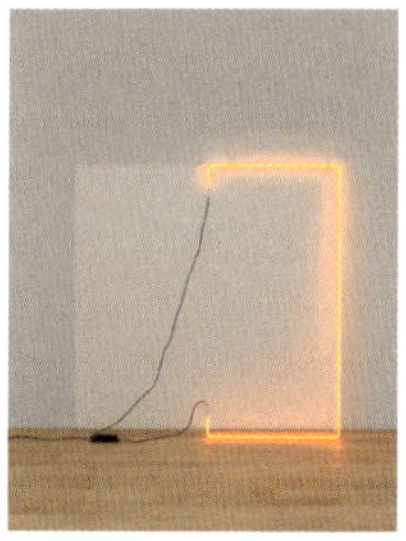

028

Keith Sonnier
Lit Square – right side variation (2-M-N)
1969 (2015)

Provenance
Galerie am Lindenplatz, Vaduz

Exhibitions
2016 Vaduz, Hilti Art Foundation / Kunstmuseum Liechtenstein, *Hilti Art Foundation – Kirchner, Léger, Scully & more. Works from the Collection*, p. 106, no. 29
2018 Vaduz, Hilti Art Foundation / Kunstmuseum Liechtenstein, *Hilti Art Foundation – Rosso, Klee, Sonnier & more. Works from the Collection*, p. 76, no. 29

Literature
Schneider 2016, p. 106, no. 29
Schneider 2018, p. 76, no. 29

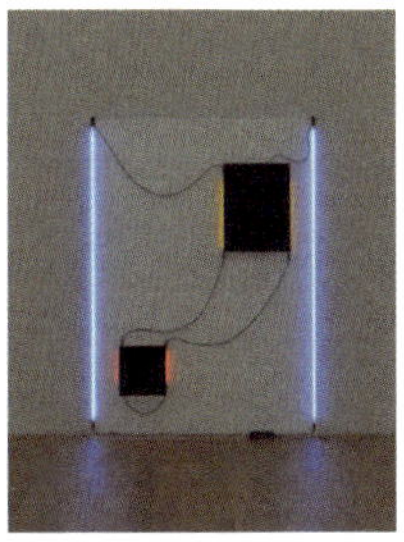

029

Keith Sonnier
Ba-O-Ba Krefeld 1B
1977 (2015)

Provenance
Häusler Contemporary, Zurich

Exhibitions
2018 Vaduz, Hilti Art Foundation / Kunstmuseum Liechtenstein, *Hilti Art Foundation – Rosso, Klee, Sonnier & more. Works from the Collection*, p. 88, no. 35

Literature
Storck 1979
Schneider 2018, p. 88, no. 35

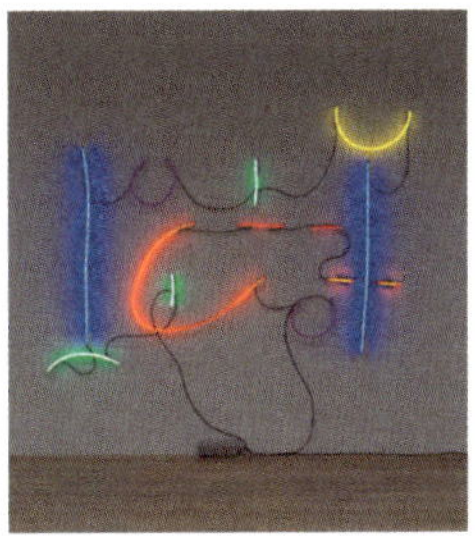

030

Keith Sonnier
Expanded SEL VII
1978 (2006)

Provenance
Häusler Contemporary, Zurich

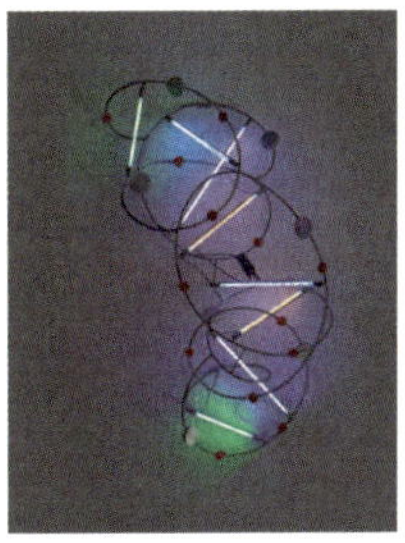

031

Keith Sonnier
Gran Twister
2012

Provenance
The artist's studio
Galerie am Lindenplatz, Vaduz

032

Sean Scully
Ada
1980

Provenance
Private collection, New York
Private collection, New York
Knoedler & Company, New York

Exhibitions
1981 New York, Susan Caldwell Inc., *Doug Ohlson, Sean Scully*

Literature
Poirier 1990, pp. 73–74, fig. 47
Price 2018, p. 35, no. 1980.16

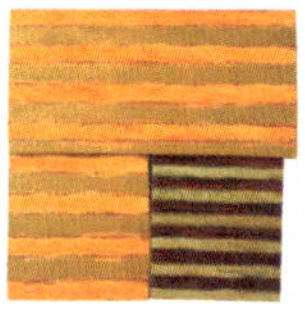

033

Sean Scully
Plum
1982

Provenance
Barbara Guggenheim Associates, Los Angeles
Private collection
Christie's, New York, 16 May 2013, lot 520
Timothy Taylor Gallery, London

Exhibitions
1983 New York, William Beadlestone Inc., *Sean Scully, Recent Paintings*
2016 Vaduz, Hilti Art Foundation / Kunstmuseum Liechtenstein, *Hilti Art Foundation – Kirchner, Léger, Scully & more. Works from the Collection*, p. 116, no. 33

Literature
Adams 1985, pp. 118–23, no. 10
Wieczorek 2016, p. 116, no. 33
Price 2018, p. 71, no. 1982.11

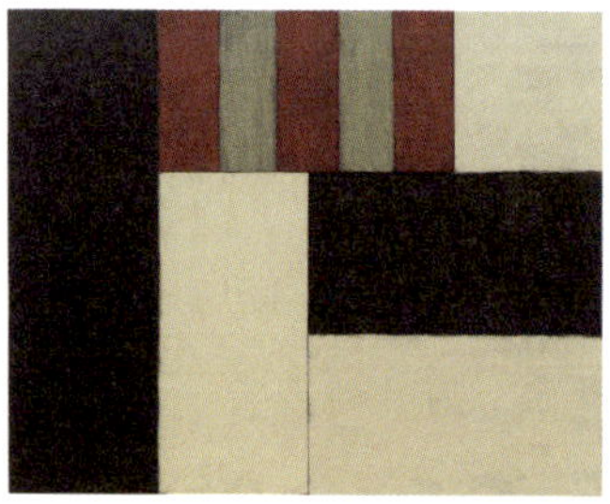

034

Sean Scully
Dreamland
1987

Provenance
David McKee Gallery, New York
Fuji Television Gallery, Japan
Private collection, Switzerland
Sotheby's, New York, 15 May 2008, lot 258
Timothy Taylor Gallery, London

Exhibitions
1987 Chicago, Art Institute of Chicago, *Sean Scully*
1988 Tokyo, Fuji Television Gallery, *Sean Scully*, no. 10
2009 London, Timothy Tailor Gallery, *Sean Scully: Paintings from the 80s*, no. 5
2009 Duisburg, MKM Museum Küppersmühle für Moderne Kunst, *Konstantinopel oder Die versteckte Sinnlichkeit. Die Bilderwelt von Sean Scully*, p. 13
2016 Vaduz, Hilti Art Foundation / Kunstmuseum Liechtenstein, *Hilti Art Foundation – Kirchner, Léger, Scully & more. Works from the Collection*, p. 118, no. 34

Literature
Wieczorek 2016, p. 118, no. 34
Price 2018, p. 198, no. 1987.07

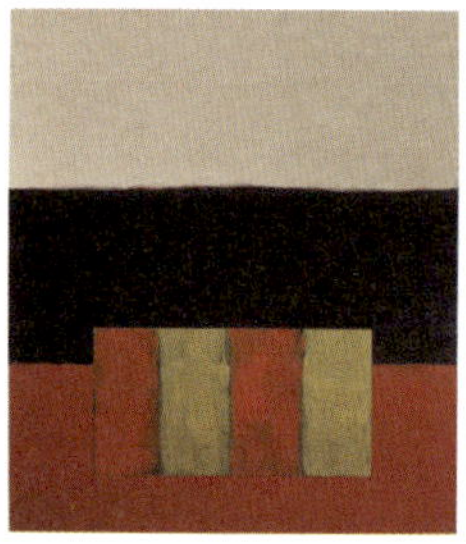

035

Sean Scully
Song of Red
1999

Provenance
The artist's studio
Galerie Jamileh Weber, Zurich

Exhibitions
2001 Düsseldorf, Kunstsammlung Nordrhein-Westfalen; Munich, Haus der Kunst, *Sean Scully*, p. 52
2001–02 Vevey, Musée Jenisch, *Sean Scully*

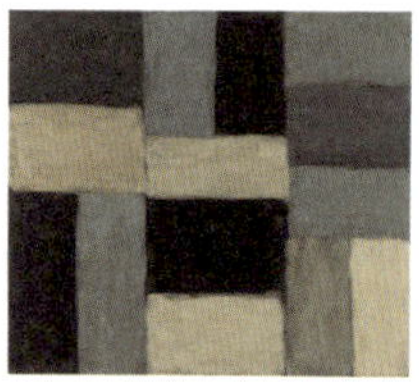

036

Sean Scully
Doric Grey
2012

Provenance
The artist's studio

Exhibitions
2016 Vaduz, Hilti Art Foundation / Kunstmuseum Liechtenstein, *Hilti Art Foundation – Kirchner, Léger, Scully & more. Works from the Collection*, p. 122, no. 35

Literature
Wieczorek 2016, p. 122, no. 35

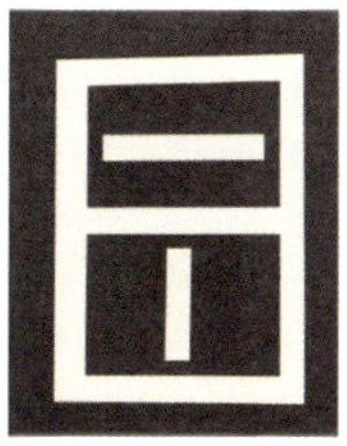

037

Helmut Federle
Zeichen der geteilten, eingeschlossenen Ganzheit
1984/1986

Provenance
Brigitte Büdenhölzer, Kunsthandel

Exhibitions
1986 Vienna, Galerie nächst St. Stephan, *Abstrakte Malerei am Beispiel von drei europäischen und drei amerikanischen Künstlern; Federle, Knoebel, Richter, Mangold, Marden, Ryman*

Literature
Bool 1985
Franz 1997
Goetz 1996
Koepplin 1985
Schwarzwälder 1988, p. 16
Zutter 1985

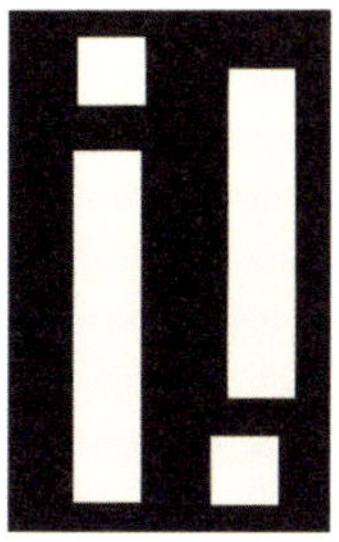

038

Helmut Federle
Two i, Undecided
1985

Provenance
Mary Boone Gallery, New York
Christie's, New York, 19 November 1992, lot 174
Spiegel Collection, New York
Peter Raczeck Fine Art, New York

Exhibitions
1986 Munich, Kunstverein, *Geometria Nova*
1986 Vienna, Galerie nächst St. Stephan
1987 New York, Mary Boone Gallery
1994 Essen, Folkwang Museum, *Symbol – Sinn – Struktur, Helmut Federle, Zwei Räume und eine Intervention in der Sammlung des Museums Folkwang*
2002 Musée des Beaux-Arts de Nantes, Nantes
2002 Museum Ludwig, Cologne, *Body of Painting – Günter Umberg mit Bildern aus Kölner Sammlungen*

Literature
Bool 1985
Franz 1997
Goetz 1996
Koepplin 1985
Zutter 1985

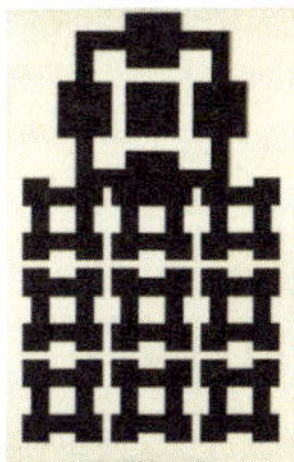

039

Victor Vasarely
Procion
1959

Provenance
Galerie Lahumière, Paris
Private collection, Switzerland
Galerie Renée Ziegler, Zurich
Private collection, Switzerland
Galerie Haas, Zurich

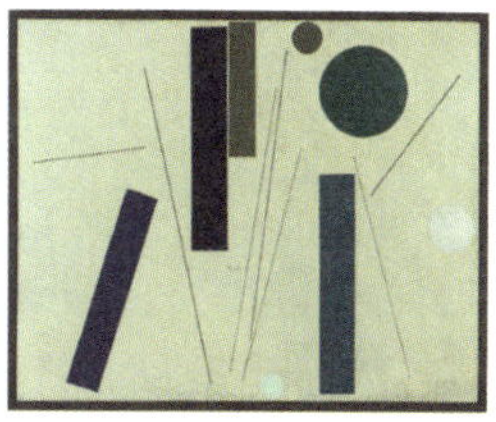

040

Günter Fruhtrunk
Untitled
1956

Provenance
Günter Fruhtrunk Estate
Edith Wahlandt Galerie, Stuttgart

Literature
Reiter 2018, vol. 1, p. 165, no. 82, vol. 2, p. 536, no. 82

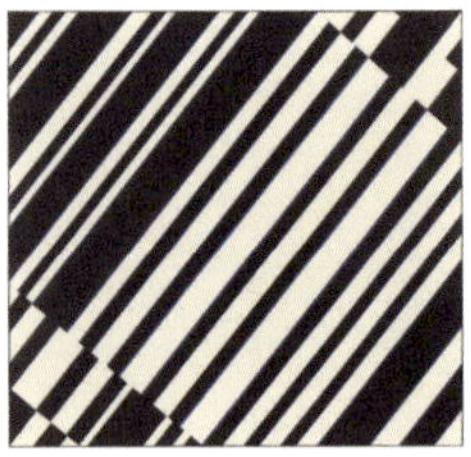

041

Günter Fruhtrunk
Diagonale Progression Schwarz-Weiss (Studie II)
c. 1970

Provenance
Günter Fruhtrunk Estate
Walter Storms Galerie, Munich

Exhibitions
2012 Vaduz, Kunstmuseum Liechtenstein, *Günter Fruhtrunk, Farbe Rhythmus Existenz*, p. 87 and p. 160
2015 Vaduz, Hilti Art Foundation / Kunstmuseum Liechtenstein, *Hilti Art Foundation – Painting and Sculpture. From Classical Modernism to the Present Day*, p. 154, no. 46

Literature
Franz 2012, p. 9
Wieczorek 2015, p. 154, no. 46
Reiter 2018, vol. 1, p. 312, no. 479, vol. 2, p. 584, no. 613

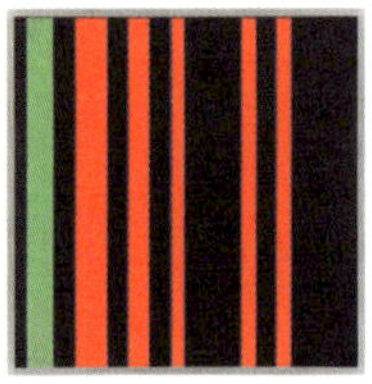

042

Günter Fruhtrunk
Exzentrisches Grün
1968

Provenance
Brigitte Büdenhölzer, Kunsthandel

Exhibitions
1979 Frankfurt am Main, Galerie Appel und Fertsch, 20 *Jahre Galerie Appel und Fertsch*, fig. p. 21, no. 3

Literature
Wendt 2001, no. 1968–07
Reiter 2018, vol. 1, p. 337, no. 547, vol. 2, p. 578, no. 547

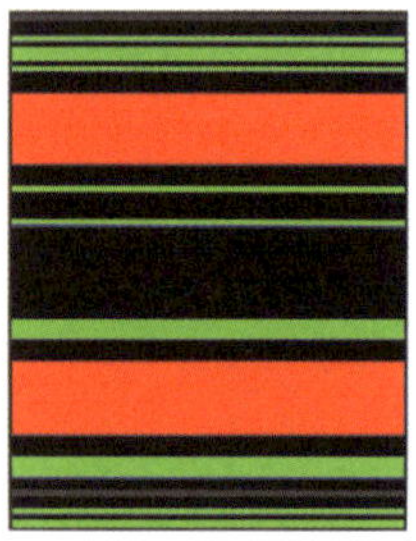

043

Günter Fruhtrunk
2 Rot: 1 Rot II
1971

Provenance
Günter Fruhtrunk Estate
Walter Storms Galerie, Munich

Exhibitions
1973 Munich, Städtische Glerie im Lenbachhaus; Karlsruhe, Badischer Kunstverein; Bochum, Museum Bochum, *Fruhtrunk. Bilder* 1952–1972, no. 67
1983–84 Braunschweig, Kunstverein Braunschweig, *Günter Fruhtrunk*, p. 171, no. 33
2012 Vaduz, Kunstmuseum Liechtenstein, *Günter Fruhtrunk. Farbe Rhythmus Existenz*, pp. 88–89

Literature
Gomringer, Imdahl, Sterner 1978, no. 245
Wendt 2001, no. 1971-08
Reiter 2018, vol. 1, p. 366, no. 641, vol. 2, p. 587, no. 641

044

François Morellet
4 Trames superposées
1959/1969

Provenance
Max Imdahl, Bochum
Imdahl Estate, Germany

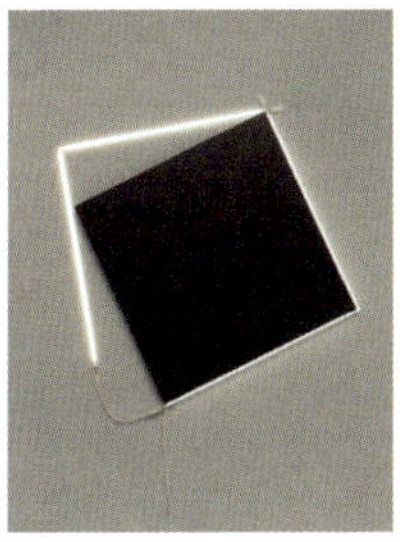

045

François Morellet
Négatif n° 14
2011

Provenance
The artist's studio
Galerie am Lindenplatz, Vaduz

Exhibitions
2016 Vaduz, Hilti Art Foundation/Kunstmuseum Liechtenstein, *Hilti Art Foundation – Kirchner, Léger, Scully & more. Works from the Collection*, p. 124, no. 36

Literature
Schneider 2016, p. 124, no. 36

046

Lucio Fontana
Concetto spaziale, Attesa
1966

Provenance
Galerie H. J. Müller, Cologne
Op Art Galerie, Esslingen
Galerie Denise René – Hans Mayer, Krefeld
Sammlung K. Schröer, Krefeld
Private collection, Germany
Galerie Thomas, Munich

Exhibitions
1981 Cologne, Galerie Reckermann, *Nice–Milano–Paris–Düsseldorf*, fig.
2015 Vaduz, Hilti Art Foundation / Kunstmuseum Liechtenstein, *Hilti Art Foundation – Painting and Sculpture. From Classical Modernism to the Present Day*, p. 130, no. 37
2018–19 Zurich, Landesmuseum Zurich, *Imagine 68. Das Spektakel der Revolution.*
2019–20 Vaduz, Hilti Art Foundation / Kunstmuseum Liechtenstein, *Epidermis – Conditio humana – Kosmos*, no. 6

Literature
Crispolti 1974, vol. II, p. 188
Crispolti 1986, vol. II, p. 651, no. 66 T 116
Wieczorek 2015, p. 130, no. 37

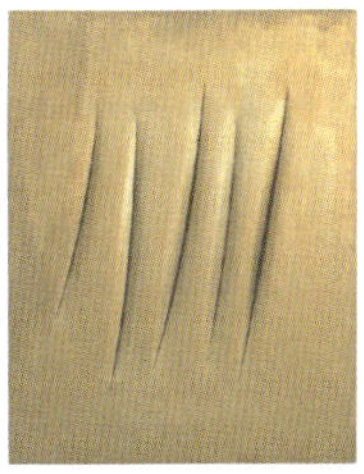

047

Lucio Fontana
Concetto spaziale, Attese
1962

Provenance
Galleria del Leone, Venice
Private collection, Milan
Galerie am Lindenplatz, Vaduz

Exhibitions
2005 Vaduz, Kunstmuseum Liechtenstein, *Werke aus der Hilti Art Foundation. Von Paul Gauguin bis Imi Knoebel*, p. 100, no. 34
2007 Hamburg, Hamburger Kunsthalle, *Das Schwarze Quadrat. Hommage an Malewitsch*, p. 78, no. 55

Literature
Crispolti 1974, vol. II, p. 132
Crispolti 1986, vol. II, p. 449, no. 62 T 41
Wieczorek 2005, p. 84, no. 34

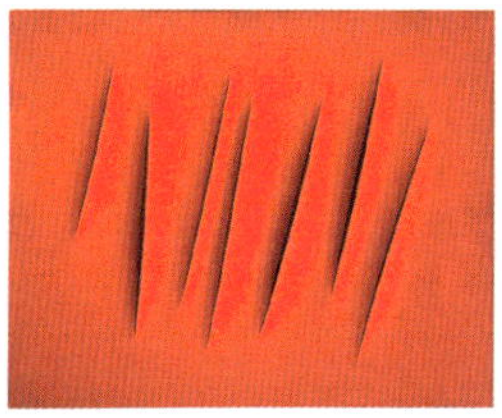

048

Lucio Fontana
Concetto spaziale, Attese
1965

Provenance
Marlborough, Galleria d'Arte, Rome
Collezione Bruno Herlitzka, Rome
Galerie am Lindenplatz, Vaduz

Exhibitions
1990 Tokyo, Tama Art University Museum, *Lucio Fontana, Spatial Conception*
2005 Vaduz, Kunstmuseum Liechtenstein, *Werke aus der Hilti Art Foundation. Von Paul Gauguin bis Imi Knoebel*, p. 86, no. 35

Literature
Crispolti 1974, vol. II, p. 162
Crispolti 1986, vol. II, p. 572

049

Yves Klein
Monochrome (IKB 180)
1958

Provenance
Rose Raymond Gaspérini, Nice
Galerie am Lindenplatz, Vaduz

Exhibitions
1994 London, Gimpel Fils, *Yves Klein*
2005 Vaduz, Kunstmuseum Liechtenstein, *Werke aus der Hilti Art Foundation. Von Paul Gauguin bis Imi Knoebel*, p. 88, no. 36
2007 Hamburg, Hamburger Kunsthalle, *Das Schwarze Quadrat. Hommage an Malewitsch*, p. 80, no. 57
2015 Vaduz, Hilti Art Foundation / Kunstmuseum Liechtenstein, *Hilti Art Foundation – Painting and Sculpture. From Classical Modernism to the Present Day*, p. 132, no. 38

Literature
Wember 1969, p. 75
Schneider 2005, p. 88, no. 36
Schneider 2015, p. 132, no. 38

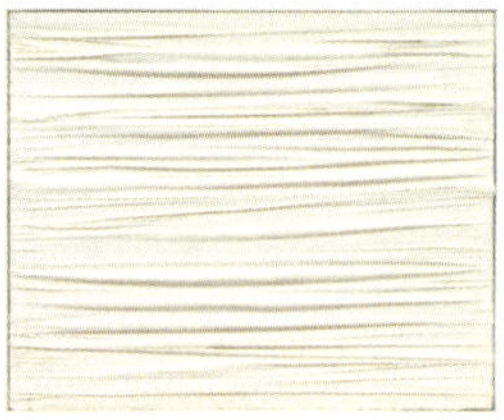

050

Piero Manzoni
Achrome
1959–60

Provenance
Private collection, Viareggio
Galerie am Lindenplatz, Vaduz

Exhibitions
2005 Vaduz, Kunstmuseum Liechtenstein, *Werke aus der Hilti Art Foundation. Von Paul Gauguin bis Imi Knoebel*, p. 92, no. 38
2008 Vienna, BA-CA Kunstforum, *Monet Kandinsky Rothko und die Folgen. Wege der abstrakten Malerei*, p. 132
2013 Wolfsburg, Kunstmuseum, *Art & Textiles. Fabric as Material and Concept in Modern Art from Klimt to the Present*, p. 190
2015 Vaduz, Hilti Art Foundation / Kunstmuseum Liechtenstein, *Hilti Art Foundation – Painting and Sculpture. From Classical Modernism to the Present Day*, p. 134, no. 39
2019–20 Vaduz, Hilti Art Foundation / Kunstmuseum Liechtenstein, *Epidermis – Conditio humana – Kosmos*, no. 7

Literature
Malsch 2005, p. 92, no. 38
Schneider 2015, p. 134, no. 39

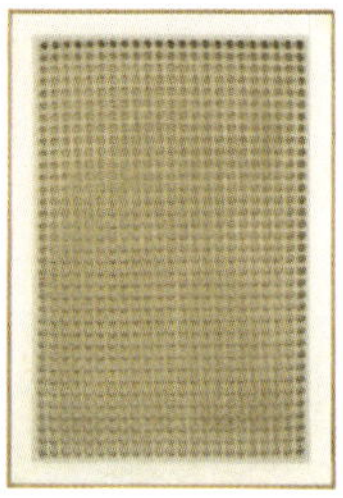

051

Dadamaino
Volume a moduli sfasati
1960

Provenance
Private collection, Milan
Galerie am Lindenplatz, Vaduz

Exhibitions
1990 Morterone, Palazzo Municipale; Ferrara, Istituto d'Arte "Dosso Dossi", *La pelle dell'arte. Riflessioni sulla superficie*, no. 5
2005 Vaduz, Kunstmuseum Liechtenstein, *Werke aus der Hilti Art Foundation. Von Paul Gauguin bis Imi Knoebel*, p. 94, no. 39
2019–20 Vaduz, Hilti Art Foundation / Kunstmuseum Liechtenstein, *Epidermis – Conditio humana – Kosmos*, no. 2

Literature
Golinski 2000
Malsch 2005, p. 94, no. 39

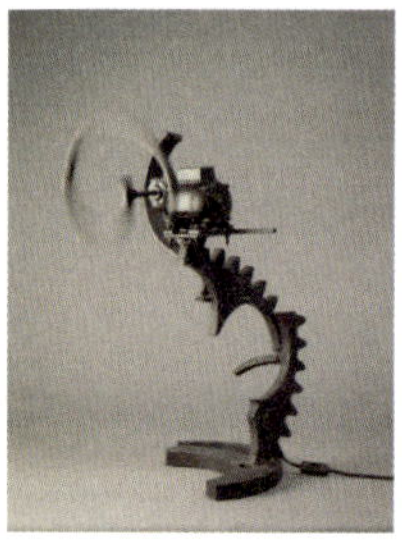

052

Jean Tinguely
Variation IV
1966

Provenance
Private collection, Paris
Kunsthandel Wolfgang Werner, Bremen/Berlin

Exhibitions
1966 Milan, Galerie Alexandre Iolas, no. 14

Literature
Bischofberger 1982, p. 264, no. 394
Violand-Hobi 1995

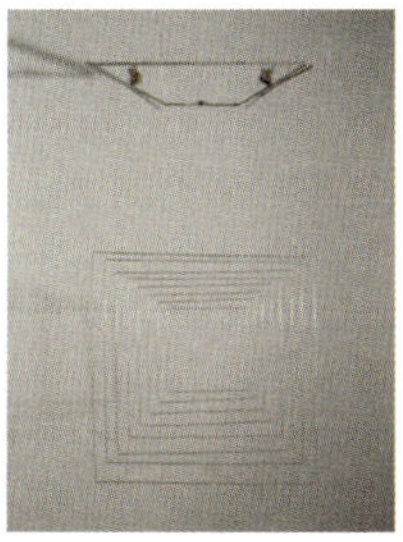

053

Gianni Colombo
Spazio elastico
1968

Provenance
Thomas Keller Galerie, Kempfenhausen, 1970
Private collection, Germany
Edith Wahlandt Galerie, Stuttgart

Exhibitions
1970 Kempfenhausen / Starnberg, Thomas Keller Galerie, *Gianni Colombo*
2009 Zurich, Haus Konstruktiv, *Gianni Colombo*
2009–10 Rivoli-Turin, Castello di Rivoli, Museo d'Arte Contemporanea, *Gianni Colombo*, p. 163 (fig.) and p. 196
2015 Vaduz, Hilti Art Foundation / Kunstmuseum Liechtenstein, *Hilti Art Foundation – Painting and Sculpture. From Classical Modernism to the Present Day*, p. 126, no. 36

Literature
Gomringer 1970
Wieczorek 2015, p. 126, no. 36

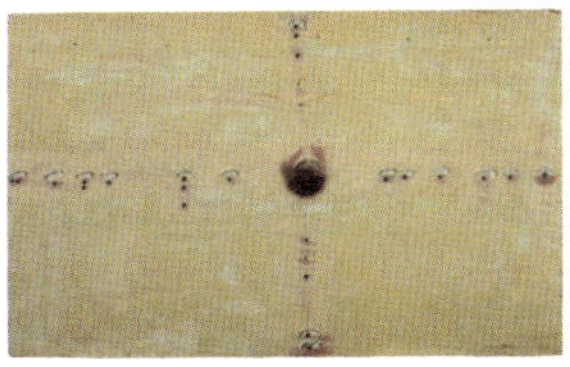

054

Hans Bischoffshausen
Zum Kreuz
1958

Provenance
Hans Bischoffshausen Estate
Galerie am Lindenplatz, Vaduz

Literature
Rohsmann 1991, p. 60

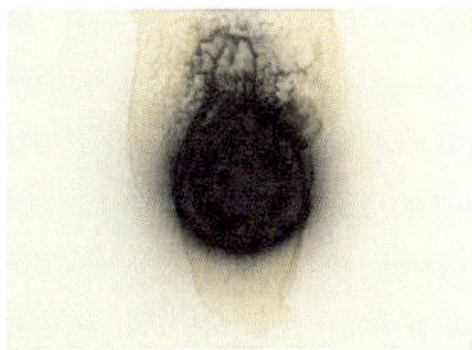

055

Otto Piene
Untitled
1962

Provenance
Private collection, Germany
Galerie Thomas, Munich

Exhibitions
2019–20 Vaduz, Hilti Art Foundation / Kunstmuseum Liechtenstein, *Epidermis – Conditio humana – Kosmos*, no. 9

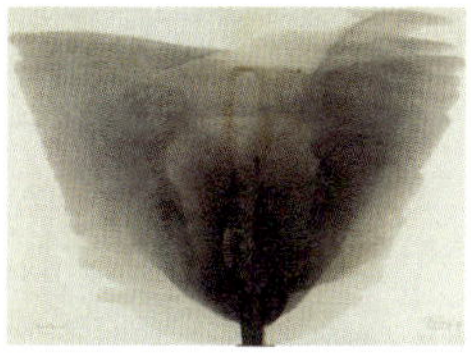

056

Otto Piene
Fire Flower
1967

Provenance
Galerie am Lindenplatz, Vaduz

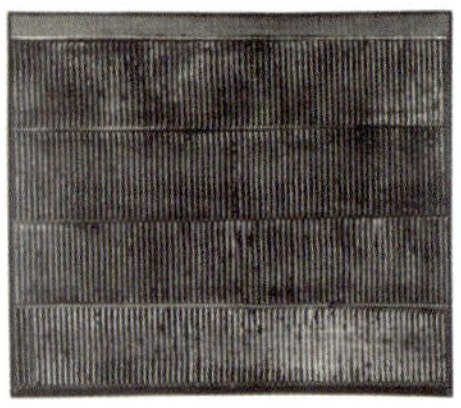

057

Heinz Mack
Untitled *(Dynamische Struktur)*
1957

Provenance
The artist's studio
Galerie am Lindenplatz, Vaduz

Exhibitions
2005 Vaduz, Kunstmuseum Liechtenstein, *Werke aus der Hilti Art Foundation. Von Paul Gauguin bis Imi Knoebel*, p. 96, no. 40

Literature
Wieczorek 2005, p. 96, no. 40
Fleck 2017, vol. II, p. 21, no. 1957–35

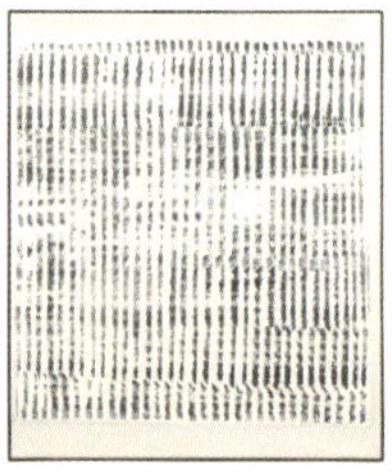

058

Heinz Mack
Untitled *(Dynamische Struktur)*
1961

Provenance
The artist's studio
Galerie am Lindenplatz, Vaduz

Exhibitions
2005 Vaduz, Kunstmuseum Liechtenstein, *Werke aus der Hilti Art Foundation. Von Paul Gauguin bis Imi Knoebel*, p. 98, no. 41

Literature
Wieczorek 2005, p. 98, no. 41

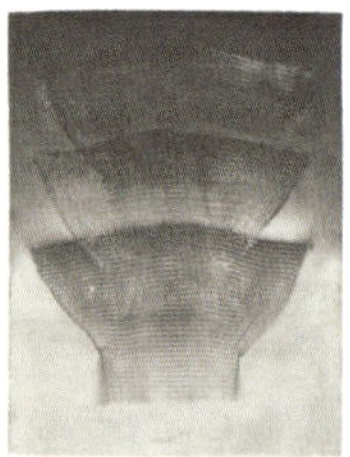

059

Heinz Mack
Untitled
1964

Provenance
The artist's studio
Galerie am Lindenplatz, Vaduz

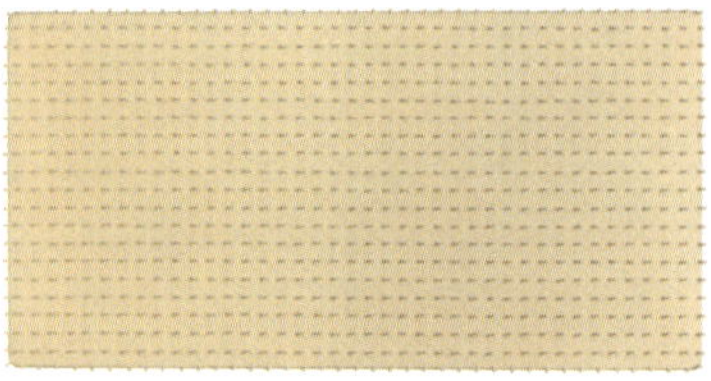

060

Günther Uecker
Serielle Reihung
1966

Provenance
Willoughby Sharp, New York (gift of the artist)
Galerie Onnasch, Cologne
Private collection, Germany
Galerie Dorothea van der Koelen, Mainz
Private collection, Germany
Hohenlohe Fine Art, Berlin

Literature
Honisch 1983, no. 489, fig. p. 207

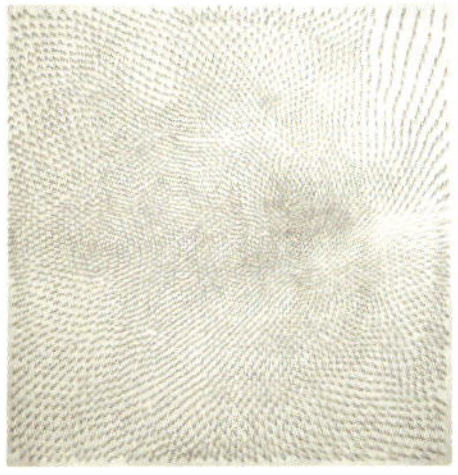

061

Günther Uecker
Grosses Feld
1967

Provenance
Galerie Schmela, Düsseldorf
Marianne and Viktor Langen Collection, Düsseldorf
TRW Collection, Düsseldorf
Galerie Thomas, Munich

Exhibitions
2015 Vaduz, Hilti Art Foundation / Kunstmuseum Liechtenstein, Hilti Art Foundation – Painting and Sculpture. From Classical Modernism to the Present Day, p. 144, no. 42
2019–20 Vaduz, Hilti Art Foundation / Kunstmuseum Liechtenstein, *Epidermis – Conditio humana – Kosmos*, no. 8

Literature
Schneider 2015, p. 144, no. 42

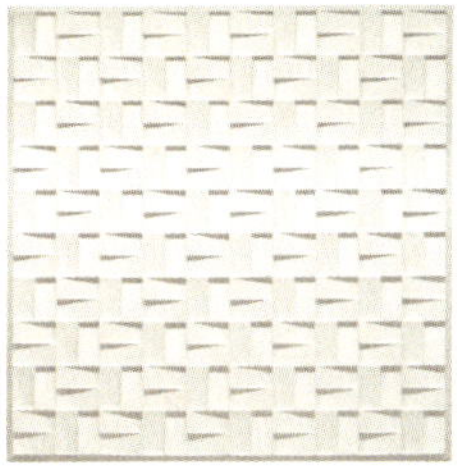

062

Jan Schoonhoven
R 72-25
1972

Provenance
Private collection, Essen
Peter Raczeck Fine Art, New York

Exhibitions
1995–96 Essen, Museum Folkwang; Maastricht, Bonnefantenmuseum; Aarau, Aargauer Kunsthaus, *Jan J. Schoonhoven – retrospektiv*, p. 142 and p. 176
2015 Vaduz, Hilti Art Foundation / Kunstmuseum Liechtenstein, *Hilti Art Foundation – Painting and Sculpture. From Classical Modernism to the Present Day*, p. 152, no. 45

Literature
Schneider 2015, p. 152, no. 45

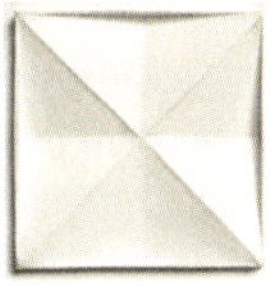

063

Jan Schoonhoven
R 69-13
1969

Provenance
Private collection, Netherlands
Brigitte Büdenhölzer, Kunsthandel

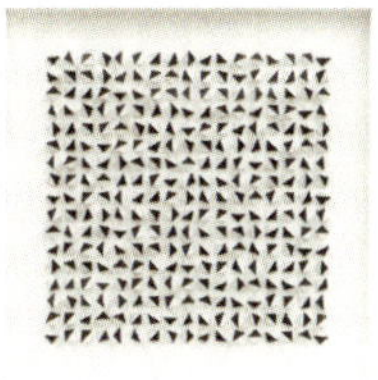

064

Klaus Staudt
S-W-R 1
1965

Provenance
The artist's studio
Galerie am Lindenplatz, Vaduz

Exhibitions
1967 Frankfurt am Main, Galerie Fischer-Steinhardt, *Klaus Staudt*
2018 Vaduz, Hilti Art Foundation / Kunstmuseum Liechtenstein, *Hilti Art Foundation – Rosso, Klee, Sonnier & more. Works from the Collection*, p. 78, no. 30

Literature
Enzweiler / Rompza 1999, p. 226, no. 1/66
Dellwing 2007, p. 15, fig. 1
Wieczorek 2018, p. 78, no. 30

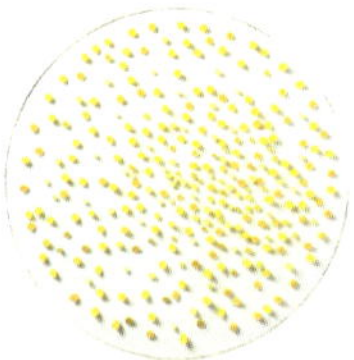

065

Klaus Staudt
Kreisformation II (FA-RE 5)
1965

Provenance
The artist's studio
Galerie am Lindenplatz, Vaduz

Exhibitions
1997 Ingolstadt, Museum für Konkrete Kunst; Frankfurt am Main, Frankfurter Kunstverein; Oldenburg, Landesmuseum für Kunst- und Kulturgeschichte, *Klaus Staudt. Retrospektive 1960–1997*, p. 35
2015 Vaduz, Hilti Art Foundation / Kunstmuseum Liechtenstein, *Hilti Art Foundation – Painting and Sculpture. From Classical Modernism to the Present Day*, p. 140, no. 41

Literature
Enzweiler / Rompza 1999, p. 226, no. 1/77
Wieczorek 2015, p. 140, no. 41

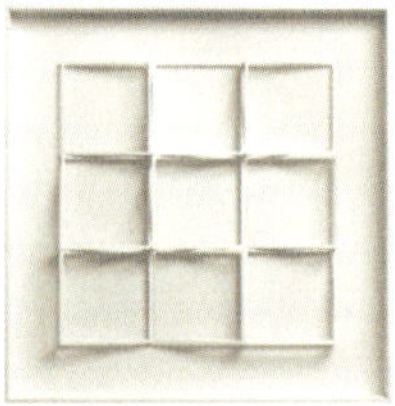

066

Klaus Staudt
Schattengitter 10 (WR-SG 10)
1983

Provenance
The artist's studio
Galerie am Lindenplatz, Vaduz

Literature
Enzweiler / Rompza 1999, p. 254, no. 1/578

067

Klaus Staudt
Verhaltenes Warm
1988

Provenance
The artist's studio
Galerie am Lindenplatz, Vaduz

Exhibitions
2018 Vaduz, Hilti Art Foundation / Kunstmuseum Liechtenstein, *Hilti Art Foundation – Rosso, Klee, Sonnier & more. Works from the Collection*, p. 80, no. 31

Literature
Enzweiler / Rompza 1999, p. 49, no. 1/659
Wieczorek 2018, p. 80, no. 31

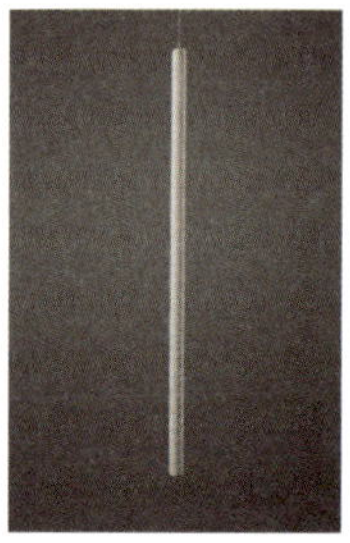

068

Gerhard von Graevenitz
Homogene Verteilung (Rundstab), Weisse Struktur
1959

Provenance
Gerhard von Graevenitz Estate, Amsterdam
Kunsthandel Wolfgang Werner, Bremen/Berlin

Exhibitions
1994 Schwerin, Staatliches Kunstmuseum, *Gerhard von Graevenitz. Eine Kunst jenseits des Bildes*, p. 166, no. 321
2014 Berlin, Kunsthandel Wolfgang Werner, *Gerhard von Graevenitz*, no. 3 (fig.)
2015 Vaduz, Hilti Art Foundation / Kunstmuseum Liechtenstein, *Hilti Art Foundation – Painting and Sculpture. From Classical Modernism to the Present Day*, p. 136, no. 40

Literature
Bremer 1984, no. 55
Berswordt-Wallrabe 1994, p. 166, no. 321
Schneider 2015, p. 136, no. 40

069

Gerhard von Graevenitz
Untitled *(horizontaler Schnitt)*
1959

Provenance
Gerhard von Graevenitz Estate, Amsterdam
Kunsthandel Wolfgang Werner, Bremen/Berlin

Exhibitions
1994 Schwerin, Staatliches Kunstmuseum, *Gerhard von Graevenitz. Eine Kunst jenseits des Bildes*, p. 166, no. 314
2014 Berlin, Kunsthandel Wolfgang Werner, *Gerhard von Graevenitz*, no. 1 (fig.)
2018 Zurich, Haus Konstruktiv, *Gerhard von Graevenitz. Eine Retrospektive.*

Literature
Bremer 1984, no. 28
Berswordt-Wallrabe 1994, p. 166, no. 314

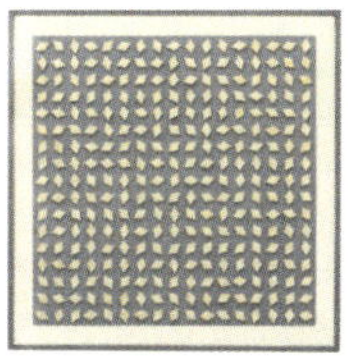

070

Gerhard von Graevenitz
Weisse Rhomben auf Grau
1961

Provenance
Gerhard von Graevenitz Estate, Amsterdam
Galerie Edith Wahlandt, Stuttgart

Exhibitions
1994 Schwerin, Staatliches Kunstmuseum, *Gerhard von Graevenitz. Eine Kunst jenseits des Bildes*, p. 168, no. 329

Literature
Berswordt-Wallrabe 1994, p. 92 (fig.) and p. 168, no. 392

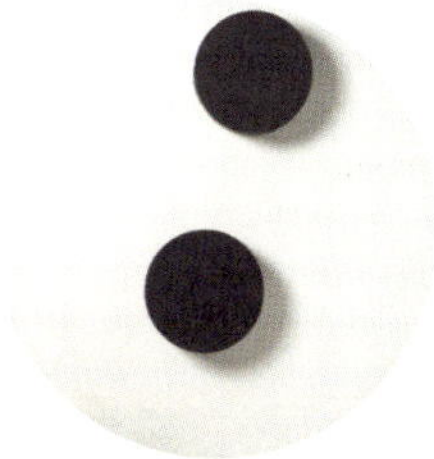

071

Gerhard von Graevenitz
Zwei schwarze Scheiben auf Weiss
1971

Provenance
Gerhard von Graevenitz Estate, Amsterdam
Galerie Edith Wahlandt, Stuttgart

Exhibitions
1972 Bochum, Galerie m Bochum, *Neue konkrete Kunst*
1974 Stuttgart, Württembergischer Kunstverein, *Gerhard von Graevenitz*
1974 Kiel, Kunsthalle Kiel, *Gerhard von Graevenitz*
1974 Hagen, Karl-Ernst-Osthaus-Museum, *Gerhard von Graevenitz*
1975 Bielefeld, Kunsthalle Bielefeld, *Gerhard von Graevenitz*
1979 Eindhoven, Van Abbemuseum, *Gerhard von Graevenitz*
1984 Otterloo, Rijksmuseum Otterloo, *Gerhard von Graevenitz. Retrospektive*
1984 Ludwigshafen, Wilhelm-Hack-Museum, *Gerhard von Graevenitz*
1994 Schwerin, Staatliches Kunstmuseum, *Gerhard von Graevenitz. Eine Kunst jenseits des Bildes*, p. 175, no. 630

Literature
Berswordt-Wallrabe 1994, p. 175, no. 630

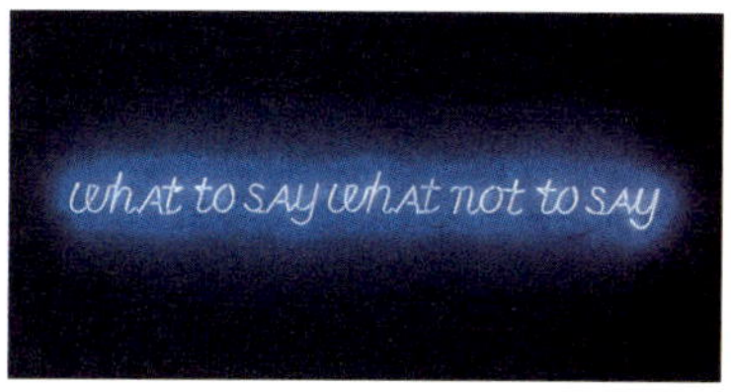

072

Maurizio Nannucci
what to say what not to say
1979

Provenance
Galerie Rieder, Munich

Exhibitions
1992 Nice, Villa Arson
1993 Rouen, Usine Fromage

Literature
Domesle 1998, p. 135
Nannucci 1999

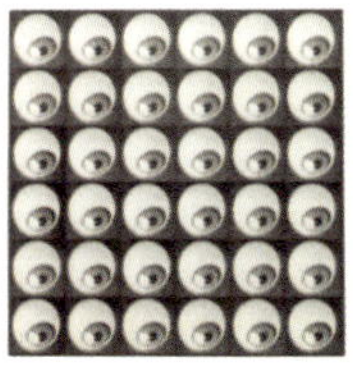

073

Peter Roehr
PR FO-34 (Untitled)
1965

Provenance
Paul Maenz Collection, Frankfurt am Main
Galerie Mehdi Chouakri, Berlin

Exhibitions
1965 Gelsenkirchen, Pianohaus Kohl, *Pop Art und Neue Realisten*
1965 Frankfurt am Main, Galerie Adam Seide, *Peter Roehr*
2000 Weimar, Neues Museum Weimar, *Peter Roehr 1944–1968*
2007 Berlin, Galerie Mehdi Chouakri, *Peter Roehr*

Literature
Wendermann 2000, p. 49 and p. 118, no. 150, fig. 162

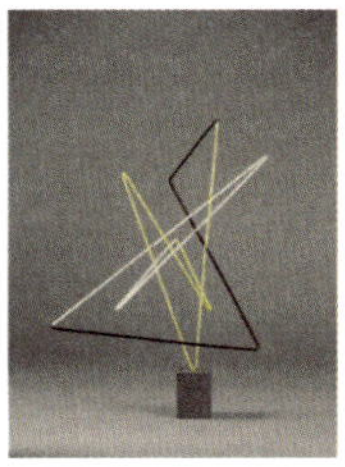

074

Norbert Kricke
Raumplastik Gelb-Weiss-Schwarz
1952

Provenance
Norbert Kricke Estate
Edith Wahlandt Galerie, Stuttgart

Exhibitions
2015 Vaduz, Hilti Art Foundation / Kunstmuseum Liechtenstein, *Hilti Art Foundation – Painting and Sculpture. From Classical Modernism to the Present Day*, p. 116, no. 34

Literature
Wieczorek 2015, p. 116, no. 34

075

Gotthard Graubner
Lichter Körper
1968

Provenance
Fritz and Ilona Busse Collection, Germany
Gmyrek Arts GmbH, Düsseldorf

Exhibitions
1969 Hanover, Kestner-Gesellschaft, *Gotthard Graubner*, no. 68
1969 Düsseldorf, Kunstverein für die Rheinlande und Westfalen, *Gotthard Graubner*, no. 81
1985 Bremen, Kunsthalle Bremen, *Kunst des 20. Jahrhunderts aus privaten Sammlungen*, no. 281
2010 Vaduz, Kunstmuseum Liechtenstein, *Gotthard Graubner. Malerei*, p. 10, no. 10
2015 Vaduz, Hilti Art Foundation / Kunstmuseum Liechtenstein, *Hilti Art Foundation – Painting and Sculpture. From Classical Modernism to the Present Day*, p. 148, no. 43
2016 Vaduz, Hilti Art Foundation / Kunstmuseum Liechtenstein, *Hilti Art Foundation – Kirchner, Léger, Scully & more. Works from the Collection*, p. 108, no. 30
2019–20 Vaduz, Hilti Art Foundation / Kunstmuseum Liechtenstein, *Epidermis – Conditio humana – Kosmos*, no. 5

Literature
Wieczorek 2010, p. 10, no. 10
Wieczorek 2015, p. 148, no. 43
Wieczorek 2016, p. 108, no. 30

076

Gotthard Graubner
Takyre I / Farbraumkörper
1974

Provenance
Private collection, Germany
Bechter Kastofsky Galerie, Vienna

Exhibitions
2019–20 Vaduz, Hilti Art Foundation / Kunstmuseum Liechtenstein, *Epidermis – Conditio humana – Kosmos*, no. 4

077

Gotthard Graubner
Herbstnacht
1990–91

Provenance
The artist's studio
Gmyrek Arts GmbH, Düsseldorf

Exhibitions
2010 Vaduz, Kunstmuseum Liechtenstein, *Gotthard Graubner. Malerei*, pp. 30–31, no. 31
2016 Vaduz, Hilti Art Foundation / Kunstmuseum Liechtenstein, *Hilti Art Foundation – Kirchner, Léger, Scully & more. Works from the Collection*, p. 110, no. 31

Literature
Wieczorek 2010, p. 18 and pp. 30–31, no. 31
Wieczorek 2016, p. 110, no. 31

078

Gotthard Graubner
Le vent du soleil I (atmo)
1996

Provenance
The artist's studio
Gmyrek Arts GmbH, Düsseldorf

Exhibitions
2010 Vaduz, Kunstmuseum Liechtenstein, *Gotthard Graubner. Malerei*, pp. 38–39, no. 39

Literature
Wieczorek 2010, p. 18 and pp. 38–39, no. 39

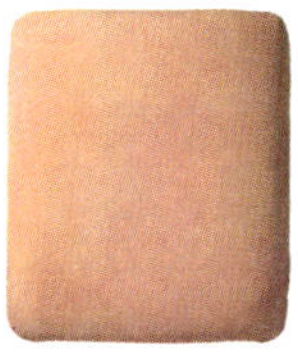

079

Gotthard Graubner
Haut
2010

Provenance
The artist's studio

Exhibitions
2016 Vaduz, Hilti Art Foundation / Kunstmuseum Liechtenstein, *Hilti Art Foundation – Kirchner, Léger, Scully & more. Works from the Collection*, p. 114, no. 32

Literature
Wieczorek 2016, p. 114, no. 32

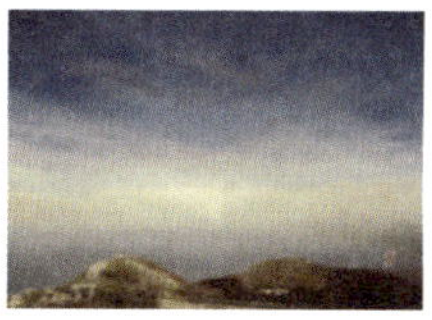

080

Gerhard Richter
Vesuv
1976

Provenance
Galerie Rolf Preisig, Basel
Private collection, Switzerland
Schönewald Fine Arts, Xanten / Anthony Meier Fine Arts, San Francisco
Anthony d'Offay Gallery, London
Private collection, London
Phillips, de Pury and Luxembourg, New York, 15 May 2003, lot 16
Galerie Gmurzynska, Zurich
Robert and Aimee Lehrmann Collection
Phillips, de Pury and Co., New York, 15 November 2007, lot 53
Schönewald Fine Arts, Düsseldorf / Anthony Meier Fine Arts, San Francisco
Galerie Haas, Zurich

Exhibitions
1997 Aarau, Aargauer Kunsthaus / Krems, Kunsthalle Krems, *Die Schwerkraft der Berge 1774–1997*, p. 197
1998 Hanover, Sprengel Museum Hannover, *Gerhard Richter. Landschaften*, p. 68
2019 Vaduz, Hilti Art Foundation / Kunstmuseum Liechtenstein, *Composition '19, Thomas Struth at the Hilti Art Foundation*, pp. 112–13
2019–20 Vaduz, Hilti Art Foundation / Kunstmuseum Liechtenstein, *Epidermis – Conditio humana – Kosmos*, no. 31

Literature
Buchloh 1977, p. 7 and p. 30
Loock / Zacharopoulos 1985, p. 44
Richter 1993, vol. 3, no. 407
Eble 2006, p. 171
Elger 2008, p. 254 and p. 307–08
Elger 2011, p. 81
Godfrey / Serota / Brill / Morineau 2012, p. 289
Elger 2013, vol. 3, p. 79, no. 407
Wieczorek 2019, p. 17

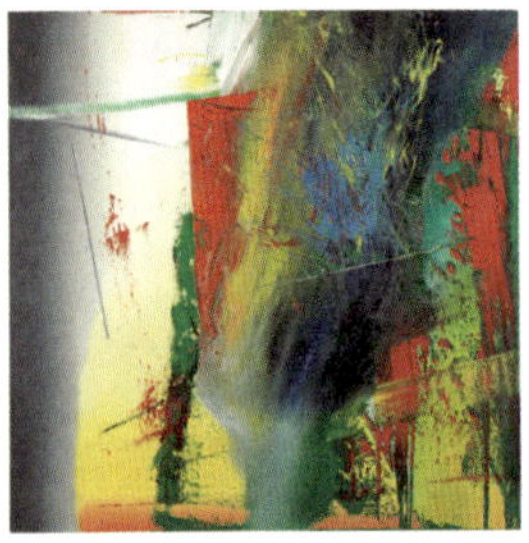

081

Gerhard Richter
D. G.
1985

Provenance
The artist's studio
Dieter Giesing Collection, Hamburg
Schönewald Fine Arts, Düsseldorf / Anthony Meier Fine Arts, San Francisco
Galerie Haas, Zurich

Exhibitions
2019 Vaduz, Hilti Art Foundation / Kunstmuseum Liechtenstein, *Composition '19, Thomas Struth at the Hilti Art Foundation*, pp. 78–79

Literature
Richter 1986, p. 325 (fig.), p. 401
Richter 1993, vol. 3, no. 407
Elger 2013, vol. 3, p. 454, no. 575–1
Wieczorek 2019, p. 16

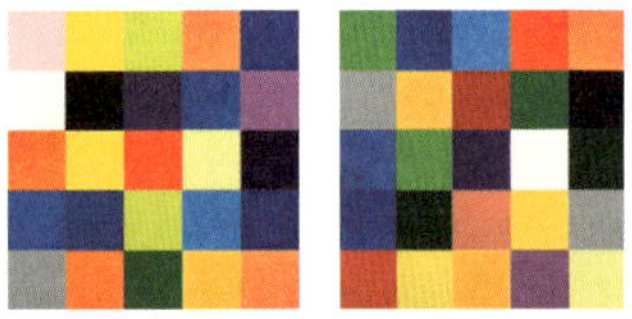

082

Gerhard Richter
25 Farben
2007

Provenance
Galerie Haas, Zurich

Literature
Richter, 2009
Garbin 2011, pp. 23, 141, 181, 190
Richter 2012, pp. 294
Elger / Butin / Mansoor 2015, pp. 12, 17
Schreier 2017, p. 23

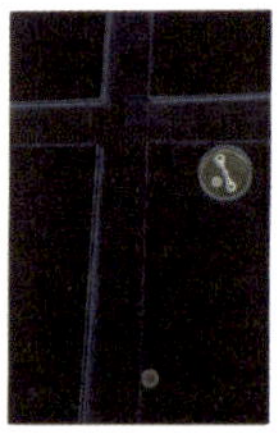

083

Konrad Klapheck
Traurige Mama
1959

Provenance
Dieter Rosenkranz, Wuppertal
Lempertz, Cologne, 27 November 2003, lot 219[R]
Galerie von Bartha, Basel

Exhibitions
1966–67 Hanover, Kestner-Gesellschaft, *Konrad Klapheck*, no. 21
1974–75 Rotterdam, Museum Boymans-Van Beuningen; Brussels, Paleis voor Schone Kunsten; Städtische Kunsthalle Düsseldorf, *Konrad Klapheck*, p. 36
2019 Vaduz, Hilti Art Foundation / Kunstmuseum Liechtenstein, *Composition '19, Thomas Struth at the Hilti Art Foundation*, p. 76
2019–20 Vaduz, Hilti Art Foundation / Kunstmuseum Liechtenstein, *Epidermis – Conditio humana – Kosmos*, no. 30

Literature
Klapheck 1974, p. 36
Hofmann / Schuster 1985, p. 38
Heymer / Wismer 2013

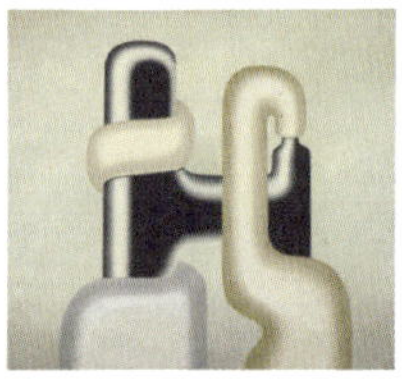

084

Konrad Klapheck
Familienleben
1961

Provenance
Sidney Janis Gallery, New York
Private collection, Monte Carlo

Exhibitions
2019 Vaduz, Hilti Art Foundation / Kunstmuseum Liechtenstein, *Composition '19, Thomas Struth at the Hilti Art Foundation*, pp. 76–77

Literature
Pierre 1970, p. 85

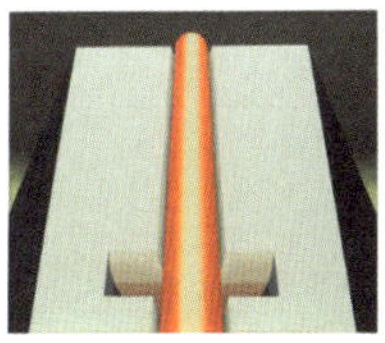

085

Konrad Klapheck
Am Ziel der Wünsche
1963

Provenance
The artist's studio
André Breton, Paris (gift of the artist)
Calmels Cohen, Paris, 15 April 2003, lot 4323
Galerie von Bartha, Basel

Exhibitions
1966 Hanover, Kestner-Gesellschaft Hannover, *Konrad Klapheck*, no. 103
1968 Prague, Národni galerie; Brno, Dům umění; Bratislava, Mladych galerie, *Princip slasti*
2019 Vaduz, Hilti Art Foundation / Kunstmuseum Liechtenstein, *Composition '19, Thomas Struth at the Hilti Art Foundation*, p. 76

Literature
Jaguer 1964, p. 62
Klapheck 2002

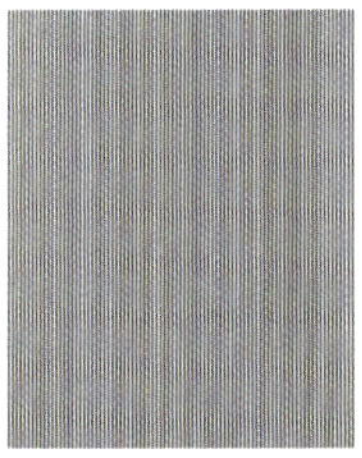

086

Imi Knoebel
s 0,6 w 1,0
1967

Provenance
Private collection, Germany
Brigitte Büdenhölzer, Kunsthandel

Exhibitions
1999 St. Gallen, Kunstverein, Kunstmuseum, *IMI KNOEBEL, Linienbilder 1966 bis 1968*, p. 29, no. 34
2002–03 Braunschweig, Kunstverein, *IMI KNOEBEL, IMI GEGEN GROBEN SCHMUTZ*, p. 36
2018 Vaduz, Hilti Art Foundation / Kunstmuseum Liechtenstein, *Hilti Art Foundation – Rosso, Klee, Sonnier & more. Works from the Collection*, pp. 86–87, no. 34

Literature
Stüttgen 1999, pp. 7 ff.
Bitterli 1999, pp. 31 ff.
Wäspe 2003, pp. 53 ff.
Wieczorek 2018, pp. 86–87, no. 34

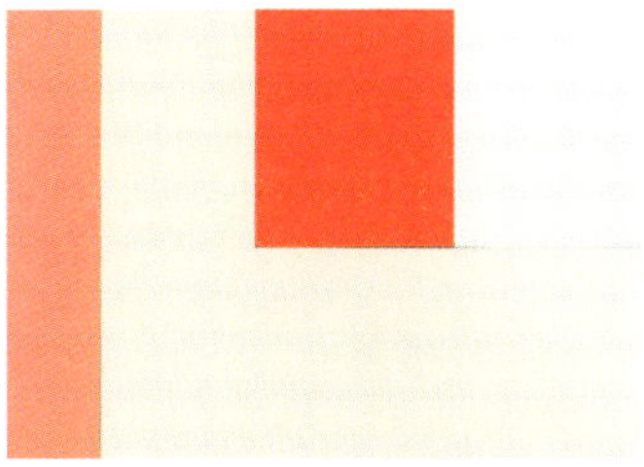

087

Imi Knoebel
Figur 49
1988

Provenance
Galerie Wilma Lock, St. Gallen

Exhibitions
2016 Vaduz, Hilti Art Foundation / Kunstmuseum Liechtenstein, Hilti Art Foundation – *Kirchner, Léger, Scully & more. Works from the Collection*, pp. 102–03, no. 28

Literature
Wieczorek 2016, p. 102, no. 28

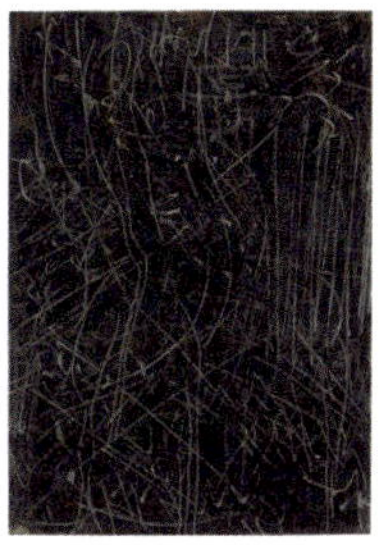

088

Imi Knoebel
Untitled *(Schwarzes Bild No. 9* [of 24], *Schlachtenbild)*
1990

Provenance
Kewenig Galerie, Cologne

Exhibitions
2015 Vaduz, Hilti Art Foundation / Kunstmuseum Liechtenstein, *Hilti Art Foundation – Painting and Sculpture. From Classical Modernism to the Present Day*, p. 164, no. 50
2018 Vaduz, Hilti Art Foundation / Kunstmuseum Liechtenstein, *Hilti Art Foundation – Rosso, Klee, Sonnier & more. Works from the Collection*, pp. 82–83, no. 32

Literature
Wieczorek 2015, p. 164, no. 50
Wieczorek 2018, p. 82, no. 32

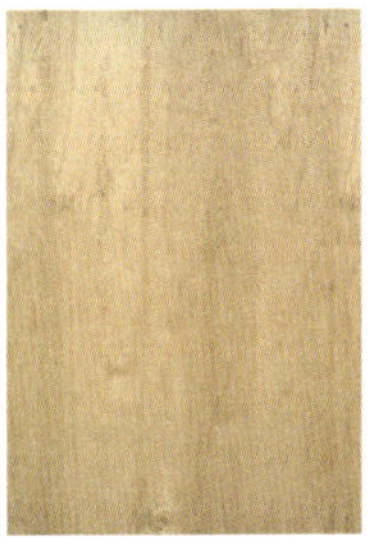

089

Imi Knoebel
Sandwich Blau-Rot-Rot-Gelb
1993

Provenance
Private collection, Germany
Brigitte Büdenhölzer, Kunsthandel

Exhibitions
1993 Lyon, 2e Biennale d'art contemporain, *Et tous ils changent le monde*
1994 London, Hayward Gallery, *Unbound: Possibilities in Painting*
2004 Hamburg, Hamburger Kunsthalle, *Imi Knoebel*
2018 Vaduz, Hilti Art Foundation/Kunstmuseum Liechtenstein, *Hilti Art Foundation – Rosso, Klee, Sonnier & more. Works from the Collection*, pp. 72–73, no. 27

Literature
Searle 1994, p. 55
Wieczorek 2018, pp. 72–73, no. 27

090

Imi Knoebel
Odyshape C4
1995

Provenance
The artist's studio
Galerie am Lindenplatz, Vaduz

Exhibitions
2016 Vaduz, Hilti Art Foundation/Kunstmuseum Liechtenstein, *Hilti Art Foundation – Kirchner, Léger, Scully & more. Works from the Collection*, p. 126, no. 37

Literature
Wieczorek 2016, p. 126, no. 37

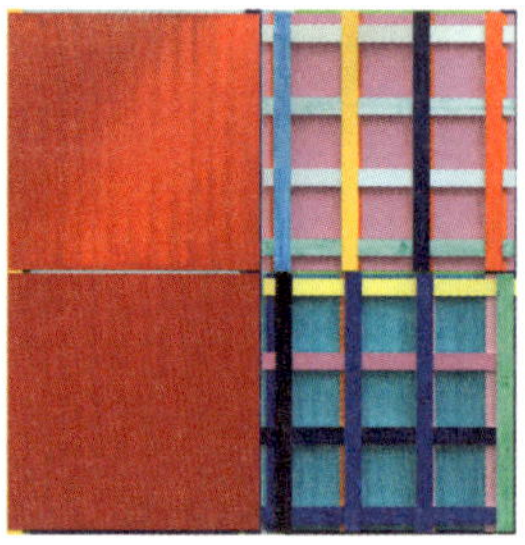

091

Imi Knoebel
LILLLI
2003

Provenance
The artist's studio

Exhibitions
2005 Vaduz, Kunstmuseum Liechtenstein, *Werke aus der Hilti Art Foundation. Von Paul Gauguin bis Imi Knoebel*, p. 118, no. 54

Literature
Malsch 2005, p. 118, no. 54

092

Imi Knoebel
Blaue Schokolade
2004

Provenance
The artist's studio

Exhibitions
2005 Vaduz, Kunstmuseum Liechtenstein, *Werke aus der Hilti Art Foundation. Von Paul Gauguin bis Imi Knoebel*, p. 118, no. 54 and p. 121 (fig.)
2016 Vaduz, Hilti Art Foundation/Kunstmuseum Liechtenstein, *Hilti Art Foundation – Kirchner, Léger, Scully & more. Works from the Collection*, p. 128, no. 38

Literature
Malsch 2005, p. 118, no. 55
Wieczorek 2016, p. 128, no. 38

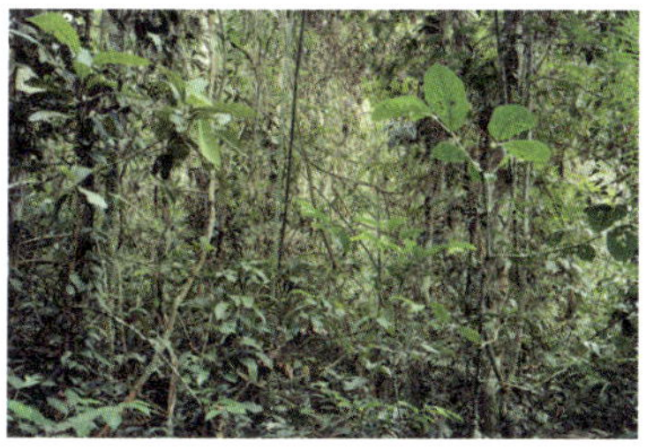

093

Thomas Struth
Paradise 29, Rio Madre de Dios, Peru 2005
2005

Provenance
Galerie Rüdiger Schöttle, Munich

Exhibitions
2019 Vaduz, Hilti Art Foundation / Kunstmuseum Liechtenstein, *Composition '19, Thomas Struth at the Hilti Art Foundation*, pp. 110–11

Literature
Struth 2017, pp. 58–59
Wieczorek 2019, p. 16 and pp. 110–11

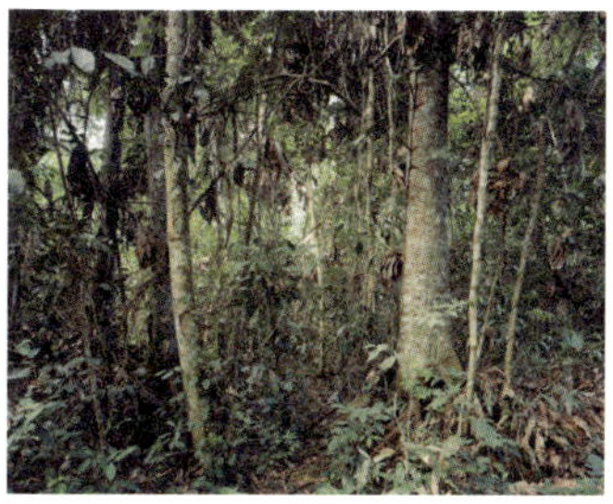

094

Thomas Struth
Paradise 30, Rio Madre de Dios, Peru 2005
2005

Provenance
Galerie Rüdiger Schöttle, Munich

Exhibitions
2010–11 Zurich, Kunsthaus; Düsseldorf, Kunstsammlung Nordrhein-Westfalen, *Thomas Struth. Fotografien 1978–2010*, p. 107 and p. 209
2019 Vaduz, Hilti Art Foundation / Kunstmuseum Liechtenstein, *Composition '19, Thomas Struth at the Hilti Art Foundation*, pp. 108–09

Literature
Struth 2010, p. 107 and p. 209
Struth 2017, pp. 56–57
Wieczorek 2019, p. 16 and pp. 108–09

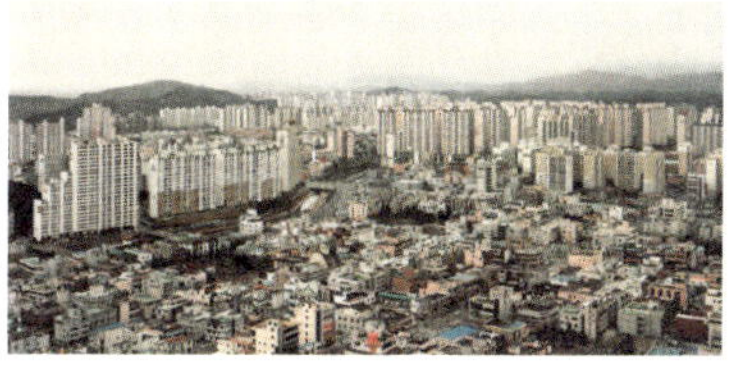

095

Thomas Struth
Ulsan 2, Ulsan 2010
2010

Provenance
Galerie Rüdiger Schöttle, Munich

Exhibitions
2016 Essen, Museum Folkwang; Berlin, Martin-Gropius-Bau; Atlanta, High Museum of Art; St. Louis, St. Louis Art Museum, *Thomas Struth. Nature & Politics*, pp. 131–36
2017 Munich, Haus der Kunst, *Thomas Struth – Figure Ground*, pp. 240–41
2019 Vaduz, Hilti Art Foundation / Kunstmuseum Liechtenstein, *Composition '19, Thomas Struth at the Hilti Art Foundation*, pp. 62–63

Literature
Struth 2016, pp. 131–36
Weski / Wilmes 2017, pp. 240–41
Wieczorek 2019, p. 14

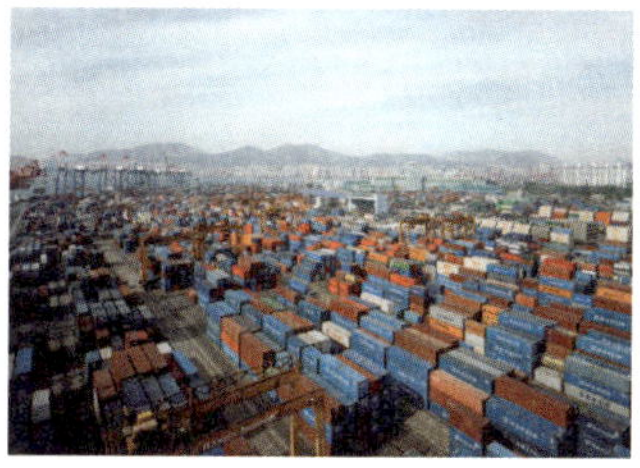

096

Thomas Struth
Hanjin Gamman, Port Busan 2007
2007

Provenance
Galleria Monica De Cardenas SRL, Milan

Exhibitions
2019–20 Vaduz, Hilti Art Foundation / Kunstmuseum Liechtenstein, *Epidermis – Conditio humana – Kosmos*, no. 28

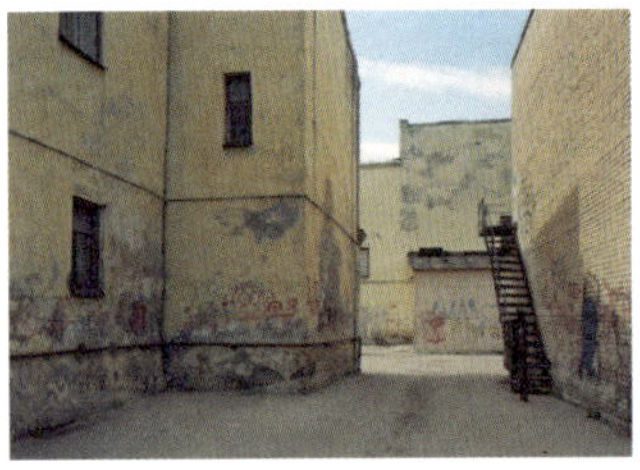

097

Thomas Struth
Kovenskij Pereulok, St. Petersburg 2005
2005

Provenance
Galerie Rüdiger Schöttle, Munich

Exhibitions
2019 Vaduz, Hilti Art Foundation / Kunstmuseum Liechtenstein, *Composition '19, Thomas Struth at the Hilti Art Foundation*, p. 116

Literature
Wieczorek 2019, p. 16

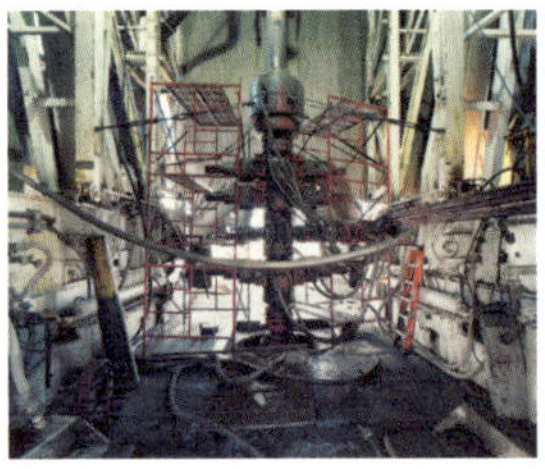

098

Thomas Struth
Blowout Preventer, Mountrail County, North Dakota 2010
2010

Provenance
Galerie Greta Meert, Brussels

Exhibitions
2016 Essen, Museum Folkwang; Berlin, Martin-Gropius-Bau; Atlanta, High Museum of Art; St. Louis, St. Louis Art Museum, *Thomas Struth. Nature & Politics*, pp. 122–23
2019 Vaduz, Hilti Art Foundation / Kunstmuseum Liechtenstein, *Composition '19, Thomas Struth at the Hilti Art Foundation*, pp. 68–69

Literature
Struth 2016, pp. 122–23
Wieczorek 2019, p. 15

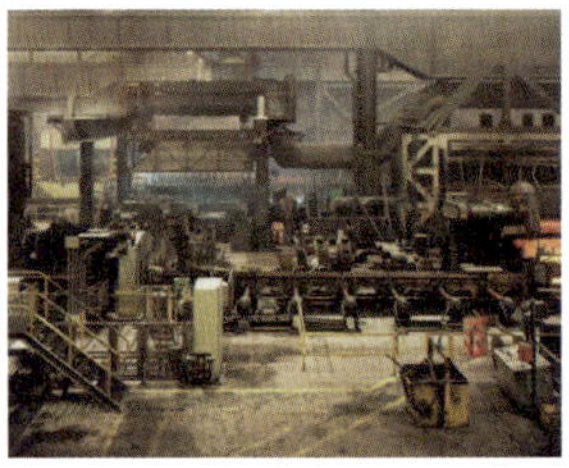

099

Thomas Struth
Seamless Tube Production, Buenos Aires 2009
2009

Provenance
Galleria Monica De Cardenas SRL, Milan

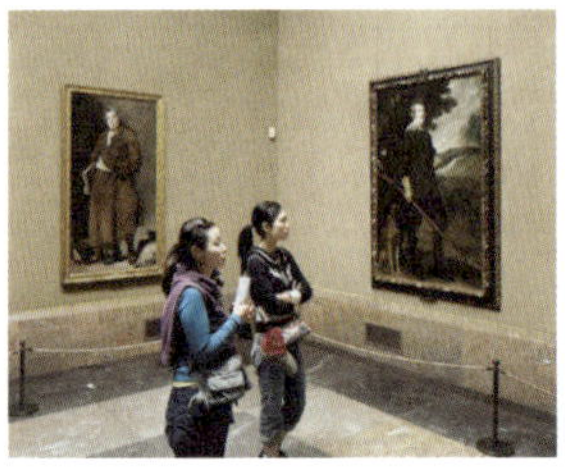

100

Thomas Struth
Museo del Prado 2, Madrid 2005
2005

Provenance
Galerie Rüdiger Schöttle, Munich

Exhibitions
2010–11 Zurich, Kunsthaus; Düsseldorf, Kunstsammlung Nordrhein-Westfalen, *Thomas Struth. Fotografien 1978–2010*, p. 221
2019 Vaduz, Hilti Art Foundation / Kunstmuseum Liechtenstein, *Composition '19, Thomas Struth at the Hilti Art Foundation*, pp. 32–33

Literature
Struth 2010, p. 221
Wieczorek 2019, p. 13 and pp. 32–33

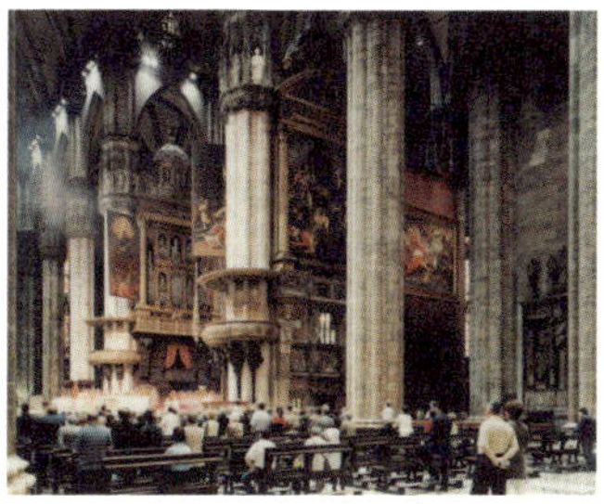

101

Thomas Struth
Mailänder Dom (innen), Mailand 1998
1998

Provenance
Christie's, London, Private Sales

Literature
Struth 2005, p. 75

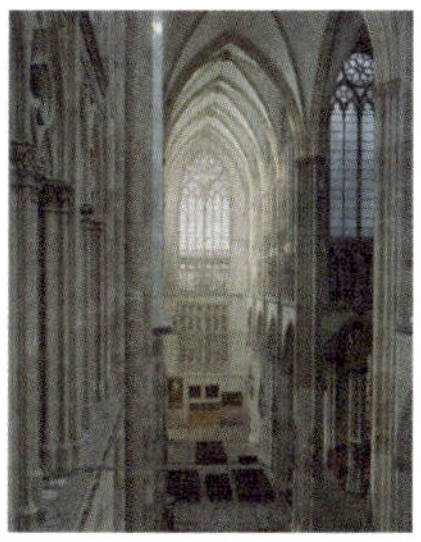

102

Thomas Struth
Kölner Dom, Köln 2007
2007

Provenance
Galerie Rüdiger Schöttle, Munich

Exhibitions
2019 Vaduz, Hilti Art Foundation / Kunstmuseum Liechtenstein, *Composition '19, Thomas Struth at the Hilti Art Foundation*, pp. 126–27

Literature
Wieczorek 2019, p. 17 and pp. 126–27

103

Willi Kopf
Random Raster 2
1986

Provenance
The artist's studio
Galerie Feurstein, Raum aktueller Kunst, Feldkirch

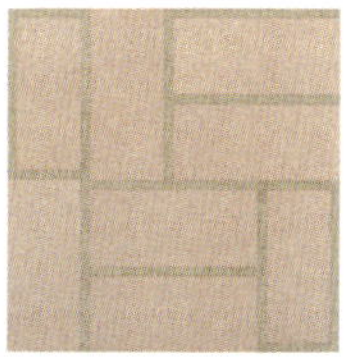

104

Willi Kopf
Red Square (Wandstück)
2003

Provenance
The artist's studio
Galerie Feurstein, Raum aktueller Kunst, Feldkirch

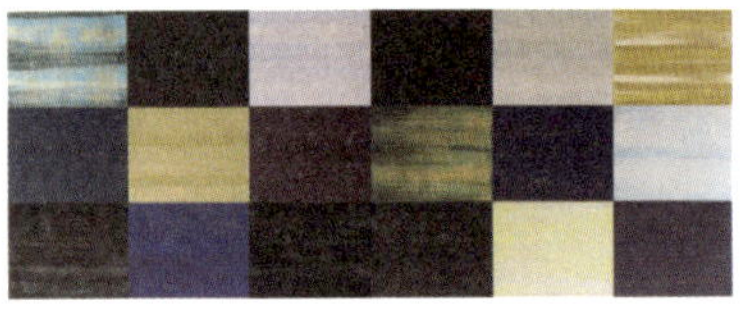

105

Hanna Roeckle
Xoana H, Chikin
2002

Provenance
The artist's studio

Exhibitions
2003 Vaduz, Kunstraum Engländerbau, *Hanna Roeckle – Fluidum und Zwischenraum*, exh. cat., n. p.
2005 Ingolstadt, Museum für Konkrete Kunst; Weimar, Kunsthalle, *Hanna Roeckle. Neue Werke, Xoana und Okulare. Malerei, Raum, Licht*, pp. 30–31
2005 Vaduz, Kunstmuseum Liechtenstein, *Werke aus der Hilti Art Foundation. Von Paul Gauguin bis Imi Knoebel*, p. 116, no. 52

Literature
Roeckle 2003, pp. 91–93
Wieczorek 2005 (1), p. 28
Wieczorek 2005 (2), p. 116, no. 52

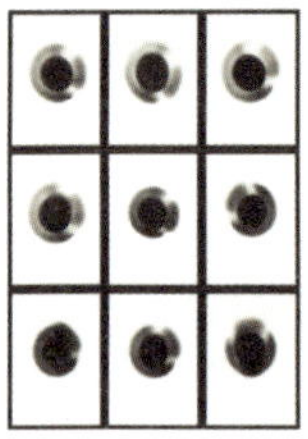

106

Giovanni Di Stefano
Punti Laser
2002

Provenance
The artist's studio
Galerie La Ligne, Zurich

Exhibitions
2008 Zurich, Galerie La Ligne, *MCBA & Giovanni Di Stefano. Punkt, Linie, Fläche*
2019–20 Vaduz, Hilti Art Foundation / Kunstmuseum Liechtenstein, *Epidermis – Conditio humana – Kosmos*, no. 10

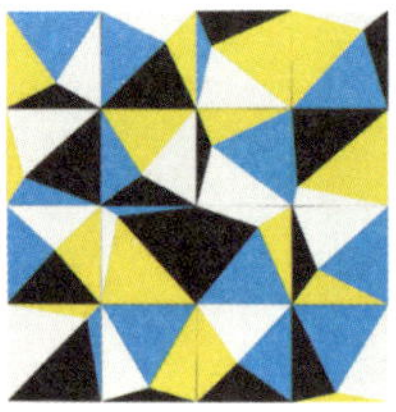

107

Giovanni Di Stefano
dArts a colori
2018

Provenance
The artist's studio

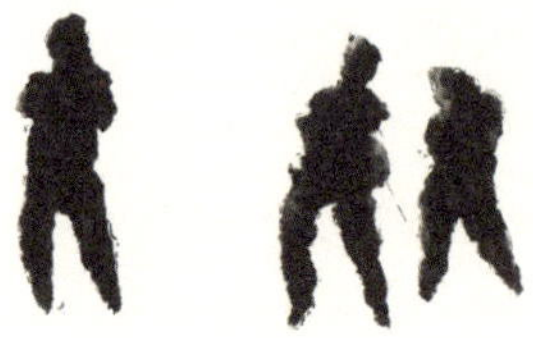

108

Karol Broniatowski
Drei schwarze Figuren
1997

Provenance
The artist's studio

Exhibitions
2005 Vaduz, Kunstmuseum Liechtenstein, *Werke aus der Hilti Art Foundation. Von Paul Gauguin bis Imi Knoebel*, p. 112, no. 50

Literature
Wieczorek 2005, p. 112, no. 50

109

Karol Broniatowski
Rote Figur
2009

Provenance
The artist's studio

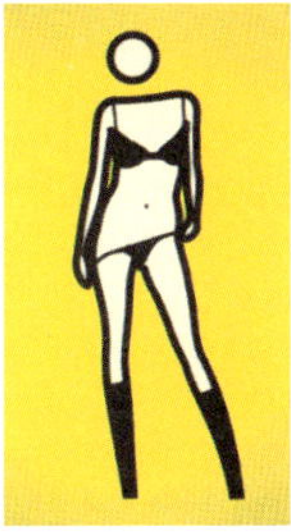

110

Julian Opie
Sara Gets Undressed
2003

Provenance
Lisson Gallery, London
Private collection
Christie's, London, 1 July 2010, lot 145
Dickinson, London

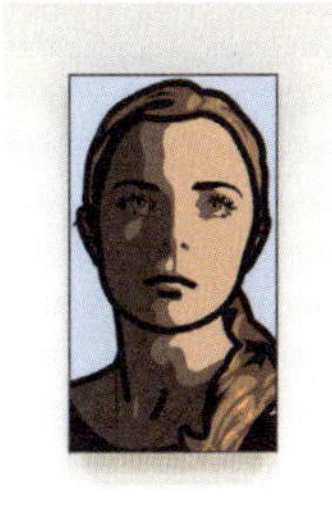

111

Julian Opie
Lily
2013

Provenance
Galerie Bob van Orsouw, Zurich

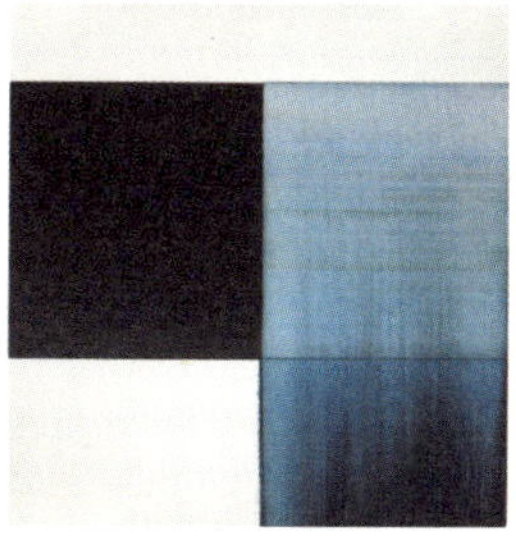

112

Callum Innes
Exposed Painting Delft Blue
2018

Provenance
The artist's studio
Sean Kelly Gallery, New York

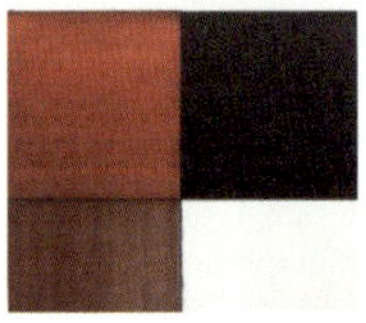

113

Callum Innes
Exposed Painting Crimson Red
2014

Provenance
Galerie Tschudi, Glarus / Zuoz

114

Hanns Kunitzberger
1. Hälfte 2017 früher
2017

Provenance
The artist's studio
Galerie Vera Munro, Hamburg

Literature
Bogner 2007
Klar 2015

115

Hanns Kunitzberger
1. Hälfte 2017 später
2017

Provenance
The artist's studio
Galerie Vera Munro, Hamburg

Literature
Bogner 2007
Klar 2015

116

Hanns Kunitzberger
2. Hälfte 2018 später
2018

Provenance
The artist's studio
Galerie Vera Munro, Hamburg

Exhibitions
2019–20 Vaduz, Hilti Art Foundation / Kunstmuseum Liechtenstein, *Epidermis – Conditio humana – Kosmos*, no. 31

Literature
Bogner 2007
Klar 2015

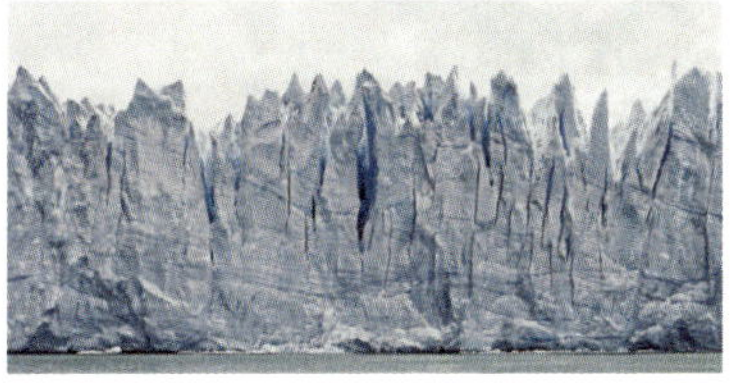

117

Frank Thiel
Perito Moreno #16
2014

Provenance
The artist's studio
Galerie Krinzinger, Vienna

Exhibitions
2019–20 Vaduz, Hilti Art Foundation / Kunstmuseum Liechtenstein, *Epidermis – Conditio humana – Kosmos*, no. 29

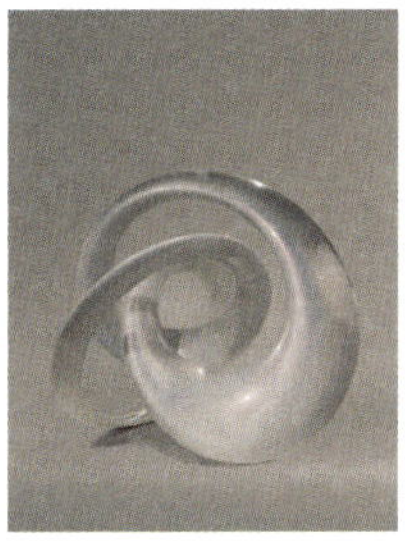

118

Mariko Mori
Cyclic I
2014

Provenance
The artist's studio
Sean Kelly Gallery, New York

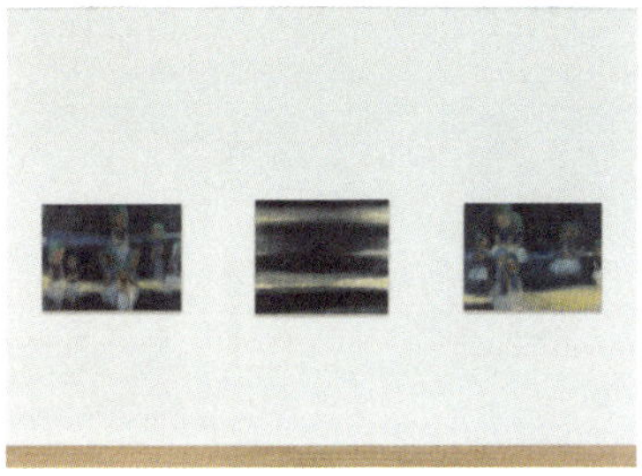

119

Leiko Ikemura
Ozean I–III
2000–01

Provenance
The artist's studio

Exhibitions
2002 Vaduz, Kunstmuseum Liechtenstein, *Leiko Ikemura. Ozean. Ein Projekt*, p. 19, pp. 45–47 (fig.)
2008 Schaffhausen, Museum zu Allerheiligen, *Leiko Ikemura. Tag, Nacht, Halbmond*, p. 211, pp. 261–63 (fig.)
2019 Tokyo, The National Art Center, *Leiko Ikemura. Our Planet. Earth & Stars*, pp. 160–65, nos. 115–17

Literature
Malsch 2002, p. 19, pp. 45–47 (fig.)
Scharrer 2008, p. 211, pp. 261–63 (fig.)
Nagaya 2019, p. 28, pp. 160–65, nos. 115–117

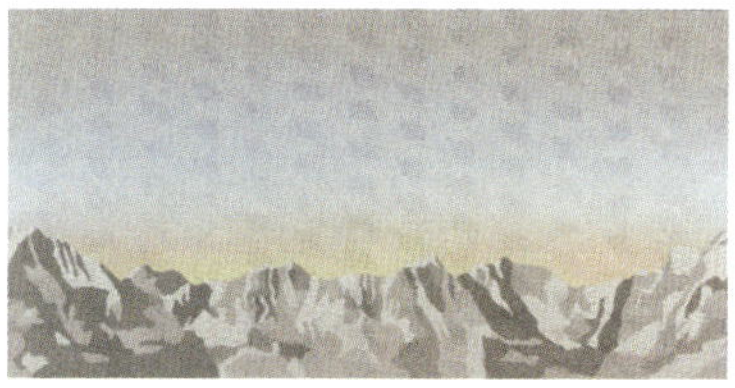

120

Stéphane Kropf
Untitled *(Tuilière)*
2012

Provenance
The artist's studio
Galerie am Lindenplatz, Vaduz

Exhibitions
2019–20 Vaduz, Hilti Art Foundation / Kunstmuseum Liechtenstein, *Epidermis – Conditio humana – Kosmos*, no. 26

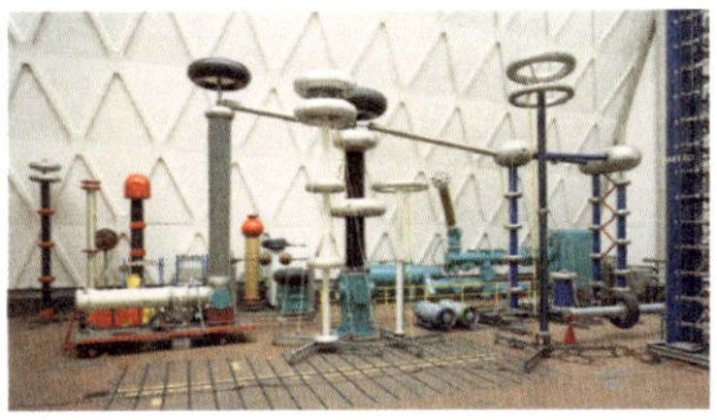

P. 267

Thomas Struth
Schaltwerk 1, Berlin 2016
2016

Chromogenic print (4/6)
Titled, dated, numbered and signed verso
Framed 198.3 × 371.6 cm
Inv. no. PH301M / Acquired 2016

Provenance
Galerie Rüdiger Schöttle, Munich

Exhibitions
2019 Vaduz, Hilti Art Foundation / Kunstmuseum Liechtenstein, *Composition '19, Thomas Struth at the Hilti Art Foundation*, pp. 28–29

Literature
Wieczorek 2019, p. 14

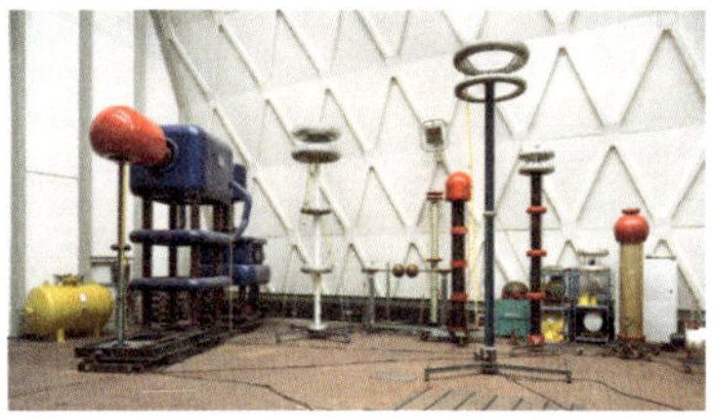

P. 267

Thomas Struth
Schaltwerk 3, Berlin 2017
2017

Chromogenic print (4/6)
Titled, dated, numbered and signed verso
Framed 198.3 × 371.6 cm
Inv. no. PH329M / Acquired 2019

Provenance
Galerie Rüdiger Schöttle, Munich

Exhibitions
2019 Vaduz, Hilti Art Foundation / Kunstmuseum Liechtenstein, *Composition '19, Thomas Struth at the Hilti Art Foundation*, pp. 30–31

Literature
Wieczorek 2019, p. 14

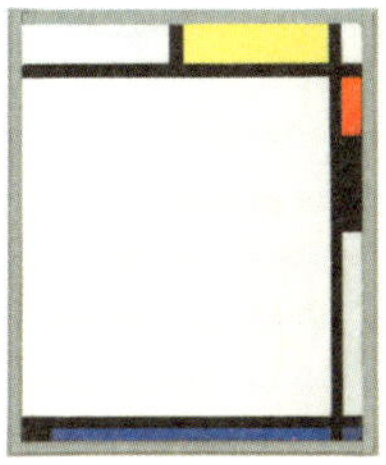

P. 43

Piet Mondrian
Tableau No. VIII
with Yellow, Red, Black and Blue
1925

Oil on canvas
Initialled and dated lower right: 25 PM
53.2 × 46.2 cm (incl. frame, not original)
Inv. no. P23T / Acquired 2002
(see vol. 1, cat. 34)

Provenance
Sophie Küppers, Hanover / Dresden, 1925, from the artist
Kunstausstellung Kühl, Dresden, 1926–27, from Sophie Küppers
Kaiser Wilhelm Museum, Krefeld, c. 1929–50
Galerie Alex Vömel, Düsseldorf, after 1950 to 1955
Karl Anselmino, Wuppertal, c. 1955–77
Private collection, Germany, on loan 1977–88 to Staatsgalerie Moderner Kunst, Munich, inv. no. L 1641
Private collection
Dickinson, London

Exhibitions
1925 Dresden, Kunsthandlung Kühl und Kühn, *Piet Mondrian – Man Ray*
1926 Munich, Galerie Goltz, *Lissitzky: Moskau, Mondrian: Paris, Man Ray: New York*
1927 Mannheim, Städtische Kunsthalle, *Wege und Richtungen der Abstrakten Malerei in Europa*, no. 261
1929 Frankfurt am Main, Kunstgewerbemuseum, *Der Stuhl*
1958 Wuppertal, Kunsthalle, *Moderne Kunst in Wuppertaler Privatbesitz*, no. 99
1966 Recklinghausen, Städtische Kunsthalle, *Variationen (über ein Thema)*, no. 154
1967 Düsseldorf, Städtische Kunsthalle, *Kunst des 20. Jahrhunderts aus rheinisch-westfälischem Privatbesitz*, no. 247
1972 Wuppertal, Von der Heydt-Museum, *Um 1930: Bild, Bau, Gerät*, no. 128
2005 Vaduz, Kunstmuseum Liechtenstein, *Werke aus der Hilti Art Foundation. Von Paul Gauguin bis Imi Knoebel*, p. 62, no. 23
2015 Vaduz, Hilti Art Foundation / Kunstmuseum Liechtenstein, *Hilti Art Foundation – Painting and Sculpture. From Classical Modernism to the Present Day*, p. 82, no. 22
2018 Vaduz, Hilti Art Foundation / Kunstmuseum Liechtenstein, *Hilti Art Foundation – Rosso, Klee, Sonnier & more. Works from the Collection*, p. 90, no. 36
2019 Vaduz, Hilti Art Foundation / Kunstmuseum Liechtenstein, *Composition '19 – Thomas Struth at the Hilti Art Foundation*, p. 64

Literature
Piet Mondrian, letter to Til Brugman, 13 November 1924
Piet Mondrian, letter to S. B. Slijper from "Dinsdagavond", c. July 1925
Piet Mondrian, postcard to M. Seuphor, 9 August 1925
Sophie Küppers, Bilderliste, Hanover, 20 December 1926, no. 6, Komposition No. VIII, 25. 51/45. Mark 400
Stuhl-Ausstellung, in: *Das Neue Frankfurt*, p. 64 (with photograph of the exhibition), March 1929
Wember 1973, p. 21
Joosten and Welsh 1998, vol. II, p. 316, no. B 160
Wieczorek 2005, p. 62, no. 23
Wieczorek 2015, p. 82, no. 22
Wieczorek 2018, p. 90, no. 36
Wieczorek 2019, p. 64

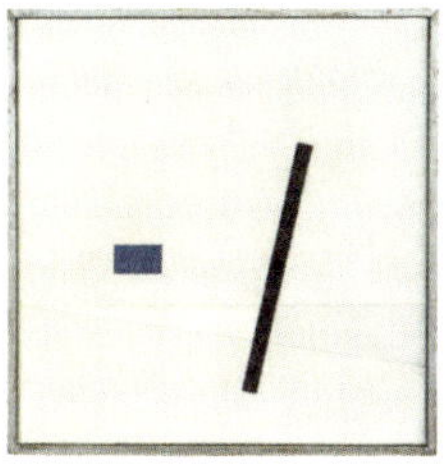

P. 253

Friedrich Vordemberge-Gildewart
Komposition 78
1933

Oil on canvas
36 × 36 cm
Inv. no. P275M / Acquired 2015
(see vol. 1, cat. 35)

Provenance
Prof. Annie Müller-Widmann, Switzerland*
Nachlass Prof. Dr. Oskar Müller-Widmann, Basel
Sammlung Petzold-Müller, Basel
Von Bartha, Basel

Exhibitions
1934 Rome, Galleria Bragaglia fuori commercio, *Vordemberge-Gildewart*
1934 Milan, Galleria del Milione, *Vordemberge-Gildewart*
1975 Ulm / Münster, Ulmer Museum und Westfälisches Landesmuseum für Kunst und Kulturgeschichte, *Vordemberge-Gildewart*, Ulm / Münster, 1975
1997 Wiesbaden, Museum Wiesbaden, *Friedrich Vordemberge-Gildewart, Retrospektive*, p. 93

Literature
Schmidt no year, unpaginated (p. 19)
Helms / Valstar-Verhoff 1990, p. 279, K78
Rattemeyer / Helms / Valstar-Verhoff, 1996–97
Valstar-Verhoff 2018, K78

*Given to Frau Prof. Müller-Widmann on 17 June 37 for hospitality for dadá and me in spring 36 and spring-summer 37 (Vordemberge-Gildewart, in: studio-book)

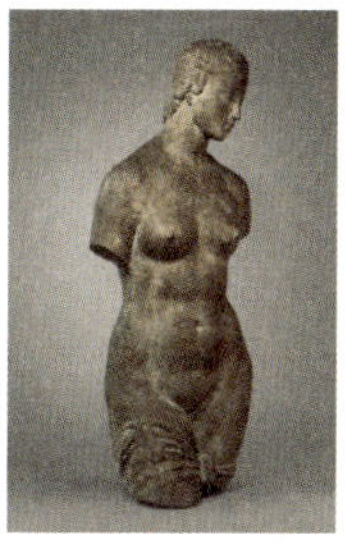

P. 266

Wilhelm Lehmbruck
Torso der Grossen Stehenden
1910

Stone cast
Signed on right thigh: LEHMBRUCK
Height: 118 cm
Inv. no. S55T / Acquired 2013
(see vol. 1, cat. 09)

Provenance
Leopold Badt
Kurt Badt and heirs
Christie's, London, 25 June 2001, lot 25
Private collection, Switzerland
Galerie Arnoldi-Livie, Munich

Exhibitions
2015 Vaduz, Hilti Art Foundation / Kunstmuseum Liechtenstein, *Hilti Art Foundation – Painting and Sculpture. From Classical Modernism to the Present Day*, p. 14, no. 1
2016 Vaduz, Hilti Art Foundation / Kunstmuseum Liechtenstein, *Hilti Art Foundation – Kirchner, Léger, Scully & more. Works from the Collection*, p. 18, no. 2
2018 Vaduz, Hilti Art Foundation / Kunstmuseum Liechtenstein, *Hilti Art Foundation – Rosso, Klee, Sonnier & more. Works from the Collection*, p. 18, no. 4
2019 Vaduz, Hilti Art Foundation / Kunstmuseum Liechtenstein, *Composition '19 – Thomas Struth at the Hilti Art Foundation*, p. 27

Literature
Badt 1920, pp. 169 (fig.), 172
Schubert 2001, p. 57
Schubert 2012, no. 7
Schneider 2015, p. 14, no. 1
Schneider 2016, p. 18, no. 2
Schneider 2018, p. 18, no. 4
Wieczorek 2019, p. 27

Bibliography

Adams, Brooks: The Stripe Strikes Back, in: Art in America 73, no. 10, 1985

Berswordt-Wallrabe, Kornelia von: Gerhard von Graevenitz. Eine Kunst jenseits des Bildes, exh. cat., Staatliches Museum Schwerin, Ostfildern, 1994

Bill, Max: unendliche schleife 1935–95 und die einflächner, Bern, 2000

Bischofberger, Bruno (ed.), revised by **Christina Bischofberger**: Jean Tinguely, Werkkatalog, Skulpturen und Reliefs, vol. 1, 1954–1968, Küsnacht / Zurich, 1982

Bitterli, Konrad: Raster und Strukturen. Imi Knoebels Linienbilder und die Erweiterung des Bildbegriffs, in: IMI KNOEBEL, Linienbilder 1966 bis 1968, Kunstverein St. Gallen, Kunstmuseum, 1999

Bogner, Peter (ed.): Hanns Kunitzberger. Die Orte der Bilder, Malerei 1996–2006, with texts by Hans Belting, Klaus Albrecht Schröder, Maximilian Schell, László F. Földényi, Johannes Rauchenberger, Vienna, 2007

Bool, Flip: Helmut Federle und die nordische Tradition, in: Helmut Federle. Bilder, Zeichnungen, exh. cat., Museum für Gegenwartskunst Basel, 1985

Bremer, Jaap: Gerhard von Graevenitz, Werkverzeichnis, in: Gerhard von Graevenitz, exh. cat., Rijksmuseum Kröller-Müller, Otterloo, 1984

Brüderlin, Markus: ArquiEscultura: diálogos entre la arquitectura y la escultura del siglo XVIII hasta el presente, exh. cat., Museo Guggenheim Bilbao / Kunstmuseum Wolfsburg, 2005

Buchloh, Benjamin H. D.: Gerhard Richter, Musée National d'Art Moderne, Centre Georges Pompidou, Paris, 1977

Caramel, Luciano / Thomas, Angela: Max Bill, Milan, 1991

Coray Loewensberg, Henriette (ed.): Verena Loewensberg 1912–1986, Katalog der Gemälde, Zurich, 2012

Crispolti, Enrico: Lucio Fontana, Catalogo Generale, vol. II, Brussels, 1974

Crispolti, Enrico: Lucio Fontana, Catalogo Generale, vol. II, Milan, 1986 (2nd ed.)

Dellwing, Herbert: Das Bild als Denkmodell, Klaus Staudt über Klaus Staudt, Harthausen, 2007

Domesle, Andrea: Leucht-Schrift-Kunst: Holzer, Kosuth, Merz, Nannucci, Nauman, Berlin 1998

Eble, Bruno: Gerhard Richter. La surface du regard, Paris, 2006

Elger, Dietmar: Gerhard Richter, Maler, Cologne, 2008

Elger, Dietmar (ed.): Gerhard Richter. Landschaften, Ostfildern, 2011

Elger, Dietmar: Gerhard Richter, Catalogue Raisonné, vol. 3, 1976–1987, Ostfildern, 2013

Elger, Dietmar / Butin, Hubertus / Mansoor, Jaleh: Gerhard Richter: Colour Charts, New York, 2015

Enzweiler, Jo / Rompza, Sigurd: Klaus Staudt, Werkverzeichnis 1960–1999, Saarbrücken, 1999

Fleck, Robert: Heinz Mack. Zero. Malerei / Painting, Catalogue Raisonné 1956–1968, vols. I and II, Munich, 2017

Forster, Kurt W.: Gottfried Honegger, Arbeiten aus den Jahren 1939 bis 1971, Teufen, 1972

Franz, Erich: Helmut Federle. Biennale di Venezia, Schweizer Pavillon 1997, Baden, 1997

Franz, Erich: Günter Fruhtrunk – Rhythmus des Sehens, in: Günter Fruhtrunk, Farbe Rhythmus Existenz, exh. cat., Kunstmuseum Liechtenstein, Vaduz, 2012

Gagel, Hanna: Verena Loewensberg – Zentriert im Wirbel der Welt, in: Hanna Gagel, So viel Energie. Künstlerinnen in der dritten Lebensphase, Berlin / Grambin, 2005

Galerie nächst St. Stephan: Jedes Zeichen ein Zeichen für andere Zeichen. Zur Ästhetik von Helmut Federle, Galerie nächst St. Stephan, Vienna / Klagenfurt, 1986

Garbin, Emanuele: Il bordo del mondo: La forma sguardo nella pittura di Gerhard Richter, Venice, 2011

Godfrey, Mark / Serota, Nicholas / Brill, Dorothée / Morineau, Camille: Gerhard Richter: Panorama, Neue und Alte Nationalgalerie, Staatliche Museen zu Berlin, 2012

Goetz, Ingvild (ed.): Monochromie. Geometrie, Munich, 1996

Golinski, Hans Günther: Dadamaino. Retrospektive 1958–2000, Museum Bochum, 2000

Gomringer, Eugen: Gianni Colombo, in: exh. cat., Galerie Thomas Keller, Starnberg, 1970

Gomringer, Eugen / Imdahl, Max / Sterner, Gabriele: Fruhtrunk, 2 vols. (WVZ), Starnberg, 1978

Gomringer, Eugen: Verena Loewensberg, in: exh. cat., Moderne Galerie Bottrop, 1982

Grossmann, Elisabeth (with Renate Holliger): Verena Loewensberg, Werkmonografie, in: Verena Loewensberg 1912–1986, published by Henriette Coray Loewensberg, Zurich, 2012

Heymer, Kay / Wismer, Beat (ed.): Klapheck. Bilder und Texte, exh. cat., Stiftung Museum Kunstpalast, Düsseldorf, 2013, Munich, 2013

Hofmann, Werner / Schuster, Klaus Peter: 1955–1959. Die Schaffung eines Vokabulars – Die Hauptthemen in ihren ersten Fassungen, in: Konrad Klapheck, Retrospektive 1955–1985, exh. cat., Hamburger Kunsthalle, Hamburg, 1985, Kunsthalle Tübingen, Tübingen, 1985, Staatsgalerie moderner Kunst, Munich, 1985, Munich, 1985

Honisch, Dieter: Uecker (catalogue raisonné, revised by Marion Haedeke), Stuttgart, 1983

Hüttinger, Eduard: Max Bill, Zurich, 1978

Jaguer, Édouard: Phases (Cahiers internationaux de documentation sur la poésie et l'art d'avant-garde), Dixième année, no. 9, April 1964, Paris, 1964

Kappeler, Susanne: Verena Loewensberg. Betrachtungen zum Werk einer konstruktiven Malerin, Zurich, 1980

Klapheck, Konrad: Meine Gegenstände, in: Konrad Klapheck, exh. cat., Museum Boymans-Van Beuningen, Rotterdam, 1974

Klapheck, Konrad: Lettre adressée à la Galerie 1900–2000 (Paris), Düsseldorf, 2002

Klar, Alexander (ed.): Hanns Kunitzberger. Bildraum – Der Blick des Bildes, Alexander Klar im Gespräch mit Hanns Kunitzberger über Musik und Bilder, exh. cat., Museum Wiesbaden, 2015

Koella, Rudolf: Camille Graeser. Bilder, Reliefs und Plastiken, Werkverzeichnis, vol. 3, Zurich, 1995

Koepplin, Dieter: Zur Form und zum Anspruch von Federles Zeichnungen, in: Helmut Federle. Bilder, Zeichnungen, exh. cat., Museum für Gegenwartskunst Basel, 1985

Lemoine, Serge: Gottfried Honegger. Tableaux-Reliefs/Skulpturen 1970–1983, Zurich, 1983

Lohse, Richard Paul: Modulare und Serielle Ordnungen, Ordes Modulaires et Sériels, Modular and Serial Orders 1943–84, Zurich, 1984

Loock, Ulrich / Zacharopoulos, Denys: Gerhard Richter, Munich, 1985

Lynton, Norbert: Richard Paul Lohse, Colour Becomes Form, Annely Juda Fine Art, London, 1997

Malsch, Friedemann: Ozean. Ein Projekt über den Raum und seine Seelenzustände, in: Leiko Ikemura. Ozean. Ein Projekt, exh. cat., Kunstmuseum Liechtenstein, Vaduz, 2002

Malsch, Friedemann: Werke aus der Hilti Art Foundation. Von Paul Gauguin bis Imi Knoebel, exh. cat., Kunstmuseum Liechtenstein, Vaduz, 2005

Malsch, Friedemann (ed.): Günter Fruhtrunk. Farbe Rhythmus Existenz, exh. cat., Kunstmuseum Liechtenstein, Vaduz, 2012

Nagaya, Mitsue (ed.): Leiko Ikemura, Our Planet. Earth & Stars, exh. cat., The National Art Center, Tokyo, Tokyo, 2019

Nannucci, Maurizio: Maurizio Nannucci. Where to start from, exh. cat., European Patent Office, Munich, 1999

Pierre, José: Konrad Klapheck, Institut für moderne Kunst Nürnberg, Cologne, 1970

Poirier, Maurice: Sean Scully, New York, 1990

Price, Marla: Sean Scully, Catalogue Raisonné of the Paintings, vol. II, 1980–1989, Berlin, 2018

Reiter, Silke: Günter Fruhtrunk, Werkverzeichnis der Bilder, 1952–1982, vol. 1: Bildmotovisch, vol. 2: Chronologisch, Berlin / Munich, 2018

Richter, Gerhard: Bilder / Paintings 1962–1985 (Catalogue raisonné), Städtische Kunsthalle Düsseldorf, 1986

Richter, Gerhard: Werkübersicht / Catalogue raisonné 1962–1993, Kunst- und Ausstellungshalle der Bundesrepublik Deutschland, Bonn, 1993

Richter, Gerhard: Texte zu 4900 Farben, Gerhard Richter Archiv Dresden / Serpentine Gallery London, texts by Benjamin H. D. Buchloh, Peter Gidal, Birgit Pelzer, Gerhard Richter, Marcus du Sautoy, Ostfildern, 2009

Richter, Gerhard: Panorama: Retrospektive, with texts by Mark Godfrey, Nicholas Serota, Dorothée Brill, Camille Morineau, Achim Borchardt-Hume, Amy Dickson, Rachel Haidu, Christine Mehring, Munich, 2012

Roeckle, Hanna: Fluidum und Zwischenraum. Bilder, Objekte, Rauminstallationen 1997–2002, with texts by Sibylle Omlin and Friedemann Malsch, Cologne, 2003

Rohsmann, Arnulf: Bischoffshausen. Struktur – Monochromie – Reduktion, Klagenfurt, 1991

Scharrer, Eva: Grenzgänger im Zwischenraum – zu den Horizontbildern von Leiko Ikemura, in: Leiko Ikemura. Tag, Nacht, Halbmond, Sturzenegger Stiftung Schaffhausen, Museum zu Allerheiligen Schaffhausen, Zurich, 2008

Schreier, Christoph: Gerhard Richter. Über Malen / Frühe Bilder, Munich, 2017

Schulz, Martin: Eine ganze Welt. Zu den aktuellen Arbeiten von Imi Knoebel, in: Imi Knoebel Weiss Schwarz, exh. cat., Galerie Bärbel Grässlin, Frankfurt am Main, 2010

Schwarzwälder, Rosemarie (ed.): Abstrakte Malerei aus Amerika und Europa, Brice Marden, Gerhard Richter, Helmut Federle, Robert Mangold, Robert Ryman, Klagenfurt, 1988

Searle, Adrian: Unbound: Possibilities in Painting, Hayward Gallery, London, 1994

Staber, Margit: Fritz Glarner, Zurich, 1976

Storck, Gerhard: Keith Sonniers neue Argon- und Neonarbeiten, exh.cat., Museum Haus Lange, Krefeld 1979

Struth, Thomas: Thomas Struth. Museum Photographs, with texts by Hans Belting, Walter Grasskamp, Claudia Seidel, Munich, 2005

Struth, Thomas: Thomas Struth. Fotografien 1978–2010, Anette Kruszynski, Tobias Bezzola, James Lingwood (eds), with texts by Armin Zweite, Anette Kruszynski, James Lingwood, Ruth HaCohen, Yaron Ezrahi, Tobias Bezzola, exh. cat., Kunsthaus Zürich / Kunstsammlung

Nordrhein-Westfalen, Düsseldorf, Munich, 2010

Struth, Thomas: Thomas Struth. Nature & Politics, with texts by Tobias Bezzola, D. Graham Burnett, Dirk Baecker, exh. cat., Museum Folkwang, Essen/ Martin-Gropius-Bau, Berlin / High Museum of Art, Atlanta / St. Louis Art Museum, 2016

Struth, Thomas: Thomas Struth. New Pictures from Paradise, with texts by Hans-Rudolf Reust, Nigel Pitman, Jana-Maria Hartmann, Munich, 2017

Stüttgen, Johannes: Bevor sich überhaupt etwas zeigt. Über die Linienbilder und die ersten Etappen der Arbeit von Imi Knoebel, in: IMI KNOEBEL, Linienbilder 1966 bis 1968, Kunstverein St. Gallen, Kunstmuseum, 1999

Thomas, Angela: Max Bill. The Early Years. An Interview, in: The Journal of Decorative and Propaganda Arts, 19, 1993

Violand-Hobi, Heidi E.: Jean Tinguely, Biographie und Werk, Munich / New York, 1995

Wäspe, Roland: IMI KNOEBEL. IMI GEGEN GROBEN SCHMUTZ, in: IMI KNOEBEL. IMI GEGEN GROBEN SCHMUTZ, exh. cat., Karola Grässlin (ed.), Kunstverein Braunschweig, 2003

Wember, Paul: Yves Klein, Cologne, 1969

Wendermann, Gerda: Peter Roehr 1944–1968. Neues Museum Weimar. Die Sammlung Paul Maenz, vol. 2, Kunstsammlungen zu Weimar, Ostfildern-Ruit, 2000

Wendt, Karin: Günter Fruhtrunk. Monographie und Werkverzeichnis. Möglichkeiten und Grenzen des konkreten Bildes. Werkverzeichnis 1952–1982, Frankfurt am Main, 2001

Weski, Thomas / Wilmes, Ulrich: Thomas Struth, with texts by Thomas Weski, Jana-Maria Hartmann, Ulrich Wilmes and a conversation between Okwui Enwezor and Thomas Struth, Munich, 2017

Wieczorek, Uwe (1): Hanna Roeckle. Neue Werke, Xoana und Okulare. Malerei, Raum, Licht, exh. cat., Kunstraum Engländerbau, Vaduz, 2005

Wieczorek, Uwe (2): Werke aus der Hilti Art Foundation. Von Paul Gauguin bis Imi Knoebel, exh. cat., Kunstmuseum Liechtenstein, Vaduz, 2005

Wieczorek, Uwe: Sean Scully – Die Architektur der Farbe, exh. cat., Kunstmuseum Liechtenstein, Vaduz, 2006

Wieczorek, Uwe: Painting as Process and Phenomenon, in: Gotthard Graubner. Malerei / Painting, exh. cat., Kunstmuseum Liechtenstein, Vaduz, 2010

Wieczorek, Uwe: Hilti Art Foundation, Painting and Sculpture – From Classical Modernism to the Present Day, exh. cat., Hilti Art Foundation / Kunstmuseum Liechtenstein, Vaduz, 2015

Wieczorek, Uwe: Hilti Art Foundation, Kirchner, Léger, Scully & more, Works from the Collection, exh. cat., Hilti Art Foundation / Kunstmuseum Liechtenstein, Vaduz, 2017

Wieczorek, Uwe: Hilti Art Foundation, Rosso, Klee, Sonnier & more, 36 Works from the Collection, exh. cat., Hilti Art Foundation / Kunstmuseum Liechtenstein, Vaduz, 2018

Wieczorek, Uwe: Thomas Struth at the Hilti Art Foundation, in: Composition '19 – Thomas Struth at the Hilti Art Foundation, exh. cat., Hilti Art Foundation / Kunstmuseum Liechtenstein, Vaduz, 2019

Zahn, Leopold: Das Kunstwerk, vol. 22, 1968–69

Zutter, Jörg: Helmut Federle. Bilder extremer Gegensätze, in: Helmut Federle. Bilder, Zeichnungen, exh. cat., Museum für Gegenwartskunst Basel, 1985

The Invisible Becomes Visible
Georg Shandor Hayde

As a restorer, my work involves assessing and conserving the physical substance of works of art, an activity that takes place largely behind the scenes. It is a great responsibility and work of a complexity that is difficult for outsiders to perceive. I have been working at the Hilti Art Foundation in this capacity for the past fifteen years and am pleased to be able to give an insight into my field of endeavour, work ethic and approach to the task at hand, thereby lending visibility to the "invisible".

Exacting ethical standards govern the way I think and act in dealing with original works of art and their restoration. The first priority is always to protect the work, to preserve the original quality created by the artist and frequently to repair later damage. Faithful to Georg Dehio's maxim of 1905, "Conserve, don't restore", I also endorse the ethical principles underlying modern restoration. My mentors Max Imkamp, Bruno Heimberg and Peter Berkes at the Doerner Institute of Munich's Pinakotheks have had a seminal influence, for instance, with such maxims as "Learn to read the works of art first". Specifically, this means assessing the original condition of the object and defining what treatment may be required. Such analysis applies not only to the holdings of the collection but also in advance, when considering a new acquisition.

The uniqueness of the work must be taken into account every step of the way, as a totality grasped down to the finest detail. Like a detective, I first examine the technique, materials, their mutual compatibility and their properties in space, time and climate. This already anticipates *preventive conservation*. My goal is to unite my personal methods with state-of-the-art standards of restoration. Occasionally, when that is not possible, one has to chart new territory, but a crucial constant remains in the form of a lived work ethic that takes responsibility for the works. Preventive conservation additionally entails in-depth enquiry into questions of handling and the materials used to protect works of art in transport and during exhibitions.

Conservation means preserving original materials subject to change and thus minimising the need for future restoration. Very little alien material is added. Renewed conservation may be necessary at a later date but is by far the lesser evil. For me, less is always more.

Restoration involves repairing damage in accordance with the original. Viewers should not be distracted by conspicuous repairs. All intervention through conservation and restoration should be reversible. In many cases, damage may be caused not only by ageing or handling but by earlier restoration, through misinterpretation, doing more than necessary, directives from previous owners or knowledge since found faulty by new findings. An important part of my work involves keeping a meticulous record of my analyses, of the measures I have taken and the materials I have used, so that everything I do can be traced and, if necessary, revised should that be required by new and better insights.

Frames and glazing protect the paintings and support them aesthetically. My ethical guideline in this case is: the frames must support but not overwhelm the work. The fact that the Hilti Art Foundation gives me considerable freedom in the choice of frames not only makes my work more interesting, it also lends greater significance to its impact.

In modern everyday life, we are swept along by a rapid succession of images and rarely have the pleasure of spending time with a single object. In museums, exhibitions and at home, however, we can engage with works of art at leisure; we can study the layering of their surfaces, their colouring, glazes, and subject matter. We can enjoy what we perceive and be touched by it, an effect ideally heightened by works that radiate the original quality generated by the artist. The most important goal, the greatest challenge, is to preserve or restore this condition to the best of my ability, to ensure that the collection of the Hilti Art Foundation continues to stimulate and school our perception. Every time I look at the works in this collection, I cannot help feeling a sense of satisfaction and even pride at having been in conversation with every single one of them and having, in many cases, contributed to recapturing the effect that so enchants us all.

One last word: to build and maintain such an outstanding collection as that of the Hilti Art Foundation requires a shared vision and the finely tuned, often invisible work of many people, too many, unfortunately, to mention here by name. It is a great privilege for me to be among those responsible for the collection at the Hilti Art Foundation and to realise, time and again, how much the voice of the restorer is appreciated and sometimes perceived as crucial. Not only has the invisible been revealed in what is visible; the invisible agent himself has also become visible.

Georg Shandor Hayde
Trained as a restorer of frames and courtly furniture. Studied museum restoration at the Doerner Institute and the Ludwig-Maximilians-Universität Munich. Conservator at Kunsthaus Zürich for three years and at the Bavarian State Painting Collections for four years. Supervising conservator at the Segantini Museum in St. Moritz for eight years and at the Wittelsbacher Ausgleichsfonds Munich for twenty-four years. Freelance work for collections in Germany and Switzerland. Guest lecturer in ethics at the Ghent School of Arts. Supervising conservator of the collection at the Hilti Art Foundation since 2005. Inventor of the Track & Slide® hanging system.

Imprint

Hilti Art Foundation
Feldkircherstrasse 100
9494 Schaan
Liechtenstein

Museum address:
Städtle 32
9490 Vaduz
Liechtenstein

www.hiltiartfoundation.li

///

Hirmer Publishers
Bayerstrasse 57–59
80335 Munich
Germany

www.hirmerpublishers.com

PUBLISHER
Michael Hilti
President
Hilti Art Foundation
Schaan / LI

EDITOR
Uwe Wieczorek
Curator
Hilti Art Foundation
Schaan / LI

PROJECT ADMINISTRATION
Michèle Frey-Hilti
Hilti Art Foundation
Schaan / LI

PROJECT MANAGEMENT
Rainer Arnold
Hirmer Publishers
Munich / DE

CLEARING ARTIST'S COPYRIGHT
Monika Bergmann
picture worx
Kranenburg / DE

TEXTS
Angela Schneider
Berlin / DE
Uwe Wieczorek
Schaan / LI
Julia Ryff
London / GB
Georg Shandor Hayde
Schaan / LI

TRANSLATION
Catherine Schelbert
Weggis, Hertenstein / CH

COPY EDITING, PROOFREADING
Miles Champion
New York / USA

REPRODUCTIONS
Günter König
Ruggell / LI
Heinz Preute
Vaduz / LI

INSTALLATION PHOTOGRAPHS
Barbara Bühler
Basel / CH
(pp. 42–43, 140–41, 200–01)
Günter König
Ruggell / LI
(pp. 98–99, 210–11, 252–53)
Thomas Struth
Berlin / DE
(pp. 224–25, 266–67)

ARCHITECTURAL PHOTOGRAPHS
Valentin Jeck
Stäfa / CH

VISUALS
prepressstudio
Günter König
Ruggell / LI

GRAPHIC DESIGN, TYPESETTING
Kurt Dornig
Dornbirn / AT

TYPEFACES
Novel Pro / Christoph Dunst
Allegra / Jost Hochuli

PAPERS
Pergraphica Classic Rough
Arctic Silk+

PRINTING, BINDING
Kösel GmbH & Co. KG
Altusried / DE

ISBN 978-3-7774-3342-4

Printed in Germany

FSC
www.fsc.org
MIX
Paper from responsible sources
FSC® C013736

COVER

Dadamaino
Volume a moduli sfasati
(cat. 51)

Lucio Fontana
Concetto spaziale, Attesa
(cat. 46)

Fritz Glarner
Relational Painting No. 58
(cat. 24)

Gotthard Graubner
Le vent du soleil I (atmo)
(cat. 78)

Callum Innes
Exposed Painting Crimson Red
(cat. 113)

Konrad Klapheck
Am Ziel der Wünsche
(cat. 85)

Imi Knoebel
Figur 49
(cat. 87)

Norbert Kricke
Raumplastik Gelb-Weiss-Schwarz
(cat. 74)

Stéphane Kropf
Untitled *(Tuilière)*
(cat. 120)

Gerhard Richter
D. G.
(cat. 81)

Gerhard Richter
Vesuv
(cat. 80)

Sean Scully
Doric Grey
(cat. 36)

Keith Sonnier
Ba-O-Ba Krefeld IB
(cat. 29)

Thomas Struth
Museo del Prado 2, Madrid
(cat. 100)